Introducing Japanese Religion

Now in its Second Edition, *Introducing Japanese Religion* is the ideal resource for undergraduate students. This edition features new material on folk and popular religion, including shamanism, festivals, and practices surrounding death and funerals. Robert Ellwood also updates the text to discuss recent events, such as religious responses to the Fukushima disaster. *Introducing Japanese Religion* includes illustrations, lively quotations from original sources, learning goals, summary boxes, questions for discussion, suggestions for further reading, and a glossary to aid study and revision.

Robert Ellwood is Distinguished Professor Emeritus of Religion at the University of Southern California. He is the author of over twenty-five books, including *Many Peoples, Many Faiths*, *The Fifties Spiritual Marketplace*, *The Sixties Spiritual Awakening*, and *Islands of the Dawn*.

World Religions series

Edited by Damien Keown and Charles S. Prebish

This exciting series introduces students to the major world religious traditions. Each religion is explored in a lively and clear fashion by experienced teachers and leading scholars in the field of world religion. Up-to-date scholarship is presented in a student-friendly fashion, covering history, core beliefs, sacred texts, key figures, religious practice and culture, and key contemporary issues. To aid learning and revision, each text includes illustrations, summaries, explanations of key terms, and further reading.

Introducing African American Religion
Anthony B. Pinn

Introducing American Religion
Charles H. Lippy

Introducing Buddhism, second edition
Charles S. Prebish and Damien Keown

Introducing Chinese Religions
Mario Poceski

Introducing Christianity
James R. Adair

Introducing Daoism
Livia Kohn

Introducing Hinduism
Hillary P. Rodrigues

Introducing Islam, second edition
William E. Shepard

Introducing Japanese Religion, second edition
Robert Ellwood

Introducing Judaism
Eliezer Segal

Introducing Tibetan Buddhism
Geoffrey Samuel

Forthcoming:

Introducing Hinduism, second edition
Hillary P. Rodrigues

Introducing Japanese Religion

Second edition

Robert Ellwood

Routledge
Taylor & Francis Group

NEW YORK AND LONDON

Second edition published 2016
by Routledge
711 Third Avenue, New York, NY 10017

and by Routledge
2 Park Square, Milton Park, Abingdon, Oxon OX14 4RN

Routledge is an imprint of the Taylor & Francis Group, an informa business

© 2016 Robert Ellwood

The right of Robert Ellwood to be identified as author of this work
has been asserted by him in accordance with sections 77 and 78 of the
Copyright, Designs and Patents Act 1988.

First edition published by Routledge 2008

Library of Congress Cataloging in Publication Data
A catalog record for this book has been requested

ISBN: 978-1-138-95875-3 (hbk)
ISBN: 978-1-138-95876-0 (pbk)
ISBN: 978-1-315-66107-0 (ebk)

Typeset in Jenson and Tahoma
by HWA Text and Data Management, London

To the memory of Professor Joseph M. Kitagawa (1915–1992)
Sensei and friend

Contents

Illustrations

Map

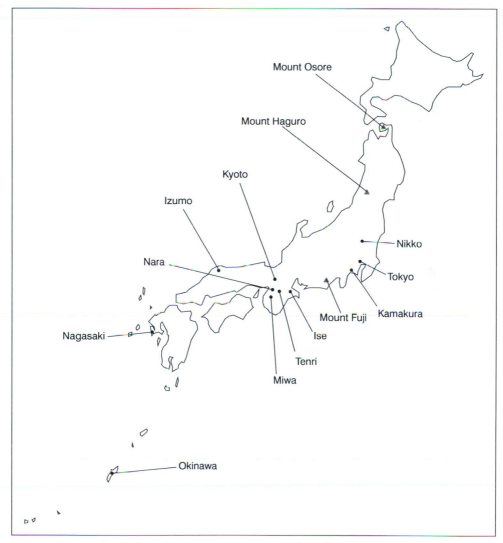

Mount Osore

Mount Haguro

Kyoto

Izumo

Nikko

Nara

Tokyo

Kamakura

Mount Fuji

Ise

Nagasaki

Tenri

Miwa

Okinawa

Major places of religious importance mentioned in the text

Preface

This volume is intended to present both information about the religion traditions of Japan and an experience of their world. For that reason it contains data, descriptions, quotations, anecdotes, and a few philosophical reflections. It is hoped also that working with this book will introduce students to some academic ways of looking at the religions of the world. *Introducing Japanese Religion* should be accessible to all motivated college and university students, whether they have had previous courses in Japanese or religious studies topics or not. Nonetheless, a little background reading in Japanese history, and in Buddhism and Confucianism, would obviously be helpful.

Some students may have had more background in European and American history than in Japanese. To my mind, at least, despite very minimal direct contact until modern times, interesting parallels between Japanese and Western social, intellectual, and religious history, from the feudal Middle Ages on up, suggest themselves; a few speculations in this direction appear.

Each chapter is followed by a list of study questions and a short representative bibliography. More specialized books and articles will be found cited in the notes; they are also generally recommended for further research. Much information can now be found online as well.

Japanese names are given in the Japanese way, with surname first, except in the case of authors of English-language, or translated, books (e.g. Susumu Shimazono), in which case the name is given as it appears on the book's title page and in library catalogs. It should be noted, however, that many premodern Japanese historical figures are normally referred to by their given name (e.g. Ieyasu rather than Tokugawa Ieyasu), and after first identification they are so named here. Also, Buddhist teachers and writers usually go by their name in religion rather than their birth-name, and to make matters more confusing, sometimes change that name to mark different ordinations or stages of life, including a posthumous (after-death) name (e.g. Saeki Mao? birth-name; Kukai, religious name; Kobo daishi, posthumous name). For the sake of clarity, the name most commonly recognized (e.g. Shinran, Nichiren, Basho) is used consistently, regardless of whether the individual actually was known by that name at the point in life under discussion.

May your studies be an adventure in the exploration of a unique world culture! It is hoped this little book will be only a beginning. Obviously, in an introduction like this many facets of the tremendously varied world of Japanese religion can only be hinted at, or pointed toward. Perhaps you will be intrigued enough to make one of those topics the subject of a paper, or even for further research later on.

Robert Ellwood

Preface to the Second Edition

In this new edition, additional material is presented on (1) certain aspects of Japanese folk and popular religion, particularly regarding the transition of death, and regarding spirits of the departed, (2) the impact on religion of the traumatic tsunami and nuclear disaster of 2011, and (3) the meaning of "religion" – or the absence of "religion" – in Japan. (The quotation marks indicate that we are not only dealing with different religions from those with which many students may be most familiar, but perhaps also with different concepts, or perceptions, of what religion is or is not.)

Bibliographies of electronic as well as print resources are also now provided for this edition. Only a sampling can be offered; many provide links or names to further material on the subject. Many of you will know how to find more on your own. As with print books, electronic material can range from excellent to awful. A critical attitude is always important.

You will also find generally good Wikipedia articles on most of the topics. I have often preferred to cite a less-obvious but interesting online source. In some cases, those are the URLs of English-language home-pages of Japanese religious institutions themselves. These are important for understanding the religion's self-interpretation; obviously they should be compared with scholarly and other perceptions.

Every good wish for your entry into the world of Japanese religion. May a spirit of exploration and adventure accompany you as you proceed.

Robert Ellwood

1 Encountering the Japanese religious world

In this chapter

We first present something of the "feel" of Japan as a special country of great interest to the student of religion and culture. Japanese religion can be studied for a variety of reasons, whether for its own sake, as an aid to understanding Japanese history and culture, or as a means to understanding religion better as a general human experience. We will see that the Japanese language helps us to comprehend this culture's complex history and religious mix. Mircea Eliade's concept of the Sacred and the Profane, and Joachim Wach's three forms of religious expression (theoretical, practical, and sociological), plus three more (art, ethics, and history), give us tools for approaching Japanese religion. However, we need to think carefully about what we mean by religion, and whether one's own prior way of thinking about religion applies fully to Japan.

Main topics covered

- Reasons for studying Japanese religion
- The Japanese language helps one see how Japanese culture is a weave of several strands, both native and imported
- Religion is not easy to define, but – with Japan particularly in mind – can be thought of first of all as symbols and experiences which enhance life and put it in a larger context of meaning
- We will look at Japanese religion in terms of its theoretical, practical, and sociological forms of expression, and then in terms of its art, ethics, and history
- Many people say that Japan is not very religious, and yet shrines, temples, and related activities seem to abound. Answers to this paradox may tell us some significant things about how the Japanese tend to think about religion.

Why study Japanese religion?

Japan is unique. No one visiting the island nation and keeping eyes and ears open for more than fifteen minutes could have any doubt of that. The language sounds like no other. As one travels, before long the distinctive *torii* or curved archways marking a Shinto shrine pop into sight, perhaps even atop a modern department store. Not long after, one espies the peaceful precincts of a Buddhist temple, with its fierce-looking but benign guardian deities. While familiar high-rise buildings appear in built-up areas, more often one sees low, graceful wooden homes, almost indefinably Japanese. Sometimes a garden may be glimpsed through a gate left open for a short while, not a flower garden but a patch of raked sand, rocks, moss, and perhaps a few miniature trees. The garden affords a glance into someone's private world; other such small paradises no doubt exist behind closed gates, as they do within the walled courtyards of temples and palaces. It perhaps tells us something about the national character that Japanese cities present few grand boulevards or vistas like those of Washington, London, or Paris. Instead, this country's great palaces and temples often just peek over the tops of drab walls. It is in what is glimpsed, hinted at, or even patently concealed, as well as through what is seen, that one recognizes this is a special place.

Japan has been heavily influenced by continental Asia and, more recently, by Europe and America. Yet the east Asian nation has generally incorporated cultural imports on its own terms, maintaining a distinct social and spiritual identity. Like the sacred *shimenawa* rope which often marks a place holy to Shinto, the Japanese

Figure 1.1 Itsukushima, a torii gate at the Miyajima shrine (© spom / Shutterstock.com)

heritage is comprised of many strands, yet somehow all manage to hold together, forming parts of a society in which harmony is highly valued.

Why would anyone want to study the religion of a society like this? Here are a few reasons. You may have others of your own.

To understand Japanese culture

In Japan, the religious and the secular are not easily separated. What looks to be this-worldly beauty may actually have a religious background – and then that religious background may turn out to be slippery by Western concepts of religion. Many people throughout the world enjoy Japanese gardens, flower arrangements, architecture, even the celebrated "tea ceremony," without fully realizing their background in Zen Buddhism – and behind Zen lies older Buddhist schools like Tendai, and Mahayana Buddhism generally. One great mystery taught by these schools, especially as interpreted in Japan, is the sacred in the ordinary. The universal Buddha-nature which infuses all things is found not only in temples, but for those with eyes to see is no less in rocks, trees, and such everyday human acts as making tea and serving it to a friend. Tendai realized that it is precisely in the seemingly empty, transitory things of this world that, for those who are in on the secret, the Buddha-nature – reality as known to an enlightened mind – can be glimpsed, moment by changing moment. (A traditional proverb says, "To a practitioner of Tendai, everything is wonderful.")

To point toward that hidden Buddha-nature, art and life should be simple, graceful, and apparently spontaneous. Japanese taste runs to *shibui*, plain and simple, even *wasabi*, suggesting poverty. Old and cracked vessels for *chanoyu*, the "tea ceremony," bring far higher prices on the antique market than newer ones. The profoundest gardens are just rock, sand, and moss, *kare niwa* or "dry gardens."

Other gardens allow grass, bamboo, perhaps the miniature bonsai trees, never flowers like a Western garden. Water flows in through contrived but natural-looking streams or springs. I once read a Japanese essay in which the writer made much of the way water in Japanese gardens is introduced: by human artifact but so as to make the garden appear a model of nature, not forced up in ways contrary to nature, as it is in fountains like those of Versailles. These gardens are not exactly nature, but like an abstract representation of the essence of nature, and therefore like a window to the Buddha-nature behind it.

> Have you ever held a bow with the string and arrow poised and pulled back, then waited till you somehow felt it was just the right moment to release the arrow and hit the target? If so, you have had a taste of the famous Japanese art of archery, taught in some temples, and the kind of awareness that lies behind it.

Figure 1.2 Zen Garden Ryoanji, Kyoto (© Chuong Vu / Shutterstock.com)

Suppose you were sitting at the edge of the famous garden of the Ryoanji Temple, in Kyoto. This Zen rectangle is nothing but fifteen rocks of irregular shape and five natural rock islands surrounded by a little moss, all on an expanse of white, carefully raked gravel. The rocks are set in no discernible pattern, yet somehow the simple, subtle arrangement has a deep contemplative effect. You feel drawn into its abstract stillness, the mystery of the place being only enhanced by the realization that there is no one spot from which one can see all the stones at once; wherever you are, at least one is hidden by another. Once, as I studied them early in the morning, I felt this arena was the universe, and the rocks were galaxies rushing off beyond space and time ...

Many Westerners are discovering these values close to home now, as Japanese spirituality expresses itself overseas in Zen centers, and the temples of other Japanese forms of Buddhism. Not a few also have come in contact with Japanese forms of the martial arts, like karate or aikido, and have realized that, however strange it may seem at first glance, spiritual preparation lies behind these fighters' blows: to strike with exactly the right timing in the right way, one's mind must be as clear as a Zen monk's, plus disciplined by Confucian loyalty to one's teacher.

To understand Japanese institutions

Japan is now a world economic powerhouse, and increasingly a diplomatic force as well. What helps in understanding a nation's economy and policies is to grasp something of that society's basic culture and values. We need to know its attitudes about the world, how its business and political leaders make decisions, and what is most important to the nation and its people. Here, religion – with the myths, symbols, and ethical touchstones it provides – are clues second to none when it comes to deep-level understanding. Not that business or political people in Japan are necessarily always guided by religion, any more than they are anywhere else, but knowing about the religion can help us to comprehend customs they are likely to respect, and principles they would not want to offend.

Many *gaijin* (foreigners) doing business with Japanese corporations or the Japanese government get frustrated trying to figure out exactly how decisions are made, and who really speaks for the institution. Not seldom those who appear to have power turn out to be figureheads, and those inside the culture have an uncanny ability to know how and when something *has* been decided by whoever *really* has power. But it's all very murky to the outsider.

Japan is a society in which individuals find their own identity by participating in a group. Decisions, from the *kamis'* (Shinto gods) through a family's to a corporation's, are made together. Everyone keeps on talking, back and forth, round and round, until a consensus is reached. (However, it may take a great deal of sensitivity to the culture, as well as thorough familiarity with the language, to get when that has happened. For Japan is also a land of understatement and indirect wording; the moment of decision may need just to be intuited, or pointed to by gesture or action, rather than pronounced.)

So then, the real decision-maker is the group, often building its consensus behind the scenes; apparent leaders, from the Emperor on down, are at best only ratifiers of the collective mind. And the *kami* are still there, as it were parts of the consensus group. The headquarters estate of the Toyota corporation, makers of cars and trucks driven by millions of Americans and Europeans, contains a shrine to the Shinto god and goddess of metal.

To understand Japanese business and government, one must also grasp how they are very much influenced by the ethical and moral values of Confucianism. Though imported from China and, in Japan, less a religion than guidelines on how life should be lived, the ways of the Ancient Sage only reinforce the emphasis on group loyalty and process stemming from Japanese clans of yore and their counterparts in the assemblies of heaven.

Confucian society is hierarchical, yet it emphasizes the crucial importance of mutual, two-way responsibility and loyalty between higher and lower, between management and workers. Each side gives a lot and expects to get a lot. Traditionally,

Here is an ancient Shinto myth that may help us understand Japanese decision-making. The beautiful sun-goddess Amaterasu, deeply offended by her brother Susano-o, the storm-god, had hidden herself in a cave to sulk. But all the other *kami* (Shinto gods), distressed at how therefore light had gone out of the world, gathered in the River of Heaven to discuss the matter. Like any Japanese family, business, or political group, they would talk until a solution emerged, as it were spontaneously or by consensus. The spontaneity was produced by a new event.

What happened was that a young goddess, Uzume, deity of mirth and dance, broke the tension by standing up to begin a humorously ribald dance, causing the other gods to burst out in laughter. That heavenly revelry so intrigued the sequestered sun-goddess that she stuck her head out of the cave to see what was going on, and then was gradually enticed back into the sky by a mirror reflecting her glory.

Figure 1.3 Amaterasu appearing from the cave by Yoshitoshi (Public Domain: Wikimedia Commons)

Japanese corporations have not only encouraged group tasking and decision-making, but have also provided very generous benefits to workers: good housing, vacation trips, retirement at full pay at as early as fifty-five, even free gymnasiums and beauty parlors. In turn they have expected lifetime loyalty. Although in the twenty-first century the system seems to be adapting in the Western direction, with workers being laid off and changing jobs much more than before, both benefits and loyalty remain important principles by European or American standards. There is a Buddhist dimension, too. Some corporations have given workers, especially promising junior executives, Zen Buddhist training to help them clear the mind of ego in order to work most effectively for the company.

The price paid, as some Japanese increasingly point out, is the way the Confucian or Zen mentality, even as it creates faithful cooperation and harmony, penalizes the individual who stands apart from the group, whether as innovator or critic. In all these matters a deep understanding of Japanese religion and its age-old values helps us to understand even seemingly secular Japan today, even if one's only object is better to do business with the land in the Western Pacific.

To better understand religion

Japanese religion is worth studying for its own sake, and that of understanding religion generally. Japan has been called a living laboratory of religion.

In this special country, as religious history rolls along down the centuries, new "layers" of religion are added one on top of the other, but the old – even the oldest forms – seem never quite to disappear. Religion just gets more and more "stacked up." Within a few miles, one can sometimes see everything from the folk-religion of neolithic farmers, to missionary-founded Christian churches, to the latest spiritual "cult" or fad.

Consider this: Buddhism came into Japan from the Asian continent around the sixth century CE by the Western calendar, roughly the same time that Christianity was introduced from the European continent into another large offshore island, Britain, then home to traditional polytheistic religions not wholly unlike Shinto. But in Japan, unlike Britain, the new did not simply replace the old (save for a few vestiges, like the Anglo-Saxon gods immortalized in the days of our week), but the two, Shinto and Buddhism, have managed to coexist down to the present.

In medieval Japan Shinto shrines were often adjacent to Buddhist temples, and it was said the *kami* were guardians or students of the Buddha's dharma or teaching, or even the same line of spiritual force as the Buddhist in distinctive Japanese guise. (Thus Amaterasu, the Shinto sun goddess already mentioned, was said to be a local Japanese manifestation of Dainichi, the "Great Sun Buddha" who represents the heart of the universe.) It is as though in Europe and North America one found temples of Wotan and Thor, or Zeus and Minerva, alongside Christian churches,

Japanese language

First as a preliminary to further study, let us look at the Japanese language. While a knowledge of Japanese is not expected of students using this book, you should want to pronounce it correctly, and a few insights into it may help in understanding the complexities of Japanese culture. The beginner will not go far wrong in pronouncing the vowel sounds in Japanese written in *romaji* (Western letters) as in romance languages like Spanish: *a* is "ah," *e* is English "a," *i* is English "e," *o* is "oh"; and *u* is as the "oo" in "too." When an *o* or *u* has a macron or long mark over it, extend the sound. (However, long marks are not used in the text of this book; they are provided in the Glossary and Index.) Try to avoid accenting, pronouncing all syllables with the same stress. Syllables with *y* like *gyo, hyo,* and *myo* are strictly one syllable, not "my-o." Diphthongs like *hei* ("hay") and *ai* ("I") are also one syllable.

The Japanese language reflects the varied origins of the culture. Its complicated writing system includes both *kanji* (Chinese characters representing words or concepts that indicate the Chinese origin of Japanese writing) and two forms of *kana* (syllabic "letters" used for the conjugated verb endings that Chinese does not possess and for simpler words – particles, conjunctions, and the like). Often the choice of *kanji* or *kana* depends on the whim or style of the writer.

Of the two kinds of *kana, hiragana* is usually used for true Japanese words and endings, and *katakana*, somewhat comparable to italics in English, is employed for modern loanwords. Loanwords, predominantly from English but some going back to the Portuguese visitors of the sixteenth century who also brought Christianity, are used for all sorts of modern and foreign things, from bread (*pan,* from Portuguese) to elevators (*erebetaa* – note that since Japanese does not have the *l* or *v* sounds, *r* and *b* are used in their place, and Japanese words do not end in consonants except *n*). The names of foreign places and persons (except Chinese and Korean) are also usually written in *katakana*, for example in newspaper stories. *Katakana* words and names, though frequently used, nonetheless stand out, indicating that what is being talked about is not, and probably never will be, assimilated into "real" Japanese.

Even "real" Japanese has two strands, roughly comparable to the Germanic and Greco-Latin strands in English. The ultimate original stems from the language in use before the Chinese cultural influx, and introduction of writing, begun in the early centuries CE. This language is not related linguistically to Chinese, has a very different vocabulary and grammar, and seems instead to be very distantly connected to such Asian tongues as Korean, Mongolian, and Turkish. Like the Germanic, Anglo-Saxon side of English, "native" Japanese governs the grammar and is used for common prepositions and everyday household words.

A second type of word, roughly the same type likely to be of Latin or Greek derivation in English (like "immediate" or "telephone"), is borrowed from Chinese. These words are of a slightly more elegant, literary, or technical quality than "original" Japanese, though like these English examples some are in very common usage. They are most often written in *kanji*, though they are pronounced in a way different from modern Chinese pronunciations of the same character.

The history of Japan, then, can be read in its language, and we will see how that includes the history of its religions: the original, perpetuated (though with modifications) in Shinto,[1] the introduction of Buddhism and Confucianism (and some Taoism) at the beginning of written history from the mainland, the development of native "scripts" for these imports, and finally the coming of modern western, and now world, culture.

and it was said those old gods were guardians or students of the gospel of Christ, or even the Spirit of Christ in an indigenous form.

The way Japanese religion works is complex in other ways too. The six or eight major schools of Buddhism make that side of religious life almost a denominational society, as the United States has been called. But most Japanese have a relationship to both Shinto and Buddhism, chiefly through allegiance to a traditional family or community shrine and temple. Shinto has been considered the only purely polytheistic (having many gods) religion surviving in a major advanced society; this alone makes it of considerable interest, and may challenge some conventional Western views of religious history. The "new religions" of Japan, which especially flourished in the postwar era, have been studied as remarkable and accessible examples of spiritual innovation. It must also be noted how Japan's tolerant religious pluralism exists within the solid framework of Confucian morality; it seems that religionists can preach and practice a variety of doctrines and methods of worship so long as they also inculcate Confucian virtues; get outside that frame, and they may find themselves in serious trouble … a lotus-pond of tolerance surrounded by an iron fence of traditional morality. All this is worth pondering.

Observing religion in Japan

Many accounts in this book are based on my own experiences. This is not because my observations in Japan are more important, or more insightful, than anyone else's, but because descriptions of religion in action always remind us that religion is not just a set of ideas. Think of religion instead as a combination of ideas about the inner nature of reality, with their outward expressions in symbol, art, ritual, and institutional life that make the inner reality more visible, and more richly experienced, than it would be on its own.

These "enhancers" of inner reality are always human constructs, though they may point to something beyond the human, just as Zen gardens though human-made point to nature and that which infuses nature. While God or the gods may dwell all through the cosmos, for us human beings it takes human skill to perceive that latent presence and then bring it out. We do so through thoughts, words, deeds, and symbols, often expressed in works that are crowning achievements of human art. The sociologist Peter Berger has spoken of religion as our audacious attempt to see the whole universe as humanly significant.[2] If religious, we want to perceive the cosmos as full of a divine life and consciousness that is our true ground of being, that can interact with ours, and is governed by laws meaningful to us. But we need to make all this visible; hence our shrines, temples, churches, rites, and all the rest which as it were are signposts. The accounts herein will, I hope, help to make evident something of this "total," not just idea-based, character of religion in Japan.

The worldviews of Shinto and the various Buddhist denominations, which might seem to be conflicting, may be held lightly, as various levels of truth or various paths to that which is beyond full human understanding. (Of course in practice many Christians and Jews take something like the same tolerant view of their many schools and denominations.) To be sure, there are exclusivist non-mixers in the Japanese religious world, some forms of Nichiren Buddhism and Christianity in particular, as well as extreme nationalistic Shinto. But the broader view, extending to the way most Japanese have a relationship with both Shinto shrine and Buddhist temple, is more characteristic – though the capacity of Japanese, like many other people, under certain kinds of pressure to "flip" to passionate, single-minded commitment to the point of martyrdom, must also be taken into account.

What is religion?

What then *is* religion, that presence and force on the human scene that can produce so many diverse manifestations? For a study like ours of Japanese religion, a definition needs to be more social and historical than personal: not, what does religion mean to *me*; but, what institutions, practices, and ideas in human history and human societies around the world can most usefully be called religious, for the purpose of studying them as religion.

Often the lines are fuzzy, and this is perhaps more the case the farther back in history we go, before people had the idea of religion as a separate compartment of human life, and a feast or a dance, say, could be at once social, recreational, and religious. Nonetheless, the track from the earliest evidences of what we would now call religious in paleolithic rock art, burials, and shamanism can be clearly traced, if we are willing to define religion as any set of ideas, practices, groups, and images

My own understanding of the general nature of religion, as over against particular religions, was greatly enriched by my first encounter with Japanese religion, which was also my first encounter with religion outside the basically Judeo-Christian culture of North America and Europe. It was when I was a chaplain with the U.S. Navy in the early 1960s, and was sent to Okinawa and Japan. Though I had only limited understanding of their meaning, I was struck by the atmosphere and color of Japanese religious sites: the rustic grace of Shinto shrines, the deep peace and soft glowing light of Buddhist temples, even the white robes and quiet power of the *noro*, or shamanesses, of Okinawa.[3] On occasion, I was thrilled by the lively energy of *matsuri*, the festivals associated with Shinto shrines, with their drums, their sacred dances, their processions with the *mikoshi* or palanquin containing the *kami*-presence. I could not help wondering how all this related to the religious world with which I was familiar.

I then read a book by Mircea Eliade, the distinguished historian of religion. Emphasizing the *phenomena* of religion – what appears, what is seen and done – this writer pointed to the way cultures everywhere separate off *sacred* space and time.[4] This is the *space* within the church or shrine or temple, where one almost instinctively thinks and acts in special, reverent ways. It is the *time* of festivals, whether Christmas or Hanukkah or the Shinto *matsuri*, which likewise feels different from ordinary workaday time. If you are at all like what Eliade called *homo religiosus*, a traditionally religious person, being inside a church or temple just doesn't feel like being on the street or in a factory, and Christmas morning, or New Year or *matsuri*-day in Japan, just doesn't feel like an ordinary Monday morning. To me, this was a way of thinking about religion that cuts through starting with doctrine – we believe this, those people believe that. Instead, this approach, technically called phenomenological and structuralist, looks for "what appears" in the practice of religion, then goes behind them to ascertain what the basic patterns or structures are, and what worldview underlies it all.

This perspective was, and is, especially important in coming to grips with Japanese religion. Western Christianity tends to start with belief, at least in theory. In Japanese religion it is above all the sacred space and time kind of experience, most often at the Shinto shrine or Buddhist temple, that comes first. It then takes account of the family and community bonding of which shrine and temple can be the hub.

(i.e. art) which work together to put human life in the largest possible context: in its relationship to ultimate reality, God or the gods (like the Shinto *kami*) or Buddhist Dharmakaya (essence of the universe), and their counterpart in the depths of human consciousness, in dreams, visions, and the wellsprings of artistic creativity.

- To spell out this definition, let us first look at it in terms of the three forms of religious expression articulated by the sociologist of religion Joachim Wach.[5] Religion, he said, may begin with a single primordial experience, but to be humanly meaningful it must be expressed in three ways:
- the theoretical (that is, its ideas, its doctrines and myths or narratives);
- the practical (that is, its practices, its ways of worship, prayer, meditation, pilgrimage; all that is done);
- the sociological (the kinds of institutions it forms: groups, denominations, churches, priesthoods, monastic orders, and so forth; and the way in which people relate to the religion, and the religion to the outside world).

The theoretical form of religious expression can be thought of as dealing with the question, What do they say? People say many things in connection with religion. First may come a basic narrative, like that of the Bible, the *Kojiki* or first collection of Shinto myths in Japan, the life of the Buddha. Then the religion will probably have secondary stories: the lives of saints, accounts of notable conversions, reports of miracles, some of which may be contemporary. It will have doctrines, more abstract statements that take the stories and say, in effect, if at different times God or the buddhas or the gods did this, and this, and this, what can we say about them that is true all the time – what general statements can we make? So it is said they are ultimately one, full of compassion, guiding the life of the world and of individuals, and so forth. Contemporary theologies and philosophies may be written to develop these ideas for our time.

The practical form of religious expression responds to the question, What do they *do*? Here "practical" refers to practices, and this form of expression covers forms of prayer, worship, meditation, pilgrimage, and the like. In Japan, the practical form is very rich, ranging from colorful folk religion practices and village *matsuri* or festivals to the mysterious rites of esoteric Buddhism and the stillness of Zen meditation. When it comes to practice, religion is more intuited by doing it than understood by thinking it, in the same way that a work of art must be seen and taken into one's life, not just described abstractly.

In relation to the practical form, it is always important to look at "the message behind the message" – at what is said, not only by what is done, but by the *way* it is done. If the ultimate purpose of religious worship is to get in touch with an ultimate reality beyond ourselves, *how* we do it tells us much about a worshiping community's view of God and human nature alike. If it is an ornate and very ancient ritual, like say a Greek Orthodox liturgy or a Japanese Shingon Buddhist rite, one "message behind the message" is that we best get outside the one-dimensionality of the present through participating in something that comes to us from far back in the past. Another "message" is that we are aided in this transcending journey by powerful sensory experience: the visual brilliance of colored vestments, candles, elaborate altars, and the like; the splendid music of hymns and chants, the aroma of incense.

If the practical form is much simpler, like a Quaker meeting or Zen meditation, the message instead is that we touch ultimate reality by taking away all else, and being in a situation where we must still the mind and look deep within. And so it goes.

The sociological form of expression asks, What kind of groups do they form, and what kind of leadership do they have? Here too the range is very great, and there is always a "message behind the message." Religious groups can vary from tiny, and perhaps unpopular, groups of the sort sometimes pejoratively labeled "sects" and "cults," to religions that are practically coterminous with a whole culture, like Catholicism in Spain or Buddhism in Thailand. In Japan the situation is complicated by the coexistence of Shinto and Buddhism, and the several "mainline" denominations of Buddhism, plus the "new religions" and Christianity. But the sociological dimension is very important because these faiths are usually based in family and community tradition. The priesthoods of local temples and shrines is generally hereditary. One "message behind the message" is the Confucian perception that family and community are the fundamental human realities. They define the self rather than the other way around. It is through them, and religious institutions based on them, that ultimate reality is reached. (Buddhism can and does speak of individual salvation or enlightenment, and many of its practices are directed toward that end. Yet, in Japan, Buddhist institutions, like Christian ones in Europe and America, are nonetheless rooted in traditional community and family commitments as well as the individual.)

Religious leadership can be of two types, institutional and charismatic. The former represents those religious leaders who emerge through institutions – churches, temples, denominations – getting regular institutional training, ordination, and appointment. In Japan, as indicated, these preferments may also be hereditary. (However, when there is no likely biological heir, a successor may be designated by adoption; this can be done in other family situations as well.) Charismatic leadership, like that of a prophet, saint, or evangelist, stems not so much from the individual's background and training, as from a certain power that seems to have appeared spontaneously, perhaps from a powerful mystical experience the individual has had.

A tradition of occasionally-erupting charismatic leadership exists alongside the institutional in Japanese religion, going back to prehistoric shamanism. It can be seen in a few great Buddhist leaders, such as Honen and Shinran of Pure Land, or

Nichiren of the medieval Lotus Sutra movement. Although they had training as monks, these outstanding individuals went far beyond that background to teach new doctrines and preach mighty revivals throughout the country. Most of the founders of the new religions are in the charismatic category as well. Many were women, as were the ancient shamanesses; there is a long tradition of charismatic female religious leaders in Japan. It may also be mentioned that some religious personages, like many great Zen masters, seem to combine institutional and charismatic roles.

*   *   *

Besides Joachim Wach's three forms of religious expression, I would like to propose three more as well. While it may be possible to find ways to include them in Wach's three, let's give them separate recognition here. They are:

- art
- ethics
- history

Art

Starting with the first, virtually all religion has some form of art. Even if, as in Islam and some forms of Protestant Christianity, sculpture is not used and pictures are generally limited to illustrations, architecture is a very important way in which the vision of the religion is expressed. Art can, of course, be expanded to include dance and the musical and literary arts, which also have wide scope in much of the religious world. Certainly in Japan all these arts are highly developed.

With a few ancient exceptions, Shinto does not have images of its *kami*, but the haunting music of its drums and flutes, the strains of its chanted *norito* or prayers, and its sacred dance, often performed at festivals by lovely *miko* or attendant maidens, are unforgettable by those who have visited shrines. The architecture of Shinto shrines, simple but graceful and suggesting harmony with nature, is in a class of its own.

Older Buddhist temples, especially in the Shingon or Tendai traditions, boast wonderful images of buddhas and bodhisattvas. Some, as of Miroku, the buddha of the future, depict an astounding lightness and grace, while statuary portrayals of Kannon, the bodhisattva of compassion, show her many-armed and crowned to suggest the many works of mercy she can perform at once. As indicated, Zen paintings, on the other hand, may be of nature, though giving nature a kind of numinous, almost translucent quality, suggesting the universal Buddha-nature behind the outward manifestations of the universe.

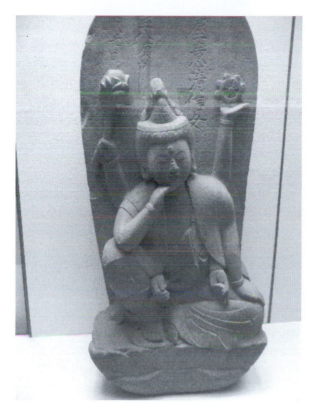

Figure 1.4 Sculpture of a seated Nyoirin Kannon, 1680 (Opal_Art_Seekers_4; CC: Wikimedia
Commons)

Ethics

Ethics – guidelines on how to organize the social order and live one's life properly –
are also major forms of religious expression. In Japan particularly, it is appropriate
to consider ethics separately from the theoretical form of expression, since in a real
sense it has a source separate from Shinto or the various forms of Buddhism, namely
Confucianism. Some Shinto teachers say that the great virtue is *makoto*, openness
or sincerity of heart; it actually comes from Confucianism. *Makoto* is the feeling of
purity and naturalness one should get in the precincts of a shrine, in the presence
of the *kami*. If one has it, one will intuitively know the right thing to do in a time of
moral or ethical decision. In somewhat the same way, in Buddhism the great virtue
is compassion, doing always what best expresses love.

Yet, as one can well imagine, it is not always easy for us fallible human beings
to know what is the way of true sincerity or love in many real-life situations, where
problems may indeed be tangled and it is hard to see all ends. Here is where
formalized Confucian ethics come in. Although in Japan it is less a religion than a
philosophy of life, since it first came in from China and Korea about the same time
as Buddhism, in the sixth century CE, it has only more and more governed Japanese

thinking about the right way to behave. Confucianism tells us that we humans are basically social creatures, finding our true human nature in relationships, first with family and then with community. Loyalty and a sense of obligation to be repaid to one's given relationships, such as to parents (in which the role of the oldest son is especially important), spouse, children, friends, and to those to whom one owes fidelity as rulers, or as employers and employees, benefactors and helpers, is absolutely basic to this tradition.

Sometimes it seems that one of the best ways to get at the values of a modern culture, and the real-life situations with which they interact in various complicated ways, is to look at the advice columns in newspapers, like those of "Dear Abby" and "Ann Landers" that have been extremely popular in the United States. An example from a Tokyo newspaper is shown in the boxed text.

Woman wonders if she should follow her heart or submit to family's wishes.

The only daughter of a traditional family; her true love bears the burden of being the oldest son

I am a woman in my early twenties, the only daughter of a traditional family in a rural area. Since early childhood I was told that I must find an adopted husband so that the family name could continue. I grew up fully accepting this condition. Two years ago I met a man that I really cared for. My parents were not enthusiastic about our union, but agreed to our engagement if he would become an adopted son. However, I found that he changed drastically after the engagement, so I ended the wedding plans some time before the date of the ceremony and returned to my parents' home.

As soon as I returned, I received many inquiries into the possibility of my betrothal and I became the center of attention. This made me uncomfortable and I returned again to Tokyo. I returned to my old job and I led what I considered a fulfilling life. Eventually I found a new boyfriend. We have been talking over our future, but the problem is that he himself is the oldest son of a traditional family. In his family it is understood that he will return in about a year and carry on the family enterprise. I want very much to follow him, but when I remember the wishes of my own family I become very confused. I am not looking forward to going home again and being accused of selfishness while being pushed into an arranged marriage.

My parents remain adamant in their wishes for me to marry for their own purposes, and it is impossible for me to talk to them about the matter. Please advise me as to what to do.

M., Tokyo[6]

In this letter we see clearly in real life a dilemma that has always intrigued the Japanese, and is reflected in countless stories, No and kabuki plays, and poems: the simultaneous push of human emotions – *ninjo* – and pull of duty or obligation, often called *giri*. *Giri* is usually understood in Confucian terms. One's primary obligation is to one's family, and above all one's parents, to whom one owes the gift of life itself – since life is beyond price, that debt is infinite and hence can never be repaid in full; the obligation to parents is life-long and indeed extends beyond the grave. Upon the system of mutual obligation society depends. To defy it in order to follow one's own heart is plain selfishness, putting oneself ahead of everyone else.

Any western idea of an obligation to be true to oneself first, and follow one's own feelings, has no place in this larger scheme of things. Rather, if one accesses true *makoto* or true compassion, instead of confused emotions, one's feelings would clarify into a proper sense of obligation to family first.

Yet, in Japan as elsewhere, certain poets and romantic heroes have put love for the beloved before *giri*, and though their life was usually not easy, they have won covert admiration; even in a purely Confucian society, it is hard to be purely Confucian. Moreover, modern young people, like this woman, have been influenced by today's global youth culture of blue jeans, movies, romance, and doing your own thing. They are less likely than their parents to embrace traditional ways without fuss. But it's a problem being in two worlds at once. Understanding all this is very important for understanding deep-level Japan, and indicates why the ethical expression of religion – and the conundrums it can create – is crucial to understanding.

History

Finally, let us consider *history* as a form of religious expression. By this we do not just mean the fact that all religions have a history, so much as the way in which that history is experienced as part of the life and message of a particular religion. This can present interesting and varied pictures. For example, in the United States, while it is predominantly Christian, the "old-time religion" really refers to little more than the religion of the great nineteenth century revivals. Some eighteen centuries of Christianity lie before those events, but most of it was in Europe or elsewhere, and though perhaps a legacy, it is, especially for Protestants, not really a living presence. In Europe, on the other hand, the Christian past is always there; the church on the town square is likely to be the oldest building around, a constant reminder of a heritage of faith, persecution, religious wars, marriages and dynasties over many centuries.

In Japan religious history is experienced more as in Europe. While temples and shrines, being mostly of wood construction and so susceptible to fire and decay, may not literally be the structures of ages ago, the site and the architecture, and often the images and gardens, are definitely the distant past in the present in a way most

American churches are not. They represent beauties and experiences that can get one outside the present, into the past and into something timeless.

Japanese religious history as a form of religious expression also bears another message different from both Europe and America. Certainly Japanese religious sites can remind one of various battles and persecutions of the past. Yet, as we have seen, the coexistence of Shinto and Buddhism bears a message contrasting with Christian Europe and North America: that new religions can be added, "stacked up," without necessarily displacing the predecessor. In such ways as this, the experienced history of a culture's religion bears its own message.

How religious is Japan?

Is Japan really a religious country? A recent poll asked people in various countries how important religion was to their lives; only 12 percent of Japanese said that religion played a very important role.[7] (In the United States, in contrast, 59 percent said it did, but then in this as in all comparable polls the U.S. stands alone among wealthy nations in its embrace of religion, although the poorer nations of Latin America, Africa, and Asia tend to have even higher figures regarding religion's importance to people's personal lives.)

Fully to answer the question of whether the Japanese are really religious one needs to think of religion in a way different from how many Westerners think about it. Here is a country in which the great majority of people have a relation to both Shinto and Buddhism, typically considering that Shinto has to do with the joyous occasions of this life, Buddhism with the ultimate mysteries of the universe and what happens after one dies. "Born Shinto, die Buddhist," they say.

So it is that Shinto *matsuri* or festivals are celebrative community affairs with a carnival atmosphere, marriages are often solemnized in Shinto shrines, and newborn children presented to the *kami* of the family shrine. Funerals and memorial services, on the other hand, are likely to be under Buddhist auspices, with interment perhaps on the local temple grounds. Probably most people would not think of Shinto and Buddhism as inconsistent with each other; as we have seen, certain medieval systems of thought made the *kami* local guardians or manifestations of the more cosmic buddhas. Confucian family and ethical values can be a powerful gird underlying them both. The Christian holiday of Christmas, at least in its Santa Claus, gift-giving aspect, is popular, as are Christian-style weddings, though most Japanese are not Christian.

Is all this religion, folk customs, or what? Does it really matter what we call it? From the point of view of Japanese culture, perhaps it does not. Japan has been called *kotoba ga aganu kuni*, the country where words need not be spoken, where indirect hints and wordless understandings often suffice, and not everything needs to be named or categorized.

It may also be a matter of how you think about religion.

Some years ago, when I was studying in Japan, my wife and I leased a house which belonged to a Japanese professor teaching in a technical field for a year at a university in Mississippi. We exchanged correspondence on matters relating to the maintenance of the house, and finally the Japanese visitor in America asked me what I was doing in Japan. I said I was doing research in Japanese religion; he replied that was an odd thing to do, since most Japanese have no religion. Surprised, I responded mentioning all the temples and shrines, the ceremonies and festivals, I saw all around that seemed to be religious. He answered those are not religion, just folk customs.

Obviously a problem had arisen as to what one means by "religion." I finally realized the other was undoubtedly thinking in terms of the Japanese word *shukyo*, usually used for religion in modern translations, but literally meaning the "teaching of a sect," such as a particular school of Buddhism. There is, significantly, no Japanese word meaning everything the hard-to-define word "religion" can indicate in English – though as W. Cantwell Smith has pointed out, our usual view of "a religion" as a separate, optional, detachable part of a culture, and of there being several different "religions" around, is a modern concept, and a modern use of the word, in all cultures.[8] (In medieval Europe "religion" meant following a rule like a monk's.)

My Japanese correspondent, then, thought that one was not religious unless one consistently followed the doctrine and practice of a particular sect, and he rightly judged this was not the case with most Japanese. (In Mississippi, he said, people really were religious. They were members of, and regularly attended, a particular church, most often Baptist; even the state legislature might debate whether certain proposals were in accordance with the Bible.) But this was not how I, as a historian of religion, had been trained to think about the subject: I was more inclined to look for religious "phenomena" – sacred spaces, sacred times, rituals and pilgrimages – and I saw them everywhere.

Toshimaro Ama, in *Why Are the Japanese Non-Religious? Japanese Spirituality: Being Non-Religious in a Religious Culture* argues that Japanese do not see their traditional practices, whether Shinto shrine *matsuri* or festivals, or Buddhist funerals, as religious because, in their understanding, to do so would commit them to a particular religious "sect," that of the shrine, temple, or folk practice in question.[9] Most attend all those which one wishes or which present a social responsibility. Yet while 70 percent of Japanese say they have no religion, 70 percent also perform such rituals as visiting a family grave or going to a shrine or temple at New Years.[10]

For them practices such as those of shrine festivals, temple rites, Buddhist funerals, or New Years are considered "natural," just part of being Japanese. They go along with growing up in a Japanese family and being part of a Japanese community. Many of these exercises are also "natural" in the sense of being closely connected to the cycles of nature, seedtime and harvest in the fields; birth, maturity, and death in the individual. Ama sees a clear distinction in the Japanese mind between "natural" religion, or customs, and "revealed" religion such as Christianity or Islam.

Rightly or wrongly, most Japanese seem to regard this "natural" view of rites as distinct to Japan, and different from the religions of most other places, which they perceive as supposed to have been revealed, as in the Bible or the Qur'an and their prophets, or through the sages of Hinduism and Buddhism, rather than just a natural enhancement of everyday life. Therefore they make special demands that may or may not be consistent with being an ordinary Japanese person. Ama makes much of the value in Japan of just being "ordinary" in one's life, and this is consistent with the emphasis in much of Japanese Buddhism as it has developed with finding the universal Buddha-nature in common things and in everyday life, for those who have eyes to see. This kind of religion does not require conversion, nor acceptance of any special revelation, but a different kind of mentality – which is *mushukyo* or non-religious even in the midst of a society permeated with temples, shrines, seemingly religious symbols, festivals, and ancestral tablets or *ihai* in the home.

One could of course respond that, however supernatural its supposed origin, most religions often function about the same way, with many people mainly relating to them through normative rites of birth and coming of age, through weddings and funerals, or holidays like Christmas and Easter. On the other hand, in the extreme nationalistic period of the 1930s and 1940s, Japan certainly acted as though an aggressive "imperial will" had all the force of divine revelation, and Ama believes that the often-cynical manipulation of religion by the government from the Meiji Restoration (1868) until 1945 had a role in creating the subsequent non-religious mindset. In any case, it is very important to understand the "natural" view of religion, or non-religion, in studying Japan.

The Zen-related poems called *haiku*, only seventeen syllables in Japanese, often convey that sense of direct seeing marvelously, and indeed can evoke the culminating Zen experience of awakening to the buddha-nature, beyond name and form, embedded in all things. Near the Ise shrine, the grandest of all Shinto shrines, dedicated to Amaterasu, Sun Goddess and ancestress of the imperial line, the great poet Basho (1644-1694) wrote:

> I know not
> From the flower of which tree it comes …
> But what perfume!

The suggestion is that the perfume may be more than natural, wafting from the divine presence within the shrine walls. Is this a religious sentiment or not? Hard to say, and certainly Basho does not care.

Another poem by Basho

> An old pond:
> A frog jumps in –
> The sound of water

has been said to encapsulate the whole meaning of Buddhism in those few words, for those who understand. (Consider that the old pond can represent this ancient universe, or nirvana; that the frog has long been taken in Japanese art – sometimes irreverently – to suggest the portly Buddha as he sits meditating; and when he enters this world, which is also nirvana, outflow the sounding waves of his dharma or teaching.)

And one by another great haiku master, Buson (1715–1783)

> As the cherry blossoms fall,
> Between the trees
> A temple appears.

This too packages much Buddhist meaning in a few syllables. Cherry blossoms, with their ephemeral beauty and poignant falling, have long been a staple of Japanese art and poetry, betokening the Buddhist perception of the transitoriness of all life and all worlds. Yet even as they fall, indeed because they fall, one can catch sight of a temple, symbol of the Buddha's teaching which can lead one from out of this passing world into unconditioned reality.

It is now time to enter directly the world of Japanese religion.

Questions for study and discussion

1. What reasons do you have for studying Japanese religion?
2. How can studying the religion help us to understand the political and economic institutions of a society?
3. Give examples of how Japanese religion is expressed in Japanese culture.
4. How can Japanese religion be said to represent several "layers" "stacked up"?
5. What does the Japanese language tell us about the history of the culture?
6. How would you define religion, as descriptive of a certain segment of human culture? How well would your definition apply to religion in Japan?
7. Explain the meaning of Joachim Wach's theoretical, practical, and sociological forms of religious expression. Give examples from Japan.
8. Explain art, ethics, and history as forms of religious expression. Again give examples from Japan.
9. Do you think the Japanese way of thinking about religion is really different from the western? Why or why not?
10. Find a haiku poem which, in your mind, expresses something important about the Japanese approach to religion or spirituality.

Key points you need to know

- Japanese religion helps us to understand Japanese culture and institutions
- The Japanese language combines native and Chinese words
- Japanese religion and ethics combine Shinto, Buddhist, and Confucian features
- Religion has theoretical, practical, and sociological forms of expression
- It further expresses itself through art, ethics, and history (understand how these forms of expression may be found in Japan)
- Answering the question of how religious is Japan requires sensitivity to the culture

Further reading

The following represent several basic textbooks on Japanese religion:

Earhart, H. Byron, *Religion in Japan: Unity and Diversity*. Boston, MA: Cengage Learning, 5th edn, 2013.

Earhart, H. Byron, *Religion in the Japanese Experience: Sources and Interpretations*. Boston, MA: Cengage Learning, 1996.

Earhart, H. Byron, *Religions of Japan*. San Francisco, CA: HarperSanFrancisco, 1984.

Kitagawa, Joseph, *Religion in Japanese History*. New York: Columbia University Press, 1966.

Kornicki, P. F. and I. J. McMullen, eds, *Religion in Japan: Arrows to Heaven and Earth*. Cambridge: Cambridge University Press, 1996.

Reader, Ian, *Religion in Contemporary Japan*. Honolulu, HI: University of Hawaii Press, 1991.

Tanabe, George, ed., *Religions in Japan in Practice*. Princeton, NJ: Princeton University Press, 1999.

Tsunoda, R., W. T. de Bary and D. Keene, *Sources of Japanese Tradition*. New York: Columbia University Press, 1971.

Yusa, Michiko, *Japanese Religious Traditions*. Upper Saddle River, NJ: Prentice Hall; London: Laurence King Publishing, 2002.

Electronic Resources

Wikipedia, "Mircea Eliade." https://en.wikipedia.org/wiki/Mircea_Eliade

Goddess Gift, "Amaterasu: Goddess of the Sun"; "Uzume: Goddess of Mirth and Dance." http://www.goddessgift.com/goddess-myths/japanese_goddess_Amaterasu.htm

Wikipedia, "Ryōan-ji." https://en.wikipedia.org/wiki/Ry%C5%8Dan-ji

Swatos, William H., jr. ed., "Charisma," in *Encyclopedia of Religion and Society.* http://hirr.hartsem.edu/ency/charisma.htm

New World Encyclopedia contributors, "Polytheism," in *New World Encyclopedia.* http://www.newworldencyclopedia.org/p/index.php?title=Polytheism&old id=988100

2 *The past in the present*

Vignettes of Japanese spiritual life

In this chapter

This chapter presents some seventeen examples of Japanese religion in expression and action, including imperial and popular Shinto, Buddhist traditions from different periods, folk religion, the new religions, Christianity, and traumatic recent experience. In all these cases, note the importance of the practical ("what is done" – ritual, meditation, and the like) form of religious expression, and of the sociological (national, community, and group life) form, as well as or more important than the theoretical ("what is said" – doctrine, teaching). Note that art, symbol, and architecture can be extremely significant too.

First, a preliminary word about these vignettes of Japanese spiritual life. These glimpses are here presented in a generally sympathetic way. This is not to suggest that Japanese religion cannot be criticized; later we will need to look at issues involving religion and violence or oppressive social structures from early times to the present, and particularly in the World War II period. But I think it is also important for an observer to try to see, and so far as possible vicariously experience, the attractive side of a religious site or practice in order to understand what it means to those for whom it is important. These descriptions are meant to assist in that endeavor.

Main topics covered

- The Daijosai, or harvest festival as celebrated by the emperor at his accession
- A *matsuri* or festival at a typical Shinto shrine
- The Great Buddha of Nara, representing Dainichi ("Great Sun") or essence of the universe; of the Kegon (Garland Sutra) school
- Toji, a major temple of Shingon, a highly esoteric form of Buddhism, in which a mandala or diagram of sacred figures is represented in three-dimensional form
- Enryakuji, the main temple of Tendai, a school embracing many paths within Buddhism

- Higashi Honganji, the main temple of a school of Pure Land, a form of Buddhism based on faith in the saving grace of Amida Buddha
- Daitokuji, a principal temple of Zen, the school emphasizing *zazen* or seated meditation
- A meeting of Soka Gakkai, based on Nichiren Buddhism with its Lotus Sutra chanting practice
- The Martyrs' Monument in Nagasaki, honoring Christians crucified for their faith in 1597
- Tenri city, headquarters of Tenrikyo, one of the "new religions" of Japan
- Jizo, a popular deity, guardian of travelers and of children, including the unborn and deceased children finding themselves in the other world
- Itako or Miko, shamanesses believed able to communicate with spirits of the departed
- Mt. Osore, a peak on the far northern tip of Honshu, where itako gather annually
- Namahage, colorful figures in demon-like masks who visit homes in parts of the far north of Honshu on New Year's Eve to admonish children to be hard-working and well-behaved; typical of many dramatic local customs based on folklore and basic Shinto, Buddhist, and Confucian values
- Obon, a basically Buddhist festival held over three days in midsummer when families gather to greet returning ancestral spirits with traditional dances and offerings
- Fukushima, site of the tragic tsunami and nuclear disaster of 2011; we will look at religious responses to this traumatic event
- Funerals and memorial services, traditionally Buddhist in Japan, are the way many people most connect with religion; here are some typical practices.

The Daijosai

The autumn evening is crisp and dark on the ground of the imperial palace, but in the light of flaring torches and bonfires we see a strange procession advance. It is probably November of the first full year of a new emperor's reign, as it was in 1990 when this ceremony was performed with Emperor Akihito in the central role. The novice sovereign is now completing his accession by a very ancient act of solemn and mysterious fellowship, in the depth of night, with his ancestral deities. This is the Daijosai, the Shinto "Great Food Festival" as first performed by the monarch after his coming to the throne. The Niinamesai or harvest festival is enacted every year by the emperor in his capacity as chief priest of Shinto, but the first celebration after his accession, when this Thanksgiving or Harvest Home becomes the Daijosai, acquires very special rituals and meaning.[1]

The sovereign walks in the midst of a small column of courtiers carrying imperial regalia. Over his head attendants hold a sedge canopy. The ruler's feet are bare.

Lest they touch the ground, orderlies unroll a mat in front of him, and others roll it up again behind him. The monarch is proceeding from the Kairyuden, "Eternal Flow Hall," where he had taken a hot purifying bath. After bathing, he had clothed himself in plain white silk and meditated until the time to begin the rite. He is now moving toward one of two ritual buildings, the Yukiden, where he will wait in an antechamber while ancient music is played.

Entering the ritual hall, the sovereign will seat himself on a mat, before which are two sets of food offerings, one for himself and one for the *kami*: rice, two kinds of rice wine (sake), seafood and other common substances. The rice had been grown in two selected fields, chosen by divination early in the year. Planted, nourished, and harvested with old Shinto ceremonies, they were then brought to the palace in great religious processions. Now, in the quiet Yukiden, solemnly as though in communion with the deity, the Emperor consumes three balls of rice and takes four sips of each kind of sake.

Constructed in a very plain and ancient style, of rough wood, thatch roof, without nails or other metal, the Yukiden takes us back to ancient Japan. But what is of most interest are the other accouterments of the interior. Before the emperor is the *shinza*, or divine bed, a couch on a slightly raised portion of the floor. Slippers wait at its feet, a comb and a fan are laid out at the head of the bed as though ready for use, and near this piece of antique furniture are set small tables bearing white and black lamps, and baskets of rough and smooth cloth.

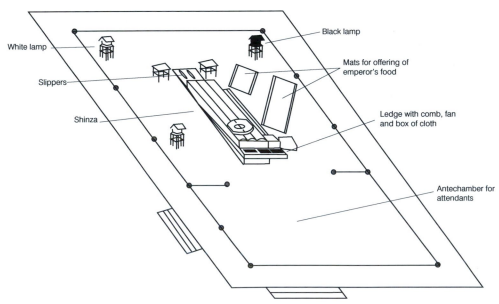

Figure 2.1 Sketch of Daijosai Hall

After completing the ritual in the Yukiden, the sovereign retires again to the Kairyuden, then processes to the identical Sukiden, where the same sacred actions are accomplished once again. In 1990, the Yukiden rite was done from 6:30 to 9:30 p.m., the Sukiden repetition from 12:30 to 3:30 a.m.

All this is just to indicate that the Daijosai tells us several important things about Japanese religion, and above all Shinto. First, the pre-eminence of the practical form of religious expression, the practices and worship. The ritual must be carried out with precision down to the last detail, though the meaning of much of it, of the *shinza* and the lamps, even the name of the *kami* with whom the new sovereign communes, is apparently lost in the mists of history and prehistory. (The Daijosai may well be the oldest state ritual still enacted today.) The loss of meaning, however, is no real loss in a land where meaning need not be spoken, and mystery only enhances our sense of something awesome and numinous in this autumnal, nocturnal drama. That feeling is the important thing. So also is the sense of tradition embodied in the Daijosai. For many Japanese, tradition – doing things the same way generation after generation

What is the meaning of these peculiar furnishings of the two halls, which – so far as is known by outsiders – have no role in the ritual as it is performed in the present day, or has been in historical times? Some have speculated that the *shinza* may derive from some former *hieros gamos*, or sacred marriage rite, such as was performed by kings in ancient Babylon and elsewhere, who consummated their divine calling by uniting physically with a priestess representing a goddess. But this has been adamantly denied by imperial officials, who say that the bed is merely the seat of the *kami* who joins the new ruler in the sacred hall. Others have pointed to ancient Japanese mythology in which the legitimate heir was recognized by his reclining at ease on a "true couch," that is, a throne.[2] Much about the Daijosai remains a mystery.

What about the black and white lamps, and the rough and smooth cloth in the two baskets? In my own thinking about the enigmas of the Daijosai, it occurred to me that they might be connected to another puzzlement: why, if the rite is supposed to celebrate imperial descent from Amaterasu, the sun goddess, is it performed – twice – in the middle of the night? Is a clue suggested by an ancient prayer, called the Nakatomi no Yogoto, recited at the Daijosai? This lofty petition refers to an envoy of the Emperor ascending to the "two peaks of heaven," from which heavenly water descends, there to speak to the imperial ancestors. This sounds like the crescent moon, not the sun! Could it be that in early Japan, as in some other early societies, the moon – giver of rain and fertility – was more important religiously than the sun, and divine descent was originally from the ruler of the night?[3]

– is an important token of continuity in a world otherwise changing with baffling speed, and the traditional religions, Shinto and Buddhism, are especially important custodians of that function.

To be sure, there were Japanese who criticized the 1990 performance of the Daijosai – the first time it had been done since the accession of the wartime emperor Hirohito; his Daijosai was in 1928, when Shinto was a state religion – and cases were brought to several Japanese courts challenging the use of state funds for it on the grounds of the postwar constitutional separation of church and state. But all were dismissed, one court ruling that so far as the government's participation was concerned, the rite merely celebrated the Emperor's secular role as "symbol of the nation," and the Shinto aspect "falls within the appropriate relationship between the nation and Shintoism as a social component of Japan's national culture."[4]

This reminds us of another important message of the Daijosai, the sociological. Virtually all important traditional religion in Japan has a significant sociological role, affirming the cohesion of the family or community which enacts it. The Daijosai, insofar as it is intended to signify the mystical union of the nation with the sovereign, and of the sovereign with the *kami*, illustrates this point to the utmost – even though it is, characteristically, scarcely a public ceremony, but one done in an almost secretive way. In Japan, that which is most sacred may be most concealed, its influence radiating out in indirect but pervasive ways.

Thus it is that after the middle-of-the-night rituals, his legitimacy confirmed in the highest quarters, the Emperor on the next day enjoys an "unwinding" banquet with his court, and – today – appears before his people and the world in appropriate photo opportunities.

A typical Shinto shrine

It is early morning; a hint of mist still hangs in the air; the *torii* or gate to the shrine, with its distinctive curved crossbeam, seems all the more like the portal to another world, as we pass through it from the this-worldly street into a precinct of grass, shrubs, a huge old evergreen tree, and in the midst of it all an unusual building fronted by a porch bearing drums, upright sticks from which fall peculiar zigzag strips of paper (*gohei*), a mirror, and a table with eight legs, four on each side. That wooden altar stands before steep steps leading up to a massive door, its heavy paneling and highly polished ornamental hinges obviously concealing something of great importance locked within. In the shrine courtyard we see on this morning, unlike all other mornings, a number of large mysterious objects covered with protective canvas. A large group of people stand in anticipation before the front of the shrine. For this is a day of *matsuri*, of a shrine festival.

Soon enough the day's activities unfold. A drum is beaten at a rapid pace, starting loud then dwindling down to faint, creating a strangely haunting effect. A priest,

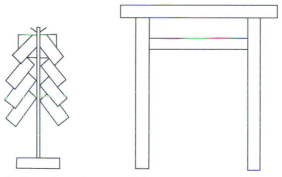

Figure 2.2 Sketch of *gohei* and *torii* (not to scale)

Honden
(Inner sanctuary)

Heiden
(Hall of offering)

Haiden
(Hall of prayers)

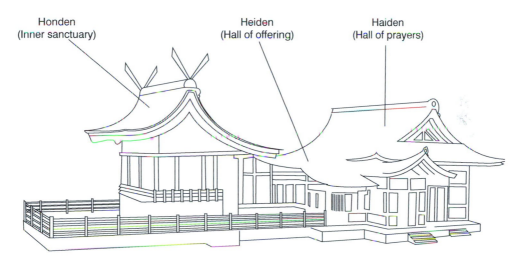

Figure 2.3 Sketch of a Shinto shrine

dressed in a white robe of archaic cut and a high rounded cap, emerges with an evergreen branch, making sweeping gestures with it around the shrine porch and over the assembled worshipers, an act of purification.

Then, with the slowness of ancient ritual, the priest, perhaps assisted by two or three others, conveys food offerings from a sideboard to the eight-legged table in the center of the *heiden*, or hall of offerings, as this part of the shrine is technically called. Placed on high-stemmed trays, the food, consisting of rice wine, rice, salt, vegetables, fruit, and seafood – rarely, if ever, red meat – is very attractively arranged, as is true also of any respectable Japanese meal. After it has been arranged, the chief priest stands before the table to read a *norito* or prayer, often chanted in a high, strained-sounding voice. In elegant language, he will thank the *kami* of this shrine for his blessings over the past season, and invoke her or him to continue them in the future. Then the offerings – probably actually consumed by the priests and their families – will be removed as slowly and solemnly as they were presented.

The steep steps and massive door lead to the *honden*, the inner sanctum of the shrine where the *kami* is said especially to dwell. In the midst of that dark room rests the *shintai*, or "divine substitute," a holy object concentrating the sacred power venerated in this particular shrine, though of course not limiting that presence to one room. The *shintai* may be an ancient sword, a mirror, a stone, or even just a strip of paper bearing the *kami* name. It will be enclosed in a box covered by many layers of brocade cloth; since these are never removed, the box may have been unopened for centuries, and in some cases the nature of the actual *shintai* object has been forgotten – another instance of how, in Japan, that which is most sacred is hidden, concealed, even pushed to the edge of memory, and for that reason become all the more mysterious and numinous. Only on very special festivals will the priests open the *honden* doors, enter, and present offering directly before the occult *shintai*.

A Shinto *matsuri* has four basic stages, which can be thought of as beginning with the letter "p":

- purification, when the shrine and grounds are ritually swept clean of impurities;
- presentation, the solemn bringing-forward of the offerings;
- prayer, the reading of the *norito*; and
- participation, when everyone gets into the act.

The first three have now transpired. Participation begins decorously as leading members of the shrine come forward one by one to present an evergreen branch on the offering table, and receive as a sort of holy communion a sip of the rice wine which has been offered to the *kami*. But after this is done, the pace changes. The canvas coverings are removed from the bulky outdoor objects to reveal a scene like a carnival midway: here booths selling souvenirs and refreshments like cotton candy, over there vendors of games of chance and skill.

Beautifully dressed miko or shrine maidens perform traditional dances for the entertainment of the *kami* and his people. Men may demonstrate sumo wrestling, a

This Buddha should not be taken as the historical Buddha, he who preached in India a millennium before his faith even reached Japan. During those ten centuries understanding of the meaning behind the world-teacher's words had, as is natural, changed, deepened, and expanded to comprehend the significance of a Buddhist worldview not just for an individual, not even just for this world, but for the way we think about the entire cosmos, with its infinite depths of space and time. That perspective – that of the Mahayana form of Buddhism prevailing in East Asia – tells us that the most fundamental reality of the universe is consciousness, endless consciousness of which our own is only an outcropping. The profoundest, and most creative, level of consciousness, we are told, is generated in meditation.

sport anciently connected to Shinto. The *kami* will be taken in a *mikoshi*, or palanquin, carried on the shoulders of young men through the streets of his parish. They will run in a fast, zigzag pace, shouting "Washo! Washo!" – for just as the opening parts of the *matsuri*, the offerings and prayer, may have seemed unnaturally slow-paced, so now, with the *kami*-presence fully ensconced in the festival, it is as though an excess of energy, more than in ordinary everyday life, is present – a real celebration, full of excitement, speed, and drive.

The "participation" part of a *matsuri* varies considerably from one shrine to another, for many pride themselves on local traditions and strive to keep them alive. Among more famous shrines, there are those that in the main annual *matsuri* mount sacred horse races, or boat races, or archery contests, or light great bonfires, or do special parades or dances. In all, though, once the "slow" portion is over, a spirit of joviality takes over; there is no shortage of eating, drinking, dancing, gaming, and clowning, sometimes with sensual innuendo. The flavor of a Shinto *matsuri* can best be compared with that of Mardi Gras or Carnival in certain Latin countries of the West; it is not religion for the puritanical. But it does what the Shinto side of Japanese religion is supposed to do: affirm the good things of this life, and cement the bonds linking families and communities to their traditions and their local gods.

The Great Buddha of Nara

Here is something else. In the ancient city of Nara, Japan's first capital, down a long gravelly path, at the back of a park-like space in which one can often spot the famous deer of Nara, rests the largest wooden building in the world, called the Todaiji. And within this structure is seated one of the most splendid treasures of Japan, the Great Buddha, the largest bronze statue in the world, rising to a total height of 72 feet; even the figure's fingers are six feet in length. When this imposing image was dedicated with great ceremony in 752 CE, the religion of the Enlightened One had been practiced in the island nation only some two hundred years. The intriguing, intrigue-laden story of its construction will be told later. Here let us focus on the figure itself, and its meaning.

Infinite creative meditation, then, is what is portrayed in this magnificent temple. For the Great Buddha seated there is none other than Dainichi, the Great Sun Buddha (Sanskrit: Mahavairocana[5]), who represents the essence of the universe itself. His eyes are turned downward in deep meditation, and out of his meditation flows the universe with all its countless worlds, all galaxies, stars, systems, and life-forms, including we ourselves.

This temple was constructed by the Kegon school of Mahayana, based on the Kegon or "Garland" (Sanskrit: Avatamsaka, Chinese: Huayan) sutra. It teaches that the universe is eternally self-creating, and entails the changing but harmonious interaction of all its myriad parts. Dainichi is seated on a lotus throne with a thousand

Figure 2.4 The Great Buddha of Nara (© Neale Cousland / Shutterstock.com)

petals, each of which is a universe like ours containing millions of worlds. Covering the wall behind him are numerous smaller Buddha images, each like a reflection of the Great Buddha in a particular world or universe, suggesting each has its own hierarchies of Buddhas able to lead sentient beings in that realm toward oneness with the Infinite Mind. But the multiverse of innumerable universes is in eternal flux and change; everything interpenetrates and reflects everything else … We shall see how and why a little later.

Toji Shingon Temple

The next stage in Japanese Buddhism is awesomely displayed in the Toji ("East Temple") in the old capital, Kyoto, beside the famous Rashomon gate.[6] (The capital was moved from Nara to Heian, modern Kyoto, in 784-94.) Toji is a major temple of the Shingon school, based on the Great Sun (Dainichi) (Sanskrit: Mahavairocana) sutra, which entered Japan under the leadership of the famous priest Kukai (774-835; also called Kobo daishi). He was given charge of the Toji in 823, and made it a remarkable visual display of his school's view of the universe.

In the center of the Lecture Hall is Dainichi, the same central consciousness-essence of all reality represented by the Great Buddha of Nara, whose profound meditations create and sustain the universe. To the four directions from this center are four more cosmic Buddhas, representing transcendental aspects of nature and consciousness. In the west, for example, is Amida, the Buddha of discriminating wisdom, who was later to step out of the mandala, as it were, to become the central, saving figure in Pure Land Buddhism.

In the Toji each of these five major mandala buddhas is accompanied by two attendants, entities embodying the Buddha in action, one manifesting wisdom (called *myo-o*, or marvelous kings), the other compassion (*bosatsu* or *bodhisattvas*, "enlightenment beings," whose full meaning will be discussed later). Technically, these personify two configurations of the mandala: the "Diamond" side, the hard clear inner core, and the "Womb" side, its soft creative merciful outward expression. For Amida, the wisdom figure is Manju, who rides on a lion and bears the sword of discrimination; the personification of compassion is the ever-beloved Kannon (Sanskrit: Avalokiteshvara, Chinese: Kuanyin), she of the many arms to display the many works of mercy she can perform simultaneously. Dainichi's *myo-o* is Fudo (Sanskrit: Acala), the Unmovable, whose sword, noose, background flames, and glaring eyes depict his unflinching enmity to error and to enemies of the Buddha's truth.

Finally, on the outer rim of the pattern stand six protector deities. Some of them are ultimately borrowed from Hinduism; guarding the mandala we see Bonten (Brahma) sitting on a lotus supported by four geese, and Taishakuten (Indra) mounted on an elephant. The Toji does indeed bring us into a fabulous universe, one that reminds us that the plain, ordinary world we see around us, even the one particular universe in which we happen to live, may be only the proverbial tip of the iceberg so far as ultimate reality is concerned: behind its manifestation, and our own minds, are layers upon layers of consciousnesses, and deeper and deeper levels of reality.

Shingon goes beyond Kegon to say, in effect, not only is the universe infinite, interpenetrating, and full of centers of enlightened consciousness ("cosmic Buddhas") everywhere, but there are secret ways in which we can learn how these figures themselves interact, and can enable ourselves to unite with their minds. Shingon is called Esoteric, "secret," *mikkyo* Buddhism. Later we will learn what some of those secrets are.

For now, let us just appreciate how the inner, esoteric universe is presented at the Toji. We first approach the temple through a beautiful, park-like space, containing lush gardens and a pond. We observe its grand five-tiered pagoda, the highest wooden tower in Japan. We press on to the Golden Hall and the Lecture

Hall. The former presents a large statue of Yakushi, the popular Healing Buddha. Characteristic of the way Shingon loves to multiply images drawn from the esoteric world are the twelve "generals," protectors of the Healing Buddha, that ornament his throne. There is also a much-worshiped statue of Kukai himself, regarded as a nearly-divine saint.

It is the Lecture Hall, however, which undoubtedly was closest to Kukai's heart. In twenty-one figures it displays an incredible life-size, three dimensional representation of the esoteric mandala, or arrangement of the cosmic Buddhas, which he taught.

Bringing it all back to everyday life, where of course Japanese Buddhism also dwells, we may note that Toji is also a "working" temple, conducting funerals and other parish ceremonies, and the site of popular outdoor markets.

The Enryakuji

On Mount Hiei, to the northeast of Kyoto – the direction from which demonic influences were thought to come – stands like a guardian the Enryakuji, the great temple complex which headquarters the Tendai sect. This denomination came into Japan from China at the beginning of the Heian period like Shingon, and like it is a highly Mahayana form of Buddhism, featuring numerous cosmic Buddhas and bodhisattvas, *myo-o* and watchdog deities. But it sees the Lotus Sutra, rather than the more esoteric Great Sun Sutra, as the highest expression of Buddhism. However, Tendai recognizes many stages of devotion and many paths on the way to profoundest enlightenment. Indeed, the school speaks of 84,000 paths to enlightenment, and has served as a broad umbrella under which later forms of Buddhism – Pure Land, Nichiren, and Zen – were first nourished in Japan. To visit Mount Hiei is like visiting a living museum of Mahayana Buddhism, in which many of its almost infinite variety of worshipful forms may be reverenced.

Now accessible by means of cable car or beautiful mountain highway, the Enryakuji is really a collection of many temples set over acres of rich deep forests and clear streams, with occasional vistas of the ancient city far below. In the middle ages as many as 3,000 temples adorned this spectacular site, but nearly all were destroyed by the warlord Oda Nobunaga in 1571, on his way to "pacifying" Japan. He had his reasons. Though long a great center of religion and learning, the Enryakuji, like the great monasteries of medieval Europe, was also a major political force which had often forced the imperial court to accede to its will, and which even fielded its own monk-army, the equal of any other in feudal wars. But while much was lost in the destruction, what remains, or was rebuilt, still gives the visitor a marvelous impression of Mahayana diversity.

On one hand a temple featuring a stunning image of Kannon may greet us. The Bodhisattva of Mercy's multiple eyes and arms illustrate her ability simultaneously to perceive those in need in many lands and worlds, then to reach out to them in pity.

She likewise hears the prayers even of the humblest for boons like healing and help in distress, for while such petitions for oneself or loved ones may not represent the highest form of egolessness to which the enlightened can aspire, this compassionate deity is also aware that love is wisdom in action. An ordinary gift, a simple prayer answered, can show there is more to this many-wondered universe than muck and misery; it can awaken the sense of awe and gratitude that guide one's first steps in the long spiritual journey.

Then, down a wooded path, we come upon a temple of Fudo, who displays another aspect of things. Holding the sword of discrimination between the real and the unreal, holding a lasso with which to snare error, backed by surging flames to illumine his fervent invincibility, he looks with piercing eye on his guests, challenging them to rise to his invincible standards. This Myo-o-do, "Hall of the Marvelous King," is home base for those who undertake a thousand-day training in self-discipline, including running a nineteen-mile marathon around the mountain daily; we will meet these adepts later.

Going on, down the road we find a wide hall dedicated to Amida, the Buddha who has promised to bring into his Pure Land all who call upon his name in faith, realizing it is ultimately beyond our power to save ourselves without the grace of the Infinite Reality of which we are only a part; Amidism or Pure Land was to become a separate school of Buddhism, but here on Mount Hiei it is one of many paths to the Other Shore.

Then over here is a grand sanctuary of Dainichi, the Great Sun Buddha of Kegon and Shingon, whose meditations sustain the cosmos, and who also holds court in Tendai. Perhaps, if Kannon is the object of devotion for those of simple prayer, Fudo of mystical athletes moved by the drive to be all they can be physically and spiritually, Amida those whose spiritual virtue is faith, Dainichi is the patron of those intellectual mystics who seek to penetrate the inner mysteries of the universe. So it goes; Mount Hiei offers these paths and many more.

It also offers the Way of the Gods, for at the base of the mountain is the Sanno, "Mountain King," shrine, whose *kami* is particularly the guardian of Mount Hiei and its mystic rites; the holy hill and protector god have long had a very close relationship.

Chionin

A pure and fabulously beautiful paradise emanates around the sublime consciousness of a great being in the class of a cosmic Buddha like Amida, or the others of the great mandala. The Pure Land (Jodo) sutras tell us that the heaven of Amida is filled with incomparable music and nets of jewels hanging from the paradisaical trees. This Western Paradise is walled with silver, gold, and beryl; its lakes have jeweled banks, and floating upon their waters an abundance of lotuses. Out of the smaller of these lovely blossoms the saved of our world emerge reborn, and in the greater flowers

Figure 2.5 Chionin Temple, Kyoto (© cowardlion / Shutterstock.com)

Aldous Huxley, in an essay entitled "Heaven and Hell," asks why it is that we humans so value precious jewels, such as diamonds and emeralds, and gleaming precious metals like gold and silver.[7] They are, after all, of no practical value; they cannot be eaten or drunk, or worn as clothing except as ornaments, or likely to be made into a house or barn. Yet people pay more than the price of a good suit of clothes or even a mansion for a fine gemstone. Pointing out that images of paradise around the world, whether the Buddhist Pure Land or the Judeo-Christian Heavenly Jerusalem, tend to be replete with jewels in abundance, Huxley suggests the real value of gems lies in their ability to evoke what he calls the "antipodes of the mind" – a realm pure, bright, glowing, the opposite of so much in this world, for which we yearn. Certainly, in entering the Chionin, one feels one is entering that "antipodes."

bodhisattvas sit enthroned. From this dreamlike terrain, with all human obstacles removed, entry into nirvana is easy.

Surely no earthly structure gives a better sense of the Pure Land's otherworldly wonder than the interior of the Chionin, the main temple of the Jodo-shu, or Pure Land school founded by Honen (1133–1212). Dedicated in 1234, it is located on a commanding hill in the east of Kyoto, boasting the largest temple gate in Japan and, at 74 tons, the heaviest of all temple bells; it is said to take as many as seventeen monks to sound it the customary 108 times at New Year. Entering the temple, however, it is the fabulous sanctuary that seizes our attention, with its rich filigrees of gold around the lotus-enthroned figure of Amida and his attendant bodhisattvas and saints, and overhead, painted on the ceiling, the colored clouds and *tenshi* (angels) of paradise.

Higashi Honganji

Hongan means "original vow," and refers to the "original vow" of Amida to bring all who call on his name by faith into his Pure Land. The Higashi Honganji is the "Eastern Temple of the Original Vow"; a few blocks away is the Nishi Honganji, the Western Temple. These are temples of Jodo-Shinshu, the "True Pure Land School," founded by Shinran (1173–1262), a disciple of Honen, the first major Japanese teacher of Pure Land, founder of Jodo-shu and of the Chionin.

In the troubled times of medieval Japan, Honen claimed he had read all the Buddhist scriptures five times, but had found no peace till he had read a commentary on the Pure Land scriptures. They awakened him to realization that salvation was not by one's own efforts, not a matter of how much one strove or meditated, but of simple faith. True salvation was willingness to put one's trust in the help of another – and this trust actually brought, far better than self-help, the ultimate Buddhist objective of egolessness and oneness with the universe. Over a long life, Honen taught and practiced Amidist faith, expressed in the simple chant, *Namu Amida Butsu,* "Hail Amida Buddha." This chant is called the *nembutsu.*

His disciple Shinran, who has been called the Martin Luther of Japan, was even more radical in his Pure Land belief, saying the important thing is not even our faith, but Amida's grace coming first, to which we respond by faith. Even if the greatest sinner in the world says the *nembutsu* only once, he can still be brought into the Pure Land, for it is not by our merits but by Amida's grace we are delivered. Recognizing that in Jodo Buddhism, where all that counts is faith and grace, celibate monkhood is pointless, like Luther then Shinran left the cloister and married.

Suggesting the austerity of this practice, compared to the Chionin the two Honganji temples are spacious but relatively plain, like simple Protestant churches compared to a traditional Catholic one. In them the main hall houses only a single image of Amida, accompanied by one bodhisattva, the beloved Kannon. Adjacent to the main hall is the founder's hall, containing only a standing figure of Shinran. But one can continually see devotees of Jodo-Shinshu reciting the *nembutsu* on a *juzu*, or Buddhist rosary. On exhibit at the Higashi Honganji are samples of rope made of human hair, donated by women from all over Japan in the 1890s, when the temple was being rebuilt after a fire, to help in lifting the heavy timbers for its construction.

Daitokuji

The Daitoku ("Great Virtue") Temple, to the northwest of Kyoto, is a prominent center of Zen. In its main temple and twenty-three sub-temples the Zen life is practiced, and in certain of them beautiful examples of Zen culture may be found: gardens worthy of compare with Ryoanji (but usually without the crowds), famous paintings, and tea houses built by the greatest tea-master of them all, Sen no Rikyu (1521–91).

For now, however, let our attention rest on Zen practice, above all the practice of *zazen*, or seated Zen meditation, such as might be observed in the *zendo*, or meditation hall, of one of the temples of Daitokuji. Here, during the hours of *zazen* one would see rows of black-robed monks, or students of Zen, seated in the lotus posture (each foot on the opposite thigh) on a round pillow called a *zafu*, back erect, hands folded in the lap with the thumbs pressed together, eyes half shut and half open. Because Daitokuji is a temple of the Rinzai school of Zen, they sit facing outward, toward the center of the *zendo*; if it were the other main school, Soto, they would sit facing the wall.

What does a Zen student meditate on? That would be made clear if we could observe another activity too: *sanzen* or *dokusan*, the interview with the *roshi* or Zen master. Entering into the presence of this teacher, after profound bows of respect, the student may be asked what *koan* or Zen "puzzle" the student is working on. Famous examples of *koan*s, assigned to the student by the *roshi*, are "What is the sound of one hand?" or "What was your face before you were born?"

The answer is not to be merely an intellectual response but, as we shall see later, a demonstration, perhaps silent, that clearly shows the student understands the inner meaning of that "case" or "precedent," which is what *koan* really means. The realization that produces an authentic demonstration, always ultimately a realization of egolessness and universal oneness, is attained not by thinking about it, but by holding the *koan* in the mind, as a mental focus, perhaps inwardly repeating it over and over, until a kind of illumination – *satori*, "surprise" – arises within one. Who has this awakening is able to live free and joyous, in the moment.

As they do *zazen*, a proctor, called the *jikijitsu*, walks up and down the silent hall, carrying a long stick on his shoulder. If a student bows to him, indicating a need to be recalled to mindfulness, or if someone appears to nod off, the *jikijitsu* will bring the stick down sharply on the student's shoulders; the latter will bow again in acknowledgment. This action is not meant to be punitive, only an impersonal aid to spiritual discipline.

At half-hour breaks in the practice of *zazen*, marked by a clapper, we will see the students rise, silently file out of the *zendo*, and walk for about five minutes before return. At the end of a *zazen* session of perhaps two hours, the Heart Sutra may be chanted, tea may be served silently, and the students leave to other labors. But in highly traditional monasteries, the *zendo* is home as well as place of meditation; the austere meals of rice and vegetables would be served there at one's place as well as tea, and the student might even sleep where he eats and does *zazen*.

At the Daitokuji or other Zen centers, one will not only see students doing *zazen*, but also working in gardens, kitchens, wherever the labors of the day call. *Zazen*, in fact, is said to be only preparation; it is in the thick of ordinary, everyday tasks that true Zen enlightenment is manifested. A real Zen person is known by the way she walks, sits, chops vegetables, or serves tea as well as by her meditation. In fact, even animals will recognize such a person; in Japan there is a saying that dogs do not bark when a Zen master passes by.

Nichiren Buddhism

For this observation let us leave the vicinity of Kyoto; indeed, let us leave Japan altogether for a hall in Santa Monica, a seaside suburb of Los Angeles. Here a group of people, of several races but predominately Caucasian and mostly young, are seated on the floor chanting in front of a dark brown cabinet-like box. The open doors reveal not an image, but a large white sheet of heavy paper on which are inscribed a number of *kanji* characters; the eye is drawn to six of them, larger than the others, running down the center of the rectangular page. The white paper is the *Gohonzon* ("Main object of worship"); the six principal characters are the words being chanted: "Nam Myoho Renge Kyo" ("Hail the Marvelous Teaching of the Lotus Sutra").

The chant goes very fast, accompanied by the dry rustle of rosaries of 108 beads, shaped roughly like a human form, with a central loop and five attached limbs; these are rubbed between the hands as the chant speeds along like an express train, leaving a resonance of tremendous energy in the air. This is Nichiren Shoshu Buddhism; no Buddhism of quiet meditation or esoteric mysteries, it sees itself as a vibrant, dynamic practice, engaged with living in the modern world. As the group I visited in this room makes evident, it is also a form of Japanese Buddhism which, especially in the 1960s and 1970s, spread itself around the world with exceptional success.

Eventually, after some forty-five minutes of chanting, the first part of the evening ended as the leader sounded a bell three times. Next came *Gongyo*, recitation from the Lotus Sutra (Sanskrit: Saddharmapundarika sutra, Japanese: Myohorengekyo, often abbreviated as Hokkekyo). *Gongyo* was also read at racing speed, in the ancient Sino-Japanese pronunciation of Sanskrit used in Japanese temples, but which probably few if any of this group understood as a language. But, with respect to both *Gongyo* and the *Daimoku* (the chant), it is not the meaning of the words, but the sound itself – its vibrations, and how they harmonize with the essence of the universe – that counts. One could not help tapping or swaying to the rhythm of this chant. The *Gongyo* was also exotic: closing my eyes, I could see ancient curved-roof temples, reflecting in lotus ponds or banked with mountain snow.

Gongyo finished, I was quickly back in contemporary California. Several vivacious girls got up and led Nichiren songs, set to lively American folk tunes, in cheerleader fashion. Speakers introduced the meaning of the practice. Nichiren Buddhism is, we were told, "True Buddhism," going back to the historical Buddha in ancient India, but fulfilled by Nichiren in thirteenth-century Japan; he recognized that the Lotus Sutra is the only valid teaching for our age, and chanted "Nam Myoho Renge Kyo", words which aligned one's inner being with the forces of the universe. Chanting could, therefore, on the one hand bring outer fulfillment, and on the other inner peace. Nichiren Buddhism does not hesitate to promise material benefits through chanting, since these would be signs one is becoming truly harmonized with the universe, but acknowledges that the outer gain is only a sign of even greater inner

Nichiren testimonies

A tall brunette, radiant with health, youth, and beauty, said that before she started chanting two years ago, she had been "down," but now she was happy. She had two problems, though: too much to do, what with work, school, and riding her horse; and her father's making it hard for her to go to Nichiren Shoshu meetings. But with the help of chanting she had been able to work it all out, and had even gotten into a ceramics class she had really wanted to take, but had been over-enrolled.

Another girl said she had been chanting for the happiness of her mother, who had been going through a hard time, and also to sell their house; the mother improved, and the house found a buyer almost immediately. A young man told of finding a good job, and getting his guitar fixed free, with the help of Nichiren Shoshu. Others mentioned getting better attitudes toward the world and others, arguing less with parents, and making friends. But all emphasized that the outward favors from the universe were not the truly important part; the greatest change was within, in their own inward happiness.

spiritual benefit. *Esho funi*, "inner and outer are not separate," is a key Nichiren tenet – by changing either one you change the other. Next came testimonies, and change was their burden.

This is Nichiren Shoshu, one of two traditional schools of Nichiren Buddhism. That denomination's impact was greatly enhanced by a lay organization called Soka Gakkai ("Value-creation Teaching Society") founded in 1930, severely persecuted before and during World War II, but which grew and flourished immensely in the 1950s. Soka Gakkai spread abroad and prospered no less powerfully in the 1960s, amid the spiritual upheavals and "youth culture" of that tumultuous decade. Always focusing on youth and what's happening now, this energetic movement shattered the serene, archaic atmosphere of traditional Buddhism with its marching bands, pop music groups, stadium-filling rallies, and cheering worthy of a football crowd. It also pursued highly aggressive recruitment tactics, often criticized, and, in Japan, formed its own political party.

A bitter split between the traditional, priestly Nichiren Shoshu organization and Soka Gakkai in 1991, together with leveling-off after the period of tremendous growth, has weakened the movement (my visit was before the split), but Nichiren Buddhism, whether as Nichiren Shoshu, Nichiren-Shu (the other traditional denomination), or Soka Gakkai, remains potent, all told among the most numerous forms of Japanese Buddhism. We will study these issues in detail later.

As for its rapid postwar growth, I was informed at this meeting that the practice (the "philosophy," they insisted on calling it) did not become freely available to everyone until after World War II, because previously the government in Japan suppressed it since it made people happy, and they found people easier to control if they were not happy. Its ultimate object, furthermore, is world peace, but world peace has to start from within. People who are truly happy do not start wars.

The Martyrs' Monument in Nagasaki

Traveling to the city of Nagasaki on the southern tip of the southern island of Kyushu, we find another kind of religious monument from those of Shinto and Buddhism, one perhaps unexpected to some. Here, on a gray and black stone wall, against a black stone cross, are twenty-six human images in bas-relief, representing twenty-six Christian martyrs.

Nagasaki has been impacted by the West in two ways. In 1945 it was the second city, after Hiroshima, to be struck by an atomic bomb. In the sixteenth century it, and nearby Kagoshima, were the first places in Japan visited by Portuguese ships bearing soldiers, traders – and missionaries. The famous St Francis Xavier arrived in 1549. At first the Jesuit and later Franciscan evangelists were welcomed by Japanese overlords, and made many converts. But by the end of the century the tide had turned. Leaders saw the new faith as destabilizing, and were all too aware that in the Philippines and elsewhere traders and missionaries were soon followed by colonial governors.

The Christian martyrs commemorated here suffered for their faith in 1597. The twenty-six included six European Franciscans, three Japanese Jesuits, and seventeen Japanese laymen, among them three young boys. They were appropriately executed by crucifixion in Nagasaki, being raised on crosses and then pierced with spears.

Many more martyrs followed. The Tokugawa shogunate (1600–1868) particularly sought to extirpate Christianity and most other foreign influence. Alleged Christians were forced to tread on crosses and blaspheme their faith, or else suffer terrible deaths. But when missionaries returned after the reopening of Japan in the nineteenth century, they found that Christian families had kept alive a sometimes garbled version of the religion for more than two centuries. These *kakure kirishitan* ("hidden Christians") still recited their versions of the Lord's Prayer, the Hail Mary, and the Creed, and would conceal a crucifix or image of the Blessed Virgin Mary within or behind a figure of the Buddha or Kannon.

Tenri City

Not far from Nara an entire city is dedicated to a religion. The city is Tenri-shi, Tenri city, and the faith is Tenrikyo, "Religion of Heavenly Wisdom." This is a good place to enter the fascinating world of the New Religions of Japan. Tenri-omi-kami, commonly called Oyagami, "God the Parent," is the patron of this faith, one of the earliest of Japanese *shinko shukyo*, "new religions." In the vast park-like city center is the main temple of the creed, itself built around a pillar, the Kanrodai, believed to mark the spot where the creation of the world began, and where the paradisal ultimate stage of world history will also commence. On festive occasions, a sacred dance re-enacting the creation is performed around the base of the Kanrodai.

Throughout the great temples and their spacious grounds one can usually see devotees, wearing a distinctive Tenrikyo jacket, cleaning, sweeping, polishing, maintaining all in immaculate condition. They are offering donated labor, an

A separate temple to the Foundress perpetuates her memory. Nakayama Miki (1798–1887), of peasant background, in the context of a very difficult life received revelations from the supreme God enabling her first to become locally famous as a spiritual healer, and finally to receive the text of the Tenrikyo scripture, the Ofudesaki, centering on the faith's account of the creation of the world. For this religion's central feature is indeed its emphasis on the fact that God the Parent created the world, guides its evolution – based on successive human reincarnation – and intends all who dwell in it to be joyous. But we human beings have forgotten, and allowed the dust of this world to blur our sight.

important Tenrikyo religious duty. A great many will be members from near and far who come to this holy city, as all members who possibly can are expected to do, for a three-months' training session. They will return as *yoboku*, missionaries, to spread the joyous life.

Around the courtyard, Tenrikyo offers educational institutions from kindergarten through a fine university, a library, museum, administrative offices, and numerous guesthouses for pilgrims on their visit for training or worship to the central city. Tenri city has in fact been compared to Mecca for Muslims, and the religion could be called a pilgrimage faith – a spiritual way in which travel, whether into the Center or back out again as bearers of joy to the world, or more metaphorically in the great journey through countless lifetimes up to one's final homecoming as children of God the Parent, is the ruling image.

Jizo

We shall now, in our vignettes of Japanese religious life, present a few examples centered particularly on death and the afterlife. These are from what may be called folk or popular religion – which in Japan, as in most places in the world, tends to be more focused on the end of life and transition to the next than intellectual religion. A good place to begin is the immensely popular bodhisattva called Jizo.

Wherever one goes in Japan, Jizo (Sanskrit: Kshitigarbha; both names literally mean "Earth-womb") is hard to miss. Along roadsides, on high mountain passes, at the entry to graveyards, the small smiling face with the shaved head and the six-ringed staff is there to greet you, and to help if he can. Along with Kannon, he is one of the two most popular *bosatsu* (bodhisattvas) in the country, and with Amida one of the three most favored Buddhist divine figures. But because Jizo, although probably introduced as part of the Shingon pantheon, is not strongly identified with any one denomination or major temple, he is easy for the outside observer to overlook.

Jizo loves to help, and especially favors travelers and women in childbirth. But he particularly aids those navigating the mysterious after-death worlds, with their six places of rebirth: hells, hungry ghosts, animals, demons, human beings, and heavenly beings. Children who have died, above all, need his assistance, and Jizo will be there, helping them counter bad *karma* they have not yet had a chance to negate, guiding them to auspicious rebirths. He will go into the deepest hell to rescue those whom he can, and his bodhisattva vow is, "Only after the Hells are empty will I become a Buddha."[8]

At many temples and burial places, one can often see numerous small images of Jizo, poignantly clothed in a red cap and a red bib such as a child would wear, placed at this site by a mother grieving for a child of her own.

Particularly significant in this respect are largely outdoor shrines called Sai no Kawara, the name of the riverbank where the souls of children gather after they die. It is said that children are often unable to cross the river to the other shore where they

Figure 2.6 Jizo Bodhisattva in Wakayama, Japan (© cowardlion / Shutterstock.com)

could be reborn, because in their short lives they haven't accumulated enough *karma* to determine what their next fate might be. What they do while so stranded is try to build little pyramids out of rocks; this task is supposed either to help them acquire a little more good *karma* by engaging in a difficult task, or ultimately provide them with a scaffold from which they could climb out of the underworld. Unfortunately, though, there are demons around who hate that endeavor, and keep knocking down the stony piles so the poor children have to start all over again. The point is that the soul has a path to take after death, and though there may be setbacks, it must be pursued until, with our help, its destiny is fulfilled.

Here is where Jizo comes in. He enters Sai no Kawara, hides children in his robes, and whisks them across the river to begin the reincarnation process before the demons or their chief, the evil hag Shozoku no Baba, has a chance at them.

There are many Sai no Kawaras, or rather simulations of it, in Japan, particularly northern Honshu, generally on the banks of a river, lake, or the ocean. Grieving parents who have lost a child frequent them to remember and pray that Jizo may help their small loved one on his mysterious journey through death and back to life. Here one will see numerous miniature statues of Jizo, about two feet tall, with his pilgrim's staff and perhaps the poignant bib of a child placed around his neck, flower and food offerings before him, and in the air many *koinobori*, the "carp banner" flown on Children's Day. In some places caves are found in the vicinity of a Sai no Kawara; these are especially venerated as suggestive of entry to the Underworld.[9] But there are other ways too in which Jizo is associated with children and death.

Today, an increasing number of popular temples are dedicated to Jizo as patron of *mizuko* ("water-child": term for miscarried or aborted fetuses). Women who have suffered such a loss attend these places of worship for a personal service called *mizuko kuyo*, in which the lost infant may be named, even fed and dressed in the form of a doll, released as at a funeral, and prayers offered for a better rebirth, all under the auspices of the understanding and compassionate Jizo.

In some parts of Japan a special children's Jizo festival is held at the end of Obon, the August holiday when spirits of the departed are said to return, and are greeted with offerings and dances. For the Jizo part, children dress in bright kimonos, set out gifts before altars of their special friend and guardian, then enjoy party-like games and treats, ending the day with sparklers and fireworks. This is one of the last summer events before schooldays begin again.

Itako

Itako, or miko, are Japaneses shamanesses who go into trance in order to communicate messages from divinities and from spirits of the deceased. Here is an itako experience, based on a visit I made many years ago to such a medium between the worlds.

You are seated in the living room of a modest house in northern Japan. Looking around, you see the wall opposite you lined with altars Shinto and Buddhist alike; popular religion tends to be syncretistic (bringing several traditions together). Your gaze is chiefly directed, however, toward the elderly, nearly blind woman seated on the floor facing those objects of worship. You see her begin to weave back and forth, her voice a low almost hypnotic chant. Gradually you sense her hymns are becoming prayers to those various deities, largely gods of peaks and places in the area.

The mood changes. In a louder and clearer voice the itako calls on Fudo, whom she says in the guardian of your family. You recall he is "the Immovable," the great bodhisattva dramatically surrounded by flames, holding a sword and lasso, whom we first met at Mt. Hiei. This mighty figure warns you that you are in danger of having a cold in the next ten days, that someone close to you will get sick in the middle of the year, and that a doctor from the south will help that person recover. (You may recall that the emphasis on direction – from the south – may reflect the place of Taoist geomancy, or the naming of harmful and beneficial directions for particular times and situations, in Japanese popular belief.)

You now think you might want to try something different. Boldly, you ask the itako to call up the spirit of your recently-deceased grandmother, just to see if she can do that. At first the shamaness is nonplussed, having never before summoned a non-Japanese spirit (if you yourself are non-Japanese). However she goes ahead, and your grandmother duly arrives, speaking Japanese whether that was her language or not. Her first message to you: "Except when it is difficult, offer me water. In this matter I am not happy. The good faith my grandchild would show in offering me water as a parting gift would make me happy." You bring to mind the Japanese practice of making offerings of such appropriate substances as incense, fruit, pastries, or water – the simplest – at the *ihai* or ancestral tablets on the Butsudan or small Buddhist shrine in a quiet corner of homes.

Your grandmother then goes on to say that a good physician was not at hand when she died, but her life had been long enough, and she was now happy in the next world. But (whatever her religion had been in this world) she now wanted to be remembered with water. Finally she asks about relatives, and tells you to be careful about pickpockets on trains. She promises to remain with you spiritually, and departs. The session ends.

You may, or may not, be able to relate to much of what the itako said. But you definitely see the experience as offering much insight into aspects of popular religion. Here as elsewhere, shamanism provides a meeting place between the living and the dead, in an appropriate atmosphere of mystery and trance. You sense that such communication, and the afterlife generally, is often more important in popular than intellectual religion. You think again of the many deities against that back wall, and perceive that systematic doctrine is far less important than practice that works and brings everything together on the popular level.

As your mind recollects more, you reflect on how Japanese shamans of this type are female and all blind or nearly so. They were brought into this vocation as young girls. The itako way of life ruled out marriage, unlikely in traditional society for a blind woman regardless. What it did was offer a respected place in village life for blind girls who otherwise would have had few options. But the ranks of itako or miko are dwindling in contemporary Japan. Despite that, you are reminded of what it would be like if you were a blind girl, and were being trained up to the itako role.

You had become an apprentice of an older adept at six or eight years of age. Perhaps living with her, you had followed a strict regimen of fasts, cold baths, and taboos. You had learned the sleepy, mystical songs that can lead one into trance. You learned all the techniques of your mysterious craft.

Finally comes the day of initiation. You put on a white gown called the "death dress." You sit facing your mistress and other elders of the art. They chant and sing the names of long lists of divine figures. Suddenly the teacher breaks in to ask, "What deity possessed you?" Hardly knowing where the name comes from, you cry out some *kami* or Buddha or bodhisattva. Hereafter that special god or goddess will be your special patron on the other side.

Then your mistress throws a rice cake at you, causing you to feel faint and fall onto the floor. The assembled women dash cold water on your head innumerable times, then revive you with their body heat by lying beside you. You finally rise up from their warmth as though coming out of the womb, for you are now indeed reborn as an itako, though blind able now to look at the world with the inner eyes of a communicator between life and death.

Appropriately, you exchange the death dress for wedding apparel. You come forward with all the excitement of a bride to a traditional Japanese wedding, and nuptials are indeed held, with the customary exchanges of cups of sake nine times nine. You are the bride – wed to an invisible groom, your deity.

A great feast of celebration is now held, shared by your friends and family, as at any wedding. As it proceeds you demonstrate, as you are expected to do, your fresh ability to communicate with spirits. All are no doubt impressed. After the banquet, you may depart to spend a week or so in a temple or shrine of your patron in a divine honeymoon.[10]

Mt. Osore

Several themes of popular religion mentioned so far, Jizo, the river between this world and the next, and itako, come together in the cultus of Mt. Osore (literally, "Mt. Fear") on the remote Shimotake Peninsula at the northern tip of Honshu. Osore is a volcano, and although it has not erupted since 1787, volcanic fumes, smoke, bubbling pits and occasional flames occur throughout the blasted landscape. The caldera, now Lake Usori, is reputedly the entrance to the underworld, and a small stream running into that depth is equated with the Sanzu River which the dead must cross. (Sanzu means "Three Crossings" – i.e., depending on one's merit, the transit may be by bridge, ford, or wading through snake-infested waters.) As with the Sai no Kawara, this stream also is patrolled by Jizo, who assists wayfarers to the realms beyond, particularly children. As elsewhere, his statues frequent the area, and are beset with offerings, particularly children's toys and clothes, and stones to help them in their pyramid-building task. There is also a small temple with a shrine to none other than Shozoku no Baba, the old hag Jizo tries to outwit, all skull and teeth, set up to jump out of a platform like a jack-in-the-box. One writer noted that this apparition looked terrifying from the front, as she tries to keep the souls of children stranded, but sad and even kind from the side angle, as though to present the two sides of death, fear and grief.[11]

Annually, beginning July 20, itako gather at Bodai-ji, the Soto Zen temple which spiritually dominates the region, for the five-day Itako Taisai, the Itako festival for which Mt.Osore is famous. During this time itako are available for consultation, and traditionally pilgrims, those in mourning for the departed, and the curious have come. However, the itako, now down to a handful, work out of tents outside since the temple insists they are not officially connected with it; there visitors line up for readings not unlike what I received.

Marie Mockett asked an engineer, a man of science, who had come for such a reading if he really believed they were accurate. He laughed as he answered, "Oh, I don't know. We Japanese. We believe. And we don't believe. Half and half." But he was still eager to consult the itako.[12]

In 2013 a new monument was erected on the shore of Lake Usori, dedicated to the victims of the 2011 tsunami. It presents a lotus blossom in which sit Jizo and a baby boy and girl, and a bell which visitors can ring called the "bell of hope." Worshipers often write the names of deceased on stones placed around the base, together with coins. One visitor noted a video game token there as well, the coming together of Japan old and new.

A kind of mushroom called O-dokuro-dake ("skull mushroom") grows in the Mt. Osore area; it is hallucinogenic and rumored to be used by itako to enhance their trance. But this has not been verified.

Namahage

You are a child at home on New Year's Eve. Like most children, you are not really bad, but have been known to fuss excessively, to be laggard about assigned tasks, even to spend too much time in front of the fire in winter – and this is northern Honshu, where cold winds out of Siberia and deep snows are not unknown. There is a clatter at the door, and when it is opened you see two or three men, or rather ogres, for they wear frightful heavy demonic masks, red with sharp teeth and glaring eyes, plus traditional straw cloaks, and they carry fake wooden knives. They yell out phrases in the local dialect like, "Any crybabies in this house?" "How about bad kids?" "We're getting our knives ready."

The parents may give the monstrous callers the traditional *mochi* or rice cakes, or even full food and drink – this is particularly expected of newlywed couples. But it is the children to whom the visit is addressed, and the younger ones may wonder if these strange and frightening guests are really *oni* or ogres, or just adults dressed up. The experience may indeed make you, as a child, think a little about your behavior. In a highly structured society like Japan, governed by Confucian ethics, behavior is very important. Children need continually to have it reinforced in memorable ways. The *namahage* do not depart without admonishing the household's young ones once again to act properly.

Sometimes the visit centers around an outdoor shrine instead. The way up to the shrine is lit with red lanterns, and men on a platform beat taiko drums louder and louder while waiting for something to happen, as many of the people gathered around a bonfire on this cold, snowy night eat and drink to keep warm. Finally a light on a nearby hillside tells us someone is coming. Then another light, and another. In a moment the demonic *namahage*, faces crimson or blue, teeth and eyes protruding, all snarling and shaking axes and swords, burst into the circle of those waiting, young and old. Small children are frightened and may cry, but their parents tell them, "The *namahage* will not hurt you if you are good." The ogres dance around the circle, admonishing each individual child, sometimes showing awareness of his or her individual faults. In the end they take off their masks and hand out auspicious food, sesame seeds and *mochi*.

This event is typical of many picturesque Japanese holiday folk customs, centering particularly around *matsuri* or festivals of Shinto shrines, New Years, and midsummer. Not a few involve mysterious visitors like these, parading, going door to door, or dancing at the shrine. Even though costumed, they remind us, if we like to think in this way, that our world is not entirely sealed off from other realms where angels and demons, gods and ancestral spirits, may abide, and that the doors and windows between here and there are especially open at such particular times as these.

Visitors like the *namahage* are found in many cultures. You may be reminded of Halloween Trick-or-Treaters, for while there it is children calling on adults and making demands of them rather than the other way around, the idea still holds that this is a day when cosmic doors stand open and beings like ghosts and witches may come through. In Holland, St. Nicholas, the original of Santa Claus, is accompanied on his gift-giving visit on Dec. 5 (St. Nicholas' Day) by Black Peter, who punishes bad children or gives them only a lump of coal.

New Years, *Oshogatsu*, as we will see later in this book, is especially important in Japan, for many the most important holiday of the year. It is a time of endings and new beginnings, a time also when perhaps there is a sort of gap between the old year and the new, when the doors between the worlds are left open, and it may be that customary rules do not apply. In some cultures this means New Year's Eve is a time when excessive revelry is permitted, though in Japan it is often more a time for formal calls, the settling of accounts, and visits to shrines – though ghosts are also said to be especially active. Clearly in their own way the *namahage* have a place in this eve of both openness and reaffirmation of the basic values of life.

Obon

It is high midsummer, and outdoors a large number of men and women are doing a traditional dance, wearing traditional dress, usually in a great circle. They have earlier visited and cleaned their ancestors' graves, and left offerings to entice those spirits to return. Very often the dances will be in the evening or at night, for the guests being welcomed by this particular dance tend most to like traveling and arriving in the dark, for they journey from the realm of the dead. Then, after the three days of the festival, they are seen off, their departure symbolized by lanterns set sailing down a river on tiny rafts, and by a great display of fireworks.

Openness to the other side, that of death and ancestors, is the fundamental premise of this midsummer festival, Bon or Obon. Though originally from China, the Bon holiday has been kept in Japan for some five hundred years, and is of interest because it displays a thorough combination of Confucian and Buddhist values: the Confucian honoring of ancestors, the Buddhist belief that through prayers and offerings the dead can be released from wherever their *karma* has sent them. The myth traditionally associated with Obon tells of a disciple of the Buddha called Mokuren in Japanese, who discovered that his deceased mother had fallen into the realm of the Hungry Ghosts, one of the six places of rebirth to be presented later. Greatly distressed, the student asked the Buddha what to do, and was told to make offerings to the monks, who had just completed their summer retreat. It worked. Delighted at his mother's release, and remembering her many kindnesses, the young monk danced for joy – hence the bon-odori.

Bon-odori, the Obon dance, takes place at different times and is done in somewhat different ways in different parts of the country. The dance is usually around a high platform called a *yagura* where the musicians and singers who perform Obon music are seated. The melodies and rhythms are generally traditional, but that does not mean they are absolutely inflexible. Today, some young people are trying to update the dances with rock beats.

While undoubtedly many people simply enjoy the dance, lanterns, and fireworks for their own sake, like the engineer mentioned above neither believing nor disbelieving in the part about the spirits of the dead, like so much in Japan Bon occupies several margins, between belief and disbelief, between this world and the next, between life and death. Probably many would debate whether it is "religion" or something else. But the return of the dead, pretend or not, is a common theme in colorful, dramatic customs on the margins of religion and folk culture around the world – think of Halloween and the Mexican *Dia de los Muertos*, Day of the Dead, though they are much more grisly, as it were like the *namahage*, than Obon.

Fukushima: Earthquake, Tsunami, Nuclear Disaster, and Religion

On March 11, 2011, at 2:46 pm, a powerful 9.0 magnitude earthquake occurred out at sea off the coast of northern Japan, some 80 miles east of the city of Sendai. By 3:12 pm the resultant tsunami began ravaging the coast with twenty-two foot waves. There were nearly 16,000 fatalities. Then, the tsunami struck the Fukushima Daiichi nuclear power plant, and by the following day, March 12, considerable amounts of radioactive water and other materials had been released. Some 300,000 people were evacuated from the area. Hospital closures were necessary, which resulted in further deaths.

What was the response of religion to this tragedy – or rather series of tragedies? In the western monotheistic religions, the emphasis might have been on a theological interpretation of the cause, asking "Why did God let this happen?" or seeing it as divine punishment for some great sin. In Japan, the view of the divine was characteristically far more impersonal, and the stress was more on spiritually motivated but practical activities.

True, Buddhism might have seen the calamity in terms of *karma*, but attempting to interpret the complex ways of *karma* in today's no less complex world is not now much in favor. To be sure, the outspoken mayor of Tokyo impulsively claimed it was punishment for Japan's "selfishness," but quickly apologized and backed away from that much-criticized judgment. Shintoists insisted that the *kami* are one with nature, but its forces are far bigger than and cannot be limited by their impact on humans. A few, recalling the Taoist influence that has affected Shinto in the past, as we will see, alleged that if the nuclear reactors had been in better accordance with geomancy, or subtle lines of force, the disaster would have been lessened.

Far more impressive, in the eyes of most observers, was response in terms of relief and rebuilding. Many volunteer groups, some from religious organizations like the "new religion" Tenrikyo and several Buddhist organizations, including Shinnyo-en and Rissho Kosei Kai, served tirelessly in the disaster area. Many identified themselves with "Engaged Buddhism," a new movement emphasizing that the faith must confront directly and endeavor to heal the suffering and social problems of the world.

One group of Soto Zen youth combined *gyocha*, "tea practice," with disaster aid. *Gyocha* properly is ceremonially taking tea in Zen temples, while deeply examining and talking about one's life. In bringing tea to refugees in the blighted landscape, they saw "Gyocha as an activity in deep listening to victims . . . holding and embracing the physical and psychological stress of the victims."[13]

Japanese volunteers in the Fukushima area attracted international attention for their perseverance and selflessness. The "Fukushima Fifty," as they were called in the media, had gone into the nuclear power plant to do cleanup work at great risk, journalists sometimes comparing them to the samurai of old. Indeed, there were those foreigners who thought, rather spitefully, that the heroic workers were almost more robots than human. A young city worker, Enki Miki, sacrificed her life by continuing to broadcast warnings of the coming tsunami until it swallowed her up.[14] A certain Naoto Matsumura has devoted himself to feeding and caring for the numerous animals, especially dogs and cats, left abandoned in the emergency.

Of course it not true that all involved were equally dedicated. Some looting, cowardice, and exploitation of victims certainly occurred. Yet overall the response to the great natural cataclysm brought out the best in the nation's Confucian values of loyalty and service, and the samurai capacity for self-sacrifice.

What about Buddhists? Not many priests worked in the volunteer cleanup groups, partly because popular mentality associates Buddhist priests with death and funerals – since that is where they are most likely to be encountered – and that would not create an auspicious atmosphere. But it was also because the priests were swamped with an overflow of funerals, burials, and of course attendant counseling. The Japanese American Marie Mutsuki Mockett, in her fascinating account of visiting the area, where some of her Japanese family lived, very soon after the tsunami, tells of visiting a cousin who was a Buddhist priest. She and other family members tried to persuade him to leave the radioactive region, if only for the sake of his children. But he refused, giving one excuse after another, including the volume of work, but finally stating simply that the family wanted to stay together and he was not afraid to die. To this there was not much more one could say. [15]

Mockett also describes a Zen priest she met called Kaneta Taio, who ministered to survivors in his own way. After the funerals and cremations were finally over in his own four-hundred-year-old temple, he set out for nearby towns, bringing such foods as udon, cakes, and coffee, and the music of the jazz musician Thelonious Monk. Kaneta called his setup Café de Monk, a pun on three meanings: himself as a monk, the Japanese word *monku* meaning to complain, and Thelonious Monk. Of the last he said that Monk has both lightheartedness and sadness in his music, the perfect backdrop for the priest's pastoral service. As he served light meals and played Monk softly, he was overwhelmed by the outpouring of grief and emotion on the part of those whose lives had been utterly disrupted, perhaps virtually destroyed, by the natural tragedy.[16]

Many survivors saw ghosts. This is not surprising given the prevalence of death, and the widespread belief, or half-belief, in ghosts in the general culture. It should be realized that this credence is more natural in Japan than in the West, where ghosts are not, strictly speaking, part of the dominant religious creeds. In Confucian societies specters could be seen as a natural extension of ancestral veneration and the corresponding assumption that spirits, familial or otherwise, happy or not, are all around, in close proximity with the living.

Kaneta told of a medium, presumably an itako, who called him in the middle of the night. She was suicidal because, she said, numerous spirits of the dead were infesting her body and she could no longer endure it. The priest spent some three hours with this woman, speaking one by one to some twenty-five entities, who had perished in the tsunami and were now wandering confusedly looking for whatever human home they could find. Kaneta explained to each that a tsunami had come, she or he was now dead, and so must leave the earth and head into the light.[17]

As for the general culture, while the following may be anecdotal and involve over-generalization, it is worth noting that some commentators have claimed that the catastrophe had a kind of shock-therapy effect on Japanese consciousness, which in some eyes had become too materialistic and self-centered. In January 2010 NHK, the Japanese Broadcasting Corporation, had presented a program called "Muen shakai," which could be translated as "An Unconnected Society." The message was that the close bonding between individuals that had once been characteristic of Japanese society was falling apart; people die alone without others even knowing.

Now it was said that this unconnectedness was, because of the tsunami catastrophe, going into reverse. People were becoming less complacent, more concerned about those who were alone, more were willing to undertake volunteer work for the good of others, and not only at Fukushima. Interest in meaning beneath the surface of life was on the rise, sale of Buddhist and other spiritual books went up, and along with it attendance at religious activities.

Jonathan S. Watts, a western Buddhist living and teaching in Japan, and who serves on the Executive Committee of the International Network of Engaged Buddhists, pointed out in the wake of Fukushima that in Buddhism the emphasis is not on evil but rather on ignorance, especially of the interconnected chain of causes and effects that lead to socially constructed suffering in our complex, interconnected world. To turn only to the human-built aspect of the catastrophe, effects like nuclear disaster cannot be blamed on any one person or cause, but rather stems from a webwork of social and economic causes, some seemingly innocent in themselves. But, from a Buddhist point of view, this interconnectedness of all could be turned the other way through individual and group meditations that lead to inner change, outer change, and finally the restructuring of society. "Yet," Watts concludes, "this process would not seek to punish any 'other' but transform the very fabric of society."[18] Or, as Rev. Shokoku Nishida, of the famous Eihei-ji Zen temple, put it, after a remark that the point is not about approving or disapproving of nuclear power, "It is not that Eihei-ji is starting an anti-nuclear campaign. The necessary evil that lurks behind the existing system of nuclear power is the lifestyle of unchecked greed. I am proposing that it is what we need to re-examine."[19]

Japanese Funerals

Although the role of the contemporary Buddhist funeral in contemporary Japan has generated controversy,[20] as we have seen in connection with the Fukushima disaster it still is the predominant way of responding to death, and the main way many Japanese encounter religion. It is therefore important to look at it. While funeral customs vary from region to region, and among different schools of Buddhism, a general outline may be presented. The rite consists of three distinct parts: visitation or wake, typically on the evening of the death, at the home or funeral parlor; the funeral proper at the temple the next day; and the cremation soon after.

Preparation of the body today is not dissimilar from usage in many cultures. For the wake, the remains are washed, dressed, and laid out for viewing in the home or a funeral hall. Belongings are displayed, including money to pay the toll across the River of Three Crossings. At the designated time the priest arrives for a preliminary service or wake at the home or funeral hall. He bows before a temporary altar, lights incense, and reads a sutra. During this reading members of the family and guests, in proper order, rise to offer their own stick of incense. This ends this service; members of the family may stay in the same room with the deceased that night.

The next day the funeral proper is generally held at a temple. The body has been removed to the temple and placed before an altar prepared by the mortuary before the main altar. A tablet inscribed with the decedent's *kaimyo*, posthumous or Buddhist name, is placed before it. As at the wake, attenders individually offer incense while sutras are being read. Afterwards, the family and others may offer thanks and condolences.

Then comes a third stage, the cremation. Most remains are cremated in Japan today. The casket is taken to the crematory, and family members watch as it is slid into the oven. Family members are told to return, probably in about two hours. Sometimes food and drink is served at the home during the interval.

After returning, the burned body is slid back out, family members take large iron chopsticks to pick out bones to place in a urn. When the urn has been filled, it is covered with white cloth and may be interred in the cemetery, or kept at the home until the 49th day memorial service and taken then. In some areas a colorful funeral procession, with banners, pictures of the deceased, and the *kaimyo* conspicuous, may even escort it to its final resting place.

The first Obon after the death is an important time of remembering. Memorial services, depending on the sect, are held on the 1st, 3rd, 5th, 7th and 13th years, perhaps more up to the 50th, of the *owakare* or great departing.

What is the meaning of these customs? Of course, as with any longstanding practice, there is not necessarily any one "right" meaning. It is clear, however, that the idea is to have the family around at the time of departure and immediately after, so that there is continuing love, support, and solemn ritual gestures of saying farewell; that while the physical body is not the fullness of the person, lasting remains from it, like the bones, may be preserved as a memento or even point of contact; and that the deceased is seen off in the context of Buddhism, which in light of a Buddha's infinite meditation embraces as one past, present, and future; life, death, and beyond.

A recent trend in Japan has been toward virtual online "tombs" or memorial sites for the deceased. Often sponsored by Buddhist institutions, accessible through a password, they enable family and friends to visit a beautifully-landscaped cyberspace, religious or secular according to preference, dedicated to the life and spirit of that individual. Although not necessarily replacing traditional tombs or rituals, these sites are beginning to move the center of gravity for remembrance from the physical remains to the visual equivalent.

*　*　*

Japanese religion is then about as varied as life itself. Always, though, it seems to add a dimension of depth to the ordinary world, suggesting that invisible realities, some near at hand, some unimaginably profound, lie beneath the surface.

Questions for study and discussion

1. What does the Daijosai tell you about one aspect of religion in Japan?
2. Summarize the structures of ordinary Shinto worship.
3. Explain the main message of Kegon Buddhism.
4. Why are mandalas important to Shingon?
5. What is the basic worldview of Tendai?

Key points you need to know

- Be able briefly to describe and interpret the sites and vignettes here presented
- Practice can be very important in Japanese religion even when original meaning is lost
- Tradition is usually an important component of Japanese religion
- The relation of religion and the state, often focused on the symbolic role of the emperor, is a frequent issue
- The place of religions perceived as "new" or, like Christianity, imported from outside Japan
- Folk religion, typified by Jizo but containing many facets, is a pervasive backdrop to Japanese religion.

6. What seems to you to be the inner experience of Pure Land Buddhism?
7. What is the nature of Nichiren Buddhism's appeal?
8. What is unique about the Zen approach to Buddhism?
9. Why was Christianity popular, and then persecuted, in Japan?
10. What are some common features of the "new religions" of Japan?
11. What does Jizo tell us about Japanese popular religion?
12. Why does popular or folk religion, like that involving the Itako, so often include deities of various traditions, and so often deal with death and the spirits of the dead?
13. Does Mt. Osore as the entrance to the Other World, and the River of Three Crossings, remind you of any other spiritual traditions?
14. Why do the Namahage present themselves as demons?
15. What is the significance of dancing at Obon, when the dead are said to return?
16. Why do you think religions seemed to be more concerned with practical response to the Fukushima tragedy, and with analyzing how it affected the Japanese mentality, than with explaining why it happened in religious terms?
17. Why do funerals seem to be mainly the province of Buddhism, rather than of Shinto, or merely secular?

Further reading

Here and under Electronic Resources, titles are given in the order the subject is presented in this chapter, rather than alphabetically. No appropriate books were found for some topics. For further material, turn ahead to the corresponding chapter and bibliographies.

Holtom, Daniel C., *The Japanese Enthronement Ceremonies*. Tokyo: Sophia University Press, 1972.

For Shinto shrines, see bibliography to Chapter 3, "The Way of the Kami."

Cleary, Thomas, transl., *The Flower Ornament Scripture: A Translation of the Avatamsaka Sutra*. Boston, MA: Shambhala, 1993. (Basic scripture of the Kegon sect, associated with the Todai-ji.)

Taiko Yamasaki, *Shingon: Japanese Esoteric Buddhism*. Boston, MA: Shambhala, 1988.

Watts, Jonathan, *Traversing the Pure Land Path: A Lifetime of Encounter with Honen Shonin*. Tokyo: Jodo Shu Press, 2005. (To go with Chion-in.)

Covell, Jon and Yamada Sobin, *Zen at Daitoku-ji*. Tokyo: Kodansha International, 1974.

Hammond, Phillip E. and David W. Machacek, *Soka Gakkai in America: Accommodation and Conversion*. New York, NY: Oxford University Press, 1999.

Dougill, John, *In Search of Japan's Hidden Christians: A Story of Suppression, Secrecy and Survival*. North Clarendon, VT: Tuttle, 2012.

Epstein, Mitch, *Fire, Water, Wind: Photographs of Tenri*. Tenri-shi: Tenrikyō Dōyūsha, 1996.

Chozen Bays, Jan, *Jizo Bodhisattva: Guardian of Children, Travelers, and Other Voyagers*. Boston, MA: Shambhala, 2003.

Glassman, Hank, *The Face of Jizo: Image and Cult in Medieval Japanese Buddhism*. Honolulu, HI: University of Hawaii Press, 2012.

Hori, Ichiro, *Folk Religion in Japan*. Chicago, IL: University of Chicago Press, 1994. (See Chapter 5, on shamanism).

Yamamoto, Yoshiko, *The Namahage: A Festival in the Northeast of Japan*. Philadelphia, PA: Institute for the Study of Human Issues, 1978.

Mockett, Marie Mutsuki, *Where the Dead Pause and the Japanese Say Goodbye*. New York, NY: W. W. Norton, 2015.

Watts, Jonathan S., ed., *Lotus in the Nuclear Sea: Fukushima and the Promise of Buddhism in the Nuclear Age*. Yokohama: International Buddhist Exchange Center, 2013.

Watts, Jonathan S., ed., *This Precious Life: Buddhist Tsunami Relief and Anti-Nuclear Activism Post 3/11 Japan*. Yokohama: International Buddhist Exchange Center, 2012.

Electronic Resources

"Akihito Performs his Solitary Rite," *New York Times*, Nov. 23, 1990. www.nytimes.com/1990/11/23/world/akihito-performs-his-solitary-rite.html (The Daijosai.)

"Todai-ji." en.wikipedia.org/wiki/Tōdai-ji

"Toji Temple." www.japan-guide.com/e/e3919.html

"Enryakuji Temple (Mount Hieizan)." www.japan-guide.com/e/e3911.html

"Chion-in English Site." www.chion-in.or.jp/e/ (The temple's own site.)

"Welcome to Higashi Honganji." www.higashihonganji.or.jp/english/ (The temple's own site.)

"Rinzai-Obaku Zen." zen.rinnou.net/head_temples/07daitoku.html (Official Site of the Joint Council for Japanese Rinzai and Obaku Zen.)

"Nichiren Shoshu True Buddhism." www.nst.org (Official site of Nichiren Shoshu in America.)

"Twenty-Six Martyrs of Japan." en.wikipedia.org/wiki/Twenty-six_Martyrs_of_Japan

"Tenrikyo." en.wikipedia.org/wiki/Tenrikyo

"Jizo Bosatsu." www.onmarkproductions.com/html/jizo1shtml

Vaughan, C. Edwin, "The Itako – A Spiritual Occupation for Blind Japanese Girls." https://nfb.org/images/nfb/publications/bm/bm02/bm0205/bm020511.htm

Fackler, Martin, "As Japan's Mediums Die, Ancient Tradition Fades," *New York Times*, Aug. 20, 2009. www.nytimes.com/2009/08/21/world/asia/21japan.html

"Oga's Namahage." www.namahage-oga.akita.jp/english/index.html

Shizuko Mishima, "Obon in Japan," *About Travel.* gojapan.about.com/cs/japanesefestivals/a/obonfestival.htm

Keishin Inaba, "Religion's Response to the Earthquake and Tsunami in Northeastern Japan. Dharma World, Oct.–Dec. 2011. www.rk-world.org/dharmaworld/dw_2011octdecreligionsresponse/aspx

McLaughlin, Levi, "What Have Religious Groups Done After 3/11?" (Part 1) www.academia.edu/4190393/What_Have_Religious_Groups_Done_After_3.11_Part_1_A_Brief_Survey_of_Religious_Mobilization_after_the_Great_East_Japan_Earthquake_Disasters (Part 2) www.academia.edu/4190405/What_Have_Religious_Groups_Done_After_3.11_Part_2_From_Religious_Mobilization_to_Spiritual_Care._

Hiroko Nakata, "Japan's Funerals Deep-Rooted Mix of Ritual, Form". *The Japan Times*, July 28, 2009. www.japantimes.co.jp/news/2009/07/28/reference/japans-funerals-deep-rooted-mix-of-ritual-form

3 *The way of the kami*

Shinto then and now

In this chapter

This chapter will survey a diversity of Shinto shrines, ancient and modern, of deities of varying types and meanings, and explain the word *kami*, designating a Shinto god. We will see how Shinto may be observed throughout the calendar year, and in individual rites of passage. Finally, major aspects of Shinto will be summarized in terms of five keynotes; the core narrative of the ancient Shinto mythology outlined; and the issue of Shinto as a religion discussed.

Main topics covered

- The Grand Shrine of Ise and its twenty-year rebuilding
- The meaning of *kami*, the term for Shinto god
- Major shrines of diverse types: Inari, Miwa, Meiji, Togo, Nogi, Yasukuni, Tenjin
- The Shinto year and life-cycle rites of passage, including New Year and weddings
- Five keynotes of Shinto: purity vs. pollution, traditionalism, importance of practice, sociological role, polytheism
- The core Shinto mythology, found in the ancient books called *Kojiki* and *Nihonshoki*
- Issues involving Shinto as a religion.

The Grand Shrine of Ise

Let us begin at the heart of Shinto.

The Ise shrine, which has been called the National Cathedral of Japan, is not located in the center of a capital ancient or modern, like St. Peter's in Rome. Its plain wooden buildings, rustic and unpretentious by most standards, dominate a lonely site near the Pacific Ocean some 225 miles south of Tokyo, 50 from Nagoya, and not much farther from Kyoto and Nara. Like ancient Japanese dwellings and granaries, Ise's edifices are set off the ground on posts, the roofs are thatched, and

Figure 3.1 The *torii* gate at the Grand Shrine of Ise (Kanchi1979; CC: Wikimedia Commons)

the timber unpainted, save for gold tips on the roof beams. They are surrounded by four wooden palisades, which block easy viewing and access. Once again, the sacred in Japan, especially in Shinto, is not clothed in glory but left lonely and obscure, and is all the more mysterious for that.

The Grand Shrine is really two shrines about five miles apart, plus several lesser, outlying places of worship. The two are the Naiku, or Inner Shrine, and the Geku, Outer Shrine. The Naiku is dedicated to Amaterasu, the sovereign solar deity who is ancestress of the imperial line; this edifice has as its *shintai* (or *mitama-shiro*), or representation of the divine presence, the *yata kagami* ("eight-hand mirror," a term probably referring to its width) which Amaterasu gave her grandson when he descended to earth to found the Empire. The Geku is dedicated to Toyouke, the

A great Western scholar of Japan in the nineteenth century wrote that Ise is "so disappointing in its simplicity and perishable nature,"[1] but modern taste has instead discovered in Ise an architecture of clean, austere effectiveness.[2] Moreover, the simplicity of style is compensated by majesty of setting. Near the cold and clear Isuzu River, amid cypress groves of wondrous and numinous beauty, Ise suggests that little could be added by human hands to provide a suitable place for worship of the greatest of the *kami*.

ancient Food Goddess. In each the Kanname-sai, or Harvest Festival as celebrated at Ise, is the most important of annual events. The offering ceremony then is presented twice, identically, in the evening and early morning.

The two shrines are roughly the same in form. Each has a *shoden* or main building containing the sacred object, two treasure houses holding imperial offerings, and a white graveled expanse for rituals, plus a partially covered pavilion for use in inclement weather. Each is rebuilt every twenty years, and with this sacred drama we enter into the mysterious and mystical realm that underlies Ise's placid exterior.

Immediately beside the rectangle of the shrine buildings and their fences is another enclosed space of the same size, spread merely with white gravel except for a tiny wooden structure in the center. This expanse is the alternative site of the shrine. The tiny structure covers the wooden foundation post, preserved after the tearing-down of the old shrine. The post is never actually seen by outside observers, and there are said to be many secrets about it.

Note that the Harvest Festival at Ise has several things in common with the imperial accession Daijosai, also fundamentally a Harvest Festival, presented in Chapter 2. Both are done at night, and both involve an odd doubling: in both the ceremony is repeated twice, in both two identical buildings sit side by side.

Ise has a number of auxiliary buildings. Outside the main Naiku and Geku buildings stands a shrine to the *aramitama* or "rough spirit" of that goddess; this is the deity in her vigorous, aggressive, active mood, in contrast to the *nigimitama* or "smooth" spirit in her main house. Buildings for preparing offerings complete the complex, together with side shrines to deities of the wind and weather, to Tsukiyomi the moon god, and to the primal parents of the mythology, to be reviewed later,

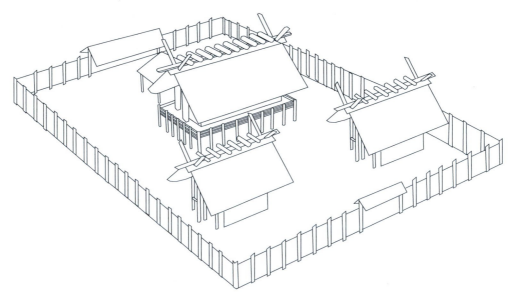

Figure 3.2 Sketch of the Grand Shrine of Ise; the main entrance is at the top

Every twenty years a new shrine is built on the alternative site; the next *shikinen sengu* or rebuilding year from the time of writing will be 2033. The construction is done by traditional means, without nails, the wood fitted together by a kind of joinery. Many of the highly skilled craftsmen employed are from families in whom the privilege of working on rebuilding the Grand Shrines goes back many generations. For a time in the fall of the rebuilding year two identical shrines will stand together, side by side. Then, at the Kanname-sai or Harvest Festival at Ise, on a crisp October evening, the *mitama shiro* will be transferred from the old shrine to the new by priests in solemn procession, including imperial envoys bearing offerings from the court – swords, bows, arrows, shields, quivers, cloth. In the center of the procession is its most dramatic entry, a rectangular wall of white silk, held and carried by twenty persons. Enclosed by it walk the two chief priests and certain other senior clerics, carrying the palanquin containing the Naiku's sacred Mirror, or the *shintai* of the Geku. The holy relic is followed by an imperial princess/priestess, called the Saishu.

When the Divine Presence is carried out, one priest makes the sound of a cock: "Kakeko" in the Inner shrine, "Kakero" in the Outer. This intriguing custom, reminding one of the cock which cried at Amaterasu's hiding and re-emergence in the myth presented in Chapter 1, immediately suggests rebirth symbolism, the dawn of a new sacred cycle. So it is that the Ise rebuilding makes the most sacred of all Shinto shrines both ancient and ever new, like eternity itself: the pattern goes back to prehistory, the actual wood is always fresh.

Izanagi and Izanami. There are barns for sacred horses, presented by the Emperor, which are led before the shrine three times a month, and a *kagura-den* or dance platform where divine dances are performed by priests and *mai-hime*, colorfully-garbed shrine maidens, who also assist in preparing materials for worship and work in the offices.[3]

In addition to sending offerings for major festivals, the Emperor informs his ancestral deities at the Grand Shrine in person of major events in the history of the nation. In 1945, Emperor Hirohito visited Ise to report Japan's defeat in the great world war.

What is a kami?

Before we go further into Shinto, the *Kami* Way, this question must be dealt with. In a sense, it might be better to leave it alone, and just let the reader intuit a kind of meaning from many accounts of Shinto shrines and their worship; this would be the poetic Japanese approach. Any general definition might be too abstract or theological. Nonetheless, for the benefit of those who expect definitions in textbooks, something will be said.

The eighteenth-century Shinto scholar Motoori Norinaga commented that a *kami* is anything that can fill us with wonder and awe. The reference can be to wonderful and awesome places – splendid old trees, waterfalls, or mountain peaks; to demarcated sacred places, especially ones that are very old, such as shrine precincts; to natural events, like the growth of plants and their harvest, or the birth of babies; to the spirit guiding an ancient tribe, or which can possess a person like a shamaness; or to an especially majestic person, such as an emperor or hero. All these objects of wonder and awe have been experienced as *kami*, and part of the wonder derives from the way they are perceived as outside oneself and greater than oneself, though still bound to a particular place: god as well as natural, something "added on" to natural glory.[4] What makes them *kami* in the traditional sense, of course, is that this is not just a personal experience, but one that belongs to a group of people, a tribe or village, and so is demarcated by a shrine with *shintai* and *torii*.

The *kami* can be spoken of as gods in the polytheistic sense, as we will see, and we have noted that Shinto can be compared to the polytheistic religion of pre-Christian Europe, such as that of the Greeks, Romans, and northern peoples. Shinto has certainly been, and still is, a civic religion as were those, in which the people of a community – family, village, town, factory workforce, nation – pray for, purify, and celebrate their common life in companionship with their *ujigami* or guardian deity. But if the ultimate meaning of *kami* is a bit elusive, that is because none of this depends on a precise understanding of the term.

The Inari and Miwa Shrines

Another face of Shinto is presented by the Inari family of shrines. These are visible everywhere by those who are aware of them, for Inari is the Shinto god of fertility, fortune, fields, and foxes. This popular deity, famous for responsiveness to ordinary human desires, has easily moved from the rice-paddy to the business districts of modern Japan's great cities, where his (or her, for this deity can appear in both male and female form) distinctive shrines are evident in shops and atop banks and department stores, as well as in urban corners, wherever a little space can be squeezed out. A recent report tells us that devotion to Inari is now especially high among firms dealing in stocks and securities. Some such companies have their own Inari shrine on the premises; some organize visits by their employees to the great Fushimi Inari shrine, to be discussed in a moment, to pray for prosperity.[5]

You can always tell an Inari shrine by its bright red *torii*, and by the two red-bibbed foxes, one holding a stick in his mouth, and the other a ball or jewel (*tama*, which can also mean "soul"), on either side of the *torii*. They are guardians or messengers of the

Figure 3.3 Fox statue at Fushimi Inari Shrine, Kyoto (© Masami Reilly / Shutterstock.com)

kami, a deity who may appear as a long-bearded old man carrying a sack of rice, or as a woman with long flowing hair carrying two sheaves of rice, accompanied by one or two white foxes. The deity is said to start the year in the mountains, to come down into the rice fields in the spring, aid in their growing to harvest, then return to the mountains again at the Harvest Festival (for the Daijosai, Kanname-sai, or Niiname-sai harvest festivals are merely state or Grand Shrine versions of what is done in every village shrine). Inari winters in the heights, away from the people and close to heaven,

The fox, *kitsune*, is an interesting entity in itself. Many are the stories told in Chinese and Japanese folklore of trickster foxes who have done mischievous or even cruel things, causing accidents or, with their shapeshifter capability, appearing as a lovely maiden who leads astray some country lad, or promises someone a bucket of gold which, come morning when the mysterious companion is gone, turns out to be nothing but dry leaves. And usually a fox, or even only the tail of a fox, will be just glimpsed disappearing out of the corner of the eye at the critical moment. (I have myself heard modern, well-educated Japanese relate that someone they knew saw a fox run across the road just before a serious auto accident ...) But this is the *kitsune* on its own, and Inari cannot be blamed for these antics; the foxes that are her guardians or messengers seem to be well under control. Nonetheless they remind us this is a deity with deep folkloric roots.

Even more archaic is the Miwa shrine, not far from Nara. The shrines of prehistory seem not to have had a structural *honden*, wherein the *shintai* or sacred object was contained, but to have worshiped the *kami* directly in nature, or at an altar in an open, set-apart sacred space. Here, at the very ancient shrine of Miwa, the *kami*-presence is still an entire holy mountain, and the shrine altar simply faces toward it. No one is allowed to set foot on Mount Miwa, save once a year, when priests ascend to its summit to present offerings.

to return again the next spring. Virtually all ancient Shinto deities ultimately have such descending and ascending features, and links to the agricultural year, as they rotate between being a *yama no kami*, mountain god, and a *ta no kami*, rice-paddy god.

The main Inari shrine, head of some 30,000 Inari shrines throughout Japan, is Fushimi Inari, in a suburb of Kyoto. The impressive main shrine edifice, with its large, stately vermilion *torii*, is at the base of a high hill. But what is most remarkable is the path up the hill to auxiliary shrines along the way and at the top; this trail is covered with countless red *torii*, becoming virtually a tunnel. All have written on them the name of the donor, most often a company, hoping for a share in the prosperity Inari is believed to bestow. The walk up this *torii*-arcaded way takes two to three hours (many joggers do it in less), and is an interesting experience in entering the archaic/modern world of Shinto.[6]

The Meiji, Togo, and Nogi Shrines

Shinto is not only about the remote past. In the center of Tokyo stands one of the most famous and impressive, and most often visited, of all Shinto shrines: the Meiji Shrine. It is dedicated to the spirits, now revered as *kami*, of the Emperor Meiji and his consort, the Empress Shoken. Meiji presided over the rapid modernization of Japan together with, not incidentally, the revival of state Shinto that accompanied the "Meiji Restoration."[7] He died in 1912 and she in 1914; the shrine was dedicated in 1920, destroyed in World War II, but rebuilt afterwards. The Meiji Shrine is set amidst a large park-like area, and beyond it the "outer garden" contains extensive sporting facilities, including two baseball stadiums, a golf driving range, a tennis club, swimming pool, skating rink, and much else.

The Meiji Shrine complex offers two important insights. First, it manifests the intimate connection of Shinto with the needs of people, above all in the vast crowded cities of today, for open air, natural beauty, and opportunities for recreation. Similar concerns are close to the heart of the *kami*, who always want their places of worship to be surrounded by at least a patch of green, and unceasingly yearn to share simple joys and earthly pleasures with their people, especially those associated with health and

Figure 3.4 The Meiji Shrine, Tokyo (© e X p o s e / Shutterstock.com)

family. Many shrines, especially since the war, have tried to develop such community service facilities as preschools and playgrounds, though none on the scale of Meiji. It is important to remember that Shinto is generally concerned with enhancing and making holy life in this world, not with otherworldly or afterdeath matters.

Second, the Shrine shows us how intimately Shinto is connected with Japan's history, especially in the State Shinto era between the Meiji Restoration and 1945. Shinto has always recognized that the *kami* are not only spirits connected with nature, or primordial mythological figures, but can also be divinized great souls of yesterday and today, particularly those who had a notable historical role. Most such men or women made *kami* are imperial, though not all.

The Yasukuni and Tenjin Shrines

Something of that world, however, still lingers in the Yasukuni ("Pacification of the Nation") Shrine, as it keeps alive memories of war and death. Located on a spacious hilltop in the Tokyo University area, this edifice honors and enshrines the spirits of all those who have died in Japan's modern wars. Grieving widows, parents, and children often worship in its precincts; so also, more controversially, have political figures. As recently as April 19, 2015, Prime Minister Abe Shinzo, a strong conservative, sent an evergreen to the shrine for its spring festival, despite ongoing protests from China and Korea, as well as domestic liberals, about Yasukuni.[8] Over a hundred members

Also in Tokyo is a shrine dedicated to Admiral Togo Heihachiro (1848–1934), a great naval hero of the Russo-Japanese War (1904–1905); despite his strongly-expressed resistance in life to being divinized after his death, he was so enshrined in 1940, at the height of Japan's militaristic surge. As it were in companionship with Togo is a shrine to General Nogi Maresuke (1849–1912), another Russo-Japanese War hero, who chose to accompany his sovereign in death, the practice known as *junshi*. He and his wife Shizuko committed *seppuku*, the ritual suicide considered honorable among samurai, shortly after the Emperor Meiji's funeral cortège had left the palace. They bathed, put on white kimonos, and shared a cup of sake before the household shrine. The General then sliced his stomach open with his sword in the approved manner, and lastly cut his throat. Shizuko stabbed herself in the chest. Faithfulness unto death fulfilled, they entered the world of *kami*, or so it was thought by enthusiasts for traditional values in those days when Japan hovered between two worlds, old and new. Apart from a few extremists, theirs is a world now largely left behind.

of parliament visited the shrine at the same time.[9] Critics understandably associate Yasukuni with Japanese militarism and assert that some of those honored therein were guilty of unspeakable atrocities, as many Japanese soldiers certainly were. Some were convicted war criminals. Detractors say the Yasukuni cultus reflects Japan's inability to come to terms with its past. Supporters see Yasukuni, though in Shinto guise, as no different in principle from the military memorials and cemeteries many countries maintain.[10]

By way of contrast to these warlike modern figures, mention should be made of the Tenjin family of shrines, which comprise no less than some 11,000 of the 80,000 Shinto shrines in Japan. They honor the deified spirit of Sugawara Michizane (845–903), a scholarly court official, historian, and poet who was advanced by the emperor to counter the all-powerful Fujiwara house. But Sugawara was outmaneuvered by rivals, who managed to have him exiled to Kyushu. There, mourning the loss of the cultured capital he loved, he died two years later.

Soon after, however, lightning struck the main Fujiwara residence, igniting a fire that destroyed much of the city. Popular opinion attributed this and other disasters to the enraged spirit of the exiled courtier. The government was forced to make elaborate amends, including the erection of a shrine, followed by many others, to him as *kami* under the name Tenjin ("heavenly *kami*"). Here then is an example of a deified historical human being in Shinto who was not warlike, but represents another side of traditional Japanese culture, that of scholarship, poetry, and aesthetics. He is considered a patron of learning and the arts of peace.

The Shinto Year

As you can probably imagine, the succession of festivals and worship occasions at a Shinto shrine keeps its priests and supporters busy. While there is no weekly service quite like the sabbath or its equivalent in Judaism, Christianity, and Islam, bimonthly offerings, originally tied to the phases of the moon, are presented regularly in many shrines; some major shrines even have daily offerings. More important is the well-packed schedule of special or occasional events, some unique to the particular shrine. January at the large Suwa shrine in Nagasaki, for example, brings not only New Year, but also, on the 5th, Chinka-sai, to control fires and protect the local fire department; Saiten-sai, the coming-of-age ritual for twenty-year-olds, on the 15th; and Kenae-sai on the 19th, when members recite poems to the *kami*. February offers special rituals for Setsubun matsuri on the 3rd, a popular festival when beans are thrown to drive away demons; Kenkoku kinen-sai, the controversial national holiday commemorating the mythological founding of the nation; and Kinen-sai, prayers for a bountiful harvest, among others. Later months bring numerous other worship events, including the ancient Oharai, or Great Purification, at the end of June and December; and in early October the Okunchi matsuri, the festival of the patronal *kami* of this shrine, lasting over several days, involving numerous rituals and the carrying of the Suwa *kami* in great *mikoshi* or palanquins to visit different areas of his domain. At Suwa, the procession becomes a parade with many floats, TV cameras, food and souvenir stalls, and a general public holiday.[11]

Another interesting perspective on the year can be seen in the spiritual life of a modern factory. David C. Lewis, in an illuminating article on this topic, has traced

As we have noted, New Year is especially important in Shinto, as befits what Mircea Eliade called cosmic religion, a religion directly dependent on the terrain and cycles of the earth, including the turn of the seasons, and of the cosmos, rather than on historical events like those defining Judaism, Christianity, Islam, or Buddhism. In Japan, New Year is a time for ceremonial visits to employers and family elders, and likewise for cleaning house, settling debts, and ritual purification (*oharai*). Countless individuals visit shrines, especially famous ones, on New Year's night, to pass through a great purifying ring of evergreen, and to purchase talismans, such as a *hamaya* ("evil-destroying arrow"), a symbolic arrow placed in one's house to repel or absorb malignant influences. Old *hamaya* from the previous year are collected in baskets at the shrine, to be burned later and so finally to destroy the evil. New Year crowds at shrines can be immense; Ian Reader tells us that at Fushimi Inari one year it took him 45 minutes to proceed from the station to the shrine gate, a walk that ordinarily would have taken only four or five minutes.[12]

the religious practices of a large synthetic fabrics plant employing some 4,000 people. On New Year's Day the three top managers of the firm go to three different shrines in the city, where they pray for the safety of their employees during the coming year, and give the shrines substantial donations from company funds. They also pray at each of five small shrines on a hillside behind the factory for which the firm takes responsibility. Then, on the first workday of the year, all employees pray together at a Shinto altar in the plant. In spring and autumn, at the times when in agricultural settings the mountain *kami* are believed to descend to the fields, and ascend back to the mountains in the fall, Shinto priests perform purifications, prayers and offerings in the plant, the offerings being presented in turn by managers, the union leader, representatives of male workers and female workers, and of the plant caterer. All then go to the hillside shrines in back of the plant for further prayers. At the end of the working year, a major purification (*oharai*) is performed by a Shinto priest, using strips of cloth to which impurities are ritually transferred; these are later burnt at a shrine.[13]

Weddings are very often celebrated with Shinto rites, with the bride wearing elaborate traditional Japanese formal garb, though today often at a Shinto altar in a hotel, where large receptions can more easily be managed, rather than a shrine. The high point is the bride and groom exchanging the "three times three" cups of sake, followed by their offering of an evergreen *sakaki* branch on the altar, and prayers by the priest. Today, the Western custom of exchanging rings is also often observed. Lately Christian weddings have also become fashionable, even among those who have no intention of becoming Christian; more on this later. It must also be noted that the Shinto shrine or hotel wedding of today is actually a modern development. Premodern Japanese nuptials were family ceremonies, held in the bride's home. If done properly, however, a Shinto priest would be brought in to do purifications, say

Shinto also has a role in celebrating stages of individual life, what are called rites of passage. About a month after birth infants (boys at 30 days, girls at 31), clad in a colorful baby kimono, are customarily taken to the family's *ujigami* (patronal or protecting deity or *kami*) shrine to be presented to that god as his or her newest godchild. This *miyamairi* (shrine visit) typically entails prayers chanted by the priest while one of the shrine maidens performs a sacred dance and gives the child a blessing.

Children visit the shrine at the Shichi-Go-San (7–5–3) festival on November 15, when girls of three and seven, and boys of five, dress up in new clothes and pray for a safe and healthy future. On January 20, a national holiday recognizes those who have reached age 20 and so are recognized as adults; though modern and largely secular, this occasion may include shrine visits.

a *norito*, and supervise the exchange of cups. A banquet would follow. For many Japanese the Shinto rite maintains the air of tradition people like to associate with matrimony, and connects well with the usual relation of Shinto and the *kami* to fertility and the good things of this life.

General features of Shinto

We have observed numerous examples of Shinto in all its diversity. What then can we say about the religion that is generally true? Five features come to mind:

- Emphasis on purity vs. impurity;
- Traditionalism;
- The importance of *matsuri* and the "practical" worship form of religious expression;
- The importance of the sociological role of religion;
- Polytheism as a special aspect of the "theoretical" expression of Shinto.

We will consider each of these in turn.

Purity versus impurity

The importance of sacred space and time is evident in the least acquaintance with Shinto. The *torii* or gate clearly demarcates the boundary between the outer world of pollution, and the *kami*-world of purity. In the same way, the time of *matsuri* or Shinto festivals is clearly, like all traditional holy days, a different kind of time from that of the workaday world. In Shinto space and time, one feels close to the purity of nature and to the ultimate essence of things in the divine spirits which animate it. In nature one is no less close to renewal, for one must in spirit return in order to renew. New Year, the great Shinto occasion, is such a time of renewal.

At shrines of any size in populated areas, one can usually see passers-by enter and approach the holy place for a moment of prayer. First the worshiper passes through

The streams, trees, and stones of nature are pure. Above all so are the hilltops and mountaintops from which, anciently, the gods descended. The human realm is less pure, which is why ideally shrines were on high ground, across a stream from the village. Particularly polluting are blood, sickness, and death, which should not be brought into a Shinto shrine; for this reason funerals are usually a Buddhist preserve, rarely Shinto. The Shinto feeling is instead the joy of happy love and marriage, of children, of green open spaces, of joyous dancing, laughing, colorful festivals, of the clean, clear peaks of sacred mountains.

Figure 3.5 Izumo Taisha (663highland; CC: Wikimedia Commons)

the *torii*, as it were leaving one world for another, the world of the street for a pure, sacred place linked to the primordial past with all its spiritual power. She (or he) then washes hands and mouth in a basin, clearly a gesture of purification. Arriving at the front of the shrine, the *haiden* or place of prayer, she then claps her hands twice, seemingly to attract the attention of the *kami*, but also, in a subtler way, letting the sharp sounds punctuate a moment of sacred time; all words or actions in a religious setting that are different from what one would do "outside" – perhaps would even look very odd if not done in temple, shrine, or church – are indicators of a special, sacred setting. The Shinto devotee bows her head for a word of prayer, probably for health, success, family welfare, one's business, or some other personal or local boon, for that is the spiritual level the *kami* know and on which they work. She then tosses an offering into a grill at the front of the *haiden*, turns, and leaves, departing the pure realm for that of the everyday world.

Traditionalism

As we have noted before in connection with the Daijosai and Ise, doing things as they have "always" been done is important to Shinto. The fire to cook the rice offerings at shrines is started by friction with the use of a kind of archaic fire-drill. Rituals like passing through the evergreen ring at New Year for purification, and clapping twice at the beginning of prayer, are done by modern people who may or may not believe deeply in them in an intellectual sense. They are more like acts of common courtesy, such as (in Japan) bowing slightly to an acquaintance, or apologizing for an inadvertent rudeness – but then gestures of courtesy are very important in Japan, keeping the wheels of interpersonal relationships well oiled, and the same applies to relations with the *kami*, and the tradition they represent, whatever one thinks the *kami* means.

Sometimes, as in the case of the Daijosai, some traditions may be so old most people have forgotten what they are supposed to "mean" – but in Japan it is not always important that religious actions have to "mean" something in an intellectual sense; it is sufficient that they express poetic or devotional feelings, and cement participation in a shrine community. In a survey conducted in the company whose Shinto rites were presented earlier, many responded that the rites have no real effect, or if they do the effect is only "spiritual" or only on one's own feelings, yet they continue to be performed.[14]

However, if Shinto were only traditionalism, it would never change, yet the evidence is clear that it has changed over the centuries. But the changes have occurred in ways which also reinforce tradition on a higher level, by invoking authority that is sanctioned within the tradition. That authority is of two types, both ultimately dependent on the existence of *ikigami*, "living *kami*," or *hitogami*, "man-gods," in our midst.

The first type is that of the state in the person of the emperor as living *kami* and "high priest" of Shinto, or of Shinto officials following general policy; as we will see later, particularly in the Meiji Shinto revival, on imperial authority state rites were constructed or restored, local shrines were combined and their rituals standardized, and new practices – like venerating the emperor's portrait in schools – promulgated.

The second type of authority is that of shamanism: persons believed to be "channeling" a new revelation from a *kami*, or responding to a divine sign. Many shrines were established in this way; the medieval amalgamation of Shinto and Buddhism was legitimated by oracles from Ise and other shrines; many new sects and religions of Shinto style derive from individual shamanistic inspiration.

The importance of practices

We have indicated that practice is often more important than subjective or intellectual belief in Shinto, and that rites are performed in a highly traditional manner. *Matsuri* or festivals, we have noted, can be thought of as following a set sequence: purification, presentation, prayer, participation, and the "participation" part will probably have a vigorous, celebrative character, like Carnival or Mardi Gras in the West, with many customary features valued by the particular community. We also noted the forms of individual shrine worship – which may also be roughly followed at home or business shrines.

Another important Shinto practice is pilgrimage. Persons will travel good distances, often in groups, to visit a shrine that is particularly important to his or her family or occupation. The Miwa Shrine, mentioned above, for example is not only extremely ancient, with its sacred mountain as the divine presence, but its *kami* is also a particular patron of *sake* (rice wine) makers, who assemble there on special pilgrimage days. The Ise shrines drew huge companies of pilgrims in the Tokugawa period.

Sacred mountains are especially ancient, famous, and important as pilgrimage sites in Japan, going back to when the *kami* were thought to dwell on their cold and lonely heights, descending into the fields during the rice-growing season – but to visit them in their mountaintop home was, and is, especially exhilarating and purifying. Of these peaks, Mount Fuji is undoubtedly best known. That incredibly beautiful and graceful mountain, the very symbol of Japan, attracts countless climbers every year, and in a sense they can be considered pilgrims, for there are Shinto shrines along the trail of ascent and at the summit.

At the same time, the syncretism, the combining of different traditions, that has long characterized Japanese religion, above all on the popular level, is evident at Fuji. Until they were largely suppressed by Meiji Restoration Shinto, the peak and access to it was controlled by *yamabushi*, "mountain priests," followers of Shugendo. This path, nominally Buddhist, involves esoteric and ascetic practices done in the mountains. It will be studied later. Shugendo surely had sources in ancient Shinto shamanism and mountain lore as well as in the imported faith. Even today, the ascent of Fuji is laid out on sacred diagrams not only in Shinto terms, but no less as entailing traversing the ten realms of existence of esoteric Buddhism, and the high summit represents Enlightenment.

The sociological role

Clearly, Shinto's foundation lies in its relation to communities: family, business, town, nation. Participation in Shinto worship is a manifestation of one's identity as a member of a community in Japan. State Shinto, and the accompanying Shinto worship in schoolrooms and on military parade-grounds, is not now what it was 1868–1945. But there remain essentially Shinto public events, like New Year with its shrine visits (including vast groups of uniformed school children), and national holidays with Shinto overtones, especially the controversial Kenkoku Kinensai ("Foundation of the Nation Commemoration Day") on February 11. Originally established as part of the Meiji Shinto Restoration under another name, it was restored in 1966; though officially secular, it is based on Shinto myth about the first emperor.

It is in its more local manifestations, however, that the sociological importance of Shinto is most evident. We have illustrated the role of company and community

Characteristically, the precise deity honored at Fuji is a little vague. The name seems to be derived from an Ainu[15] fire-god, appropriately given the mountain's volcanic character, but was later replaced by a goddess called Konohana ("Flowering Tree"), of whom a romantic myth is told. Taking human form, she was beloved by and married a husband. In time she felt required to return to the realm of the immortals atop the peak, but out of compassion for his sorrow gave her spouse a mirror in which she could always be seen. However, unable to contain his love, he followed her to the peak. There he jumped off a precipice, and the smoke issuing from the volcano is the burning ardor of his passion. On the other hand, sectarian Shinto groups that organize Fuji pilgrimages, of which the principal are called Jikko-kyo and Fuso-kyo, believe on the grounds of their own revelations that the sacred mountain was the dwelling place of three gods of creation, and so truly the spiritual center of the world.

matsuri, and family occasions. Mention might also be made of the importance of such Shinto ceremonies as dedicating new buildings, when priests are brought in to perform cornerstone-laying rites, and purifying edifices before use; this too can get into a "gray area" when it comes to dedicating public structures such as schools and government offices. As always, the question remains whether Shinto is "a religion" in the Western sense, or something else unique to Japanese culture and almost indefinable in outsider terms, but undoubtedly very important to Japanese identity.

Polytheism

As a religion, if so it is, Shinto is of great interest for a further reason: it is the only thorough-going polytheistic religion – having many gods – still extant in a major advanced society today. For while Hinduism and Taoism, and in a sense Buddhism, have plural deities, the emphasis is always on how they are but manifestations of the One, and the distinct religious experience of polytheism as a way of seeing the sacred universe seems to be lost.

To be sure, in medieval and early modern times various schemes were developed, some in conjunction with Buddhism, some based on Neo-Confucianism, to bring the Shinto *kami* into philosophical oneness. But the real focus in Shinto still lies in the gods' distinctiveness and local character. The distinguished theologian Paul Tillich once commented that the difference between monotheism (one god) and polytheism, like that of ancient pre-Christian Europe, is not a matter of quantity but of quality. It is not just that the former has but one deity whereas the latter has two or more. Rather, polytheism means the sacred world is experienced in a different way: as varied, nuanced, pluralistic, not reducible to a single entity or a single all-powerful will. There is a god for love and for war, for this sacred waterfall and that holy hill, each with distinct mood and myth, and as one moves from one to the other in time and space, one can intuit the difference.

The modern Shinto theologian Hirai Naofusa once told me that Shinto is the most democratic of religions, because in it the *kami* decide matters by discussion and consensus, not arbitrary fiat. It creates, in the title of one of the great American philosopher William James' books, *A Pluralistic Universe*. Even though, as we know, one also finds strong conformist messages in Japanese society, the relativistic and reaching-a-consensus mentality is certainly part of the national character.

A polytheistic system requires cycles of mythology to give embodiment to its deities. Shinto has them in its two ancient books, the *Kojiki* (*Chronicles of Ancient Times*) from 712 CE and the oldest extant Japanese book, and the *Nihongi* or *Nihonshoki* (*Chronicles of Japan*), 720 CE. Both were written by order of the court at a time of rising Buddhist influence to keep alive a pre-Buddhist narrative of the country, and to present accounts legitimating imperial rule. While Chinese models were clearly used, and the propagandistic mission exerted its influence, the two works surely contain much very ancient and important material. The longer *Nihongi* in particular is remarkable for its ability to present, almost in the manner of a modern folklore scholar, several variant and even contradictory versions of the same story.

The core narrative goes like this. The two primal parents, the male Izanagi and his consort Izanami, came down from the High Plain of Heaven on the Floating Bridge of Heaven; the earth was then all empty ocean as far as they could see. Izanagi dipped his spear into the watery waste and stirred it until it congealed into a bit of land, with the spear as a central pillar. The two *kami* deemed this a suitable place to dwell, and therein, after an initial disastrous experiment, began begetting much that was beautiful: the islands of Japan, *kami* of the mountains, sea, rivers, trees, and rice. But then, when Izanami gave birth to a fire-god, she burned herself terribly and had to descend to Yomi, the underworld land of the dead. Distraught, Izanagi followed, but found she had decayed and could not return again. Repelled by the horror and filth of the place of death, the male deity returned above.

He bathed in the ocean by way of purification. From the washings of his left eye the beautiful goddess Amaterasu of the sun came forth; from his right eye the moon god Tsukiyomi; from his nose the wind god Susanoo. This last deity, however, was rambunctious and unpredictable; a real trouble-maker, like the typhoons that ravage Japan. He went up to visit his lovely sister, and after a contest of procreation between them became enraged, violently destroying her rice fields and weaving-hall, together with other outrages. Distressed, Amaterasu retreated to the rock-cave of heaven.

The "eight hundred myriads" of *kami* gathered on the banks of the heavenly river to seek a way to bring Amaterasu back out of the cave. They placed cocks, her sacred bird, normally the herald of dawn, near her cave. One *kami* manufactured a special mirror; he waited with it near the entrance of her hiding-place. Then the goddess of dawn, Ama-no-Uzume, standing on an upturned tub, began doing the lewd dance mentioned before which caused the *kami* to laugh uproariously. The sun goddess, curious as to what was going on, put her head out of the cave. The roosters crowed; the god with the mirror held it before her face. Entranced by the brightness of her own reflection, she emerged further out, and a *kami* put a sacred straw rope (*shimenawa*) across the entrance to the cave so she could not return.

Susanoo was barred from heaven and exiled below. However, in a later mythical episode, he redeemed himself somewhat by rescuing a maiden from a dragon and, marrying her, establishing a divine land around Izumo, in the western part of Japan. The Izumo shrine is now second only to Ise in antiquity and mythological fame. He and his descendant Okuninushi, "Lord of the Land," are there enshrined; he and Izumo are the subject of intriguing myths that in some ways present alternatives to the core myth just outlined. It was during the time of Okuninushi's rule in Japan that Amaterasu became disturbed by the chaos, the struggles between good and evil *kami*, here below, and sent down her "Divine Grandson," Prince Ninigi, to establish a dynasty to settle matters. She gave him the sacred mirror to remember her by; this is the mirror that drew her out of the cave, and is now hallowed at Ise. According to the myth, his great-grandson in turn, Jimmu, was the first emperor, enthroned in 660 BCE by the Western calendar; Emperor Akihito, who succeeded in 1989, would be the 125th in that line.

The meaning of Shinto

What does all of this mean? Is Shinto really a separate world-class religion, to be set alongside others like Christianity and Islam, as it is in some world religions textbooks? Is it really the ancient, pre-Buddhist religion of Japan still extant in modern times? Or is all of this a sort of delusion, or at worst deliberate deception? This has been a matter of much scholarly controversy. Some still contend that Shinto is, at least to a significant extent, primordial Japanese religion. Others argue that it was anciently so influenced by Chinese religion, in the Middle Ages so reconfigured by its symbiosis with Buddhism (when the same priests might service both the buddhas and the *kami*), and in modern times so reconstructed by the Meiji Restoration, with its "invention of tradition" and its drastic separation of Shinto and Buddhism, as to be little more than a new religion passing itself off as old.

We cannot settle this issue here. My own inclination would be to take a middle ground, acknowledging much of what revisionist critics say, but pointing out that nonetheless all through the centuries, in places like Ise and Izumo, even in the imperial court, as well as in numerous local traditions, something distinctively Shinto, or at least not explainable in any other terms, can be found, whether in texts, or in rituals, or in sacred places.

In any case, for us what is important to understand is Shinto in Japanese social and spiritual life today. Here it is separate from Buddhism and has a distinct "flavor" and life of its own, even though most Japanese may relate to both it and Buddhism.

Questions for study and discussion

1. How do you explain the meaning of the word Shinto, both literally and religiously?
2. What is the meaning of *kami*?
3. What is the significance of the Grand Shrine of Ise? Of Inari shrines and Tenjin shrines?
4. Discuss the relation of Shinto to Japanese history, especially 1868–1945.
5. What are the central values of Shinto?
6. How is Shinto worship typically conducted?
7. Why is the "practical" form of religious expression so important to Shinto?
8. How does Shinto express the sociological bases of religion?
9. Discuss the meaning of polytheism and relate it to Shinto.
10. Relate purity vs. pollution to Shinto.
11. Summarize the core Shinto myth, as presented in the *Kojiki* and *Nihonshoki*.

Key points you need to know

- The Grand Shrine of Ise is the main national shrine, dedicated to Amaterasu, mythological ancestress of the imperial line
- Other representative Shinto shrines include those of the Inari, Miwa, Meiji, Yasukuni, and Tenjin types
- Basic Shinto terms include *kami, honden, shintai, torii, gohei, oharai,* and *shimenawa*
- The Shinto year, beginning with New Year, contains many special occasions, some special to particular shrines, though most will include planting and harvest festivals, and the *oharai* or great purification twice a year
- Shinto also offers individual rites of passage, including the dedication of children as *ujiko* and weddings
- Five keynotes of Shinto are: purity vs. pollution, traditionalism, importance of practices, the sociological role, and polytheism
- The core Shinto myth is found in the *Kojiki* and *Nihonshoki*.

Further reading

Ashkenazi, Michael, *Matsuri: Festivals of a Japanese Town*. Honolulu, HI: University of Hawaii Press, 1993.

Breen, John and Mark Teeuwen, ed., *Shinto in History: Ways of the Kami*. Honolulu, HI: University of Hawaii Press, 2000.

Hardacre, Helen, *Shinto and the State, 1868–1988*. Princeton, NJ: Princeton University Press, 1989.

Kageyama, Haruki, *The Arts of Shinto*. New York: Weatherhill, 1973.

Kasulis, Thomas, *Shinto: The Way Home*. Honolulu, HI: University of Hawaii Press, 2004.

Nelson, John K., *Enduring Identities: The Guise of Shinto in Contemporary Japan*. Honolulu, HI: University of Hawaii Press, 2000.

Picken, Stuart, *Essentials of Shinto*. Westport, CT: Greenwood Press, 1994.

Plutschow, Herbert, *Matsuri: The Festivals of Japan*. Shrewsbury: Roundwood Books, 1996.

Ross, Floyd, *Shinto: The Way of Japan*. Boston, MA: Beacon, 1965.

Electronic resources

Encyclopedia of Shinto. http://k-amc.kokugakuin.ac.jp/DM/dbTop.do?class_name=col_eos (A reliable resource.)

Wikipedia, "Ise Grand Shrine." https://en.wikipedia.org/wiki/ise_Grand_Shrine

Junko Edahiro, "Rebuilding Every 20 Years Renders Sanctuaries Eternal – the Sengu Ceremony at Jingu Shrine in Ise." www.japanfs.org/en/news_iDO34293.html

BBC "What are kami?" www.bbc.co.uk/religion/religions/shinto/beliefs/kami_1.shtml

"Inari." www.onmarkproductions.com/html/oinari.shtml (Also contains interesting material on fox folklore.)

"Yasukuni Shrine." www.yasukuni.or.jp/english (The controversial shrine's own site.)

Yonei Teruyoshi, "Tenjin Shinkō" [Tenjin Faith], *Encyclopedia of Shinto*. http://eos.kokugakuin.ac.jp/modules/xwords/entry.php?entryID=1081

Todd Jay Leonard, "Traditional Japanese Weddings are Beautiful." www.toddjayleonard.com/Todd_Jay_Leonard/Traditional_Japanese_weddings_are_beautiful,_Blog_Archives.html

"Festivals of the Four Seasons." www.jinjahoncho.or.jp/en/festival (A guide by the national shrine association.)

"New Year in Japan," *Japan Monthly Web Magazine*, Winter 2011.12. http://japan_magazine.jnto.go.jp/en/1112_newyear.html

Wikipedia, "Kojiki." https://en.wikipedia.org/wiki/kojiki

Interlude

Introduction to Buddhism

In this section

As background to understanding Japanese Buddhism, we will survey Buddhism as a whole, beginning with the traditional life of the Buddha, then going on to the Buddha's basic teachings, and finally the Mahayana and Yogacara schools which most influenced Japanese Buddhism.

Main topics covered

- The traditional life of the Buddha
- His four noble truths: suffering, the cause of suffering, the end of suffering, the path
- His eightfold path, last of the four noble truths
- The three refuges: the Buddha, the Dharma, and the Samgha
- The Middle Way and Nirvana
- Mahayana Buddhism and its principal features, especially the cosmic buddhas and bodhisattvas
- Yogacara, the school of consciousness only.

The Enlightened One

Many years ago, in ancient India, a young prince set out on a quest for the greatest prize of all. For this prize he was willing to give up a kingdom with all its wealth and palaces, a place of honor in his father's court, even a lovely young consort and son. In the search for this prize he would instead wear only the coarsest of robes, beg for his meager meals, and suffer temptations that could have been devised by demons. But in the end he found that for which he was seeking, and accordingly he was called the Buddha, the Enlightened One, the Awakened One. He was the one who has woken up and is in the know; compared to him the rest of us are like persons asleep, lost in the world of dreams. The reverberations of his awakening, like the sound of water in Basho's poem, resounded across the planet, finally reaching Japan.

The traditional story of this exceptional individual's life is no doubt mostly legend, but it is significant nonetheless: it reflects the way the Buddha has been understood by the hundreds of millions of persons over some twenty-five centuries for whom he has represented the summit of human attainment, and has been the supreme guide in matters of the spirit. It goes like this.[1]

He who came to be called the Buddha (approx. 563–483 BCE according to some modern scholarship) was born as Siddhartha Gautama of the Sakya[2] clan. He was born, it is said, in a park at Lumbini, about where the border of India and Nepal now lies, north of Banaras; his mother, a queen, was on a journey away from the palace.

It was no ordinary birth. This infant was a bodhisattva (future buddha), and accordingly he had undergone countless previous lifetimes in preparation for his final entry into our troubled world. Eons ago, he had made a vow before Dipankara, the "Silent Buddha," the Buddha of a previous world before ours, that however long it took, however great the obstacles, he would himself attain full and perfect enlightenment. His last life had been as a white elephant with four tusks. Then his mother, Queen Mahamaya, had a dream in which this beast pierced her side with one of his tusks, and in this way the future buddha was conceived. He was likewise born out of her side.

Siddhartha's mother died only eight days after giving birth, and he was raised by his aunt, Mahaprajapati. Wise brahmins came to see the child, saw certain signs on his body, and predicted two possible futures for him: if he stayed home, he would become a *chakravartin*, a world emperor; if he left home, he would become a Buddha, an enlightened being, who would show humankind the way out of suffering. The king his father, apparently more politically than spiritually motivated, preferred that he take the first option, and bring undying renown to his house by ruling over the entire earth. But the monarch was apparently just perceptive enough to grasp that if such a child saw anything of the anguish of the

---

At Siddhartha's birth wondrous signs appeared. Music was heard in the air, blossoms fell around the babe, and sweet rain descended from heaven. The remarkable child immediately walked, pacing to the four directions, then stood in the center, pointed to the zenith, and said, "This is my last incarnation. In this life I will accomplish what I have set out to do." This event is celebrated in Japan every April 8 as *hanamatsuri* (literally, "flower festival") when in honor of the Buddha's birthday small images of the marvelous infant are placed out of doors, if possible under falling cherry petals, and children pour sweetened water over it from ladles.

world, he would be so moved by compassion as not to be content to reign from a throne, but would want to show all beings the way out of pain. Thus the king built for his son three pleasure palaces, with everything to delight the heart of a young prince, horses, chariots, music, dancing girls, later a beautiful wife, and high walls to keep out any sight or sound of ill.

By the time the prince reached 29, however, the restless call that had long stirred within him grew more insistent. He could no longer restrain his desire to know what life was like outside the palace walls. He persuaded his charioteer to take him on four expeditions beyond home. On these he saw four sights, all apparently new to him.

- On the first outing he saw an aged man, bent over his staff, senile, blind, and deaf, yet still tottering down the highway.
- On the second he saw a man dying horribly by the side of the road, full of disease and pain.
- On the third he saw a funeral procession conveying a corpse toward the burning ghats.
- And on the last he observed a holy man with his staff and begging bowl.

The future Buddha immediately recognized that the first three visions represented the true ends of life in this world: old age, sickness, death. Large disturbing thoughts and unanswered questions swirled through his mind. What is the meaning of a world of pleasure such as his if, in the end, it came only to this? In the face of these three ends, how could it be possible to enjoy a productive and peaceful life?

Siddhartha was honest enough to acknowledge that he did not know the answer to these questions, but he also knew that now he could live for no other purpose than to find that answer. The last sight gave him the inspiration: the ideal of a life devoted to nothing but dealing with the ultimate issues of life and death, setting all else aside. Therefore, not long after, kissing his wife and son farewell, he bade his charioteer take him on one last journey outside the palace. By the banks of a river he discarded his princely garb, gave it to the charioteer, and taking for himself only a monk's robe, together with a staff and bowl, he set out utterly alone.

For six years he wandered northern India, seeking, studying with various teachers. He spent time with brahmin philosophers, who no doubt at this time were developing the non-dualist philosophy we now call Vedanta. But the seeker felt in the end they were only playing intellectual games, and were not as passionately concerned as he to gain real, practical wisdom. As he would say, he needed his answers as badly as a man shot by the arrow of suffering needs to have it removed. In his desperate quest, he practiced extreme asceticism with another group, until he became so emaciated he looked like a skeleton, but found this path was only a sort of spiritual athleticism which did not yield ultimate answers either. He went on alone.

Finally the bodhisattva seemed to realize the time had come. He seated himself under a giant fig tree and, touching the ground, swore by the earth itself that he would not stir from that spot till he had attained full and perfect enlightenment. During that night, Mara, a demonic adversary utterly opposed to change, came to the Buddha and tried to prevent his final realization in three ways: through tremendous distracting storms, by sensual temptations, and finally by telling him to get enlightened but tell no one about it. The Enlightened One rejected all these by holding up his hand in a gesture of refusal, familiar in Buddhist art, saying he was meant to be teacher of gods and men, and would not swerve from that calling. Mara finally left, and early in the morning the Buddha moved into the highest states of unlimited consciousness, consummated when he saw the morning star.

His fundamental teaching[3], which he called the Middle Way (the point of equilibrium between all extremes, from indulgence and asceticism to being and non-being) came to him together with enlightenment. It is expressed simply in what are called the Four Noble Truths:

The Four Noble Truths

- The truth of suffering (Sanskrit: dukha): that suffering pervades all life as it is ordinarily lived, both physical pain and suffering in the forms of anxiety, despair, frustration, and dissatisfaction.
- The cause of suffering: desire (Sanskrit: tanha, literally "thirst"), craving, clinging, attachment. The reason desire causes suffering is that this "thirst" always wants to grab on to something, whether an object of pleasure, status, power, or even an idea or belief, whereas the world is continually changing, we ourselves are changing, and nothing to which we cling holds still. The ultimate attachment, of which all others are merely symptoms, is to ourselves as separate individual egos. But Buddhism teaches that the ego itself is an illusion (the truth of Sanskrit *anatman*, "no self"), for we are made up of transitory parts, both on the physical and psychological levels, which come together and then go apart, driven by the winds of *karma* or cause and effect.
- There can be an end to desire. The good news is that *tanha* can be stopped.
- The Noble Eightfold Path: The way to end it is to live according to these eight principles: right views, right intentions, right speech, right conduct, right livelihood, right effort, right mindfulness, right concentration or meditation. Basically, what these say is that the real way to reverse ego-attachment is by meditation, that is, stilling the mind to free it of all thoughts of self; the other seven are intended to create a lifestyle and state of mind that supports meditation.

As the Buddha went around teaching these things, he attracted disciples who practiced meditation, aspiring to become liberated beings (Sanskrit: arhat; Japanese: *Rakan*). In time they formed the Samgha, the Buddhist order of monks. Those who joined that company took the Three Refuges or Three Jewels:

I take refuge in the Buddha,
the Dharma,
and the Samgha.

That is, I accept the Buddha (*Butsu* or *Hotoke*[4]) as the supreme teacher, I accept his Dharma (*Ho*) or teaching as the ultimate truth insofar as it can be put into words, I accept his Samgha or Order (*So*) as the supreme spiritual fellowship.

*   *   *

What did it mean to become liberated? The term for the liberated state is nirvana (*Nehan*); the best way to think about it is as unconditioned reality. What is this?

Most of what we experience is conditioned, that is, limited, reality. If we are in one place, we are not also in another. If we are in the twenty-first century, we are not also in the twenty-fourth with *Star Trek*. Most of us cannot think of more than one thing at a time, or do more than two-digit multiplication in our head. Moreover, as the Buddha would have been the first to say, we are conditioned in all sorts of ways by our fears, our angers, and our desires. It is all this conditioning, Buddhism says, that blinkers our minds and keeps us tied down to the realm of suffering and repeated rebirths.

But what if there were a state the absolute opposite of conditioning? In which we had total freedom from every limitation, and therefore our minds were as horizonless as infinite space and time itself? We would be hard put to describe that state in words, since language itself comes out of conditioned reality and the need to distinguish its separate, limited things. But surely it would be a realm of peace, clarity, and calm joy, beyond all that can upset, beyond all limits. This is what is called nirvana.[5]

Mahayana Buddhism

These precepts – the Middle Way, the Four Noble Truths, the Eightfold Path, meditation, and conditioned reality and unconditioned nirvana – were among the essentials taught by the Buddha and the early Samgha. But in time some who had taken refuge wanted to dig further into Buddhist truth, and expand the practice and sociology of Buddhism to take into account the deeper levels of Buddhist reality they believed they had uncovered, or had been revealed to them. This move produced Mahayana (*Daijo*; "Great Vehicle") Buddhism, the form of Buddhism that entered Japan and has overwhelmingly prevailed in that country down to the present.[6] (The alternative form, Theravada, the "Way of the Elders," is the Buddhism of the southern tier of Buddhist countries: Laos, Cambodia, Thailand, Burma or Myanmar, and Sri Lanka. This tradition believes itself more firmly based in the Buddha's original teaching.)

Wanting to understand more deeply, early Mahayana thinkers asked themselves, "What kind of ultimate reality does the Buddha's experience of enlightenment really imply"? In what kind of universe could this happen? What does it say about mind and matter that is true all the time?[7]

The Buddha himself seems not to have been given to such speculation. He was more like an ancient version of psychotherapist than philosopher, content to show people the way out of suffering, and its immediate causes in their lives, than a seeker of metaphysical truth. But it was hard to keep people from wondering what it all meant. If you carry the Buddhist vision to worlds without end, what kind of cosmos do you see on the way?

Basically, Mahayana – perhaps influenced by Indian Vedanta philosophy – turned Buddhist *psychology* into *ontology* (i.e., the study of the nature of ultimate reality, and of levels or kinds of reality). Thus, if there is an experience of enlightenment such as a Buddha and the *arhats* have, enlightenment must be something that is within us, and within our universe, all the time; we just need to realize it.

If that is the case, the universe, and all worlds in it, must be full of consciousness and enlightenment, or at least the potential for them. For we obviously are children of the universe, profoundly interrelated with it all the time, as we are to the air we breathe and the thoughts we think in response to what we see and hear. We did not drop into it from some other sphere, for the universe is infinite and all there is; what is in us must be everywhere.

If even one enlightened consciousness has existed on earth – the Buddha's – it stands to reason other even deeper and greater buddhic consciousnesses undergird the infinite universe as a whole: beings like some we have already met – Dainichi, the "Great Sun Buddha" of the Todaiji in Nara, whose super-profound meditations sustain the cosmos, or Amida, in whose aura all who seek liberation can find a Pure Land. Soon these great beings were known not only by reason, but also by revelation in newly-discovered sutras or texts, often sermons purportedly given by the Buddha but reserved until the time was right to reveal them to the world.

These "cosmic buddhas" can take human form at the interface between human consciousness and the infinite universe, though ultimately they should perhaps be thought of more as great vortices of wisdom and compassion in the consciousness field underlying the universe's physical expression. Being part of a rational order, they work together and form interlocking patterns or mandalas (*mandara*); think of the five cosmic buddhas in the Toji temple. In it, as we saw, the five each have bodhisattvas (*bosatsu*), like Kannon or Jizo, as their agents. With one foot in unconditioned reality and one in conditioned, guided by wisdom and compassion and using skill-in-means, the bodhisattvas bring ultimate values into our muddled planet, and to all other worlds.

Let us now summarize some basic principles of Mahayana Buddhism that distinguish it from Theravada, and go beyond – or, Mahayanists would say, spell out the implications of – the earliest dharma.

The sutras

A voluminous body of additional scriptures or sutras, written in Sanskrit rather than the Pali (a kind of dialect of Sanskrit) of the *Tripitaka* (*Three Baskets*, the scriptures of Theravada containing basic teachings about the Middle Way, the Four Noble Truths, No-Self, Rules for Monks, etc.). The Mahayana sutras, undeniably later, include such important texts as the Garland, Great Sun, Lotus, Heart, and Pure Land sutras, immensely influential in Japan.[8]

Nagarjuna's Two Principles

Nagarjuna (c. 150–250 CE) was an Indian Buddhist philosopher who was the most important intellectual force in early Mahayana.[9] He said that *samsara* (the wheel of cause-and-effect, *karma*, and rebirth; what we have called conditioned reality) and nirvana were the same; nirvana is not some place you "go to" but is here and now; it's just a matter of looking at things differently and seeing your life as an enlightened buddha's life and your world as nirvana, instead of a life of suffering going round and round on the wheel of *samsara*.

Second, he said such a universe is void or empty because it's really nirvana or unconditioned; though things are out there, they are continually changing and there's nothing to grab hold of, either materially or intellectually; the way is to let go rather than grab. Reality is real, but what it is cannot be held by hand or head; it is *tathata*, "suchness," "thusness." See it, appreciate it, love it, but know that once you think you understand it, it has become something else. This is the way of *prajna*, wisdom, or *prajnaparamita*, the wisdom that has gone beyond, to the other shore, the shore of unconditionality. (*Prajnaparamita* (*Hannya haramita*) is the name of a

> Mahayana might be called "multimedia" Buddhism. The Great Vehicle also speaks of relative and absolute truth, and of skill-in-means. The absolute truth is that we are already enlightened buddhas; relative truth, accepting that we don't know this and are not yet ready to know it, tells us that for now, as a "skillful means," follow whatever teaching and practice helps you keep moving, and regard it as provisionally true.

great early Mahayana sutra; the Heart sutra, *Shingyo*, beloved of Zen especially, is a summation of it.)

Universality

If nirvana is all around us, and we are already enlightened beings without knowing it, then enlightenment must be available to all, whether monk or layman, wise or foolish, educated or not, rich or poor.[10] This was an original issue between Theravada and Mahayana, and remains essential to such teachings as Pure Land – that all can be saved by faith – or in Zen that enlightenment can come as *satori*, "surprise."

Devotion and faith

So it is that in Mahayana one does not need a long series of auspicious reincarnations, or a lifetime of practice, to attain liberation. The Lotus Sutra tells us that a simple offering of flowers or a tiny clay *stupa* presented by a child in self-forgetful devotion and love is of far more worth than years of self-centered effort. If one just lets oneself drop away in a childlike sense of wonder and giving, one is already there; in that moment ego has vanished. In its place there stands an enlightened buddha. Any means that helps us get one of those moments, whether the golden-lotus beauty of the Chionin temple or the many different buddha and bodhisattva figures of Mount Hiei, whether Pure Land faith or Zen quiet sitting, is as good as any other.

Accommodation with other religions

In the same broad-minded way, Mahayana generally coexists with other faiths – Confucianism and Taoism in China, Shinto and Confucian ethics in Japan – finding tactics for incorporating their deities and doctrines into its own.

Cosmic Buddhas

These have already been considered.

The Mahayana Bodhisattva

Just as in Theravada only one buddha exists for our age of the world, so is there only one bodhisattva, the buddha in preparation for the next world, after the dissolution of this one. But in Mahayana buddhas and bodhisattvas are countless because they come out of the infinite consciousness of the universe itself.

Bodhisattvas are buddhas in training. It is said they have vowed not to enter nirvana till all other sentient beings have been saved; they are also agents of a buddha's wisdom and compassion, just as a graduate student can both be a learner at an advanced level while teaching and helping undergraduates. Indeed, bodhisattvas are guided supremely by wisdom and compassion (compassion being the ethical expression of wisdom, which above all is seeing the interrelatedness of all things); these two together, in turn, endow the bodhisattva with *upaya* or skill-in-means, knowing precisely the right way to exercise compassion in a particular situation, and having the ability which comes from deep wisdom to do whatever it takes, even apparently miraculous means, to apply that compassion.[11] (The trouble with many of us is that, although we may sincerely want to be compassionate, we often do so unskillfully and mess things up, because we don't fully understand all aspects of a situation. Of course it's better to try to be compassionate than do nothing; that's how we get on the bodhisattva path and slowly learn.)

Figure I.1   Sanjusangendo Temple, Kyoto (*Japanese Temples and their Treasures*. Shimbi Shoin, 1915; Public Domain: Wikimedia Commons)

Yogacara

In the fourth and fifth centuries CE, after the basic Mahayana teaching of Nagarjuna and the Prajnaparamita sutras was in place, a further philosophical movement arose. It is called Yogacara ("practice of yoga," referring to the importance the school put on deep practice as a means to realizing its truths) or Vijnanavada ("way of mind"), or sometimes, in English, "Mind only" Buddhism.[12] (The Japanese is *Hosso*, literally "dharma character.")

If Nagarjuna had taught that the universe is void, emptiness, or "suchness," to be seen but not held onto, Yogacara wants to go beyond saying what it is not, to ask what it is, or at least what positive reality it is most like. Yogacara philosophers said it is most like mind, consciousness. It is quick, hard to grasp, yet real, like thoughts. The universe is really just thoughts, projected out of our minds and greater minds than ours. We need to understand how much we make our own world out of our feelings, desires, and *karma*, or carryovers from this and previous lives. If we are given to fear, we see much to be afraid of. If anger, we see much to make us angry out

Think of the movie projector again, and of the interdependence of all things ...

Donald Ritchie, the eminent western interpreter of Japanese film, has observed that its cinematic composition is often "bottom-heavy," like conventional Sino-Japanese landscape paintings, which leave realms of sky and empty space above the scenery to suggest the infinite void framing all "solidified" reality. The empty space above the filmic action, Ritchie said, "was there to define what was below; it had its own weight." In a western movie, a character and his or her emotions might be established by a close-up, where every individualizing detail is more than apparent; in a Japanese picture, it's more likely to be a long shot, where one is drawn in toward the character by distance, and the environment is part of what explains him or her.[13]

The buddha-nature in all things ... The great Ozu Yasujiro, considered the "most Japanese" of the modern directors, whose pictures are inevitably about "ordinary" families and people, can spend a seemingly inordinate amount of time recording a character doing a common act such as wrapping a package or peeling a piece of fruit; he has said he has a profound respect for the ability to do simple, everyday actions well.[14]

One thinks of the Tendai idea of many paths and ways. The classic Japanese film probably best known in the West, *Rashomon*, by the celebrated director Akira Kurosawa, presents a crime (set in the Onin War era) through the eyes of several persons: the victim, the perpetrator, a would-be avenger, a bystander. Who is right? And the film is enveloped in pounding, almost blinding rain.[15]

there. But if, like a buddha, we live in wisdom and compassion, we are united with those great beings, and live in love and inner peace whatever happens.

Think of it as like a movie projector. The light is the universal consciousness within, the screen the field of universal consciousness without; the reel of film, or cassette or DVD, or download into our minds, which actually projects out the scenario of our life and how we see the world, is stained and colored by the *karma* of our previous actions. Yogacara practice can help us understand this and change the movie, as it were taking out one film and putting in another, better one.

In Japan, Yogacara has had a major impact, especially in the Hosso, Shingon, Tendai, and Zen schools. But the influence of Mahayana and Yogacara is not limited to sects and doctrines, or even to religion, or to words.

Questions for study and discussion

1. Outline the traditional tale of the Buddha's life. What is the significance of this narrative?
2. What is the significance of the four sights the Buddha saw?
3. Explain the meaning of the Four Noble Truths in your own words.
4. Do the same for the Eightfold Path.
5. And for the Three Refuges or Three Jewels.
6. What are the essentials of Mahayana Buddhism? What do you believe Mahayana thinkers were really trying to get at?
7. Explain the cosmic buddhas and bodhisattvas of Mahayana Buddhism.
8. How does Yogacara or "Mind Only" Buddhism explain the universe, and your own life?

Key points you need to know

- The outline of the traditional life of the Buddha
- The Buddha's basic teachings are contained in the four noble truths, the three refuges, the middle way, no self, liberation and nirvana
- The fundamentals of Mahayana and their meaning: Sanskrit sutras, Nagarjuna's two principles (*samsara* is nirvana, emptiness), universality of buddhahood, the role of devotion and faith, accommodation with other religions, cosmic buddhas, the bodhisattva in Mahayana.
- The Yogacara or "mind only" school teaches that reality as we perceive it is a projection of mind, influenced by our *karma* and basic thought-forms.

Further reading

Chen, Kenneth, *Buddhism: The Light of Asia*. Woodbury, NY: Barron's Educational Series, 1968.

Cone, Edward, *Buddhism: Its Essence and Development*. New York: Harper Torchbooks, 1959.

Cone, Edward, *Buddhist Wisdom Books*. London: George Allen & Unwin, 1958.

Deal, William E. and Brian Ruppert, *A Cultural History of Japanese Buddhism*. Hoboken, NJ: Wiley-Blackwell, 2015.

de Bary, William Theodore, Ryusaku Tsunoda and Donald Keene, *The Buddhist Tradition in India, China, and Japan*. New York: Modern Library, 1969.

Percheron, Maurice, *The Marvelous Life of the Buddha*. New York: St. Martin's Press, 1960.

Prebish, Charles, and Damien Keown, *Introducing Buddhism*. New York: Routledge, 2006.

Robinson, Richard H., and Willard L. Johnson, *The Buddhist Religion*. Belmont, CA: Wadsworth, 1982.

Stone, Jacqueline Ilyse and Mariko Namba Walter, *Death and the Afterlife in Japanese Buddhism*. Honolulu: University of Hawaii Press, 2008.

Williams, Paul, *Mahayana Buddhism: The Doctrinal Foundations*. New York: Routledge, 1989.

Electronic Resources

"Following the Buddha's Footsteps." http://online.sfsu.edu/rone/Buddhism/footsteps.htm

"Dharma Data: Nirvana." www.buddha.net/e-learning/dharmadata/fdd43.htm

"Mahayana Buddhism," *Encyclopædia Britannica*. www.britannica.com/EBchecked/topic/358037/Mahayana

"Five Buddha of Wisdom" [The Cosmic Buddhas]. www.onmarkproductions.com/html/godai-nyorai.shtml

"Bodhisattvas of Compassion," *Buddhist Studies*. www.buddha.net/e-learning/historyb_fbodi.htm

"Mandala in Japan." www.onmarkproductions.com/html/mandala1.shtm

"Nagarjuna (c. 150-250)," *Internet Encyclopedia of Philosophy*. www.iep.utm.edu/nagarjun/

Wikipedia, "Yogacara." https://en.wikipedia.org/wiki/Yogacara

4 *Early times*

Pre-Buddhist Japan and how Buddhism arrived

In this chapter

This chapter will survey religion and society in Japan before the coming of Buddhism, noting their several stages – Jomon, Yayoi, "horse-rider," and Kofun – and the role of female shamanistic rulers in the earlier stages, giving way to male sovereignty. The introduction of Buddhism in the sixth century CE, and the conflicts it produced, will be described. We will then look at the work of the great pro-Buddhist ruler Prince Shotoku, the Taika reform of 646, and the Taiho Code of 702, noting the balance they attempted between Shinto and Buddhism. Finally, we examine the religious history of the eighth century Nara period, with its brilliance, scandals, and divisions between aristocratic and countryside Buddhism.

Main topics covered

- Japan before Buddhism: the several stages and outside influences, shamanism, and consolidation around the Yamato clan
- The introduction of Buddhism
- The role of Prince Shotoku
- The Taika reforms and the Nakatomi house
- The Nara period: its six schools, the construction of the Great Buddha, the Empress Koken and the priest Dokyo, the split between court and countryside Buddhism, the end of the Nara era.

Japan before Buddhism

The traditional date offered by the *Nihonshoki* for the introduction of Buddhism into Japan can be calculated as 538, or some say 552, CE in the Western calendar. While this year may not be precisely accurate, certainly it reflects the era the great religious change began.

What had been going on in Japan up to this time? Although Stone Age remains many thousands of years old have been found on these islands, the earliest culture that appears to have much continuity with historic Japan is the Jomon, dated approximately 8000 BCE to 200 CE and, some have speculated, ancestral to the later Emishi and the Ainu of today. Jomon society is considered neolithic, possessing villages and some agriculture, as well as hunting, fishing, and gathering. Jomon religion is not fully understood, but seems, like that of many neolithic cultures, to have emphasized fertility. Female clay figures, perhaps goddesses, have been found at Jomon sites, as have male phallic representations and serpent designs. Clay masks, possibly used by shamans, have also appeared.[1]

Jomon culture produced remarkable clay figures known as *dogu* – exquisitely crafted half-animal, half-human forms with peculiar slit eyes. Perhaps they had some magical or religious meaning, but since the Jomon left no written record it is not known. In any case, we may already see the brilliant fusion of religion and art that has always characterized Japanese culture. Broadly speaking, Jomon culture seems comparable to that of traditional Polynesia and Melanesia, and that connection is one strand in later Japan.

Between about 200 BCE and 250 CE another strand entered the mix, arriving in the south and gradually moving up the Japanese islands. Called Yayoi culture, it was characterized by wet rice agriculture; metal also appeared in this period, probably from Korea. Indeed, it seems that another influence, perhaps a wave of conquering immigrants bringing horse-riding and metal, entered in the early centuries CE via Korea, but with antecedents further inland. One theory is that if horse-riders came in from the northwest, with a language at the root of modern Japanese, that would explain aspects of Japanese language and religion reminiscent of Mongol and Turkic culture. This final invasion would also explain the increasing unification of the nation in those years under a ruling house based in the Yamato clan. The "horse-riders," though perhaps not numerous, probably had superior technology and military prowess.

In sum, then, we see traditional Japanese religion and culture as having four sources or connections, coming from the four directions to Japan. The Jomon culture may have links to Polynesian and Melanesian societies, like them possessing fertility and trance-state emphases, together with a "horizontal" mythology, featuring deities coming in from sacred lands across the sea.

The Yayoi wave, bringing rice agriculture from the south, stressed the agricultural cycle of seed-time and harvest festivals still characteristics of Shinto today.

The northern influence, with links to Korean and Mongol culture, added shamanism and "vertical" cosmology, its gods descending from a heavenly realm far above, in the sky.

Finally, as we will see, at the beginning of written history there came, via Korea and China to the west, literacy, Buddhism, and Confucian and Taoist texts and practices.

We get a vivid picture of Japan around this time from accounts of Chinese visitors. The most important is from the early third century. It tells us that people ate raw vegetables from bamboo or wooden trays, clapped their hands for worship rather than kneeling, were fond of liquor, long-lived, and generally honest. (All this is still largely true of Japan today.) We are also told the country was ruled by a woman named Himiko or Pimiko (probably "Sun-Princess"), who was clearly a shamaness-queen. She lived in seclusion, was never married, served by a thousand female attendants plus one man who mediated between her and the outside world. This mysterious queen "occupied herself with magic and sorcery, bewitching the people."[2] When she died, she was buried in a great mound and was succeeded by a relative, a girl of thirteen named Iyo.

Some scholars have identified Pimiko with a shamanistic empress called Jingu Kogo in the ancient chronicles. Probably both intriguing women can be taken as representative of a number of ruling shamanesses governing various clans in ancient Japan. In the chronicles, however, Jingu was preceded by the Emperor Sujin, called "the emperor who first ruled over the state." The "horse-riders" invasion theory could make him first of a new line, and in any case there is reason to think he actually followed Himiko and represents a religious as well as political new beginning, from female rulers of Pimiko's type, whose power was based in magic and mystery, toward what one might call a more "modern" style of male sovereignty.[3]

Although we perceive them through the lens of a later era, the Yayoi period and then the "horse-riders" are reflected in the earliest *Kojiki*[4] and *Nihonshoki* myths, where the rice-paddy cycle and the Harvest Festival dominated religion (as it still does in the Daijosai and at Ise), and in which metal, as in Amaterasu's mirror, had magical significance before it was given much practical use. (In tombs from this period, obviously magical mirrors and swords are often found, containing and protecting the spirit of the deceased.)

The period 250–552 CE is called the Kofun, meaning "great burial mounds" like Pimiko's in which important people were interred; many remain, often attributed to some mythological emperor, and when excavated (permission is only now being given to touch those said to house deified sovereigns of old) have yielded important grave-goods, including mirrors, swords, and curved stones (*magatama*) like those now regarded as imperial regalia.

All in all, Japan before Buddhism was no doubt at a culture-level like that of Native America at the time of first European contact, or Britain at the time of the first Roman incursion. There was some agriculture and large-scale building of the megalithic or mound-building sort, and society was divided into tribes or clans each governed by a chieftain who also served as priest of the clan's patronal god or *kami*. Shamanism remained important; a chief's sister or wife would serve as shamaness, giving advice on matters of state out of trance; this arrangement remained in Okinawa until as late as the nineteenth century. Literacy was lacking, but political unity was beginning to take shape around 350 CE under rulers of the most powerful clan, the Yamato in what is now the area of Kyoto, perhaps starting with the figure later called the Emperor Ojin.[5] Ancestors of the present imperial house then more and more asserted a leadership role. They seem to have been like what is sometimes called a Paramount Chief in a federation of tribes, such as the Iroquois in North America.

The coming of Buddhism

We are told in the *Nihonshoki* that in the year 538 or 552 a Korean king sent the Japanese sovereign a Buddhist image, scripture, and other paraphernalia, saying in a letter that all the rest of East Asia worships the Buddha; why not Japan?[6] The date (whichever it is depends on how one reads the *Nihonshoki* chronology) and the details may not be historical, but undoubtedly reflect the approximate time Buddhism began to make an impact, through Korean immigrants and perhaps also diplomatic contacts, on Japan.

The story goes on to say that the emperor was intrigued, but cautious. He asked his principal counselors for advice. One, of the powerful Soga family, urged that Japan should be up to date and accept the latest thing. Two others, of the Nakatomi and Mononobe families, both hereditary Shinto priests, said that the *kami* would be angry if this intruder was welcomed. The ruler hit upon a cunning solution; he asked the Soga minister to take the image to his house, worship it, and see what happened.

What happened was that his house caught on fire, and voices were quick to say the *kami* were angry. So the image was thrown into a river. But then an epidemic broke out, and the cry was that the Buddha was outraged. The altar was restored. It is clear that, in Japanese eyes at the time, Buddhism was nothing more than another form of magic, and the situation soon deteriorated into civil war between the Soga and Nakatomi clans. The Soga initially prevailed. Soga no Umako completed his seizure of power in 592 by arranging for the assassination of the emperor and placing his own niece on the throne as the Empress Suiko. She was a devout Buddhist and appointed as her regent an imperial prince, Shotoku (573–621).

However devious the means by which he came to power, Shotoku was among the most admired and influential rulers in Japan's history. Under his auspices, Buddhism became a major cultural influence and a national religion, as the prince strove to consolidate Japan politically and spiritually. Though seriously Buddhist, Shotoku

Figure 4.1 Horyuji Temple, near Nara (© KPG_Payless / Shutterstock.com)

was a practical layman more interested in what the imported religion could mean for the life of the nation than in doctrinal squabbles. His own essential interests are suggested by the three sutras on which he is said to have written commentaries: the Lotus Sutra, with its theme of universal salvation; the Vimalakriti Sutra, emphasizing the path of the devout layman; and the Srimala Sutra, chanted for the protection of the state.

He quickly grasped that, as an outside force, the new faith could unify Japan because it was not identified with particular clans as were Shinto *kami*, but only with the imperial house. He founded the first national temple, the famous Horyuji outside of Nara, in 607. This great complex, of which one building remains as the oldest wooden structure in the world, is a magnificent treasure-house of early Buddhist art, some from overseas. There is also a small octagonal edifice called the Yumedo ("Hall of Dreams") where the prince is said to have liked to meditate.

According to tradition, it was in 604 that Prince Shotoku issued the document called the Seventeen Article Constitution. Some scholars say it is actually much later, but in any case this remarkable work perhaps reflects Shotoku's vision for the nation. Not a constitution in the modern sense, the text is largely a set of moral principles, chiefly for officials, couched in Confucian language, beginning with an appeal for harmony borrowed from the *Analects* of Confucius. The second "article" or paragraph, however, exhorts its readers to "Sincerely reverence the three treasures, the Buddha, the Dharma, and the Samgha," before going on to admonish ministers to "Chastise that which is evil and encourage that which is good," and to "Be not envious!"[7]

The Constitution reminds us that in this sixth and seventh century period of rapid change in Japan, not only Buddhism but much else – Confucianism, Taoism, fine art, the Chinese writing system, and many practical devices, including printing – was coming from the continent. The bulk of these imports were undoubtedly brought by Korean immigrants, who left their homeland for Japan partly because of unstable conditions there, but also because of the exceptional opportunities for skilled craftsmen and teachers in the new Japanese environment. The sudden appearance of something as astounding as the Horyuji temple, in a land whose previous architecture amounted to little more than modest thatch-roofed houses and granaries, was certainly due to outside help. So also was the magnificent Buddhist sculpture of the period.

The struggle over the place of Buddhism was not over, however. Buddhism continued to be favored by Soga rulers during the first half of the seventh century, although subsequent ministers of that house had few of Prince Shotoku's gifts. They suffered increasing popular opposition because of their high-handed ways and favoritism toward the foreigners who served their cultural revolution. Resentment came to a head in 645, when Nakatomi Kamatari led a coup which overthrew the Soga regime.[8] (As his name indicates, Nakatomi was of the earlier pro-Shinto faction; part of this family later took the surname Fujiwara and became all-powerful in the Heian period.) The upshot was the so-called Taika Reform of 646, which endeavored to centralize the government under the monarch and a Chinese-style bureaucracy, excluding the Soga and favoring Shinto as well as Buddhism.

A favorite subject for sculptors was Miroku (Maitreya, the coming buddha of the future), whose image, based on Korean models, appears in both the Horyuji and the nearly contemporary Koryuji in Kyoto. These figures, clad only in soft and simple robes, convey remarkable lightness and peace. One senses a state of infinite awareness so sublimely perfected as to have the appearance of casual ease. Yet Miroku's is a calm state worn with the gentle grace only the enlightened attain in this world of anxiety and woe. The Future Buddha's poise and equilibrium are hallmarks of transcendent spirituality. Breathtaking even in the twenty-first century, one can only imagine what sacred art such as this must have meant to Japanese only emerging from the Neolithic Age. Before long, though, they had made it their own, and produced native works equal to anything created by foreign craftsmen.

The subsequent Emperors Tenchi (reigned 661–671) and Temmu (r. 671–686), together with the latter's widow, Empress Jito (r. 686–697), were strong sovereigns who promoted Buddhism but also made sure that Shinto, under Nakatomi leadership, would have an enduring place in the court and the nation. It was during this time that the Ise Grand Shrine, with members of the Nakatomi clan as chief priests of the Naiku dedicated to Amaterasu (a position they held till 1872), came into prominence as the main imperial shrine. Temmu also ordered the compilation of the *Kojiki*, the official record of ancient Shinto myths legitimating the imperial lineage, though the book was not completed until 712.

These and many other reforms were institutionalized in the Taiho Code of 702, a comprehensive organ of government which, together with commentaries, became known as Ritsuryo (laws and regulations). It not only clarified the new bureaucratic structure, but also regulated Buddhist priests, monks, and nuns, showing they were ultimately dependent on the state, and provided for various Shinto rites. Here we find early documentary, as opposed to mythical, references to such Shinto concerns as the seasonal ritual cycle culminating in the Harvest Festival, the Daijosai of a new emperor, and the practice (to be discussed later) of sending a princess to the Ise Shrine to serve as a priestess. The court, though not necessarily the countryside, was now ensconced in a rationalized system in which Buddhism and Shinto, together with Confucian morality and sometimes Taoist mystical ideas, were delicately balanced against each other.

The Nara Period (710–794)

Up until 710, despite the state's growing sophistication and complexity, the court was moved after the death of each emperor because of Shinto taboos against the pollution left by a sovereign's demise, and Japan had no real metropolis. By the early eighth century, however, dreams of a Japanese city to rival the splendid capital of the Tang dynasty then reigning in China overcame those scruples. Nara was planned. Now, in this new model city, the full richness of the island nation's imperial wealth and emerging Buddhist culture could be put on display. It was to be a showplace of opulent palaces and lavish temples, spaced by lovely parks.

Even today, Nara is a wonderful place in which to walk as one absorbs its unique cultural atmosphere, almost that of an Asian fairyland. One can wander through the famous Deer Park, with its scattered pagodas, temples, and tame deer, and up the path of stone lanterns leading to the vermilion-porched Kasuga Shrine, home to the patronal *kami* of the great Fujiwara clan. Not far away, down a long walkway, stands the immense wooden Todaiji. Within it reigns the Great Buddha of Nara, massive and inward-looking, representing the mind whose meditations maintain the universe.

Let us look for a moment at the political meaning of Buddhist Nara.[9] Considering that faith to be its greatest instrument of national unification and advancement, the government supported Dharma priests and institutions generously. Much was put into building, and moreover the state sent promising young clergy to China for education. They, together with visiting clerics and teachers, brought in new forms of Buddhism and many other cultural gifts.

The upshot was, first of all, the so-called six sects of Nara Buddhism, actually little more than intellectual schools imported from the particular temple in China where a scholar had studied, to one he then founded back in Nara. Two were based on Theravada teachings, and are now extinct in Japan. Two more, though Mahayana, are also almost extinct as separate sects: they are Sanron (Sanskrit: Madhyamika, based on Nagarjuna's teaching) and Ritsu (Sanskrit: Vinaya, emphasizing monastic discipline and proper ordination lineages; in the Nara period certain Ritsu priests were influential, and gave lay ordination to members of the imperial family).

The two others were Hosso, the Japanese expression of Yogacara, and Kegon, based as we have seen on the "Garland" or Avatamsaka Sutra. Hosso, although small today, is associated with several old and famous temples, including the Horyuji, the Kofukuji with its pagoda and several edifices in the Deer Park of Nara, and the Kiyomizu on a spectacular hillside setting above Kyoto.

Kegon, though also small today, is the school of the Todaiji of Nara with the Great Buddha, as we have seen. It emphasizes the interrelatedness of all things, and the worship of Dainichi, who represents unlimited absolute reality itself.

The Kegon School

The Kegon school, as Huayan, was influential in China during the Tang period. It is said that the great master Fazang (643–712) was once trying to explain the idea behind the Garland sutra to an empress of that dynasty, who was having difficulty grasping its subtleties. Finally he told her to wait, and in another room he placed an image of the Buddha on a small table and a lamp behind it. Then he completely covered the walls, ceiling, and floor of that room with mirrors. When the empress entered the room, she gasped in amazement, for she saw the Buddha reflected in all the mirrors in every direction – and not once, but reflections of reflections of reflections, an infinite series in each of the many mirrors. Then Fazang took from his sleeve a crystal ball, held it up, and lo! the endless hall of Buddha images was reflected over and over again, this time in miniature. The empress smiled; she understood.

Elite and popular Buddhism

The realities of Nara during its golden age were not as idyllic as these temples and stories suggest. For the elite Buddhism of the six schools in Nara was not the only Japanese Buddhism of the period. Far from the capital, out in the countryside, something else was happening. Popular Buddhist teachers and wonder-workers, often called *ubasoku* from a Sanskrit word for disciple, went about combining Buddhism with native shamanism. Their Buddhism may have been only superficially understood as a potent kind of magic giving them ability to heal and work miracles, and they may not have been properly ordained, especially by strict Ritsu standards. But they and their admirers regarded them as something much better than an ordinary ordained monk.

They were like bodhisattvas, and their path was called *bosatsu-do*, the "way of the bodhisattva." For the *ubasoku*, like the bodhisattva of the Mahayana ideal, were not content merely to live a life of careful piety; combining wisdom with compassion, they went from village to village, healing the sick, consoling the afflicted, counseling the oppressed, and directing such practical works as building bridges and irrigation systems. These charismatic figures also spoke out on the side of the common people, giving voice to their anger at the grasping and hypocrisy of the upper classes, and of the complacent orthodox monks who served them.

Much there was to complain about, for the social divide of the Nara era ran deep. As the palaces and pagodas of the splendid new capital rose higher, the common people only felt more downtrodden as they sank deeper into poverty. The new bureaucratic, rationalized government brought with it regimentation and heavier taxes, collected more efficiently. Temples themselves were given vast gifts of land by devout noblemen, and were no less assiduous than their donors in collecting onerous rents. In those days only sons and daughters of the aristocracy could aspire to the orthodox priesthood or the convent.

In short, the gulf between rich and poor, between those who enjoyed the fine new Buddhist culture of the capital and those whose toil made it possible, through taxes and coerced labor, became a canyon. It is not surprising, then, that the peasantry turned to a form of Buddhism whose leaders seemed sympathetic with their lives, and whose forms reminded them of the shamanistic religion with which they were familiar.

By mid-century it was evident that these two levels of Buddhism and of society would have to be reconciled. The devout Emperor Shomu desired to build the Great Buddha as a supreme national temple, but donations of money and labor from outside the capital were skimpy. Clearly, confidence in the court and its religion had fallen to a low level. In a dramatic gesture, Shomu appointed a certain Gyogi Bosatsu (670–749), Gyogi the bodhisattva, a recognized leader of the countryside shamanistic Buddhists, as chief priest of the nation. This was despite the fact that earlier (in 717) the same Gyogi had been arrested for preaching the heretical doctrine that one could be saved through good works.

In return, as was no doubt intended, Gyogi won his followers over to the emperor's cause. Moreover, according to tradition he visited the Grand Shrine of Ise, and there received through an oracle the blessing of the goddess Amaterasu (esoterically identified with Dainichi) on the building of the Todaiji with its Great Buddha. (This was also a step toward the reconciliation of Shinto and Buddhism.) The temple was dedicated in 749, the year of Gyogi's death. The Emperor Shomu himself then took the monastic robe, abdicating in favor of his daughter Koken.

The abdication of Shomu led to a scandal which did much to discredit Nara Buddhism. Koken herself abdicated in 758, leaving the throne to a young prince named Junnin. She then became romantically involved with an ambitious priest called Dokyo. He persuaded his imperial mistress to depose Junnin. This she did, and for good measure had him strangled. She took the throne again for herself in 764, now calling herself Empress Shotoku. She made Dokyo prime minister and, in 766, chief Buddhist priest of the nation. Not content with these elevations, Dokyo plotted to marry her, seize imperial power for himself, and establish a dynasty. But by this time the lay aristocracy, especially the Fujiwara house, was thoroughly alarmed at what was going on, and not least by the overweening power the Nara priesthood seemed to have, or to want. A timely oracle from the Shinto *kami* Hachiman thwarted Dokyo's conspiracies. The Empress died in 770, and Dokyo in 772. With one or two minor exceptions, no empress was again allowed to reign in Japan.

The Nara sects never attained more than local importance in terms of membership, though some of their fabulous temples attract multitudes to this day. The Fujiwara and their allies were in time convinced the capital should be moved from the superheated religious atmosphere of Nara, with its scheming priests and wealthy temples. A new start should be made in a new place, with the Fujiwara of course well in control behind the scenes. So it was that in 784 the new Emperor Kammu moved the government out of Nara. After ten years in a town called Nagaoka, the court settled in Heian, modern Kyoto, another planned city modeled on the Chinese capital of Changan, in 794. The colorful Nara period was at an end, and the Heian era began.

Key points you need to know

- Before Buddhism, Japan's religion was based on fertility, agriculture, and shamanism. Shamans and shamanistic rulers may often have been women in earlier stages
- Buddhism was introduced from Korea in the sixth century CE. Around the same time writing, Confucian thought, and new forms of art and architecture arrived from the continent
- Under Prince Shotoku particularly, Buddhism provided a religious means for unifying the country
- The Taika reform of 646 led to greater balance between Shinto and Buddhism
- In the Nara period, 710–794, a brilliant aristocratic Buddhist culture emerged in the capital, centered around six schools, especially Kegon and Hosso, based respectively on the Garland sutra and Yogacara
- But the gulf between the city and the countryside was great; outside the capital *ubasoku*, followers of the bodhisattva way, were influential
- The split was partly resolved when Gyogi was made chief priest of the nation, and the Great Buddha was completed in 749. But then scandals involving the Empress Koken (Shotoku) and the priest Dokyo brought the Nara period to an end.

Questions for study and discussion

1. Interpret the worldview of Japan before Buddhism.
2. How and why was shamanism important in ancient Japan.
3. How did Buddhism come to Japan?
4. What were some early effects of Buddhism on Japan?
5. What was the significance of Prince Shotoku and his times?
6. What were the achievements and problems of Nara Buddhism?
7. What was the significance of Gyogi for his own times and the later development of Japanese religion?

Further reading

Blacker, Carmen, *The Catalpa Bow: A Study of Shamanistic Practices in Japan*. London: George Allen & Unwin, 1975.

de Visser, Marinus Willem, *Ancient Buddhism in Japan*, 2 vols. Leiden: E. J. Brill, 1935.

Eliot, Sir Charles, *Japanese Buddhism*. London: Edward Arnold, 1935.

Kamstra, J. H., *Encounter or Syncretism: The Initial Growth of Japanese Buddhism.* Leiden: E. J. Brill, 1967.

Kidder, J. Edward, *Early Buddhist Japan.* New York, NY: Praeger, 1975.

Kidder, J. Edward, *Japan Before Buddhism.* London: Thames & Hudson, 1959.

Matsunaga, Alicia, and Daigan Matsunaga, *Foundation of Japanese Buddhism*, 2 vols. Los Angeles, CA: Buddhist Books International, 1974.

Meeks, Lori, *Hokkeji and the Reemergence of Female Monastic Orders in Premodern Japan.* Honolulu, HI: University of Hawaii Press, 2010.

Mizoguchi, Koji, *The Archaeology of Japan: From the Earliest Rice Farming Villages to the Rise of the State.* Cambridge and New York: Cambridge University Press, 2013.

Ooms, Herman, *Imperial Politics and Symbolics in Ancient Japan: The Tenmu Dynasty, 650–800.* Honolulu, HI: University of Hawaii Press, 2008.

Piggott, Joan R., *The Emergence of Japanese Kingship.* Stanford, CA: Stanford University Press, 1997.

Saunder, Dale, *Buddhism in Japan.* Philadelphia, PA: University of Pennsylvania Press, 1964.

Tamura, Yoshiro, *Japanese Buddhism: A Cultural History.* Tokyo: Kosei, 2000.

Electronic Resources

"The Jomon World of Ceremony and Ritual." https://heritageofjapan.wordpress.com/customs-of-the-jomon-people/

"The Yayoi Years." https://heritageofjapan.wordpress.com/yayoi-era

Wikipedia, "Himiko." https://en.wikipedia.org/wiki/Himiko

"Shōtoku taishi." www.onmarkproductions.com/html/shotoku-taishi.html

"Tenji and Temmu's ritsuryo religion: 'There is only one imperial way'." https://heritageofjapan.wordpress.com/tenji-and-temmus-ritsuryo

Wikipedia, "Nara period." https://en.wikipedia.org/wiki/Nara_period

"The Establishment of Buddhism [in Japan]." http:// countrystudies.us/japan/8.htm

James Mark Shields, "Gyogi bosatsu" in Phyllis G. Jestice, ed., *Holy People of the World: A Cross-cultural Encyclopedia*, vol. 1. (Santa Barbara, CA: ABC-CLIO, Inc., 2004) www.facstaff.bucknell.edu/jms/Z-Unpublished Work/Gyogi.pdf

"Kōken: Empress of Japan," *Encyclopædia Britannica.* www.britannica.com/EBchecked/topic/321233/Koken

5 *Magic mountains and the old court*

Heian Buddhism and its culture

In this chapter

This chapter will present the atmosphere of the Heian court and its literature, infused as it may be with Buddhist values. The two major schools of Heian Buddhism, Shingon and Tendai, will be surveyed, together with Heian Shinto and popular religion, influenced by features taken from Confucianism, Taoist, and folk shamanism.

Main topics covered

- The world of the Heian court
- Shingon, Kukai, and esoteric Buddhism
- Tendai, Saicho, and the Lotus school
- The cultural significance of Heian Buddhism
- Court and popular Shinto in fusion with Buddhism
- Heian popular religion: Confucian moral values, Taoist beliefs, *goryo* or spirits of the dead.

The world above the clouds

The Heian period (794–1185) was the golden age of imperial court society. In its immortal works of literature, we see a world of consummately refined men and women who saw themselves as eschewing the grosser forms of violence, but whose lives centered around the love of art and the arts of love. We envision women seated sedately behind screens, perhaps waiting for the sweet intrusion of a lover; and we recall delightful parties centered on "verse-capping" or moon-viewing, and fashionable excursions to romantic mountain temples.

The incomparable elegance of the Heian court has always evoked moments of yearning in cultured Japanese. In more frenetic and violent years to come, its timeless world of poetry and love behind palace walls, a realm always as much ideal or dream as reality, has offered nostalgic surcease. Much later, the great haiku poet Basho (1644–1694), on visiting Kyoto (literally, "Old Capital," the Heian city), jotted these lines:

> Even though in Kyoto
> I still long for Kyoto –
> O, the Bird of Time!

(The bird of the last line is the *hototogisu*, the Japanese cuckoo, which in literature has somewhat the romantic, evocative overtones of the nightingale in Western poetry; here *hototogisu* is written in characters which also mean "Bird of Time.")

Of course, like all times, the Heian era also had its harsh political and social realities. The emperor reigned nominally, but real power was in the hands of the Fujiwara house. That family's leading men were usually the chief ministers of state. The dominant clan continually arranged to marry its daughters into the imperial house, ideally as consort to the sovereign, so that the monarch often had a Fujiwara as both wife and mother, and not seldom as regent too. The real rulers tried to keep the emperors minors, or at least young and inexperienced, encouraging them to abdicate once they had performed their one important function in life, begetting an heir by a Fujiwara empress. Many such sovereigns were not sorry to abdicate, since their role as figurehead consisted mainly of tiresome ritual and social duties, while in retirement a man could enjoy relatively more freedom, sometimes even more power.

The greatest of all the Fujiwara ministers was Fujiwara Michinaga (966–1027), during whose span as virtual dictator no less than eight youthful emperors reigned, each giving up the throne after producing an imperial heir; at the same time, the years of his life are reflected in several of the greatest works of Heian literature. Michinaga himself enjoyed supreme contentment, complete with a private temple designed to imitate the wonder of a Buddhist paradise; this duplication of the Pure Land displayed networks of jewels interwoven through the trees and placed peacocks on the islands in its reflecting pond. "My aspiration," he allegedly said, "is fully satisfied like a full moon in the sky."

Others were less well pleased with Fujiwara domination. Some emperors, especially in retirement, sought to exercise real authority from behind the scenes. The peculiar system of *insei* ("retirement rule") grew in importance as the Heian era advanced and gradually weakened the hold of the Fujiwara. That ministerial dynasty's slow decline was abetted by increasing dissatisfaction in the provinces with the apparently luxurious but non-productive capital. Out there, in the farther reaches of the empire, a rising class of *buke* (samurai or warriors) was beginning to realize that decisive force of arms could be in their hands, if they chose to seize it, rather than in what they saw as the effete, over-cultured court.

This was the classic era of traditional Japanese culture. Some of the nation's greatest works of art and literature, such as the poems of the *Kokinshu* (*Anthology of Poems Old and New*, issued 905), the *Makura no Soshi* (*Pillow Book*; a collection of witty and penetrating observations of life, c. 1002) of the Lady Sei Shonagon, and the *Genji Monogatari* (*Tale of Genji*) by Lady Murasaki (c. 1010) come from that age; the massive *Genji* is to Japanese literature what Homer was to the ancient West, or Shakespeare to English letters.

These new men were by and large not traditional clan chieftains, but exiles from younger branches of aristocratic Heian families, including the imperial family, who could not hope for a meaningful place in the rigidly rank-bound court, but were bought off with tax-free estates and military duties in outlying areas. The time was coming when they would turn against their betters. But we must first understand the world of the Old Court and its relation to religion.

The literary works reflect the world of the *bijin* (the "beautiful people") who saw themselves dwelling *kumonoue* ("above the clouds"), devoted to *miyabi* (courtly elegance and taste). Needless to say, they were only a tiny percentage of Japan's overall population, and the lives of those whose toil supported this elegance were far less advantaged. Of their lives, religious and otherwise, we learn little from the court literature.

On the other hand, Heian literature reveals countless details of court life and the nuances of its values. Few societies so far in the past are known so intimately. Much of the writing is by women, such as Shonagon and Murasaki. That is partly because, while men felt constrained to display their classical Chinese education by composing in *kanji*, an alien and cumbrous vehicle for Japanese, women wrote largely in *kana*, in which Japanese feelings and conversation flowed freely. Moreover, the importance of beautiful and gifted daughters to Fujiwara marriage politics meant well-bred women were highly esteemed. Yet theirs was a strange society by modern standards, a culture in which it was thought that skill in poetry and calligraphy really could affect social or political advancement, in which entertainment included games comparing flowers or kinds of incense, and in which semi-ritualized courtship was a major preoccupation, regardless of a lover's marital status. On the other hand, court society's rigid rank and class structures, dependent on birth, could be harsh.

The literature reflects a looming, almost intoxicating sense that such beauty and love is fleeting, and will be gone once one tries to grasp it. Heian people had a deep sense of *mono no aware*, "sensitivity to things." This sweet/sad feeling came out of attention to the transitoriness of human life and of all else is this "dewdrop world," while at the same time appreciating beauty all the more in realizing it was passing away. We will see how a feel for the inner sadness of beauty was influenced by Buddhism, especially Tendai. First, however, let us look at some poetic examples. Here, in a verse by Lady Murasaki, is a play on the word *yume*, the name of a scenic spot on the Yoshino River, but also meaning "dream":

> As I walk across the bridge
> That spans the Ford of Yume,
> I see that this world of ours too
> Is like a floating bridge of dreams.[1]

Genji himself, in the *Genji Monogatari*, is presented as a paragon of the man about court. He was admired not as a warrior or a statesman, but as a supreme exemplar of *miyabi*, and above all as an adept in the arts of love. The essence of the long work is Genji's relationships with a succession of women. The distinctive personality of each companion is splendidly portrayed, and the prince's relationship with each is subtly different, as the sensitive hero adapts his own manner to hers. A wonderfully insightful and almost infinitely complex man, he is able to play innumerable roles. Yet he somehow remains convincing, true to a fundamental vision of life as a mosaic of many nuances and shadings. His princely path calls not for rigidity, but flexibility of character guided by deep awareness of each person and setting; that could be called the way of insight, even of love.

Overt religion is fairly superficial in the novel, consisting of socializing visits to temples or observing various taboos, but one could argue that on a much deeper level Genji himself reflects something of the Mahayana Buddhist, and particularly Tendai, view of the world as endlessly varied, always malleable and changing, yet precisely in its many appearances manifesting the indefinable "suchness" of the eternal buddha-nature.

Heian Buddhist schools

The Buddhism predominant in the Heian period can be thought of in terms of the number two: two founders (each going by two names) who traveled to China to study, two scriptures, two schools, two mountains. Kukai (773–830), whose posthumous name was Kobo daishi (*daishi* is a title meaning "great teacher") studied Shingon or esoteric Buddhism based on the Mahavairocana sutra (Japanese: Dainichi, or "Great Sun"). He established a great monastic center on Mount Koya. Saicho (767–822, posthumously Dengyo daishi) studied the Lotus Sutra and established the Tendai sect (named after Mount Tiantai in China where an eminent school based on its teaching was based). In Japan Tendai was headquartered at the Enryakuji, previously presented, on Mount Hiei just northeast of the Heian capital. We will look at each of these denominations in turn.

The Shingon and Tendai schools

Name	Shingon	Tendai
Founder	Kukai	Saicho
Posthumous name	Kobo daishi	Dengyo daishi
Main temple	Mount Koya	Enryakuji on Mount Hiei
Main scripture	Mahavairocana (Dainichi)	Lotus Sutra
Essential quality	Esotericism, mandalas	Many paths

Shingon

If half the stories about him are true, Kukai, founder of Shingon, was among the most brilliant and versatile individuals in Japanese history. He is said to have been not only a consummate religious teacher and ritualist, but also a gifted artist, master calligrapher, inventor of the *kana* writing system, and worker of countless miracles as he traveled about the country. Living at the time of transition of power from Nara to the new capital at Heian, when new Buddhist foundations could conveniently be laid, he had ample opportunity to exercise his creative ability.

He was originally trained for government service, but in the course of his studies his interests turned to religion. As early as 797 he wrote a characteristically wide-ranging book, *Sango shiki*, which compared Confucianism, Taoism, and Buddhism. (He was later, around 830, to pen the *Jujushinron*, a remarkable survey of all known religions and schools of Buddhism arranged according the level they represented, to his eyes, in the quest for total enlightenment. This was entirely in accord with Kukai's syncretizing and systematizing thought; he constantly strove to unite all religion and all aspects of human experience into one vast but coherent pattern or mandala.[2])

As a student the young seeker discovered the Mahavairocana sutra, which helped crystallize his devotion to the esoteric path. It taught a faith oriented not only to the historical Buddha, but to the truth behind his enlightenment, the Dharmakaya or essence of the universe, personified by Mahavairocana, Dainichi in Japanese, whom we have already met as the Great Buddha of Nara and in connection with Kegon. Dainichi is neither the historical Buddha nor God, but the Buddha as the Dharma or universal reality body, without beginning or end and inherent in all things, all the rising and falling appearances of reality being manifestations of this undying substance. Jacqueline Stone put it this way: "All visible forms are the Buddha's body, all sounds the Buddha's voice, and all thoughts are the Buddha's mind, though the unenlightened do not discern this."[3]

The Buddha preached conditional doctrines for the sake of those not ready for the fullness of truth but, "What was expounded by the Dharmakaya Buddha for his

Kukai himself wrote, "There are three bodies of the Buddha and two forms of Buddhist doctrine. The doctrine revealed by the Nirmanakaya Buddha [the historical Buddha] is called Exoteric; it is apparent, simplified, and adapted to the needs to the time and the capacity of the listeners. The doctrine expounded by the Dharmakaya Buddha [Dainichi] is called Esoteric; it is secret and profound and contains the final truth."

own enjoyment, on his innermost spiritual experience, is called Esoteric."[4] It will be noted that for esoteric Buddhism the historical Buddha, he who lived and taught in ancient India, is relatively unimportant compared to Dainichi, who is here and now and in all things; the former is significant only in that he showed the possibility of enlightenment in this world and his teachings pointed in the right direction.

This Dainichi orientation was shared with Kegon, but the mikkyo ("esoteric teachings") went further than the Nara school. They not only celebrated the interaction of all things in the "body" of Dainichi, but also taught practices by which one can become one with the essence of the universe he manifests, and so achieve buddhahood in this body, in this lifetime (*sokushin jobutsu*).

In the *Jujushinron*, Kegon is rated second highest and Shingon the highest expression of Buddhism; the esoteric school not only tells, but also shows and does.

Figure 5.1 Kompon-daito (Kompon Great Pagoda), Mount Koya (©Francesco Dazzi / Shutterstock.com)

The distinctive Shingon teaching, then, is that one can become a Buddha in this very life, and that there are secret, esoteric means of doing so. They center on the *sanmitsu*, "three secrets": *mudras* (hand gestures), *dharani* (chants aligned to spiritual beings), and yogic visualization meditations. These are aligned to another esoteric arena: the great mandalas or diagrams showing the relative positioning of cosmic buddhas, bodhisattvas, and deities.

In 804 Kukai formally took Buddhist orders, and the same year was sent to China, where he studied esoteric Buddhism intensively for two years. On his return, after some difficulties he was able to establish Shingon as an independent denomination around 812 or 813, and its center on Mount Koya beginning in 816. In the last decade of his life Kukai also became very popular and influential in the capital, initiating emperors into esoteric practice and performing theatrical esoteric rituals before the court.

We have looked at basic examples of the mandalas and their personifications of realities in the Toji temple (where Kukai founded a school in 828), with its array of such figures radiating out from Dainichi: the cosmic buddhas of the four directions, their attendant bodhisattvas of wisdom and compassion, their protective "Dharma kings" and guardian deities. The mandalas have many further complexities which cannot be detailed here, but one distinction which must be made is between the Diamond (*Kongo*) and Womb (*Taizo*) mandalas. The figures of the former are hard and clear like diamonds, inward-looking, meditating on the profoundest levels of truth. The Womb (or Lotus) mandala expresses truth looking outward in compassion, expressing itself in service that represents the interrelatedness of all beings.[5]

Shingon offers elaborate rituals demonstrating the dynamic relationships between these two mandalas. Above all, the mandalas tell us that there is, just below the surface as it were of the world of appearances, a vast and deep sea of consciousness, where the cosmic buddhas, bodhisattvas, and wisdom kings dwell like vortices within that sea, even as our own smaller individual consciousnesses are more like wavelets or ripples on its surfaces. Yet we are able to feel and, if we know how, to use the energies of the greater whirlpools and currents as we sail toward the farther shore. In the end all is thought; not a single divine mind so much as an infinite field of consciousness within which arise many centers of wisdom and compassion.

How does one become a buddha in this life, in this body? Essentially by working with one of the figures in the mandala until one becomes united with that deity, and so shares his or her enlightenment. The deity may be assigned by one's teacher, or sometimes the right figure is indicated by throwing a flower on a diagram of the mandala, and regarding the one on which the flower lands as chosen. The student is then initiated into the practice of this deity. The most dramatic of the initiatory rituals is the *goma* or fire ritual, in which, to the accompaniment of chants, various kinds of wood and other flammable objects are placed in a fire on an altar to represent burning away all delusions and impurities.

Once initiated, the student can be given the secrets – the hand gestures, chants, and meditations that pertain to the deity with which one is uniting, and so facilitate that process. If you make the secret movements, say the secret words, and think the secret thoughts of a buddha or bodhisattva, you are well on the way to becoming one; you are finally what you do, say, and think. A close working relationship between master and disciple is very important to Shingon; this is a religion which must be practiced, not just studied, even to be understood.

At this point, a word about what is meant by esotericism, *mikkyo*, and secrecy in religion may be of help. Many spiritual and religious groups east and west have insisted that certain practices of theirs are esoteric and secret, to be transmitted only to those with proper training and initiation. Needless to say, this stance often produces controversy and criticism.

Those who support esotericism do so on several grounds. First, just as a textbook on calculus would likely be esoteric to someone who had not yet taken algebra, some levels of spiritual training, by their own nature, are not accessible to one who has not mastered the preliminaries. They would most likely be seriously misunderstood, and could very well lead to dangerous confusion.

Second, some esotericists contend that, just as one would not allow a child to play with power tools, advanced practices do release real power, which should be evoked and used only under the supervision of experts and in a controlled setting.

Third – and this was the issue most often cited by Kukai and the Shingon tradition – it is held that these are teachings which can never be mastered just by study alone, but can only be understood in conjunction with practices which in turn must be taught "hands on" by a teacher who has himself mastered them. The cosmic buddhas of esoteric Buddhism, for example, are lifeless and one-dimensional on the pages of a book; only by evoking them through right techniques, with the help of a living guide, can one know them as they are, three dimensional, each bearing powerful and distinctive energies.

In one meditation process, the student begins by visualizing the seed syllable (a Sanskrit letter) of the deity with which one is working imprinted on a circle or "moon disk," then seeing oneself in the center of the disk, and finally mentally expanding the disk to embrace the universe. One can expand and contract the disk over and over. At some point, it is said, one makes a "quantum leap" into the realm of wisdom, where it is no longer a matter of the student's own effort, but of losing oneself in the life and transhuman consciousness of the divine personality which is his guide and inner life, nearer than hands and feet.

In another practice, the "circulation technique," the student envisions a stream of energy leaving his body with his breath, entering the deity who is facing him, and returning through the opening at the top of the head. This stream may be seen as like a pulley, drawing the student and the deity closer and closer together until the two become one.[6]

This practice of the moon disk and the breath-energy stream is basic to the Morning Star Meditation, referring to the tradition that the Buddha became fully enlightened on seeing the Morning Star, a demanding practice usually attempted only by advanced Shingon priests. It entails spending fifty days in an isolated temple set amidst a natural landscape. The practitioner arises very early, worships Venus, the Morning Star, who here symbolizes the universe itself as one, and spends the day alone in rituals, chants, and moon-disk and energy-chain meditations of uniting with the bodhisattva Kokuzo (Sanskrit: Akasagarbha[7]). Food is very ascetic and none is taken after noon.

Taiko Yamasaki, a modern Shingon adept, relates certain interesting experiences that came to him during his intensive Morning Star practice. At first he felt pain in the legs and back from long hours of sitting, and peculiar hallucinations, undoubtedly tempters, visited him in his lonely hermitage:

[A] mysterious priest "appeared," and offered to teach me a secret *mudra* The image was so vivid that I had difficult realizing that it was not real ...

Gradually, however, my body and mind came into harmony, creating within me a feeling of lightness and tranquility. During meditation, my body came to feel almost transparent, while my mind and what I saw around me were clear, like crystal. Far from being a hallucination, this came from increased clarity of consciousness – as though I had come to a place where heaven and earth join. Coming out of meditation and leaving the practice hall, the sense of the vastness of the universe remained, as though I were seeing the world for the first time ...[8]

Art, like ritual, is of great importance to Shingon because it is a way of showing the buddhahood in all materials, in all "bodies." In a piece of wood, the buddha-nature may be concealed beneath what appears to be natural, but let the artist carve it into an image of a buddha, and its true essence becomes outwardly manifest. Moreover, artistic portrayals of the mandala deities, whether two or three dimensional, were crucial to the visualization practice.

It is not surprising, then, that Shingon made very important contributions to the development of Japanese religious art and, even more crucially, to the spiritual attitudes toward art that have shaped artists' approaches to their craft down to the present, whether the work is explicitly sacred or secular. In this tradition, art becomes meditation, because the artist himself or herself must be in touch with inner buddhahood in order to draw the same out of the medium, with the help of one's own buddha-eye. Many Japanese artists, whether religious or not, still begin work with a period of meditation. Japanese art also remains very medium-oriented, concerned to find the essence that needs to be expressed in the ink, paint, wood, or stone before them. The artist strives to work with rather than against grain, texture, or flow, so as to bring out what is already there.

Shingon's emphasis on sacred art, together with its exaltation of states of mystic power, had great consequence for the popularization of Buddhism. We have already talked about the rift between elite "six schools" Buddhism and popular *bosatsudo* Buddhism in the Nara period. This split remained in the Heian period, but began to be alleviated by the way in which the new Shingon and Tendai Buddhism came closer, even at elite levels, to the faith of the countryside, centered on images and the *hijiri* or person of inner spiritual power acquired by tremendous effort.

Let us consider for a moment religion's great and little traditions, as the anthropologist Robert Redfield called them.[9] The former is the religion as it is known to books, scholars, intellectuals, and the hierarchies that run its great institutions; usually the great tradition also has important expression in the culture's formal arts, music, and architecture, and may well have close ties to the political, economic, and educational establishments. It is likely to be learned, cool, able to take a long historical view.

The little tradition, on the other hand, means folk religion, popular religion, peasant religion. It is not really religion of books and scholarship, though certain scriptures may be venerated in an almost talismanic way. But its primary means of transmission is through family, community, and local priests or preachers. Charismatic shamans and evangelists may be important. Field and village look to miracles, local shrines, and festivals of seedtime and harvest, rather than to reason, history, or the faith put into national or world perspective.

In Nara and Heian Japan, the Buddhist great tradition was of course that of Prince Shotoku, the six schools, and then Shingon and Tendai. The little tradition was that of the *ubasoku* and the countryside. Shinto showed comparable contrasts. The distinguished folklorist Hori Ichiro divided Japan's "little tradition" into two themes, *ujigami* and *hitogami*: the first revolving around the *kami* of one's *uji*, clan, or home community with its settled shrine; and the other centered on *kami*-possessed individuals ("*hito*"), wizards, shamans, and diviners like the *obasoku*.[10] By all accounts persons possessing an individual relationship to a *kami* or buddha were prominent in Nara and Heian Japan, and it is interesting that it took one of them, Gyogi, to bring about a reconciliation between the great and little tradition.

At the same time, aided by the Shingon talent for art, several figures in the rich Shingon pantheon, from buddhas and bodhisattvas to the imported deities of India, stepped out of the mandala, so to speak, to become quasi-independent gods of folk religion, especially Amida, Kannon, and Jizo.[11]

Kukai himself, as Kobo daishi, became a major figure in popular religion. To this day his shrines are noted for bestowing healing and boons. Thus, however elite, professional, and esoteric the "great traditions" of Shingon and Tendai were, their influence the other way, on the popular "little traditions" of Japan down to the present, can hardly be overestimated.

The most colorful folk movement was Shugendo ("the way [*do*] of gaining spiritual power"), the path of adepts who, practicing austerities and esoteric rites in the mountains, then came down into the villages to serve as healers, diviners, exorcists, dispensers of charms, and guides (*sendatsu*) of groups of laypeople on pilgrimage to their mountains. They were popularly called *yamabushi* (literally, "those who lie down [i.e. dwell] in the mountains"; one might label them "[spiritual] mountaineers").

The *yamabushi* are clearly continuous with the *ubasoku* of Nara-era *bosatsudo*. Traditionally Shugendo was founded by a certain En no Ozunu of the early eighth century, who is said to have practiced both Buddhist and Taoist occultism, acquiring such magical powers as the ability to fly. Eventually more than a hundred local Shugendo centers were established. They served no central organization nationwide, honored various individual traditions, and held only tenuous affiliations with Shingon or, more often, Tendai centers. Essentially the movement is an indigenous Japanese syncretism of ancient Shinto shamanism with Taoist magic and esoteric Buddhist occultism. The Shingon concept of becoming a buddha in this body, in this lifetime, through intensive religious practice is central to it from the theoretical point of view. Later we will examine Shugendo rites and practices in more detail.

Tendai

The other great Heian school, Tendai, takes its name from the Chinese Tiantai, after the mountain upholding its principal center. Its great Chinese exponents were Zhiyi (538–97)[12] and Zhanran (711–82), whose writings reached Japan in the eighth century. There they so impressed the young Japanese monk Saicho (767–822) that he traveled to China to study further on the monastic mountain. On his return in 805, Saicho became the effective founder of Tendai as a Japanese denomination with imperial patronage, though the court seems to have been more interested in his performance of esoteric rites – even if he could not equal Kukai and Shingon in this regard – than in his philosophical teaching.

Nonetheless, during the Heian period Tendai's influence, and its esotericism, grew significantly. Its great monastic center on Mount Hiei, where Saicho had established a hermitage as early as 788, before going to China or before the Heian capital was moved conveniently nearby, came to embrace thousands of temples. There Tendai competed successfully with Shingon.

It appears that during their lifetimes in the opening years of the Heian era the brilliant, charismatic Kukai far outshone the intellectual but retiring Saicho. (One modern student put the difference this way: "Saicho is the type of person you would ask for help with your homework; Kukai is the fellow you would invite to a party to stir things up."[13]) But later, with gifted leadership and easy access to the court, Tendai made its way to parity or better. The radical new religious movements that changed the face of Japanese Buddhism in the next period, the Kamakura, first took root in Japan amidst the rich diversity of practice encouraged on Hiei.

Tendai offers a very expansive Mahayana vision. It affirms the deep unity of all Buddhist teachings and practices, and indeed of all existence as manifestations of the innate buddha-nature. To this end its teachers, like Kukai, ranked Buddhist schools on various levels of truth, but Tendai put the Lotus Sutra at the top, as the profoundest expression of the dharma in words. This powerful scripture emphasizes the universality and eternity of buddhahood or nirvana. Its expansive reality is not limited in space or time. All sentient beings can find buddhahood, indeed on a deeper level *are* buddhas, always have been and always shall be. The historical Buddha and all other buddhas are themselves but particular manifestations of this absolute reality for a particular time and place. But, the Lotus says, the true buddha-nature continually showers its grace over the entire earth like rain.[14]

That universal buddha-nature was quickly personified in Tendai, as in Shingon, as Dainichi. Many, perhaps countless, paths there are to this realization, but they exist only as expedients to help people till they reach the point where they understand there is no path and the buddha-nature is everywhere here and now, age after age. The Lotus tells the famous parable of a father who, returning from a long journey, was appalled to see that the house in which his children awaited him was on fire. But he possessed enough presence of mind to realize that if he shouted fire, they might not believe him or, alternatively, would panic and fall over each other trying to get out. So he cried out that he had brought them beautiful toy carts to play with. Squealing with delight, the children rushed out of the house to see the carts, and were saved from the fire. But then they learned there were no carts after all.

The fire represents the destructive passions and energies of this world, and from them the children were liberated. The sutra next goes into a lengthy argument as to whether the father was morally justified in lying to free them. It concludes that he was, since the carts or vehicles (Sanskrit: *yana*, in Buddhism a means to convey one to liberation, as in Mahayana) do have reality insofar as one believes in them in one's mind; they are expedient means to deliverance, like all specific spiritual teachings. In the end, though, the Lotus tells us, there is but one vehicle to salvation. Significantly, it is never defined. Clearly, the One Vehicle beyond words represents the All, the universe within which we find ourselves. Knowing the eternal oneness in depth is itself the means by which all the world's children are delivered from fire. This reality is there before, or beneath, all illusion, and therefore is known as *hongaku*, "original enlightenment."

Central to the expression of this truth is the dialectical statement known as the "perfectly harmonious threefold truth." It goes like this. All separate things are empty of individual reality or self-nature, because any entity's only true reality is as a part of the whole; its apparent separateness depends on causes. (For example, the biological causes that brought you and me into existence.) But at the same time, because causes have an effect, the things they produce do have an existence, though transitory. The third truth, then, is that all things are *at once* empty, temporary, and real.

In short, the phenomenal world, just in its transitory forms, is *also* ultimate reality, and all beings in it are buddhas. A single flower or snowflake, a lover's smile, a fleeting thought, your life and mine – all these are passing, yet also manifest the eternal.

The other side is represented in another famous Tendai phrase: "Three thousand things in one thought." For all reality, being interpenetrating and inclusive, is contained in every thought that flashes through our minds, however momentary, rather as a turning, faceted jewel can receive and reflect light from all directions at once.[15]

This way of thinking had a profound impact on Japanese art and letters. Consider, for example, Heian poetry. A theme that recurs in certain verses of the great *Kokinshu* (*Anthology of [Poems] Old and New*, issued in 905) is the distinction between reality (*utsutsu*) and dream (*yume*), the latter meaning seeing things as they appear in our minds conditioned by attachments and illusion, the former as they really are, at once transitory and eternal. Contemplate these Tendai-flavored lines by Lady Komachi, the greatest woman poet of the anthology:

> On the path of dreams
> My feet have run after you without rest.
> But that is not worth
> Catching a single glance
> Of you in reality.[16]

The lover we pursue in dreams can never truly satisfy us, because he or she is only a phantasm concocted out of our own desires and needs, not a real person. But seeing a lover in the flesh, if only for an instant, is an experience which gets one outside of oneself to confront something of the larger and more real interpenetrating universe, in which (as in a hologram) a single part is also the whole, and the whole is in any single part. Hence a single glance of the beloved can even be a flash of ultimate enlightenment, the one thought in which all the three thousand things are seized. As Dante said of Beatrice a few centuries later, "Her least salutation/ bestows salvation on this favored one/ and humbles him till he forgets all wrongs."

In another direction, as we will see later in more detail, the "easy path" of Amidist or Pure Land faith also developed under the wide Tendai umbrella. Devotional or faith approaches to Buddhist salvation are likewise expounded in the Lotus Sutra as expedient means. We are told that even a child bringing a flower or a crudely-made picture to a Buddha out of love is close to liberation, for a moment of self-forgetting love

One interesting example of Tendai esoteric practice is the *Kaihogyo*, monks running around Mt. Hiei, stopping at a series of shrines on the way for brief devotions, is still performed today. This is no leisurely pilgrimage, but an intense marathon for which monks train assiduously, then run a course of increasing length for one hundred days a year over seven years; in the seventh year the daily run is 84 km or 52.5 miles.

So the best runners in the world are probably not Olympic champions, but these marathon monks of Mount Hiei, who in the seventh year of their *kaihogyo* run a course twice the length of the Olympic marathon – not just once before cheering crowds, but every day for a hundred days, training on a vegetarian diet and with hand-made straw sandals as their running shoes. Moreover, in the fifth year had come the greatest trial of all, the *doiri*, a nine-day period of fasting without food, drink, or sleep, while reciting the Lotus Sutra and a mantra to Fudo, the latter 100,000 times.[17]

These are of course very exceptional practices, carried out by only a small minority even of Tendai priests and monks. Yet they are widely admired. They display a drive for testing one's endurance and resolution to the extreme that not seldom surfaces in Japan, not only in Buddhist asceticism but also in the martial traditions, and elsewhere.

is enlightenment. Likewise, "If persons with confused and distracted minds should. … once exclaim, 'Hail to the Buddha!' then all have attained the Buddha way."[18]

Heian Shinto

In a real sense this expression is a misnomer. No Heian Japanese would have said, "I am a Shintoist," and few would have thought of Shinto and Buddhism as separate religions or even distinct traditions. The spirit of *shinbutsu shugo*, seeing buddha and *kami* as two faces of the same thing, was almost universal. Important shrines were *gongen* (Sanskrit: avatar) shrines, making the *kami* like an incarnation of a buddha or bodhisattva. Some even housed images of *kami* such as Hachiman dressed as Buddhist monks, or serving as guardian deities. Often these sculptured or painted *kami* displayed exaggerated strength and unique, even eccentric, individual characteristics as well as unmistakably Japanese courtly or monastic dress. That was to make clear they were special local manifestations of a line of spiritual energy in its distinctly individual Japanese form, in contrast to the usually more stylized, "generic" buddhas.

But Shinto and Buddhism were then all one religion, Japanese religion. Buddhism in the Shingon or Tendai form (and they were nearly indistinguishable on the level of public rites and iconography) was outwardly that religion's most visible shape, with its lavish temples and eminent monks preaching to distinguished audiences. Buddhist ideas like *karma* and transience were entering conversation and influencing literature. As the Heian period advanced, belief in the Buddhist Pure Land of Amida became more and more important.

Yet one could also make a case that, if Shinto was absorbed into Buddhism, much of Japanese Buddhism was also Shinto under another name. *Gongen* shrines functioned on the local level as shrines of a local *kami* with a buddha standing behind him; before them as always communities prayed for fertility, offered thanks for bountiful harvests, and celebrated local *matsuri*. *Yamabushi* and other *hijiri*, though perhaps at the same time esoteric Buddhist practitioners, came calling in the old shamanistic tradition of the adept who goes into the mountains to gain supernatural powers, then returns to heal and divine.

Some unmixed Shinto rites were maintained by the court as tokens of its ancient past and as reminders of the divine descent of the imperial house. The liturgies for these, together with a valuable register of Shinto shrines, are found in the *Engishiki*, an imperial document of 927. The four principal rituals are the Toshigoi, or spring prayers for the crops; the rituals and customs associated with the Saigu, the residence of the imperial princess stationed at Ise, and two special versions of the Niiname-sai or harvest festival, both already presented: the Shikinen-sengu or twenty-year rebuilding of the Ise Shrine; and the Daijosai, or imperial accession harvest rite. It will be noted that all of these have a close connection with the ideology of the divine sovereign as descendant of Amaterasu, the goddess enshrined at Ise.

The Saigu may be of particular interest. An imperial princess was selected by divination to proceed, after long preparation, to the Grand Shrine of Ise, where she would live a life of isolation and purity in the Saigu (literally, "pure palace"), performing many rituals. It was probably not a welcome fate for a young woman used to the glamorous court; in *The Tale of Genji* we are told that a sentimental emperor wept as he consigned his niece to this lonely destiny. However, the Saigu princess could return to Heian after her mother or the emperor who had appointed her died, once again enjoy the sparkling capital, and probably marry.

One fascinating section of the Saigu chapter in the *Engishiki* involves *imi-kotoba*, or forbidden words. According to it, any reference to Buddhism was taboo in this shrine dedicated to pure Shinto. The Buddha was to be called "middle child," a sutra "stained paper," a Buddhist temple "tiled roof," and a Buddhist priest "long hair" (ironic). It is apparent that in this one place the court wanted to be seen in the sight of the ancient gods as it was before the coming of the imported religion, pure and unstained, in the person of the Saigu princess.[19]

Heian popular religion

How did lay people in the Heian era think about religious topics? Themes present themselves from all three major influences, Confucian, Shinto, and Buddhist. Confucian teachings go back to the so-called Constitution of Shotoku, and the classics of that tradition dominated formal education in Heian, inculcating such virtues as sincerity and magnanimity. The practical impact of Confucius' moral precepts, however, seems to have lain mainly in the area of family loyalty, including the virtue of filial piety – the honor that children owed their parents, and members of a clan or extended family to its *kacho* or patriarchal head. The meritocracy China was already developing, by selecting candidates for public office through an examination system which tested their classical education, never took hold in Japan where basing rank on birth, and promotion on family connections, was too deeply ingrained.

Of much more actual influence, judging at least from such literature as *Genji*, was a complex of quasi-Taoist beliefs that had been introduced with Confucian literature from China, but were much more oriented toward divination and taboo than the virtues of the Great Sage. These had to do with *onmyo-do* ("the way of yin and yang"), which included also study of the five elements, astrology, and directional taboos. An influential government office, the Onmyoryo, was dedicated to such matters. Its scholars made pronouncements on portents, and recommended ritual adjustments required to restore the order of nature. Under its guidance, no less than about fifty *onmyo-do* rites were regularly observed at court during the Heian height of that school's influence. These included honoring Chinese deities of the dead, propitiating mischievous spirits whose seasonal movements had to be followed closely, and placating entities believed to have brought disease or disaster.

The fundamental idea was that nature is divided into two forces, yin (the female, dark, passive, watery, earthen energy) and yang (the male, light, active, mountain, heavenly force). These always need to be balanced out. A structure or grave should ideally be located between high ground and a pond. But the additional role of the five elements (water, fire, wood, metal, earth), dominating successive days, calendric considerations, together with moving planets and other astrological signs, made matters much more complicated, often requiring professional consultations.

Of particular interest in connection with Heian writing is *kataimi* (forbidden directions). At certain times it would be unwise to travel in a particular direction; this could also vary depending on one's age and gender. Very often, the taboos were personified in the form of malevolent deities, sometimes astral or planetary, who had moved for a time into that line of sight. In the literature, not seldom clever individuals use *kataimi* and their avoidance, sincerely or as a convenience, to explain their movements or as an excuse to skip an otherwise requisite but tedious obligation. Young gallants, on the other hand, might employ directional obstacles as justification for spending the night at a lady's house. On one occasion the government felt *kataimi* considerations required delaying an army to crush a rebellion for a full month.[20]

Professor Hori Ichiro has pointed out that belief in *goryo*, the spirits of departed aristocrats, especially those who had died in political intrigue, was likewise important in the Heian world. These powerful ghosts were assumed to be malevolent, seeking vengeance against those who had wronged them. They were capable of devastating a city with fire or epidemic in the process. Often rumors that such an angry specter was abroad could create widespread panic; it would then need to be propitiated, often with gestures originating at the highest level. A good example is the spirit of Sugawara Michizane, already mentioned, who was worshiped, first in fear but eventually as a benign *kami* of calligraphy and culture, at the Kitano Tenjin or Tenmangu shrine, and finally throughout the Tenmangu family of shrines. Hori believed that *goryo* belief was significant because it was one aspect of Heian spiritual culture that cut across social lines, and eventually because it encouraged such practices as chanting the *nembutsu*, or relying on the magic of *yamabushi*, both able to counter the power of *goryo*.[21]

Heian religion may appear very diverse, eclectic if not chaotic, wanting to preserve everything from ancient Shinto to esoteric Buddhism to astrology all together without much rhyme or reason. Perhaps so, but there is another way of looking at it: the Heian mind seemed to want to bring all human experience, and all human thought, into a vast medley in which both mind and heart, both the social and the spiritual order, had a place. Inevitably, this was a work in progress, with many loose ends at any given moment. But such a view helps us to see Heian Japan, for all its faults, as the great civilization it was.

Key points you need to know

- The Heian era was a high point in classic Japanese literature; it was influenced by Buddhist values
- The main schools of Buddhism were Shingon and Tendai
- Shingon is esoteric Buddhism, centered on mandalas of cosmic buddhas and bodhisattvas, and techniques of mantra, mudra, and meditation for realizing them within
- Tendai, centered on the Lotus Sutra, is an inclusive Buddhism presenting many paths of enlightenment and the Buddha-nature in all things; also acquired esoteric practices
- Shinto was generally conjoined with Buddhism, except for a few court rites
- Heian popular religion included Confucian morality, Taoist beliefs such as *kataimi*, directional taboos, belief in *goryo* or spirits of the dead, and shamanism developing as Shugendo.

Questions for study and discussion

1. Describe the relation of the imperial and Fujiwara houses in Heian times.
2. Articulate the overall values of the Heian court and its culture.
3. Summarize the essentials of Shingon.
4. Explain the religious meaning of esotericism, or *mikkyo* in Japan.
5. Summarize the essentials of Tendai.
6. Describe the main themes of the Lotus Sutra.
7. Explain the role of art in Heian Buddhism.
8. Interpret the meaning of great and little tradition in religion, giving examples both from Japan and from your own country.
9. Discuss a) the assimilation of Shinto and Buddhism in Heian Japan, and b) the significance of those court rituals in which Shinto was ostensibly kept "pure."
10. Summarize the role of popular Confucianism and Taoism in Heian society.

Further reading

Bargen, Doris G., *A Woman's Weapons: Spirit Possession in the Tale of Genji.* Honolulu, HI: University of Hawaii Press, 1997.

Bowring, Richard John, *The Religious Tradition of Japan, 500–1600.* Cambridge: Cambridge University Press, 2005.

Caddeau, Patrick W., *Appraising Genji: Literary Criticism and Cultural Anxiety in the Age of the Last Samurai.* Albany, NY: State University of New York Press, 2006.

Groner, Paul, *Saicho: The Establishment of the Japanese Tendai School.* Honolulu, HI: University of Hawaii Press, 2000.

Hakeda, Yoshito S., trans., *Kukai: Major Works.* New York, NY: Columbia University Press, 1972.

Kiyota Minoru, *Shingon Buddhism: Theory and Practice.* Los Angeles, CA and Tokyo: Buddhist Books International, 1978.

Matsunaga, Alicia, *The Buddhist Philosophy of Assimilation.* Tokyo: Sophia University Press, 1969.

Matsunaga, Alicia, and Daigan Matsunaga, *Foundations of Japanese Buddhism, vol. 1, The Aristocratic Age.* Los Angeles, CA and Tokyo: Buddhist Books International, 1974.

Morris, Ivan, *The World of the Shining Prince.* New York, NY: Columbia University Press, 1964.

Sango, Asuka, *The Halo of Golden Light: Imperial Authority and Buddhist Ritual in Heian Japan.* Honolulu, HI: University of Hawaii Press, 2015.

Ten Grotenhuis, Elizabeth, *Japanese Mandalas: Representations of Sacred Geography.* Honolulu, HI: University of Hawaii Press, 1998.

Electronic Resources

Ethan Segal, "Heian Japan: An Introductory Essay." www.colorado.edu/cas/tea/curriculum/imaging-japanese-history/heian/essay.html

"Summary of the Tale of Genji." www.davidmoreton.com/echoes/pamphlet-short.html

"Kukai." www.shingonbuddhism.org/information/kukai (An official Shingon site.)

Wikipedia, "Tendai." https://en.wikipedia.org/wiki/Tendai

"Dengyō daishi's Life and Teaching." www.tendai.or.jp/english/ (An official Tendai site.)

"Mandala in Japan." www.onmarkproductions.com/html/mandala1.shtml

"The Lotus Sutra: An Overview." http://buddhism.about.com/od/mahayanasutras/a/lotussutra.htm

"Shinto-Buddhist Syncretism in Heian Japan." https://faroutliers.wordpress.com/2006/04/23/shinto-buddhist-syncretism-in-heian-japan

JREF, "Sugawara no Michizane." www.jref.com/articles/sugawara-no-michizane.201

6 *Warrior culture, simple faith*

The Kamakura Buddhist reformation

In this chapter

This chapter notes the end of the Heian era, the rise of the samurai and their values, and in religion the yearning for a simple, sure key to salvation or enlightenment, exemplified in new Pure Land, Nichiren, and Zen Buddhism.

Main topics covered

- The sense of *mappo*, a difficult last age of the dharma, as the Heian world fell
- The samurai class and its values
- The meaning of Pure Land Buddhism
- Honen and his Pure Land teaching
- Shinran and his more radical Pure Land teaching
- Nichiren and his message.

The end of an age

The old order was slipping away. One could feel it in the air, and see it in distressing events on every hand. No more than 150 years after the *Tale of Genji* had been penned, the world of timeless elegance that classic depicted was brutally disrupted by rough warriors fighting, burning, and slaughtering in the undefended streets of the old capital. It was the beginning of the age of the samurai, colorful but violent men who enabled their class, for all intents and purposes, to replace the tired Heian aristocracy at the top. Religiously, their needs, and that of the land they dominated, were not the same as those of former times. Powerful new spiritual movements swept across Japan to reflect the change.

It was an age of anxiety. Perhaps most ages are ages of anxiety for many people, but now thoughtful Japanese seemed particularly to think uneasily of times present. Buddhists spoke of our now entering the *mappo*, the "last age of the dharma." Assuming (mistakenly, according to modern scholarship) that the Buddha had lived

Yoshida Kenko, a relatively secular writer (even though he was a hermit-monk), in his celebrated *Tsurezuregusa* (*Essays in Idleness*) of about 1340 expressed deep nostalgia for the lost elegance of the old court, and put forth a chastened aesthetic based on *furyu*, appreciation of the beauty of that which is old, flawed, cracked, and unbalanced, as relics from Heian prime were by now likely to have become.[1] Poignantly imperfect objects invoke feelings of *yugen*, yearning, and *sabi*, the sweet sadness of something lonely and disordered which nonetheless draws one toward it, as toward an abandoned child. Michinaga, at the height of the Heian prime, had compared himself to the full moon; Yoshida Kenko, much more aware than he of desolate times and a damaged world, declared that only the unsophisticated admire a moon perfectly full on a clear night; the person of true taste prefers instead to see the moon behind clouds or in the rain, past or prior to fullness, or just visible before sunrise. The new Kamakura faiths were religions for an age when the moon (an old Buddhist symbol of enlightenment) was behind clouds, or not quite at its best, or awaiting a new dawn.

around 1000 BCE, some said that in the first thousand-year age of the dharma, one could be liberated by hearing living teachers. In the second millennium the dharma had declined to the extent that living teachers were no longer available, but those still remained who could understand the scriptures well enough to be liberated by reading. However, in the present degenerate age, beginning around 1000 CE by the Western calendar, the third and last age of the dharma, the world was so depraved that even scriptures could not be adequately comprehended. If one were to be saved at all, it would now need to be by faith alone. (Paradoxically, though, faith alone opened up salvation to vast numbers of the uneducated and unmonastic who would never have been saved by guide or book. The Kamakura period with its sense of *mappo* was swept by a great salvationist movement based on faith alone.)

The new men

Troubles escalated in the eleventh century. Upcountry military factions, most importantly those linked to the rival Minamoto and Taira clans, began to demand greater and greater influence at court. The established Fujiwara ministers temporized by making alliances with importunate warlords, bringing their representatives into the government. But by the twelfth century the hegemony of the old aristocrats was clearly going terminal; it was merely a matter of time before a decisive move by one or another of the warlords would effect radical change in the political order. That disruption, inevitably, would be on a scale to turn society, culture, and religion upside down.

The end of the old order can be dated from 1156, when ongoing war between the Minamoto and Taira for supreme strength swept into Kyoto itself. The Minamoto had gained a level of influence in the capital resented by the other house. Heian, the city which for more than three hundred years had been, at least in the eyes of its courtly elite, a haven of peace and gentility, was suddenly the scene of incredible violence and destruction. Palaces were burned and their inhabitants slaughtered by the ravaging contenders; prisoners were beheaded, though capital punishment had long been abolished out of Buddhist scruples.

In this stage of the Gempei War, as the struggle between the Minamoto and Taira was called, the latter, under the commanding Taira Kiyomori, emerged victorious. His minions seized control of the imperial family and the central government, hoping to govern in the name of the throne as the Fujiwara had done. But those days were to be no more. Once in the timeless city, the Taira samurai tried to adapt their rough demeanor to its elegant life, only to become overly seduced by Heian's charms. Amid incense and lovemaking, they forgot the war was still on, and failed to engage the foe as he continued to battle in the outlying provinces. By 1180 the other house had regrouped and was ready to challenge Taira pretensions.

In 1185, forcefully led by Minamoto Yoritomo, the Minamoto prevailed in the dramatic and much-sung sea battle of Dannoura. At this time the eight-year-old emperor was effectively a hostage of the Taira forces. He was in a doomed ship with his grandmother, also the widow of Kiyomori, together with the sacred jewel and sword of the imperial regalia. Tears in her eyes, the woman told him to worship Ise in the east, and Amida in the west; she then said he had a beautiful capital beneath the sea. They leapt into the waves with the regalia, and all were lost to this world.

It is worth noting that 1180–1185, the five culminating years of the Gempei War, the supreme samurai event, have been the focus of an astonishing proportion of traditional Japanese culture. Innumerable No and kabuki plays, epics, and poems, as well as folklore, tell and retell the dramas of that half-decade.

Like the Taira, Yoritomo was unwilling to usurp the imperial role, recognizing the sun-descended ruler's divine status and his importance as a source of political legitimation. Instead, the Minamoto lord had the sovereign make him shogun (commander-in-chief, in effect military dictator), with power to rule in the emperor's name, restricting the latter to ceremonial and cultural duties. Moreover, Yoritomo did not make the mistake of establishing his *bakufu* ("tent government," the designation of the shogun's military/political regime) in Kyoto, where it might easily be corrupted by the allurements of the old court as were his rivals.

He placed it instead some four hundred miles to the north, in the town of Kamakura near what is now Tokyo Bay. The shogunate, as unusual and seemingly temporary an arrangement as it may seem to be, lasted almost seven hundred years as Japan's national polity, until 1868. During this time, the imperial house, though sometimes impoverished and almost forgotten, survived in the old capital, the dweller behind palace walls still performing his one essential administrative function of appointing the ruling dictator, then retiring to engage in poetry readings and Shinto rites.

The world of the samurai

The Kamakura revolution brought a new class to full power, the samurai (literally, "servers") and their feudal *daimyo* or lords. They have been compared to the European knights who were their contemporaries, but differences as well as similarities obtained.[2] Both honored above all loyalty to their liege in similar feudal systems. Both fought on horseback, in contrast to the common soldiers on foot, and both were clad in armor – though the Japanese armor, made of steel strips held together by thongs, was considerably lighter and more flexible than the European, even as the well-tempered samurai swords, of which their bearers were inordinately proud, were perhaps the best in the world.

But the samurai, though some later were to adopt Zen practice as a means toward self-discipline and indifference to life or death, were not knights of the Round Table or crusaders driven by ideals of chivalry or religious devotion. Their motivation, like that of many Europeans as well in actuality, was simple devotion to their master, their family, and their honor. In confronting an enemy, a samurai would seek to disconcert him by shouting out the names of his own famous ancestors, and his own claims to fame.[3] His religion was victory, or faithfulness unto death – and he valued nothing so highly as an honorable death, if need be by his own hand – at least until he chanced to peek over the limited horizons of that creed.

For another view of life and glory also colored the world of the samurai. The great epic *Heike Monogatari* (c. 1240), or *Tale of the Heike*, tells the story of the rise and fall of the Taira or Heike house in the era of the Gempei wars, setting all against the backdrop of a profoundly Buddhist sense of evanescence. Its descriptions of the great battles and political issues of the era are lucid and dramatic. Swords and armor flash in the noonday sun; courtiers whisper intrigue in palace corridors at midnight.

But the book is deepened by a further motif – a somber, elegiac tone that evokes the ultimate futility of striving for power and glory on the field of honor, even though it does not deny the heroism and splendor of the samurai endeavor. This grand narrative makes clear that the reason for the final fall of the Taira, and especially of their leader Kiyomori, was failure to realize that all human life and glory is but vanity. In their pride they thought themselves exceptions to the lot of mortals. But the oft-quoted opening lines of the *Heike* tell us:

> In the sound of the bell of the Gion temple echoes the impermanence of all things. The pale hue of the flowers of the teak tree shows the truth that they who prosper must fall. The proud ones do not last long, but vanish like a spring-night's dream. And the mighty ones too will perish in the end, like dust before the wind.[4]

The Gion Temple was in Kyoto, and reminds us that many samurai, finally sickened by the carnage which was the cost of their glory, turned in the end to religion, taking Buddhist vows. A flowering teak tree was said to have stood at each of the four corners of the Buddha's death-bed.

One of the most popular heroes in Japan is Yoshitsune, brother of Yoritomo. A brilliant commander, Yoshitsune had incurred the wrath, or perhaps the jealousy, of Yoritomo, and was often on the run from his sibling's henchmen. The estranged brother had as his faithful companion Bankei, who though a monk was extremely strong and without fear. Many tales are told about them, but in the end Yoshitsune was betrayed, surrounded by his enemies, and forced to commit suicide. Much later, the poet Basho, looking on the now-peaceful scene of those horrific events, wrote:

> Summer grasses:
> All that is left
> Of warrior dreams.

In the twelfth and thirteenth centuries, the country sometimes enjoyed uneasy peace under the Minamoto, and soon enough, after the death of Yoritomo, obeyed a further surrogate, the Hojo house. (During much of the century, the actual government was at the end of a remarkably long chain of delegated power: from the emperor, often a minor, to the *insei* retired emperor, usually his father, who was regent; to the shogun, a figurehead after Yoritomo; to the Hojo chief minister, the individual holding real authority.)

The main events of the thirteenth century were two attempted invasions of the Mongols, who now controlled China under Genghis Khan's grandson, Kublai Khan. That potentate desired to extend the world-conquering rule of his race to the island nation. The vast fleets of the aggressor came in 1274 and again in 1281. Both times the alien was fought to a standstill by samurai forces, then defeated when the Mongol armada was wiped out by a typhoon – storms called by the Japanese *kamikaze*, "divine wind." Nonetheless an anxious sense of *mappo* lingered in religious consciousness as the world of the Old Court gave way to dangerous and uncertain times, and wars and rumors of war disturbed the ancient peace. It was a time for new questions, and new answers.

Motifs of Kamakura religion

An age is often better understood by the questions it asks than the answers it gives. Although the comparison can doubtless be pressed too far, the transition from the Heian religious world to that of Kamakura can be suggestively illumined by comparing European religion in the Middle Ages to the deepest concerns of Martin Luther and the Protestant Reformation.

Heian culture, like the medieval Europe of Dante and Thomas Aquinas, seemed to be asking: "How can all human experience, all aspects of religion and all that we know of the universe, be fitted into a vast but unifying system in which everything finds its place?" The rather disorderly pattern of Heian beliefs and observances, Confucian, Taoist, Shinto, and Buddhist, appeared to want to include everything. In a far more sophisticated way, so did the complex mandalas, and graduated hierarchies of religions, in the grand intellectual constructions of Shingon and Tendai.

The new movements of the next era, the Kamakura, sought with Martin Luther to ask instead: "How can I know that I am saved?" Not "What is the world like?" but, "How can *I* find peace?" Three movements, new to Japan in the independent form they now took, gave their answers: Pure Land, Nichiren (Lotus Sutra), and Zen Buddhism. In this chapter we will deal with the first two, popular movements based essentially on faith. In the next chapter we will look at Zen, which found its peace in *zazen* meditation instead, and was based in the rising samurai class.

In a troubled time of change, a troubled individual may well put finding a single, simple, sure key to personal peace of mind, understood as assurance of personal salvation or liberation, ahead of a comprehensive, intellectually satisfying world-system. In both Reformation Europe and Kamakura Japan, the answer to anguish was salvation based on simple faith, the one thing anyone can have, faith alone – the *mappo* means.

Faith alone meant a new way of looking at religion and experiencing it. For one thing, faith put all believers on a more equal footing than did vast complicated systems requiring training and sophistication. One practically needs to be a priest or monk to have the time and education to manage elaborate rituals or philosophical systems, but anyone can express trust in a savior or single sure key, whether priest or peasant, monk or merchant, woman of the court or warrior facing death on the field of battle. Thus the new faiths newly sanctified the lives of ordinary laypeople. There were those who soon realized that if what is important is inner faith, it does not matter whether one is celibate monk or householder. The Pure Land leader Shinran, like Martin Luther, gave up the monastic life to marry and have a family.

The analogy between the Protestant Reformation in Europe and the Buddhist Reformation in Kamakura Japan should not be taken too far.[5] The older forms of Buddhism were not entirely decadent or closed off from the common people, but Shingon and Tendai, even Kegon and Hosso, had their popular teachers and movements in the Kamakura period.[6] (But the same could be said of Catholicism in Reformation Europe, which responded with its own popular revival or "counter reformation.") Nonetheless, new teachers and new patterns of spiritual life were being talked about in shops and palaces alike. We must now find out what the talk was about.

Kamakura Buddhism

Class	Group	Founder	Main practice	Keynote
Pure Land	Jodo-shu	Honen	Nembutsu	Faith in Amida
	Jodo-shinshu	Shinran	Nembutsu	Faith in Amida's grace alone
Nichiren	Nichiren-shu	Niko	Daimoku	Faith in Lotus Sutra; Nichiren as bodhisattva
	Nichiren-shoshu	Nichiko	Daimoku	Faith in Lotus Sutra; Nichiren as buddha
Zen	Rinzai	Eisai	*Zazen, koans*	*Koan* practice
	Soto	Dogen	*Zazen*	Quiet sitting

Pure Land

What is a Pure Land? It was originally a buddha-land, a region in which the pure dharma had been purely preached and received, so that it became a land of bliss. But, since only one buddha could so transform a particular place, and the number of buddhas in Mahayana Buddhism was as infinite as the worlds and galaxies of endless space and time, buddha-lands or Pure Lands (Japanese *Jodo*) were uncountably numerous throughout the universe. Each was a kind of aura around the consciousness of a buddha in profound meditation, and was the place of residence of his dependent bodhisattvas, and of believers brought there by his grace or compassionate power. Though above ordinary space and time, a Pure Land could be thought of as reaching billions of miles in all directions, every one of its vistas even more incredibly delightful than the Chionin temple.

A Pure Land is not one of the heavens of the *devas* or gods. These one enters through accumulation of good *karma*, but they are far from eternal since tenancy lasts only as long as one's finite amount of good *karma* holds out. Nor is a Pure Land Nirvana, which is beyond all conditioned reality, even reality "conditioned" by heavenly beauty as rapturous as a Pure Land's. But entry into nirvana is easy from a Pure Land since, unlike the situation in the Impure Lands of ordinary life, full of distractions stemming from attachments and desires, nothing in the buddha-land distracts one from making those final meditations that lead to ultimate release.

One of the most accessible of Pure Lands is that of Amida (Sanskrit: Amitabha). That is because, according to the "Original Vow" (*Hongan*) of Amida, all who call upon his name in faith will be brought by grace, out of infinite compassion, into this Pure Land after death.

Figure 6.1 Amida, the Great Buddha of Kamakura (© stepmorem / Shutterstock.com)

Salvation thus *depends* not upon one's deeds or merits or good *karma* – though of course these are beneficial in themselves – but upon the grace or gift of Amida received through intense concentration on that all-powerful buddha, or simply through faith. Concentration is realized or faith expressed through recitation of the *nembutsu* ("remembering the Buddha"), in Japanese the words *Namu Amida Butsu*, "Hail Amida Buddha."

The basis of this belief is three scriptures, the longer and shorter Sukhavati ("paradise") scriptures and the "Visualization" scripture.[7] They tell us that eons ago a king heard a buddha preach, and was so moved that he became a monk, and vowed to reach that same supreme state of buddhahood, however long it took and however great the effort required. After innumerable ages the monarch attained his sublime goal, becoming none other than the Buddha Amitabha or Amida.

It was indeed a glorious accomplishment. Out of the cosmic splendor of his buddhahood this godlike being radiated a Pure Land, in the midst of which he sits enthroned on a lotus, surrounded by an aura wider than a billion worlds, a splendor which to human eyes crystallizes into incomparable paradises. Out of the compassion of his buddhahood he vowed to bring all who call upon his name in faith into those paradises by his grace. The Pure Land texts then offer lavish descriptions of the fabulous Realms of Bliss, and of the bodhisattvas who abide there.

The first two Pure Land sutras were originally composed in northwest India around 100 CE, but Amidism did not take hold as the basis of a religious movement until reaching China, where the third scripture was written. There, perhaps supported by Taoist belief in paradises of immortals, and by a trend in intellectual Buddhism toward "sudden" as against "gradual" enlightenment, the Pure Land idea captured popular imagination to become in time the dominant form of lay Buddhism in mainland East Asia, though it was never exactly a "denomination" there, as in Japan.

Regarding "sudden" enlightenment, Chinese teachers in the Chan (Zen) and Pure Land traditions both agreed that enlightenment has to be an immediate, all-or-nothing experience (compare the Japanese Zen term *satori*, "surprise"). Daosheng (312–385), for example, insisted one can no more reach nirvana in several steps than one could cross a canyon in several jumps; one either makes it in a single leap or falls to the bottom. In Pure Land the single leap is in the act of faith, the single vow, the brief recitation of the *nembutsu*, the dependence on divine grace.

The whole point is that liberation is not arduous, but surprisingly easy. Yet the easiness is what, paradoxically, makes it hard for some people. If all it takes is one jump, what does that say about all the effort some put into their salvation? Perhaps the humility a simple practice required was part of it, for the "easy way" demanded putting aside one's intellect, pride, and ego. Then, as soon as a person has discarded those fetters by faith, has not she or he already gotten to Buddhist enlightenment, which is nothing but egoless joy in the present moment? Moreover, is it not the corruption of degenerate times that wants to make things complicated? Another Chinese Amidist advocate, Tanluan (488–554?), taught that a simple path was most suitable for an evil age.

Nonetheless, when it first came to Japan as a part of the vast Tendai collection of practices, Pure Land was less a distinct, single way to salvation than a form of meditation. *Nembutsu zammai* (Sanskrit: *samadhi*) meant reciting the *Namu Amida Butsu* over and over while meditating, making those sacred words a kind of mantra to focus the mind. But as the Heian period advanced, belief in the Pure Land on the basis of Amida's vows – yearning to see the savior at the moment of death, and enter the buddha's paradise – took hold of general consciousness, first among the nobility. None other than Fujiwara Michinaga, the strongman who outlasted many emperors, believed in Amida's Original Vow, and built the wonderful Byodoin Temple, with its gold and soaring angels, to replicate a corner of the Pure Land on earth.

Ordinary people as well quickly realized the worth of the simple faith. A wandering monk named Kuya (903–972) was said to be the first preacher to extend Pure Land practice to the peasants and the poor. The popular Nembutsu dances he organized, in which the chant was accompanied by cymbals and drums, became a vogue throughout the countryside. On a more intellectual plane, the monk Genshin (942–1017), in his *Ojoyoshu* (*Essentials of Pure Land Rebirth*) set out two levels of *nembutsu*: meditative *nembutsu*, which can bring enlightenment in this life; and the *nembutsu* of faith, invocational recitation of the sacred words by laypeople in the midst of ordinary activities, which can result in rebirth in the Pure Land after death.[8]

Honen and Jodo-Shu

It was Honen (1133–1212) who was the real founder of Jodo as a separate school or denomination in Japan, and he was the pre-eminent teacher of the *nembutsu* as the superior means to salvation for virtually all. A Tendai monk of Mt. Hiei, the quiet, scholarly Honen studied Pure Land texts, including Genshin's *Ojoyoshu*, and personally practiced *nembutsu zammai* for many years. He claimed to have read the texts of all the other major Buddhist schools five times over. But he said that he found no peace of mind in them till, in 1175, he had a sudden realization that the only path to salvation was to put total faith in Amida's vow, and to engage in "single practice *nembutsu*" (*senju nembutsu*). Giving up his private life, he then went into the city preaching Amida and the *nembutsu* alone as the way to liberation for our time, for all persons and all social classes.[9]

Honen's book *Senchaku Hongan Nembutsushu* (*Passages on Choosing the Original Vow and the Nembutsu*, 1197) was highly influential.[10] It was first important work to propose that this practice, however and by whomever done, was supreme. Honen divided Buddhism into two gateways to liberation: the *shodomon* ("Gate of the Saintly Path") and the *jodomon* ("Gate of the Pure Land"). The former depended on one's own power (*jiriki*), the later on the power of another (*tariki*). Honen contended that the "holy" path was very difficult, especially in our degenerate times, and that in the *mappo* throwing oneself on the power of another, Amida, was not only easier but better.

As the Lotus Sutra also makes clear, self-reliance as a means to Buddhist salvation is not just hard. It can also be highly deceptive. The ultimate point of salvation is negating attachment to one's illusory ego, and becoming one with the interdependent universe. Yet if practices intended for spiritual advancement are looked at as achievements, like getting promotions and degrees, they may only reinforce that ego and make one proud of one's holiness – which puts the "saint" back at the beginning again. On the other hand, simply putting trust in the grace and compassion of another, "choosing" Amida's original vow, is nothing other than forgetting one's ego, and acknowledging interdependence with the universal buddha-nature which Amida really represents.

We might pause for a moment on the word *senchaku*, "choosing," in Honen's title. This word seems to go with the Kamakura "reformation" theme of finding and accepting one single, sure key to salvation, rather than relying on a comprehensive system, and on countless buddhas and bodhisattvas acting through "skill in means" in all sorts of diverse ways. "Choosing" transfers some responsibility to the individual seeker. One must find and accept the Pure Land "gateway" through one's own choice. Why a choice? The complex world of religious "truth-claims" is full of conflicting "facts" and arguments. At some point, it appears, one must simply make a decision. The Western philosopher Søren Kierkegaard (1813–55), called the father of existentialism, proposed that in the end arguments for and against the existence of God balance out, with as much to be said on one side as the other; one must finally just *choose* whether to believe or not – and this is the way God *wants* it, because God desires belief that is a freely-given "leap of faith," compelled by nothing, not even human logic.

Perhaps it would be too much to call Honen a medieval Japanese existentialist, but his use of the word *senchaku* does suggest he was moving in the "modern" direction of seeing religious commitment as a matter of individual "choice" or decision, oriented toward a single simple practice (*senju*) available to anyone, rather than based in a complex religious culture or on elaborate reasoning.

Honen advocated constant recitation of the *nembutsu* as a means to purification. Having it continually on one's lips could lead to an experience of enlightenment (*satori*) in this lifetime as well as rebirth in the Pure Land after death. He insisted the *nembutsu* was now really the only way of salvation, not simply one expression of faith out of many. In those troubled times, *nembutsu* practice became popular throughout society. The Jodo-shu, or Pure Land sect based on the teaching of Honen alone, is one of the two major Pure Land denominations in Japan to this day.

Inevitably, Honen and his growing movement attracted opposition from the older and established Buddhist schools. After various forms of harassment, Honen's teachings were banned and he with most of his disciples exiled in 1206. (Enemies said that certain of his monks had behaved improperly with court ladies.) However, five years later he was pardoned and allowed to return to Kyoto, where he died in 1212. His school continued, as did another, Jodo-Shinshu, founded by his best-known and more radical disciple, Shinran (1173–1263).

Shinran and Jodo-Shinshu

Shinran, like Honen, was originally a Tendai monk of Mount Hiei. However, at age 29, experiencing deep spiritual disquiet, he went on a hundred-day retreat. During this time, a vision led him to become a disciple of Honen, in 1201. At the time of Honen's exile in 1206, Shinran was also expelled from Kyoto, though he was sent to a different remote province and never saw his teacher again. It was during this exile that Kannon appeared to him in a dream, in which that great female bodhisattva told him it would be all right for him to marry, and that she would take the form of a woman who would be his wife, and help him in his mission to spread the Pure Land teachings. It was apparently not long after, still during his ostracism from the city, that he met and married the promised companion, Eshinni.

They moved to the Kanto (modern Tokyo) area in 1213, gradually building up a sizable community of Pure Land believers by creating a number of small *nembutsu* groups, which met to recite and study in members' homes. Some twenty years later Shinran returned to Kyoto, where he strengthened the oppressed Pure Land community there. He also had to deal with various "heretical" interpretations of the doctrine, including that of his son, Zenran. Shinran had to expel Zenran from the movement; this was a tragic episode for the now-aging patriarch of True Pure Land.

Shinran's Jodo-Shinshu ("True Pure Land School"), as his denomination came to be called, went beyond Honen in several ways. Shinran emphasized *tariki*, or faith in the power of Amida rather than oneself, to the point of saying, by some reports, that a single sincere recitation of the *nembutsu* was sufficient for rebirth. Honen and his group had encouraged repeated recitation as a means of deepening faith, but Shinran wondered if repetition might lead to *jiriki*, reliance on one's own power – of repetition – and so in effect claiming salvation by something one did oneself, rather than pure *tariki* faith in the grace of Amida.

The True Pure Land teacher rejected the worship of any Buddha other than Amida (and Kannon as his bodhisattva agent); even the historical Buddha, Shakamuni, was important only as a means of transmission of the Original Vow, and not to be worshiped for his own sake. Ethical and intellectual labors, or strenuous seeking for enlightenment by study and practice, were worthless in themselves; what was needed in these areas would effortlessly come by itself as consequences of true faith, Shinran maintained.

Shinran's Pure Land is not even salvation by "our" faith in the last analysis: like the European Protestant reformers, the Japanese Buddhist stressed that faith is not a "state" we achieve on our own. It is a gift or grace of Amida; we trust Amida because the universal Buddha first gave us the light and power to do so. For Shinran, Amida was not just the buddha of the west in the great mandala; suffused with infinite light and life, he was for all intents and purposes the universal buddha-nature, or God in the western sense, bestowing grace and salvation upon all.[11]

It was not that Shinran was indifferent to good or bad behavior, for he thought that *nembutsu* faith would lead to good behavior on its own, and indeed that those reborn in the Pure Land could return to earth as bodhisattvas living out of compassion

Shinran was sometimes given to rhetorical provocation. Some argue, he said, that if even a wicked person can be reborn in the Pure Land, how much more a good person. But according to Shinran, it is really the other way around: if even a good person can be reborn in the Pure Land, how much more a wicked person! For "Amida made his vow with the intention of bringing wicked men to Buddhahood. Therefore the wicked man who depends on the power of another is the prime object of salvation."[12]

> Picking up on the *senchaku* theme, Shinran said, "I can only say that, whether
> you are to accept this faith in the *nembutsu* or reject it, the choice is for each
> of you to make ... Whether the *nembutsu* brings rebirth in the Pure Land or
> leads one to Hell, I myself have no way of knowing. But even if I had been
> misled by Honen, and went to Hell for saying the *nembutsu*, I would have no
> regrets. If I were capable of attaining buddhahood on my own [*jiriki*] through
> the practice of some other discipline, and yet went down to Hell for saying the
> *nembutsu*, then I might regret having been misled. But since I am incapable
> of practicing such disciplines, there can be no doubt that I would be doomed
> to Hell anyway."[13] Lines reminiscent of the "leap of faith."

for all beings. But he insisted that one-time faith, not good works or even multiple recitations, was sufficient for salvation, since salvation depends not on us but on the *tariki* grace of Amida. This "choice" to depend on the grace of Amida as alone sufficient was profoundly important to him.

After Shinran's death his remains and his tomb became the center of the movement. Ten years later, his youngest daughter Kakushinni built a mausoleum near Kyoto where the founder's ashes and statue were enshrined; she stipulated that this edifice – now relocated and known as the Honganji – and Pure Land services at it were to be maintained by her and her descendants forever. This was the beginning of the hereditary leadership of Jodo-Shinshu down to the present, although at the time the lineage was not meant to be authoritarian, for the movement did not yet have much organizational structure.

Shinran himself had preferred small informal *nembutsu* groups; he did not intend a new denomination, but considered himself merely a follower of Honen. However, differences with those who considered themselves strict disciples of Honen, and with the Tendai organization which wished to regard the entire Pure Land movement as a subsect within itself, as well as regional issues, led to a complex history.

A major figure was Rennyo (1415–1499), eighth hereditary leader of the Honganji. Despite violent opposition from Tendai monks, Rennyo revitalized the venerable temple containing Shinran's memorial as a Jodo-Shinshu center, uniting around it many scattered groups of Shinran followers throughout the land, and making Jodo-Shinshu into a well-disciplined, militant sect based on strict loyalty to its leaders.[14] Rennyo has been called the "Second Founder" of Shin Buddhism.[15]

One remarkable development of Rennyo's tumultuous times and after was *Ikko ikki*[16] or Jodo-Shinshu rebellions. Beginning in the aftermath of the destructive Onin War (1467–1477), when much of the country was in chaos, bands of armed Jodo-Shinshu peasants and low-ranking samurai marched out against those they regarded as oppressors. Though untrained and ragtag, they were an awesome sight and sound. Imagine thousands of men marching in rows, each holding high a white banner inscribed with the *nembutsu* – *Namu Amida Butsu* – while chanting the sacred words over and over in an unearthly drone as they advanced.

Desperate combatants with nothing to lose, believing that if killed in battle with the *nembutsu* on their lips they would go straight to the Pure Land, they overwhelmed highly trained samurai armies with their numbers and fearlessness. By around 1500 *Ikko ikki* forces controlled several provinces, including the city of Osaka, whose temple-fortress was their strongest redoubt. Their power was not broken until the ruthless warlord Oda Nobunaga waged war to the death against them in the 1580s. But the struggles of the *Ikko ikki*, and the memory of Rennyo's early support of their campaigns on behalf of the oppressed, secured the lasting allegiance of many common people to the True Pure Land School.

Nichiren

The third of the great Kamakura Buddhist reformers who wished to encapsulate the faith in a single, simple sure key was Nichiren (1222–1282).[17] His focus, however, was not Amida and the Pure Land, but the Lotus Sutra (in Japanese *Myoho-Renge-Kyo* or often, for short, the *Hokke-kyo*). This mighty scripture was, of course, regarded by Tendai as supreme in a great hierarchy of texts and spiritual practices. Nichiren, like Honen and Shinran, began as a Tendai monk. But for him the Lotus was not merely supreme but unique, the one doctrine for the *mappo* age, and moreover virtually a sacred power in itself, in the very sound of its words. That is why the central devotion of Nichiren Buddhism is chanting the *daimoku*, the words *Nam myoho renge kyo*, "Hail the marvelous teaching of the Lotus Sutra." The *daimoku* is properly recited before a *gohonzon*, a sheet containing in *kanji* the names of the principal buddhas and bodhisattvas of the Lotus Sutra, and down the center in bolder characters the six *kanji* of the chant: *Nam myoho renge kyo*.

Nichiren was of humble birth, the son of a fisherman. His original name was Zennichimaro, but he took in religion the name Nichiren, meaning "sun-lotus," combining the symbol of Japan with that of the sutra so central to his mission. That combination well sums up Nichiren's story, for he was both a patriot and a revivalist, seeing Japan as potentially the world center of a great spiritual renewal. If, he profoundly believed, the nation would accept the Lotus teachings, making that text the heart of its spiritual life, the energies of a new and wonderful age would spread out from the island empire to cover the planet.

Zennichimaro/Nichiren was ordained a Tendai monk at the age of 16. These were times of unrest, civil war, and disturbing change. An intelligent and questing youth, he was, he said, unsettled by two questions, "How can I be sure of salvation?" and "Why was it that, in the civil wars, the imperial forces were often defeated despite the many prayers and incantations offered on their behalf by Shingon and Tendai priests?" These two queries, it may be noted, probe two major areas of spiritual inquiry: the religious meaning of personal life, and the religious meaning of history. In his search, Nichiren studied the tenets of various schools – Shingon, Zen, Pure Land – in their temples.

But he became convinced in the end that the Lotus Sutra *alone* provided the answers. Ironically, that discovery brought him into conflict with his own Tendai hierarchy, who expelled him for his radical view that there is only one truth and the Lotus alone is it. But Nichiren, embodying samurai determination, and the Kamakura need for an absolute answer to the question of saving truth, could not be content with the relativistic "skill-in-means" mentality of the older schools. He required uncompromising commitment in himself no less than in others.

In the 1250s, after leaving Hiei, the passionate preacher took his message of national regeneration through unequivocal acceptance of true religion to the streets of Japan. He proclaimed that true Buddhism was to be found only in the Lotus, all other forms having been at best only temporary and provisional teachings of the Buddha to prepare people for the final truth. Now they are obsolete. Now, in the *mappo* age, only the full and final doctrine, the Lotus, was valid, only it was to be proclaimed.

Nichiren's way was centered on "three great hidden truths" – the *daimoku* or practice, the *gohonzon* or object of worship, and the *kaidan* or ordination platform, which he wished to erect on a sacred mountain, or some say more esoterically within himself – meaning that his faith would be established as an independent form of Buddhism, free from control by any other sect. Though the right to a *kaidan* may seem a bit more obscure today than the other two points, it was significant in Nichiren's time. The right to ordain in a recognized lineage had been a longstanding issue in Buddhism, and was a greatly-prized privilege when gained.

Not only that, but in this age, Nichiren said, a teacher – indeed, a new bodhisattva or even Buddha – would be sent to declare this truth to the nation and, through it, to the world. There was little doubt he saw himself as that teacher, and indeed the legatee of two bodhisattavas who, according to the Lotus Sutra, heard the Buddha deliver the Lotus sermon. One was the supreme custodian of the sacred text; the other a disciple of the Enlightened One destined to great suffering, but out of whose ordeal would come proclamation of the true faith to the world when it was needed. Thus Nichiren had an explanation for the abuse he endured.

So it was that on April 28, 1253, the same day he took the name Nichiren, he confronted the monks of his original monastery with the notion that all other forms of Buddhism than his should be forbidden, for they were erroneous and deceptive. His message was not well received by either his fellow monks or by feudal lords enamored of "erroneous" doctrines. Nichiren had to flee for his life to Kamakura. There he preached on street corners, declaring the Lotus truth as he understood it and attacking other schools of Buddhism. His well-known saying was, "The *nembutsu* is hell, Zen is a devil, Shingon is the ruin of the nation, Ritsu is treason." In the shogunal capital he received hostility equal to his own assaults.

At the same time, the country was being afflicted by epidemics, earthquakes, and internal conflict. In 1260 Nichiren wrote a tract called *Rissho ankoku-ron*, (*Establish righteousness and pacify the country*) in which he contended that the evils Japan faced were due to its failure to acknowledge the Lotus-truth. If the country would accept his doctrine and banish all others, Nichiren said, all would be well. But if not, worse would befall, climaxing in a foreign invasion. He was exiled by the shogunal government to a distant province in 1261, but pardoned two years later and, nothing daunted, renewed his attacks.

When the Mongol ultimatum came in 1268, the fiery prophet understandably claimed to be vindicated, but his interference in state matters was not appreciated by the *bakufu*. He was condemned to death in 1271, only to have the sentence commuted at the last moment. He wrote his second major work, *Kaimokusho* (*The Opening of the Eye*), a systematic exposition of his teachings, in 1272. He returned to Kamakura in 1274, now moving in high government circles owing to influential friends. He was treated with respect, but his demands were still not granted. Finally retiring to a mountain retreat, he wrote and instructed his close disciples until his death in 1282.[18]

Nichiren is undoubtedly the most controversial religious figure in all Japanese history. Sometimes compared to a Hebrew prophet, he does not fit the usual stereotype of Buddhist monks as mild and meditative. His spiritual practice was dynamic chanting of the *daimoku*, not meditation. Incapable of compromise, he saw truth in black-and-white terms, and contended in season and out, at the cost of exile and even death, that error should be extirpated. His followers were given to disrupting the meetings of other sects with loud protests and brutal action, on several occasions burning Pure Land temples. This method is called *shakubuku*, "break and subdue," based on Nichiren's idea that by deliberately provoking people to anger they will be caused to reconsider their beliefs.[19]

Oneness on several levels was important to Nichiren: one sutra, one practice (the *daimoku*), one time (the present, the time of the radical new revelation), one man (himself), and one country (Japan), were crucial to the new Buddhism. At the same time, Nichiren's letters show him to be compassionate and understanding toward disciples with spiritual problems.[20]

He truly loved Japan, and wanted his nation to fulfill a world-saving mission. It must be remembered that in the Middle Ages, in Japan as in Europe, the concept of patriotism, or of a nation with a distinctive national purpose or destiny, was much less well developed than later. People ordinarily thought of their identity in terms of local community and the feudal lord to whom they owed fealty, rather than to a nation in the current sense. In this as in other respects Nichiren, who called himself "the pillar, the eyes, and the great vessel of Japan," anticipated some aspects of the modern.[21]

Six places of rebirth

This may be a good place to introduce the six places of rebirth (*rokudo* or "six paths") of conventional Buddhism's wheel of existence. The concept of these six *lokas* or places of potential rebirth came into Japan with the earliest sutras, but seem to have been more widely emphasized in medieval times than before; then the six became a part of popular Buddhist lore, reflected in No plays and other literature.[22]

The idea is that varying *karma* can lead to rebirth in one of the following realms:

- The hells (*jigoku*), where one suffers excruciating tortures in retribution for cruelty and other extreme offenses – but hell, like all the other of the six realms, is not eternal, lasting only until the bad *karma* which has put one there is paid off;
- The realm of the *gaki* (Sanskrit: *preta*) or hungry ghosts, pathetic beings often pictured with huge bellies but tiny mouths, so they are always hungry and never satisfied – *karma*'s answer to greed and gluttony;
- The animal realm, that of creatures who suffer without having the discernment to know why, a result of giving way to "animal passions";
- The realm of the *ashura* (Sanskrit: *asura*, or titans), warriors of more brawn than brain who continually fight for no better reasons than anger, jealousy, and inordinate pride – in Japanese literature, often the destination of samurai fighters motivated in life by those same drives above all else;
- The human realm, the only world in which good and evil, joy and sorrow, can be experienced in their fullness by creatures who at the same time have the capacity to analyze the meaning behind that changing thought-experience, recognize the unsatisfactoriness of all transitory life, and therefore seek liberation from this wheel of existence into nirvana – liberation is ordinarily only possible from the human realm, and therefore rebirth as a human is a priceless gift, not to be wasted;
- The heavens (*tendo* or *tengoku*) of the *devas* or gods, paradisal realms of continual delight, the reward of good *karma* – but not nirvana or even a buddha's Pure Land, and ultimately unsatisfactory because these heavens last only as long as the good *karma* holds out and in them one is so consumed with continual pleasure as to take no thought for liberation.

The prophet of the Lotus was also perhaps modern in his interpretation of the Lotus Sutra as it inculcated the absolute unity of reality; all differences of time and space, inner and outer, spirit and matter, were illusory. This is a common Buddhist concept, of course, but Nichiren carried it to characteristic extremes, especially in terms of practical application. A key principle for him was the Tendai tag, *ichinen sanzen* – "one thought, three thousand" – that is, all realms of reality coexist simultaneously in a single moment of meditation. So it was that Nichiren emphasized that the three aspects or "bodies" of buddha-nature, as taught by conventional Mahayana (the *dharmakaya* or essence body, the *sambhogakaya* or heavenly body, and the *nirmanakaya* or manifest in-this-world body), are all one, and the believer must experience, and incarnate, all three at the same time. Other forms of Buddhism, he said, have become unbalanced by emphasizing one over the other – Zen the *nirmanakaya*, Pure Land the *sambhogakaya*, and so forth. The Nichiren believer is to be at once united with the absolute essence of the universe, while experiencing inwardly the bliss of heaven or the Pure Land, and living actively in the manifested world.

According to Nichiren (and some other liberalizing Buddhist preachers) all the places of reincarnation are really in the mind, here and now. In the course of a single hour, as you sit in class, in the library, hang out with friends, wherever you are, you may have moments of heavenly joy, of titan-like anger, of animal stupidity, of hungry-ghost unsatisfied hungers, of feeling like you're in the pits of hell – and of being just plain human. So also are all stages of the bodhisattva path capable of realization here and now. All stations of rebirth, and enlightenment itself, are not places, but states of consciousness, as in much modern psychologizing of religion.

Related to this grand unification of all things in the present moment of consciousness is *esho funi* ("inner and outer not two"), the principle important to Nichirenism that affirms one's inner, subjective life and the outer environment around it are deeply interwoven. A subjective cause, such as strong faith in the Lotus expressed by chanting the *daimoku*, can affect outer realities, and one's outer environment can shape one's inner life. Modern followers of Nichiren, as we have seen from the earlier description of a Soka Gakkai meeting, have strongly emphasized these ideas to make the faith a "practical" one which molds one's life, health, prosperity, and joyousness here and now. In the Nichiren tradition, they say, religion is not just about life after death or nebulous mystical states, but a modern movement involved in everyday happiness and success in this world. Like many modern preachers in other faiths, Nichirenists offer peace and prosperity today, in this world, through right inner faith.

After Nichiren's death, his following grew, despite persecution and division. Two major Nichiren groups emerged, under two of his disciples. The more conservative, led by Niko (1253–1314) was Nichiren-shu, which held that the founder was a bodhisattva; it was and is relatively moderate.

The letter of Hojo Shigetoki

A final perspective on Kamakura spirituality may be gained by a glance at a letter of advice by Hojo Shigetoki, a member of the Hojo family of "regents" under the Kamakura shoguns, to his son. Penned between 1256 and 1261, this document balances the single-mindedness of some Kamakura religion with a busy layman's understanding tolerance. Though a devout Jodo-shu Amidist, Hojo enjoined worship of the gods and buddhas alike every morning and evening, and speaks of honoring parents and superiors in the Confucian manner, but at the same time goes out of his way to extend patience and respect toward those less advantaged than oneself. He tells his son not to punish servants when angry, but "wait until you are calm, and think of their past service as well as their present error." His consideration reaches out to all living beings: "Do not take the life of a creature that to you seems useless. You should know that the lowest insect clings to life as strongly as a man."[23]

Nichiren-Shoshu, founded by Nichiko (1246–1332) contends instead that Nichiren was himself no less than a buddha for a new age, a new dispensation beginning in his time. After his proclamation of the Lotus truth all other Buddhism, like all other religion of any sort, became way out of date. Only the Lotus is valid now. It was from this strict form of Nichiren Buddhism that Soka Gakkai arose, first as a lay organization within Nichiren-Shoshu, to make it one of the larger forms of Buddhism in postwar Japan.

Key points you need to know

- The passing of the Heian era brought anxiety and a feeling of impending disaster; many considered it the *mappo*, the last age of the Dharma, when faith alone would be means to salvation
- A key religious question was, "How can I be saved?"
- Pure Land Buddhism said it would be by faith in Amida Buddha
- Honen taught Pure Land as an independent spiritual movement, based on saying the *nembutsu*
- Shinran taught a form of Pure Land emphasizing it is really by Amida's grace we are saved
- Nichiren called for faith in the Lotus Sutra, and declared all Japan should accept this faith.

Questions for study and discussion

1. Why does salvation through faith make religion accessible to a very wide range of people?
2. What were the dominant values of the samurai?
3. What is the "Original Vow" of Amida Buddha?
4. What is a Buddhist Pure Land?
5. Why was the "choice" of faith in Amida's vow important to Honen?
6. How did Shinran's Jodo Shinshu differ from Honen's Jodo-shu?
7. How would you interpret Shinran's character?
8. How and why did Pure Land Buddhism become politically important?
9. How would you characterize Nichiren's personality?
10. What were Nichiren's fundamental questions and how did he resolve them?
11. How did Nichiren combine religion and nationalism?
12. Describe the six places of rebirth, and interpret the significance of each.

Further reading

Adolphson, Mikaei, *The Teeth and Claws of the Buddha: Monastic Warriors and Sohei in Japanese History*. Honolulu, HI: University of Hawaii Press, 2007.

Andreasen, Esben, *Popular Buddhism in Japan: Shin Buddhist Religion and Culture*. London: Routledge Curzon, 1998. [Selections by various writers from Kamakura to the present]

Anesaki, Masaharu, *Nichiren, The Buddhist Saint*. Cambridge, MA: Harvard University Press, 1916.

Bloom, Alfred, *The Essential Shinran*. Oxford: Blackwell/World Wisdom, 2007.

Bloom, Alfred, *Shinran's Gospel of Pure Grace*. Tucson, AZ: University of Arizona Press, 1965.

Dobbins, James, *Jodo Shinshu*. Honolulu, HI: University of Hawaii Press, 2002.

Dobbins, James, *Letters from the Nun Eshinni: Images of Pure Land Buddhism in Medieval Japan*. Honolulu, HI: University of Hawaii Press, 2004.

Lee, Kenneth Doo Young, *The Prince and the Monk: Shotoku Worship in Shinran's Buddhism*. Albany, NY: State University of New York Press, 2007.

Matsunaga, Daigan, and Alicia Matsunaga, *Foundations of Japanese Buddhism*. 2 vols., Los Angeles, CA: Buddhist Books International, 1974.

Meeks, Lori, *Hokkeji and the Reemergence of Female Monastic Orders in Premodern Japan*. Honolulu, HI: University of Hawaii Press, 2010.

Sakashita, Jay, ed., *Writings of Nichiren Shonin*. Honolulu, HI: University of Hawaii Press, 2004.

Sansom, Sir George, *A History of Japan to 1334*. Stanford, CA: Stanford University Press, 1958.

Stone, Jacqueline, *Original Enlightenment and the Transformation of Medieval Japanese Buddhism*. Honolulu, HI: University of Hawaii Press, 1999.

Tanabe, George Joji, and Willa Jane Tanabe, eds., *The Lotus Sutra in Japanese Culture*. Honolulu, HI: University of Hawaii Press, 1989.

Wakita, Haruko, *Women in Medieval Japan*. Melbourne: Monash University, 2006.

Watts, Jonathan, and Yoshiharu Tomatsu, eds., *Traversing the Pure Land Path: A Lifetime of Encounters with Honen Shonin*. Tokyo: Jodo Shu Press, 2005.

Yamamura, Kozo, ed., *The Cambridge History of Japan*, vol. 3, *Medieval Japan*. Cambridge University Press, 1990.

Electronic Resources

"Samurai and Bushido." www.history.com/topics/sanurai-and-bushido

John R. Wallace, "Main Navigation Page of the Web site for *The Tale of the Heike* (*Heike monogatari*)." http://sonic.net/~tabine/heike081003/Heike_mainpage.html

"Japanese Pure Land Philosophy," *Stanford Encyclopedia of Philosophy*. http://plato.stanford.edu/entries/japanese-pure-land

"About Pure Land Buddhism." www.jodo.org/about_plb/what_plb.html (Official Jodo Shu site.)

"About Honen Shonin." www.jodo.org/about_hs/ho_life.html (Official Jodo Shu site.)

"Our Founder – Shinran Shonin." http://buddhistchurchesofamerica.org/shinran-shonin/ (Official site of the Buddhist Churches of America, which are Jodo Shinshu.)

John Paraskevopoulos and George Gatenby, "A Primer of Shin Buddhism." www.nembutsu.info/primshin.htm

"Life of Nichiren." www.sgi.org/buddhism/life-of-nichiren.html (Official site of Soka Gakkai International.)

"Nichiren-shu." www.nichiren.or.jp/english/teachings (Official site of this denomination.)

"Nichiren Shoshu True Buddhism." www.nst.org (Official site.)

"Cycle of Suffering, Cycle of Samsara." www.onmarkproductions.com/html/six-states.shtml (On the six places of rebirth, with useful material on *karma* and Kannon as well.)

7 *Swords and satori*

Zen and its culture

In this chapter

This chapter will look at the particular role Zen Buddhism has had in Japan and Japanese culture, and also its reception outside of Japan. Major Zen teachers and schools will be presented, as will the main traditional arts associated with Zen.

Main topics covered

- A Zen experience
- Basic Zen teachings
- Eisai and Rinzai Zen
- Dogen and Soto Zen
- The Ashikaga period
- The arts traditionally associated with Zen: gardens, tea, flower arrangement, painting, No drama, and the martial arts
- Bushido, the Way of the Warrior
- Later Zen poets and teachers: Ikkyu, Basho, Hakuin
- Zen in the West.

A Zen experience

Zen Buddhism is only one Buddhist strand in Japan, and only one of the three major movements – Pure Land, Nichiren, and Zen – resultant from the Kamakura spiritual upheavals. Actual members of temples of the two or three Zen denominations represent less than ten percent of the total population. Nonetheless, Zen is allotted a separate chapter in this book for two reasons: first, that school has had a widely-recognized distinctive role in Japanese culture; and second, Zen has attracted particular interest outside of Japan.

Why the twofold interest? Zen is associated with several arts in a way emphasizing nature, "minimalism," and what might be called "trained spontaneity." Challenging concepts. Fascinating also is a school some inquirers have thought to be, in the opening words of one of the most influential modern books on Zen, "a way and a view of life which does not belong to any of the formal categories of modern Western thought."[1]

However, it is important to realize that, despite presentations which put Zen in a sort of spiritual stratosphere, the tradition is in fact simply an East Asian form of Buddhism as grounded in history, culture, and religious institutionalization as any other. It has its rituals, has had its scandals, its wealthy temples and set attitudes – as well as its glorious art, its tales of marvelous spontaneity, and the inner freedom of those who have found the secret of *satori*.

Perhaps, to introduce the real life of Zen, a personal story would be of help. Many years ago, I visited an evening *zazen*, or seated meditation, at an American Zen center. The *roshi* or master was from a Japanese monastery, but most of the members of this center were Euro-American. As I crossed the flagstoned courtyard of the old mansion which was now the center's main edifice, I was met by a woman who welcomed me courteously and, rightly taking me for a newcomer, showed me how to enter the *zendo* or meditation hall, bow to the image of a Buddha on the altar, and take a seat on one of the two rows of mats and cushions on either side of the long room. This I did, sitting cross-legged in the "half lotus" posture (one foot on the opposite thigh, the best I could attain) with spine erect, and eyes pointed toward the floor three feet in front. (This being a center in the Rinzai rather than the Soto tradition, the two rows faced each other rather than toward the wall.)

Most of the others, regular members or attenders, wore black robes. One such individual was the *jikijitsu* or proctor, who walked up and down the rows with a flat paddle, the *kyosaku* or awakening stick, on his shoulder. When he saw someone whose mindfulness seemed to be lagging, or whose posture – like mine – was poor, he would pound the stick sharply on the floor in front of that person to get attention, then make the correction. If she or he was a stable and experienced member, he would slap the drowsy meditator smartly on the shoulders with the stick, then bow as the recipient also bowed to acknowledge the favor, and pass on silently.

At the end of a half hour, everyone silently arose, filed out into the courtyard, circled around in single file for a few minutes of "walking zen" to loosen up, then returned to the *zendo* for another half hour of sitting. After that, another moment of exercise, and more sitting.

By this time, to my uninitiated mind, Zen was becoming tedious, and my body was feeling the effect of sitting too long in an unaccustomed position. But then the *jikijitsu* approached and, whispering in my ear, asked if I would like to have *sanzen*, an interview with the *roshi*. Being willing to try, I consented, and was led to a small anteroom.

A low table, with a gong on it at one end, was the only furniture; three or four people were seated in *zazen* posture on cushions beside the table. Beyond this room the *roshi* waited in a private audience chamber. When he had finished an interview, he would ring a bell; the next student in line responded by sounding the gong. That person would then enter, kneeling to bow touching the forehead to the floor as he entered the room, and again just before the master.

The small rotund monk from Japan was seated high on a vast cushion. He wore a sashed gray robe with wide winglike sleeves, and held a fan in his hand. Taking a note of introduction from my hand, he eyed me shrewdly.

"So," he said. "You're a professor of religion. Do you believe in God?"

Stumbling around, having no real idea how to express such things to a Zen master, I tried to say something about God as the ground of my being and the source of my life.

I was cut short. I was surprised by a sting on my thigh as he brought the folded fan down on me. "Not good!" he said strictly. "*Now* how do you know God?"

This time I stumbled even more. "Perhaps in the immediacy of the experience …"

"Not good!" he retorted, slapping me again with the fan. "This is your Zen *koan*: *Now* how do you know God?"

I knew that the Zen *koan* is a riddle with no obvious answer. Famous ones are, "Where was your face before you were born?" or "What is the sound of one hand?" The ultimate answer to both lies in the Oneness that is prior to all differentiated, manifested phenomena, but just to say so would hardly satisfy a Zen teacher. The student has to demonstrate that she or he *knows*. For the *koan* is meant to bring the mind up against the limits of its rational, verbal way of thinking, and to shift gears to immediate awareness expressed in direct, spontaneous action without words or ideas. If asked, for example, about the sound of one hand, the student who *knows* might just silently thrust out one hand in a single, unified gesture, putting all his energy into that one movement, with no flicker of doubt or hesitation.

I thought I knew what "*Now* how do you know God?" meant: How do I encounter God in the immediate Now? Not how did I know God in some past religious experience, or as a result of theological study or reflection, but Now, before I even have a chance to find words for the experience. How do I know God before I know I am knowing God, in what the Japanese would call *naka ima*, the "middle now"? Perhaps the *roshi* used the term "God" because I was a Westerner; it might have been the Buddha-nature or the Dharmakaya; but the purport was the same. How does the ultimate interface with the passing moment, and how could that be expressed without thinking? How do I push awareness outside the verbal and conceptual boxes into which we put all experiences as soon as we have them, or only a split second later?

I knew that the idea was not to cogitate on the *koan*, trying to figure it out rationally, but just to hold it in my mind, perhaps just saying it over and over, sinking into deeper and deeper levels of consciousness, until it had an effect beyond the reach of ordinary mind. Then I began, if only dimly, to have some feeling for the potential of Zen practice. I seemed to be lightly floating, as though a half-inch above the cushion.

All times except the Now shrank away, like something seen through the wrong end of a telescope. I might have been in that Zen meditation hall two hours, which was actually the case by then, or two weeks, or two years, or two centuries; it didn't matter and wouldn't have made much difference whatever it was. The present was my life, the center of my being, and that was enough.

But soon enough we were brought back to the normal space-time continuum. The meditation was over, tea was served, and the *roshi* came out to give a brief *teisho* or sermon. (The Japanese-American interpreter was a simple gardener by day, but some in the temple said he was secretly a bodhisattva.) Finally, the evening ended with chanting the Heart Sutra. ("Form is emptiness, and emptiness is form …The wisdom that has gone beyond, and beyond the beyond; O what an awakening, all hail.")

Note two thoroughly integrated sides to this experience: structure and freedom; one might even say form and emptiness. Of structure and tradition there was plenty: bows, robes, chants, bells and drums, altar and incense. The *roshi* was in his position because he had been certified by his *roshi*, and so on back in a kind of apostolic succession supposedly leading to the Buddha himself. In Japan many Zen temples have at times been powerful institutions, with heavy political and cultural influence.

At the same time, the final point of that traditional structure was, ideally, to release within myself and the other students an inner freedom that would go beyond even the fetters of words, to express itself in a shout of awakening, or perhaps through one of the Zen arts: in the natural lines of an ink-wash painting, the clear seeing of a haiku poem, or the direct thrust of a martial artist's sword. Extreme constraint and liberty nurturing each other: that is the Zen model.

Philip Kapleau, in his invaluable *The Three Pillars of Zen*, gives a number of Zen accounts, by both Japanese and Westerners. Here are some of the closing words of one attributed to an "American schoolteacher" as she recorded her experiences during *sesshin*, a time of intense Zen training. On this last day, despite great fatigue, she awoke early:

with a bright 'Ha!' and realized I was enlightened."

A strange power propelled me … I arose and calmly dressed. My mind raced as I solved problem after problem … At *dokusan* [the interview with the *roshi*] I rushed into the little cottage my teacher was occupying … and let loose such a torrent of comical verbosity that [we] laughed with delight. The *roshi* tested and passed me, and I was officially ushered through the gateless gate.

A lifetime has been compressed into one week. A thousand new sensations are bombarding my senses, and a thousand new paths are opening before me. I live my life minute by minute, but only now does a warm love pervade my whole being, because I know that I am not just my little self but a great big miraculous Self. My constant thought is to have everybody share this deep satisfaction.

I can think of no better way to end this account than with the vows I chanted at *sesshin* every morning:

> All beings, however limitless, I vow to save. Fantasy and delusion, however endless, I vow to cut off. Dharma teachings, however immeasurable, I vow to master. Buddha's Way, however lofty, I vow to attain.[2]

Now on to the story of Zen in Japan.

Basic Zen

Heian Japan cut off commercial and diplomatic relations with China in the mid-ninth century, as the once-brilliant Tang dynasty (681–907), whose early phase had represented a golden age of Chinese Buddhism, deteriorated into warlordism and persecution of the Dharma. The unique culture of the Heian era, though at first inspired by Chinese Buddhism, Confucianism, Taoism, and secular poetry, thereafter flourished on its own and in its own way. So it was also that Japan knew the Buddhist faith in the forms in which it had crossed over to the island nation before the break – the six Nara schools, the two Heian versions – but had little awareness of subsequent developments on the mainland. Shingon, Tendai, and the other schools continued in Japan as though nothing had happened since their arrival, save their accommodations with the *kami*, and the exfoliation of growths whose seeds were already embedded in Tendai: Pure Land, and Lotus or Nichiren Buddhism.

But beginning in the mid-twelfth century, as the Heian era gave way to the Kamakura, Japanese priests and others began traveling to China once more. They found a quite different religious world from what they had expected. The dominant monastic form of Buddhism was no longer esoteric schools like the originals of Shingon and Tendai, but Zen, known as Chan in China. Chan prevailed partly for political reasons: a great persecution, launched in response to complaints that most monks and nuns were idle parasites on society, had devastated Chinese monastic Buddhism in 845. Most monasteries and convents were emptied, their inhabitants returned to lay life. But Chan temples were much simpler, often located in backcountry areas, and in principle these monks could not be accused of lassitude because they already worked with their hands.

On a deeper level, the success of Chan can undoubtedly also be attributed to the way that school, really an amalgam of Buddhism with Taoist simplicity and naturalism, and a bit of Confucian respect for hard work thrown in, went well with the Chinese temperament. At one and the same time, Chan was commonsensical and mystical, self-disciplined and life-affirming – all virtues the Chinese admire.

Figure 7.1 Japanese Buddhist monk in Zen posture (Marubatsu; Public Domain: Wikimedia Commons)

According to tradition, Chan was brought to China by Bodhidharma (ca. 470–532; Daruma ["Dharma"] in Japanese), a south Indian who journeyed to the Middle Kingdom around 520. Allegedly he was the last in a series of Indian patriarchs of a silent style of Buddhism begun when the Buddha handed his favorite disciple, Ananda, a flower and merely smiled. This legend is no doubt apocryphal, but for whatever reason a new Chinese interpretation of Buddhism, Chan, coalesced around Bodhidharma's name.

Many are the stories about Bodhidharma. It is said he meditated in front a wall until his legs atrophied; a round-bottomed Japanese toy representing a man who, when you push him over, comes back up again, is called a Daruma. According to legend, he once fell asleep while trying to do *zazen*, and in his anger cut off his eyelashes, which fell to the ground to become tea leaves – a drink which ever since has kept sleepy monks awake. The first patriarch is said to have answered an emperor impudently, declaring the sovereign's good works on behalf of the dharma had won him no merit, and that he, Bodhidharma, did not know why he was standing there before him. Somehow he got by with it.

He left four principles which – whether actually by him or a later hand – have since governed Zen:

- A special transmission outside the scriptures;
- No reliance on words or letters;
- Direct pointing to the mind;
- Seeing into one's own nature.

This is the heart of it: direct experience of reality here and now. Zen masters were insistent their docents abjure buddhas and sutras outside themselves, and see the buddha-nature as much in the hedge at the back of the garden, and in themselves, as in book or temple. They would say such things as that a sutra was toilet paper, or "If you meet the Buddha on the road, kill him." You might become enlightened when, after you had eaten breakfast, your master told you to wash your dishes.[3]

Zen took the basic Mahayana premise that *samsara* is Nirvana all the way. The wheel of existence, the world as it is, is also the Buddha-nature or eternal Reality – not a philosophical idea but something to be experienced directly, within oneself and in all that is. Words and concepts only get in the way of this direct experience. That's why sutras are for toilet use and any buddha you meet – that is, outside of yourself – is an enemy. So one Chinese master said, "Eat when you are hungry, sleep when you are tired" – that's enlightenment if you can really do it without bondage or self-deception. Again, "Cutting wood, drawing water – how wonderful, how miraculous!" For this radical Chan everyday life was the Path: "The only difference between a buddha and an ordinary person is that a buddha realizes he is a buddha and the ordinary person does not."[4]

Some Western interpreters of Zen may have given the impression that Zen was mostly just this kind of talk. But although these and many other good lines, preserved as *koans* or *mondo* (teaching stories), may suggest that Chan was a rather freewheeling, even chaotic, way of life, in fact they come out of the context – like my experience, such as it was – of highly structured monastic practice. Discipline is not at odds with spontaneity and "everyday life." Rather, the stick and the *zendo* frame the freedom at Zen's heart. To play or sing great music so well that it *sounds* free and easy takes a lot of practice, as any performer knows. So does eating, sleeping, and living everyday life with enlightened joy rather than hassles in your heart.

Eisai and Rinzai Zen

The first Japanese teacher to discover and transmit this new Chinese Buddhism in the Kamakura era was Myoan Eisai (1141–1215). To be sure, he did not represent Japan's first meeting with Zen, but no earlier contacts had taken hold. One or two Chinese Chan masters visited Japan in the Nara period; Saicho of Tendai had also studied Chan meditation. The eminent Tendai monk Ennin, Saicho's disciple and successor, was in China 838–847 as a member of the last official Japanese embassy. There he witnessed the persecution of 845. But though he must have been aware of Chan, he was apparently not impressed; on his return he introduced esotericism instead to Mount Hiei.

Like so many other creators of the new Kamakura religious era, the aristocratic Eisai began as a restless Tendai monk. In 1168 his restlessness carried him to China as he embarked with a Shingon priest on a tour of the mainland, intending mostly to sightsee and make a pilgrimage to the main Tiantai temple. The pair was disconcerted to find that once-great monastic center seriously deteriorated. On the other hand, Chan was everywhere. Nonetheless, on his return the young Tendai cleric continued Tendai practice for some twenty more years.

In 1187 Eisai went again to China, this time studying with an aged master of the Linji (Rinzai) lineage on Mount Tiantai. He returned to Japan in 1191 with a certificate of enlightenment. Even so, his commitment was less than total, for he brought an array of other Buddhist and Confucian teachings as well, together with tea plants. (Zen, at its best intellectually alert and curious, conveyed Neo-Confucian as well as Buddhist philosophy to Japan – and tea has always had an important role in Zen to revive drowsy monks in *zazen*; recall Bodhidharma's eyelashes. There is a Japanese saying, *Cha no aji, Zen no aji*, "The taste of tea is the taste of Zen.")

However, Eisai did establish a Rinzai Zen temple in southern Kyushu, and wrote a lively defense of Zen as good for Japan. In "Propagation of Zen for the Protection of the Country," he tactfully emphasized Saicho's earlier introduction of the practice, and the simple purity of its way, saying, "Outwardly it favors discipline over doctrine, inwardly it brings the Highest Inner Wisdom. This is what the Zen sect stands for."[5] A skillful religious politician, Eisai also got permission to start a Zen temple in the new capital of Kamakura, and later in the old imperial capital of Kyoto as well. He ended his life as abbot there.

Eisai was a complex individual with wide-ranging interests. He was not a passionately single-minded missionary for Zen, but he seriously believed its practice could have a reforming effect on his own sect, Tendai, and on Japan as a whole. Ironically, although Rinzai is often thought of as a strict, intense form of Zen, with frequent use of *koans* and the stick, its Japanese founder also embodied that other, cultural side of the tradition which is no less celebrated. Eisai is famous not only for "Propagation of Zen," but also for a treatise called "Drink Tea and Prolong Life."[6] While allegedly written for the benefit of an alcoholic shogun, this work did much to promote the beverage in Japan, and indirectly the famous "tea ceremony" which has become almost a Zen sacrament.

With his cultured and cosmopolitan background, Eisai laid the foundations of Zen as a favored religion of the emerging samurai class. The match was right: on the one hand the discipline of Zen, including ability to endure pain and privation, went well with the warrior spirit; on the other, the austere but elegant arts of Zen suited the rising warriors' aspirations to refinement. We will examine some features of this culture in a moment. First however, a look at a rather different personality, the other great founder of Zen in Japan, Dogen.

Dogen and Soto Zen

The leading Western historian of Zen, Heinrich Dumoulin, has called Dogen "the strongest and most original thinker that Japan has so far produced."[7] Probably more than any other traditional Japanese intellectual, Dogen would be entitled to take his place as a world-class philosopher. Yet he did not seek fame, nor did he receive much in his own lifetime. All he wanted was to find enlightenment by living a completely natural and ordinary life as a monk.

Dogen (1200–1253) was, like Eisai, of aristocratic background. He was the illegitimate son of a Fujiwara mother and a princely father, nurtured and educated amid the elegance of the Old Court. However, his parents both died while he was a child. Thus made acquainted with the dark as well as the sunny side of life, he desired to become a monk. After some difficulty he entered the Tendai center at Mount Hiei.

But like Honen, Nichiren, and others of his age he was troubled by apparent unanswered paradoxes in conventional teaching – in his case the question of why, if a person is born with the Buddha-nature within, does he nonetheless have to seek enlightenment? In this quest, Dogen first worked with a disciple of Eisai, Myozen, in Eisai's old Rinzai temple, Kennin-ji. But though he always spoke of Eisai with great respect, little by little the younger disciple, Dogen, was becoming dissatisfied with Rinzai Zen. To him, the *koans* in which Rinzai put such stock were too much directed toward inducing particular mental and emotional experiences, rather than ultimate unconditioned liberation.

In 1223 Dogen sailed for China with Myozen, desiring to visit Buddhist centers. He found his way to Caodong (Soto) monasteries, where he appreciated the way they emphasized quiet sitting and living Zen in the context of all one's life, including ordinary labor, more than *koans* and intense breakthrough experiences.

Later, Dogen was to write a whole book on working in the kitchen as Zen practice, though he also insisted on much *zazen*.[8] Dogen also declared that not only cooks, but

> Even a little girl of seven can become the teacher of the four classes of Buddhists and the compassionate mother of all beings; for [in Buddhism] men and women are completely equal. This is one of the highest principles of the Way.[9]

This was not, however, a principle widely recognized in practice in traditional Buddhism. In this, as in so many things, Dogen was far in advance of his times, and often ours.

It was in China, in 1225, that Dogen had his enlightenment experience. While doing early morning *zazen*, a monk next to him fell asleep. The master, Rujing, walking by, raged, "Zen means the dropping away of mind and body! What will you get by sleeping?" Dogen was first startled, then felt a tremendous calm and inner joy at these words. He went in to the master who, recognizing him as enlightened, imparted patriarchal succession to the young Japanese.

Dogen learned an important lesson, he said, from the aged cook of a monastery who had visited his ship to purchase some Japanese mushrooms. They fell to talking, it became late, and Dogen suggested that instead of walking the ten miles or more back to the monastery, the cook should just stay on board overnight. When the old monk insisted on returning to his duties, Dogen took him to task, saying there must be other monks who could cook, and pressing him on why he wanted to be a cook anyway instead of spending more time practicing *zazen*. At this the other just laughed, telling the brash young Japanese that if he could ask that, he hardly understood the real meaning of Buddhism.

On returning to Japan in 1227 Dogen went first back to Kennin-ji, then lived at other temples, but finally established Eihei-ji, where he was able to lead a temple following his own concept of pure Zen. There he completed his great book, *Shobogenzo* (*Treasure of Knowledge of the True Dharma*).

Dogen emphasized in all his philosophical works the unity of practice and enlightenment – and practice is not only meditation, but the whole life of the practitioner: eating, sleeping, working, recreation. Buddhist enlightenment, like that of the old cook, is nothing exotic and otherworldly. It's just living ordinary life – though in a way in which mind and body are unified, all together in the here and now. Dogen said, "[T]hink of neither good nor evil, right nor wrong. Thus, having stopped the various functions of your mind, give up even the idea of becoming a Buddha. ... *Zazen* is not 'step-by-step meditation.' Rather it is simply the easy and pleasant practice of a Buddha, the realization of the Buddha's Wisdom."[10] To become a Buddha, give up *wanting* to become a Buddha, and be one.

One of the most difficult and celebrated parts of the *Shobogenzo* is its discussion of *uji*, often translated "being-time." Time, Dogen proposed, is a series of discrete moments, and each moment also includes the state at that moment of the world's ever-changing forms. Each moment, one might say, is an encapsulation of that point in the space-time-matter continuum. Dogen mentions mountains, oceans, and a sixteen-foot statue of the Buddha. In each being/time capsule, time, matter, all that *is* in that moment, coexists as a unit, separate from past and future. Moreover, each unit exists in its motion, for time, while inseparable from being, *is* motion. You can't have matter that isn't moving (that is, not in time), or time without something in it to move. Time then really makes and *is* the universe. Different objects are, as it were, just different times.

Paradoxically, though only time exists, we know time and the universe as a present moment which simply *is*, complete in itself, having no bridge to past or future except those built by our desire-ridden clingings to memory, and the future-fantasies of our minds. Memory does not, of course, simply record everything in the past equally;

what we remember of our own past is like a story we are telling ourselves to explain who we are today. As Dogen was well aware, most of our memories are not the past as it really was, but selective images pulled out of the past by our attachments, conceits, and hatreds; and our fantasies of the future are probably even more off-base. The point of Zen is to eliminate these connections to past and future and to live wholly unified in the present.[11]

Some recent commentators have compared Dogen's "being-time" to concepts in modern existentialist philosophy or to Einstein's relativity theory. Such comparisons are not out of place; but we should not forget that in his own mind attachment to metaphysical games was no better than any other attachment. The real test is the connection of ideas to enlightenment and oneness in the midst of ordinary life.[12] It is worth noting that his term *uji*, literally "being-time" and so often translated, can also, if the same characters are read *aru toki*, simply mean "for the time being," or "now and then. ..." So Dogen sometimes used the expression. What this suggests is that everything is temporary, in continual flux and flow, and enlightenment means just to live for the time being with the whole mind and body, in the way things are right now, then let go.[13]

Muromachi Zen culture

The Ashikaga shoguns who replaced the Kamakura rulers came to power in this way. Emperor Go-Daigo (1287–1339, r. 1318–1339), more ambitious than most of his immediate predecessors, plotted to replace the Kamakura shoguns with direct imperial rule. A complicated civil war, with much switching of sides, ensued. In 1333 Ashikaga Takauji, supporting the emperor, decisively overthrew the Hojo "regents" and their forces to take Kyoto.

But soon the new conqueror had a falling out with Go-Daigo, who had unwisely refused to make him shogun. By 1335 open war broke out between Ashikaga, who proclaimed himself shogun, and Go-Daigo, who was forced to flee the capital. Ashikaga set up his own puppet emperor; from 1336–1392 two imperial courts existed, the so-called Northern Court of the Ashikaga's sovereign, and the Southern Court of Go-Daigo in the Yoshino mountains, now famous for their incomparable spring cherry-blossoms. (It is interesting to note, given the quasi-priestly character of the Japanese emperor, that this split in the imperial house was contemporaneous with the so-called Papal Schism in Europe, when rival popes reigned in Rome and Avignon, France, each with his own feudal supporters.)

The Ashikaga period, also called the Muromachi after the district of Kyoto where that house set up its palace, was troubled. After Takauji the Ashikaga shoguns were ineffectual rulers; the imperial schism was a sore point, and their power steadily drained away until some sixty regional warlords, as often as not fighting one another, had virtually free rein.

Nonetheless their day was a cultural high point, for the Ashikaga made up for political failure in patronage of the arts, above all those connected with Zen. Despite horrendous conditions outside monastery and palace walls, Zen culture reached its golden age under Ashikaga Yoshimitsu (1358–1408) and Ashikaga Yoshimasa (1435–1490; shogun 1449–1473). The latter withdrew from active political leadership as the terrible Onin war destroyed much of Kyoto in a dispute over his successor, retiring in 1473 to become the great architect of what is known as Higashiyama ("Eastern Mountains") culture. His residence, on the eastern side of Kyoto, faced the Higashiyama range. There he built the Ginkakuji ("Silver Pavilion Temple"; the famous Kinkakuji, or "Golden Pavilion Temple" was built by his grandfather, Yoshimitsu), encouraged Zen gardening, practiced the "tea ceremony," watched No drama, promoted Zen floral arrangement (*ikebana*), and painting.

Certainly Zen, especially the Rinzai school, was then the most influential Buddhist sect. Its monks were the most educated men of the society; while burning and killing raged outside, scholarship, including the beginnings of Japanese Neo-Confucianism as well as Buddhist philosophy, flourished in the five main Zen monasteries of Kyoto under patronage of the shogun – the *gozan* ("five mountain") system.[14]

Higashiyama styles of art have been greatly admired. They had about them attributes Yoshida Kenko would have loved: *sabi*, a feeling of being aged or antique, and *wabi*, the "poverty" quality of being simple, rough-hewn, imperfect, asymmetrical.

Figure 7.2 Ginkakuji ("Silver Pavilion Temple"), Kyoto (© cowardlion / Shutterstock.com)

Now the Zen eye saw these virtues stemming from the Buddha-nature in all things, even the most ordinary, best perceived when an object is most truly natural and itself. Let us look at a few of these arts in light of Zen.

Gardens

Any photographic album on the beauties of Japan will feature numerous shots of famous gardens. The observant viewer will quickly pick up certain distinctive characteristics. Unlike Western gardens, classic Japanese ornamental landscapes display no showy flowers, but only rocks, gravel, moss, grasses, and neatly-trimmed greenery, together with perhaps a stream and lotus-pond. Some, in fact, like the Ryoanji Zen garden mentioned in Chapter 2, are *kare-niwa*, "dry gardens," with no water or plants except moss. Moreover, these plants and other features are not lined up in geometrical rows or shapes as in a formal western garden, but paths seemingly wander and objects are scattered at random. Nonetheless, somehow the arrangement seems right and ultimately harmonious, just as the stars in the sky appear "thrown" and are not in straight lines or regular patterns (as an enthusiast of the Age of Reason once allegedly said God should have put them), yet we would not have it otherwise.

The point is that these gardens, like so much Japanese art combining both aesthetic and spiritual meaning, are neither raw nature nor human geometry, but rather like minimalist abstractions of nature. (The rocks can represent mountains, the raked sand waves surging against them, the moss and miniature *bonsai* trees fields and forests.) Meditating on them – and they were meant to be objects of contemplation – we penetrate in mind and heart to the essence of nature, and finally find the buddha-nature at its core. Too much clutter gets in the way of this focus, which is why the Zen arts all present things as they are, but with as little fuss as possible: a few sure lines in a painting, a turn of the head in No drama, a scattering of rocks and green in a garden.

Other transcendent signs also present themselves. The Taizoin garden of the Myoshin temples in Kyoto is one of the most pleasing and philosophical of Zen gardens. One enters it by passing between two rock gardens, one featuring vertical rocks, the other horizontal, representing respectively *yang* and *yin*. The garden-pilgrim then walks through landscaping from paradise to a lovely pond, where benches allow the entranced visitor to sit and meditate. One can imagine this final pond stands for the great Tao itself, the unity between all the polarities of *yin* and *yang*.

Tea

Talk of the celebrated *chanoyu* (literally, "hot water for tea") or "tea ceremony" logically grows out of talk of gardens, for the tea rite ideally takes place in a traditional garden, where the one obvious human artifact will be a tea house. It is set at the back of the mossy garden and is reached by stepping stones called the *roji*, "dewy path." The house is a simple, rustic structure of bare wood and plaster. The door is low, so guests however exalted must stoop to enter. The only ornaments are an *ikebana* or flower arrangement, and a *kakemono* or hanging scroll, both highly traditional.

While the tea ceremony may include a light repast and several kinds of drinks, its essence is the graceful making and serving of whipped green tea, a frothy liquid with a fresh astringent taste. Each guest in turn takes two sips from the large cup in which it is served, wipes the rim of the cup, and passes it on, commenting on the beauty of the bowl. The bowl and service should be elegant in the old, cracked *wabisabi* spirit, and is lovingly held by host and guests.

The tea ceremony can be virtually regarded as a Zen sacrament. Spiritually, the idea is to receive and appreciate the tea and the atmosphere by just being in the present moment, letting go of past and future and of anything outside the tea house. A true tea-maker prepares the services with the simple, graceful movements of a

Figure 7.3 Traditional Japanese tea ceremony. Note portrait of Daruma (Bodhidharma) on the *kakemono* in back (renfield kuroda; CC: Wikimedia Commons)

Father João Rodrigues (1562–1633), one of the early Portuguese Jesuits and one who attained an exceptional insight into Japanese culture, wrote that everything in the tea ceremony "is as rustic, rough, completely unrefined and simple as nature made it, after the style of a solitary and rustic hermitage," and the purpose of the rite "is to produce courtesy, politeness, modesty, exterior moderation, calmness, peace of body and soul without any pride or arrogance, fleeing from all ostentation, pomp, external grandeur, and magnificence."[15]

past master, like a dancer or musician who has endlessly practiced and accomplished a piece, and can perform it in a way that looks effortless and yet perfect, without a single wasted motion. To one for whom *cha* becomes *chado*, the "way of tea" as a way of life, that is how all of life ideally should be lived.[16]

Ikebana

The practice of artistic flower arrangement is considered another *do*, *kado*, the way of flowers. Like the others it has its own traditions of refined aesthetics, its hereditary masters, and its schools. In Japan mastery in any craft is admired, and excellence in one of the classic Higashiyama arts is seen as a sure sign of cultivation. While the arrangement of cut flowers may seem a relatively trivial skill in most cultures, in Japan it is taken as seriously as any other art, at its height possessing philosophical and spiritual significance as well as visual delight.

A flower arrangement may be seen as the smallest and most abstract of gardens, a garden indoors, the ultimate miniaturization of nature. Its principles are the same as the others: simplicity, asymmetry, and form considered more important than color. Styles range from the very old and elaborate *rikka* (standing) form to modern constructions that are often very free, "flowing," and highly imaginative, the floral equivalents of surrealism. Most popular and conventional is the Tokugawa-era *ten-chi-jin* (heaven-earth-man) style, which is expected to contain three elements, one high, one low, and one in the middle, representing these three constituents of the universe. Without ostentation, then, a bouquet of flowers can hint at mysterious inner meanings.

Painting

The form of painting most closely related to Higashiyama Zen was *sumie* or *suiboku*, ink-wash brushed on paper, treatments of nature or portraits of Zen masters. Ink is a difficult medium because it cannot be erased or covered over, and because it ideally does not employ color, calls for perfect control of fine gradations of shading; *suiboku* requires quick, deft, absolutely sure strokes. For this reason it is an excellent art for a

Zen adept, who is supposed to see the world just as it is with a buddha's eye, and be able to act without a second thought out of the center of his being.

The idea is to bring out the essence or buddha-nature of an object with a few elegant strokes, and as in the Chinese landscapes that inspired much of this art large areas may be left white, for the Unconditioned Reality of Nirvana lies directly behind all the world of appearances. Thus a bird on a bamboo branch may be a few upright lines and a shaded squiggle coming out of the Void, and a Zen worthy like Bodhidharma seem mostly big eyes and the suggestion of face and beard – but in those eyes an incomparable Zen combination of sternness and humor, like a firm teacher who knows he has to discipline his docents, but can hardly keep from bursting out in laughter at the cosmic absurdity of it all, since whether they know it or not they are all buddhas already.

No drama[17]

Few forms of drama are more subtle than the No plays of Japan. They are another product of Higashiyama culture. To the accompaniment of shrill flutes piercing the air, hand drums beating a complex rhythm, and strange (to Western ears) recitations like an eerie atonal chant, actors in hard white wooden masks move with slow, almost abstract gestures on a stage bare except for two traditional evergreen branches on low tables. The perfectly controlled movements, however, say more to the aficionado in a single movement or a tilt of the head than many players could express in a whole scene of talk and pacing. A turn of the face, and the casting of new shadows on the carefully carved mask, can bespeak love, aspiration, or despair. A movement of the hand is anger or fear, courage or cowardice.

No has been called a combination of Greek tragedy and liturgy: that is, it has the themes and earmarks of tragic drama, yet it is enacted in a stylized, symbolic manner embodying a society's deepest values and worldview, as would the worship of its religion. (Indeed, in the Tokugawa period No drama was regarded as the Japanese equivalent of the "rites" and "music" with which the well-tempered Confucian state was supposed to complement the ancient sage's philosophical and moral teachings.)

The major No plays, usually fairly short, lasting only about an hour, are about tragic themes, but like all great tragedy present them in a way which is moving and cathartic for the audience. Very often they are ostensibly ghost stories. They center on two characters. The first to appear, the *waki*, is likely to be a traveler bound on some mission that recalls haunted memories. He encounters a strange figure, the *shite*, who may be a *karma*-laden hero from the past, a woman enmeshed in hopeless love, or even a contemporary person, drawn to this place and time by some deep power or attachment whose hold has not released him or her. As the *shite* recites and dances with symbolic motions it slowly becomes clear that she or he is supernatural,

A No drama

In *Tsunemasa,* a Taira scion of that name, killed in the great sea battle of Dannoura, returns. The warrior is in the realm of *asuras* or titans for his many acts of violence but, poignantly, he is not a fighter at heart, but a lover of music and the lute. The emperor had asked that a lute which he himself had given to Tsunemasa be enshrined in a temple built in his honor. The *waki* is a priest dedicating that temple; during the ceremony a vision appears, a revenant in the brilliant court dress of a samurai, his face frozen by a small white mask bearing a quiet smile. It is Tsunemasa, drawn by the mention of his name, and when the lute is struck he has a few moment's respite from his suffering by performing a slow, hieratic dance to its notes. But soon he must lament that the horrible passions of the other realm to which he is condemned are rising with him, and he cannot stay. He vanishes, and the chorus sings the pathos of his fate.

coming to us from the other world for a brief time, but must soon return to the fate from which he cannot yet escape.

The greatest writer and theoretician of No was Zeami Motokiyo (1363–1443), patronized by Yoshimitsu. Zeami said that the main features of No were *monomane,* the "imitation of things" type of acting, good and important in its place, and the even more important transcendent quality of *yugen. Yugen* is almost beyond definition, but it suggests that sense of wonder, mystery, and almost shuddery awe that great drama, especially great tragedy, conveys – a sense that the depths of meaning in life are so profound they can hardly ever be fully probed, but whenever one truly looks into them, one can be touched by feelings well beyond ordinary emotion.

In No the ghost theme supports *yugen* with its sense of the unexpected and enigmatic. The issue is not, of course whether one believes in ghosts. In such abstract, dreamlike drama the specters could well just represent deep, half-forgotten memories or attachments, the depth-charges we all carry in our unconscious. Our inner ghosts are vehicles to bring to light the deepest conundrums of human life. In No they do so in the Zen way, through acting that is like a *suiboku* painting or a Zen garden: austere so that nothing but what is really important appears; skillful to the point that the maker or actor disappears into the meaning.

The martial arts

Quite another side to Zen is shown by its relationship to the so-called martial arts, and to the code of Bushido (a later term), the "Way of the Warrior," the values supposed to guide the samurai in life and death. *Budo,* the martial arts, are not exactly a creation of Zen, much less of Buddhism. But they came to be connected with that school in the Kamakura period, as the newly-powerful samurai class tended to embrace Zen, especially Eisai's Rinzai with his cultural as well as strictly religious interests, as their spiritual path. They liked to send their sons to Zen monasteries for training, and themselves found that *zazen* could help steel a fighting man for battle. Inevitably, then, the fighting skills and attitudes samurai practiced professionally came to be deeply entangled with the religion they professed, till it seemed that each side supported or expressed the other. To be sure, these warlike skills, taken as arts or exercises rather than means of shedding blood, can well demonstrate Buddhist concentration and Zen awareness.

The arts of *budo* take many forms. Some, such as *judo* ("the way of the gentle or weak"), *karate* ("empty hands"), and the modern *aikido* ("way of balanced spiritual energy") employ no weapons. As the names imply, they do not depend on physical strength or main force, but skill in using what force one has, often by turning the opponent's strength against himself.

Others, especially *kyudo*, "the way of the bow," and *kendo*, "the way of the sword," place an instrument in the warrior's hand. One of the most famous early books by a Westerner on Zen is Eugen Herrigel's *Zen in the Art of Archery*, describing the German disciple's study under a Japanese teacher of the art in the 1920s.[18] While Herrigel's accuracy on some matters has been questioned,[19] and the fact that he became a confirmed Nazi found disturbing, there is no doubt his book had a remarkable impact on Western awareness, especially European, of an approach to sport and skill entirely different from what many had taken for granted. What fascinated them was the idea that skill began with breath control, which in turn was based in meditation, and that when it came to shooting, the point was not screw oneself up by aiming anxiously and carefully, but rather to release the arrow with a kind of spontaneous intuition, almost casually, when something greater than the conscious mind knows the time and direction are right.

The way of the sword is no doubt the most important of all the martial arts, for the sword was the samurai's supreme weapon, the mark of his rank, forged with excruciating care, tested on a corpse, captive, or criminal due for execution, and considered virtually an extension of the wielder's arm. Training in the art of its use was a long and difficult process. It entailed unlearning as much as learning, for as with *kyudo* the point was to leave behind conscious effort and acquired skills. The adept cuts and thrusts with his sword without thought, instinctively, reacting or taking advantage of an opening before he would have had time to think. This gives him an insuperable advantage over an opponent who must think, however quickly, what move to make next.

The master's guidance comes not from the mind but from the *hara*, the center of energy just below the navel. Here is centered the *ki* (Chinese: *qi* or *chi*), that quasi-spiritual energy which is the real ally of all true proficients in the martial arts.

Like the Force in *Star Wars* (which is undoubtedly based on *ki* and the East Asian martial arts), it arises to be employed when one is first truly calm and centered, then totally alert to the moment and the environment in all directions, able to act without thought but with the flow of *ki*. The true warrior should raise his sword in a state of *munen*, "no thought," complete innocence. It is said that a trained swordsman can so intimidate just by his visage that he need not strike a blow; a lesser foeman will simply turn and run.[20]

Nonetheless, the ideal warrior was not afraid of death, for living in the moment he was to be non-attached to life or death. Indeed, that the way of samurai is death – to die nobly and honorably – was a byword. The manner of death should reflect no stain of dishonor, and such a death is the true warrior's constant concern. Given the Japanese preoccupation with what has been called "the nobility of failure," it would hardly be too much to say that dying honorably was, in theory and often in fact, more important than winning – and facing all the ambiguities with which the survivor of a battle must deal.

Bushido

All this was the realm of the celebrated code of Bushido, the way of the warrior and military honor, often invoked and extolled or, by the less well impressed, excoriated. (It derives as much or more from Confucianism and Shinto, and the universal warrior spirit, as Zen.) But for all that, Bushido is no single document or set of precepts. Although there have been, since the early Tokugawa period, books attempting to put it down in writing, they all have their own angle, and the way of the *bushi* (warrior) was talked about before then. The essence of Bushido can only be intuited or described in one's own way.

Nonetheless, a few principles can be given. First, Bushido meant total loyalty to whomever one owed loyalty, beginning with one's lord, extending to filial piety, and in modern times of course loyalty to the emperor above all. Second, Bushido meant being perpetually prepared for battle: alert, sword at the draw, ideally prepared with the Zen facility to act directly with *ki* out of the *hara*. Third, and perhaps most important of all, the *bushi* must always be conscious of death and prepared to die at any time, with no more concern for dying than for living.

The early eighteenth-century *Hagakure* of Yamamoto Tsunetomo (which exists in several versions), a classic Bushido text, says, "Meditation on inevitable death should be performed daily"[21] for "The way of the warrior is fulfilled in death." The warrior knows that sooner or later he will probably die violently, either in battle or if need be by *seppuku*, to atone for some wrong or to accompany his lord in death. To die in bed is far less worthy of the warrior. This mentality implies living simply, without attachment or pretense. It also means being as ready to kill as to die in the line of duty, without a second thought. "Once a warrior has made up his mind to

> One passage in the *Hagakure* faces the clash of values between Bushido and Buddhism directly. It says:
>
> > A warrior can take sword in hand and charge into the midst of an enemy's camp. But do you think a priest with a rosary in hand can crash through a wall of enemy spears armed with only love and mercy? This would require a great amount of courage indeed ...
> >
> > It is unseemly that they [priests] encourage warriors to follow the same path. This leads a warrior to follow two paths and turns him into a useless coward. Unless a warrior is totally committed to Bushido, he is of no consequence. Old men and retired warriors may follow the priest's path, but not active warriors.[22]

kill someone, he should charge straight in and kill him. ... The way of the warrior is direct and immediate."[23]

The *Kokutai no hongi*, a document issued by the Ministry of Education in 1937 to put forth what the then-dominant nationalists and militarists considered the essence of Japaneseness, showcased Bushido and spoke of "meeting death with a perfect calmness. ..." saying the warriors of old "tried to fulfill true life by way of death."[24] These values were deeply instilled in Japanese military training, including that of soldiers and sailors in World War II.

Bushido then could certainly mean, and often did, death by suicide – ideally the warrior's ritual *seppuku* or cutting open the belly with his sword[25] – if that was the only way of honor, or as we saw in the case of General Nogi, of *junshi*, accompanying one's lord in death. A few years after the *Kokutai no hongi*, in the Pacific War, *kamikaze* pilots exemplified these precepts in their suicide missions, as did thousands of Japanese troops who committed mass suicide in the so-called *banzai* charges rather than surrender.[26]

Later Zen

In the latter Ashikaga/Muromachi period and after, we can treat of Zen only through a few representative figures. But if nothing else, they show how lively, creative, and possessed of a rich inner life those truly transformed by Zen can be. Let's start with Zen's crazy man, the priest and poet Ikkyu Sojun (1394–1481).

Ikkyu

This individual was said to be the natural son of a nominal emperor (of the pro-Ashikaga faction in the split imperial house) and a court lady. But at the age of five he was placed in a Rinzai Zen temple, largely to keep him from being a pawn. Because of his birth and imperial infighting, being a prince could be a highly dangerous role in those days. He did not see his parents again, and became a monk, one recognized early for talent in music and verse.

Soon enough Ikkyu was exceptional in other ways as well. Refusing to take to ordinary monastic discipline, which his poems denounce in no uncertain terms for hypocrisy and stifling conformity, he developed a way of life entirely his own. During part of the year he would live as a monk, but in a hermitage of his own on monastery grounds, and the rest of the year would wander around the country, mixing with ordinary people, appreciating their pleasures. In the hermitage he followed with an eye of wonder the cycles and beauties of nature; while out and about he scarcely adhered to conventional Buddhist morality, but ate meat, drank wine, and enjoyed sexual encounters. Yet of all this he wrote powerful and impressively original verse – some of it highly erotic – which suggests that he directly saw and experienced something of the buddha-nature in the highest and lowest (by commonplace standards) of human life.

Even during his own lifetime people recognized that, though his way may not be for everyone, there was something authentic in this Zen eccentric. Neither he nor his powerful poems have been forgotten. To his own surprise and that of many others, he was selected to spend his last few years as abbot of the great Daitokuji monastery in Kyoto.

His preparation? Here is one of his hermitage poems:

> Who needs the Buddhism of ossified masters?
> Me, I've spent three decades alone in the mountains
> And solved all my koans there,
> Living Zen among the tall pines and high winds.[27]

And from the other side of life:

> With a young beauty, sporting in deep love play;
> We sit in the pavilion, a pleasure girl and this Zen monk.
> Enraptured by hugs and kisses,
> I certainly don't feel as if I am burning in hell.[28]

Basho

Another Zen poet was Matsuo Basho (1644–94), major creator of the *haiku*, the pithy 17-syllable (in Japanese) poem often associated with Zen that, in a few words, stabs an object down to its buddha-nature as surely as a *kendo*-master's sword, or captures it without comment like a garden or a *suiboku* painting. The ideal *haiku* sees with *mushin*, "no mind," all eye and no wordy interpretation. If something can be seen wholly and just as it is, *haiku* tells us, it speaks for itself without words beyond those which just make us see it.

Basho's first famous haiku:

> On a dry branch
> A crow settles –
> Autumn nightfall.

Not much is said – but we immediately feel the mood, see the darkening colors: black dead limb, black crow, dark time of the year, night coming. Note the "spring" in the last line, when the image suddenly jumps from a particular branch and bird to something much larger, even cosmic: autumn and night. This is a vital switch that makes a *haiku* "work" well; so is the more conventional seasonal allusion good *haiku* are supposed to have.

We have already read Basho's most famous poem, about the frog jumping into the old pond, as well as another about summer grasses and warrior's dreams. Here is a further Basho poem, which I have translated a little more freely:

> It's the first day of spring.
> And already, because my thoughts are lonely –
> Autumn nightfall.

Basho was probably often lonely. Though as a boy he was page to a young samurai, with whom he had a close and friendly relationship, when his lord died suddenly in 1666, Basho entered a monastery. But, like Ikkyu, he did not stay there, undertaking a life of wandering, studying, practicing Zen in temples, writing travel narratives and scribbling poems about what he saw and felt.[29] As the *Lord of the Rings* says, "Not all who wander are lost."

Hakuin

Zen artist, formulator of the Rinzai *koan* system, and remarkable autobiographer, Hakuin (1685–1768) was also a popular preacher with a large following. From the beginning he showed signs of a special religious destiny. As a young boy, he recited long sutra passages from memory, and meditated on the transitoriness of all things as he watched passing clouds. One day, his mother, a devout Nichiren Buddhist, took him to hear a preacher who expounded on the agonies of hell. The boy was so terrified he ran out of the temple, physically shaking. A bath his mother had made a little too hot made him no less fearful of the infernal fires, and he had to be calmed down. Finally, at age fifteen, he was able to enter a Zen monastery, a longtime dream goaded by religious aptitude and hell-fear.

At twenty-four, Hakuin had his first breakthrough. He had been working on the *koan* "Mu." ("Does a dog have the buddha-nature?" Answer: "Mu! [Nothingness, the Void, the All]") He experienced what he called the Great Doubt, and it was as though he was "frozen solid in the midst of an ice sheet extending tens of thousands of miles." Then he heard the temple bell ring, and he felt transformed, as though "the sheet of ice had been smashed." All his former doubts vanished.[30]

Finally, at thirty-two, Hakuin experienced what he considered his decisive enlightenment. He said that in a dream his mother came and presented him with a purple robe of silk. The sleeves seemed very heavy, and he found that in each of them lay an ancient mirror. As he looked into them, each revealed to him his inner nature. One reflected all the world, mountains and rivers, and the great earth; the other was apparently pure and shining, like the Void. He now understood, he said, the saying, "The enlightened person sees the buddha-nature within his eyes."[31]

Hakuin described the journey to enlightenment in terms of three stages: the Great Doubt, the Great Death, and the Great Joy. He organized the *koans* in sequence, so that Zen students could progress through them in order of difficulty. He lived in poverty among the peasants, sharing their life. As an evangelist, he taught that direct knowledge of truth is open to all, even the lowliest, and he also emphasized that a moral life must go along with spiritual practice.

He himself devised the most famous *koan* of all, the sound of one hand. (Two hands clapping make a noise. What is the sound of one hand?)[32]

Kyoto School

Mention should also be made of the twentieth century academic philosophy known as the Kyoto School which, inspired chiefly by Zen, endeavored to create a modern Japanese way of thought in interaction with Western existentialists, such as Martin Heidegger, and other philosophers. Principal figures were Nishida Kitaro (1870–1945) and Nishitani Keiji (1900–1990).[33]

Overseas Zen

Zen has had a distinctive social and cultural impact outside of Japan. Among Westerners, the influence has taken two forms, which Alan Watts, in the jargon of the 1950s, labeled "Square Zen" and "Beat Zen."[34] The former represents those who have followed formal Zen practice, doing *zazen* and *koan* work, with a master in one of the centers which have sprung up outside Japan. The First Zen Institute of New York was established by Sokei-an in 1930.[35]

Many more centers opened after the World War II, some started by former Allied occupation soldiers who, once in Japan, had come under the spell of Zen, as they discovered the beauties of its gardens and temples in the land of the erstwhile enemy. The postwar Zen vogue also included "Beat" Zen, the spirituality embraced by those of the "Beat" writers, like Gary Snyder and Jack Kerouac, who (mainly inspired by the writings of D. T. Suzuki, R. H. Blyth, and Alan Watts[36]) identified with the old sages they called "Zen lunatics," like Ikkyu or Basho. In a decade of conformity, they saw in Zen a spiritual path for rebels against convention, who wandering freely watched the world through poet's and artist's eyes. A great classic of this type is Kerouac's novel, *The Dharma Bums*, the semi-autobiographical story of his and his comrades' freewheeling life in San Francisco and environs.[37]

Though not always a polished writer, Jack Kerouac was capable of lines which explore the mysteries of Mahayana Buddhism as well as any Eastern sutra. Here are two sentences from *The Dharma Bums* about sleeping outdoors in the southwestern desert:

> The silence is so intense that you can hear your own blood roar in your ears but louder than that by far is the mysterious roar which I always identify with the roaring of the diamond of wisdom, the mysterious roar of silence itself, which is a great Shhhh reminding you of something you've seemed to have forgotten in the stress of your days since birth. I wish I could explain it to those I loved, to my mother, to Japhy, but there just weren't any words to describe the nothingness and purity of it.[38]

Key points you need to know

- Zen intends an experience of inner freedom based on *zazen* and interviews with a *roshi*
- The tradition formed in China around the legend of Bodhidharma
- Eisai and Rinzai Zen emphasized *koan* work
- Eisai also brought Neo-Confucian works and tea to Japan
- Dogen, an important philosopher as well as Zen teacher, and his Soto Zen taught quiet sitting
- Dogen also emphasized Zen in the midst of ordinary life and work
- The Ashikaga period was a time of civil war but also of significant cultural development, much of it associated with Zen
- Higashiyama or Ashikaga-period Zen arts include gardens, tea, ikebana, painting, and No drama
- The martial arts and Bushido also came to be associated with Zen
- Later Zen poets and teachers included Ikkyu, Basho, and Hakuin
- In the West, Zen is represented in a number of practice centers and also in the work of writers like Gary Snyder and Jack Kerouac.

Questions for study and discussion

1. What would you say is the essence of Zen experience?
2. What is a *koan* and what is its purpose?
3. If Zen is "a special transmission outside the scriptures," why is there so much formality connected with it?
4. Describe the life and work of Eisai.
5. What was Dogen's greatest concern?
6. Why did Zen appeal especially to the samurai class?
7. What do all the Zen-related arts have in common?
8. What is Bushido and how would you characterize its relation to Zen?
9. Try writing a few *haiku*.
10. Give your interpretation of the course of Hakuin's life.
11. Why did Zen appeal to many in the "Beat Generation"?

Further reading

Arai, Paula Kane Robinson, *Women Living Zen: Japanese Soto Buddhist Nuns*. New York: Oxford University Press, 1999.

Barnhill, David Landis, trans. *Basho's Journey: The Literary Prose of Matsuo Basho*. Albany, NY: State University of New York Press, 2005.

Besserman, Perle, and Manfred Steger, *Crazy Clouds: Zen Radicals, Rebels, and Reformers*. Boston, MA: Shambhala, 1991.

Dumoulin, Heinrich, *Zen Buddhism: A History*. 2 vols., New York: Macmillan, 1990.

Heine, Steven, *Dogen and Soto Zen*. New York: Oxford University Press, 2015.

Hoover, Thomas, *Zen Culture*. New York: Random House, 1988.

Hoover, Thomas, *The Zen Experience*. New York: New American Library, 1980.

Kapleau, Philip, *The Three Pillars of Zen*. Garden City, NY: Doubleday, 1980.

Sanford, James, *Zen Man Ikkyu*. Chico, CA: Scholars Press, 1981.

Suzuki, D. T., *Essays in Zen Buddhism*. New York: Grove Press, 1984.

Suzuki, D. T., *A Manual of Zen Buddhism*. New York: Grove Press, 1960, and other works.

Waddell, Norman, and Masao Abe, trans. *The Heart of Dogen's Shobogenzo*. Albany, NY: State University of New York Press, 2002.

Electronic Resources

Wikipedia, "Japanese Zen." https://en.wikipedia.org/wiki/Japanese_Zen

"The Rinzai Zen Community." www.rinzaizen.org (Official site.)

"The Soto Zen Buddhist Association." http://szba.org (Official site.)

Metropolitan Museum of Art, "Muromachi Period (1392–1573)," *Heilbrunn Timeline of Art History*. www.metmuseum.org/toah/hd/muro/hd_muro.htm

"7 Japanese Aesthetic Principles to Change your Thinking." www.designprinciplesftw.com/collections/7-japanese-aesthetic-principles-to-change-your-thinking

Ken Bolt, "Zen Garden History and Defining Characteristics." http://feelingsandflowers.com/255/zen-garden-history-and-defining-characteristics

"Ikebana International." www.ikebanahq.org/whatis.php (Site of a leading ikebana organization.)

"What Is Sumi-e?" www.sumiesociety.org/whatissumie.php (Site of a leading sumi-e or ink-brush painting organization in America.)

"Noh Theater." www.japan-guide/e/e2091.html

Wikipedia, "Budō." https://en.wikipedia.org/wiki/Budō (Links to articles on the major martial arts.)

"Reflections on Ikkyu." http://emptyskysangha.org/ikkyu.htm

"Hakuin Ekaku (c.1685–1768)." http://blog.shambhala.com/2013/08/15/hakuin-ekaku-c-1685-1768

Alan Watts, *Beat Zen, Square Zen, and Zen.* http://enlight.lib.ntu.edu.tw/FULLTEXT/JR-ADM/watts.htm (Text of this influential booklet.)

8   *Christ and Confucius*

The West arrives, and then Japan turns inward

In this chapter

The situation in Japan during the *Sengoku*, or country at war, period will be surveyed in this chapter, including religious responses such as the rise of militant Buddhist groups, new Shinto ideologies, and pilgrimages. Then, wholly unexpected, came Western visitors and Christianity. We will examine the impact of that new religion, and the condition of Japan in the subsequent Tokugawa period, when the nation was largely sealed off from the rest of the world.

Main topics covered

- The Country at War period
- Three warlords
- The coming of Christianity
- The Tokugawa peace
- A Neo-Confucian society
- Peasant philosophies
- Shinto revival
- Popular Shinto and the Ise *mairi*
- Religion and popular culture

The Country at War period

Let's go back to the Onin War of 1467–1477. Call it a suitable catastrophe with which to begin examination of the tumultuous events that wrenched Japan into the modern world. This terrible and almost pointless struggle devastated the capital, Kyoto, ending what peace there had been under the weak Ashikaga shoguns.

The conflict began with rivalry between two powerful houses, the Hosokawa and Yamana. They were in dispute over their respective candidates for successor to Ashikaga Yoshimasa, he who had withdrawn from government to live as a Zen aesthete. The fighting soon spread from Kyoto throughout the countryside, as various clans lined up with one side or the other. It all ended in stalemate, with Yoshimasa finally naming a compromise heir. But by then the Bakufu was virtually meaningless, the reclusive ruler's edict barely extending beyond his elegant estate.

That ruinous warrior rampage was only the beginning of a period known in Japanese history as *Sengoku*, "warring states," when real power lay with the many local *daimyo* or feudal lords. With no central restraint, each built up strong military bases and fought freely against the others for spoils and territory, or for the sake of "honor." Nor were the proud *daimyo* themselves secure: it was also the period of *gekokujo*, "inferiors overthrowing superiors." Retainers took power from their masters, lesser branches of a house usurped the greater, and commoners, even peasants, asserted themselves against their usual state of oppression in *ikki*, uprisings, often mounted under religious banners.

One example we have noted was the *Ikko ikki*, the Jodo-Shinshu army of peasants and low-ranking samurai. Hungry and embittered, with the *nembutsu* on their lips and emblazoned down their flags, these legions of Amida took over provinces and established fortresses. In such chaotic times, closely-knit, well-organized religions that provide identity and support to the vulnerable are likely to be notably successful. As we have seen, Rennyo (1415–1499) of Jodo-Shinshu well understood this. He stood with the faithful in persecution. In response to dangerous times, he organized *ko* or associations of believers; these not seldom evolved into *Ikko ikki* armies.

The Hokke or Nichiren school likewise gained adherents for its adamant, uncompromising faith in the Lotus despite persecution, and on at least one occasion fielded its own *Hokke ikki* force (see Chapter 6, note 19). On the other hand, the hegemony of the older denominations of Buddhism, Shingon and Tendai, declined through their loss of support by any viable central government, and perhaps on a deeper level because of the need in such times for strong, simple faith rather than esotericism, or broad, comprehensive world views embracing many paths.

In the fifteenth and sixteenth centuries pilgrimage to holy places grew in popularity despite the confusion, or perhaps even because of the unsettled times. When one is nearly as safe on the road as at home, and supernatural aid seems the only hope, why not set out with the pilgrim's staff? Famous shrines of Kannon attracted columns of petitioners from across the country. Mount Fuji, the spectacular volcano visible from much of central Japan, began to draw thousands of hardy climbers who found its ascent spiritually renewing. Perhaps most significantly of all, the Ise Daijingu, once restricted to the prayers of the imperial family, now turned around to become one of the most popular of all places of worship for Japanese of every class. That was because the priesthood of the Grand Shrine, responding to loss of support in those troubled times from the ruling house, promoted mass pilgrimage in compensation.

On another level, the growing appeal of Ise gauges a perceptible increase in the strength of Shinto in the late Middle Ages. Buddhism was discredited in some eyes

Figure 8.1 Mount Fuji (© Vacclav / Shutterstock.com)

as either corrupt or too sectarian. The old Nara and Heian schools now appeared to critics to be only shadows of their former selves whether in spiritual, intellectual, or political integrity; Zen was, despite exceptions like Ikkyu, too close to the inept Ashikaga shoguns; and the new mass movements, Pure Land and Nichiren, seemed, to the unenthused, mere fanaticism.

Certain of the old Shinto priestly houses, especially at Ise, tried to seize the day. They encouraged the establishment of local Ise *ko*, or support groups, who would support pilgrimages led by *oshi*, or guides, to the Grand Shrine. Often *ko* members pooled their resources to send individuals or families selected by lot each year. On the intellectual side, in a thirteenth-century work called the *Shinto Gobusho* (*Shinto Five Books*, inspired by the Five Books of Confucianism), theologians like Watarai Tsuneyoshi (d. 1339) and Watarai Iyeyuki (d. ca. 1355), of the Watarai family (who were priests of the Ise Outer Shrine), labored to develop doctrines for the religion separate from the Buddhism with which it had usually been merged. Their school, called Ise or Watarai Shinto, shows Taoist and Confucian influences instead; it held that the *kami* are all manifestations of a universal Way, and that the *kami* religion's central virtues are purity and honesty. By stressing Japan's role as a uniquely divine nation and the symbolic importance of the imperial house and regalia, Ise Shinto gave ideological support to the Emperor Go-Daigo's effort to annul the shoganate and rule directly.

Yoshida Kanetomo (1435–1511), priest of the Yoshida shrine in Kyoto, taught a more esoteric form of Shinto called Yoshida, Urabe, or Yuiitsu Shinto. Developing elaborate genealogies and hierarchies of the *kami*, his school declared that the shrine-gods represented the primal nature of the universe and – turning the former Buddhist-Shinto lore on its head – claimed it was the buddhas and bodhisattvas who were conditioned manifestations of spiritual forces, and the *kami* the originals. On a practical level, Yoshida and his house, as officials in the Jingi-kan or imperial shrine office, did much to organize shrine associations and rankings to help them maintain their place in the disturbed society of a country at war. At the same time, a dramatic new factor was about to enter the political and religious world of Japan.

The warlords and the coming of Christianity

The Sengoku ended with the successive rule of three great warlords, each of whom managed to emerge above all other lords to unify Japan under a single authoritarian government in his day. They were Oda Nobunaga (1534–1582), Toyotomi Hideyoshi (1537–1598), and Tokugawa Ieyasu (1543–1616). Each was a man of strong individual character, and each had a distinctive attitude toward religion.

Nobunaga, a cold, ruthless warrior, generally hated religion. To him monks and believers, with their armies, were nothing but particularly devious and contemptible obstacles to his total dominion. It was he who, in the process of bringing all Japan under his sway, slaughtered the monks of Mount Hiei and burned their temples in 1571, and who received the surrender of the *Ikko ikki* in 1580.

Ironically enough, it was also during Nobunaga's heyday that a totally unexpected new politico-religious force arrived in Japan: Europeans and with them Christianity. The great age of European expansion and missionizing had begun. Across the globe, from the Americas to the Indies, visitors without invitations were planting new flags and beside them the cross, symbol of a new faith.

The first Westerners to arrive in the war-torn country of Japan were Portuguese sailors shipwrecked off Kyushu in 1543. Soon enough, St Francis Xavier arrived with a party of fellow Jesuits in 1549. The Jesuits and Portuguese traders brought faith and firearms, both of which greatly interested Nobunaga and other *daimyo*. The Jesuits wanted first to convert the samurai class, starting at the top if possible, rightly seeing they were a wedge: if the rulers went over to Christ, the ordinary people would follow.

In this venture they were initially successful. Some lords and not a few others were baptized; by the death of Nobunaga, less than thirty-five years after the missionaries first came, as many as 150,000 Japanese were Christians. Nobunaga was not among them, although he seemed more sympathetic to the foreigners and their creed than to the despised native Buddhists. Indeed, he reportedly said of the missionary followers of the one-time soldier Ignatius Loyola, "These are men I like: upright, sincere, and who tell me solid things."[1] In part, of course, he saw the new religion, and those *daimyo* who had gone over to it, as counters to the political power of the Buddhist establishment.

However, a deeper affinity between Jesuit and samurai can be discerned as well. Both were men who lived by the demands of total loyalty and dedication to a cause greater than themselves, who admired simple living, self-sacrifice and a high sense of honor, who each fought to the death in his own way and by his own code. Even Japanese who were not of samurai rank, in those days of so much political and religious turmoil, could admire guests who, though of another faith and nation, seemed to embody the best of the Japanese spirit.

At the same time, the Jesuits did their part to facilitate the crossing of boundaries. They took the trouble to learn the Japanese language and culture, to promote trade with the Portuguese as advantageous both to Japan and the foreign merchants, and to adapt as best they could to Japanese society. Catholic Christianity did have a profound spiritual appeal for many Japanese in the sixteenth century, who once they had accepted the faith were prepared to adhere to it to the end with true samurai resolve: if it were not so, there would not have been so many Christian martyrs a little later.

The Jesuits reciprocated the feeling, in turn finding much to admire in their hosts. Francis Xavier's own words of praise for the Japanese have often been quoted:

> I do not think you will find their match among the pagan nations. They are very sociable, usually good and not malicious, and much concerned with their honor, which they prize above everything else … They have one characteristic which is not to be found in any part of Christendom: however poor a noble may be … they pay him as much honor as if he were rich.[2]

The visitors' Iberian culture, with its own high view of honor and nobility, may be speaking here as much as Christ. Nonetheless, the Jesuits and the Japanese were a good fit. But more was to come.

He who lives by the sword will die by the sword, it is said, and so it was with Nobunaga, who died quelling a fairly minor rebellion in some of his own following. He was succeeded by his most brilliant general. Hideyoshi, sometimes compared to Napoleon, though no less sanguinary than his master, was a more varied person. Despite his military reputation, he was a small man with an almost comically monkey-like face, and of peasant rather than samurai antecedents. But he had clawed his way to the top, was a brilliant strategist, and ready to complete Nobunaga's work. Then he could, and would, live life his own way.

By 1590 Hideyoshi had unified the country, and turned his attention to making up for his disadvantaged background. With almost endless resources now his, he built palaces marked by lavish architecture, with an almost un-Japanese extravagance of red and gold ornamentation. The greatest was at Momoyama, just outside Kyoto, and it is after it his age is sometimes named. At the same time, he tried to educate himself secretly, liked to perform in No plays, and studied the tea ceremony with Sen no Rikyu, considered the greatest master of all, and as we have seen noted for his emphasis on extreme simplicity and naturalness – the opposite of Hideyoshi's values in other areas

Figure 8.2 Castle in the Momoyama style (© KPG_Payless / Shutterstock.com)

of life. (There was eventually a falling out between them.) Hideyoshi was a complex man of many contradictions, not least in his attitude toward Christianity.

At first this dictator seemed complacent toward religion, without the vindictiveness of Nobunaga. He allowed Tendai, Pure Land, and Nichiren groups to become active again, and remained on cordial terms with the Christians. Then, suddenly, in 1587, he turned against the missionaries in an edict forbidding their activities; why is not entirely clear, but it is likely he came to fear the faith's growing power. However, the foreigners became more discreet, and the edict was not enforced. During the 1590s, in fact, Hideyoshi embarked on a fruitless attempt to conquer Korea; of his two principal generals, one was a Christian, the other a Nichiren Buddhist.

Then, in the wake of that disappointing venture, Hideyoshi again rejected Christianity, and this time the results were more serious. The ruler seems to have had advice that, as the example of the Philippines and the Americas made clear, missionaries were not seldom followed by European regiments and colonial governors. He also no doubt believed that Christian *daimyo*, and perhaps even the independence of character that some Christians showed in their loyalty to a power greater than the state, might present centers of opposition. Moreover, by this time Spanish Franciscans had joined the Portuguese Jesuits in Japan. The two orders often quarreled and disparaged the other to their Japanese hosts; the rivalry was unedifying, creating a negative impression of their whole church. The twenty-six martyrs of Nagasaki described in Chapter 2, both European and Japanese, both

Franciscans and Jesuits, perished on crosses at Hideyoshi's order in February of 1597. Hideyoshi himself died the following year. Christians were given a short respite as power shifted, after some vicissitudes, to the third great warlord, Tokugawa Ieyasu.

Tokugawa Ieyasu (1543–1616), the most powerful of Hideyoshi's *daimyo* supporters, had emerged on top of his rivals in 1600 after the great battle of Sekigahara; he was soon appointed shogun. Interestingly, it was in the same year, 1600, that another portentous event took place: a Dutch ship arrived, a strayed member of a fleet of five that had set out from Rotterdam for the Indies via the New World. One member of the crew was from England. He was Will Adams (1564–1620), the first known Englishman to see Japan.

He and his Dutch companions were unlike the other Europeans the Japanese had met so far. They had red hair and blue eyes, or at least were so caricatured in pictures. Moreover, they were Protestants, not Roman Catholics like the Spanish and Portuguese and, in those days of bitter religious conflict in Europe, not adverse to warning their hosts about the insidious plots of which Iberian Catholics, above all priests, were capable. At the same time, the North Europeans, themselves laymen, showed no interest in missionizing; their only concern was trade.

The new shogun, Tokugawa Ieyasu, was much taken by these visitors, above all with the capable Englishman, who taught him and his men the latest European technology in such skills as shipbuilding and cannon-making. In turn, Ieyasu made Adams a *daimyo* and gave him an estate, together with a wife. Adams' letters, the earliest first-hand accounts of Japan in English, provide an interesting outsider's picture of Japan in his twenty years as friend of the shogun.[3]

Ieyasu entertained yet another European visitor in those years. Don Rodrigo de Vivero y Velasco, former Spanish governor of the Philippines, was shipwrecked in Japan in 1609 on his way back to his homeland via Mexico, and was received by the shogun, with Adams as his mentor. The Spaniard described the Tokugawa ruler as "a stout, heavily built old man between sixty and seventy years old, with a most dignified bearing and a pleasing expression."[4] Vivero did have certain petitions to make, however: that Catholic priests be allowed the same freedom in Japan as Buddhist, and that Spanish trading ships be welcomed. Contradicting the North Europeans' biases, he informed the shogun that it was actually the Dutch, enemies of Spain and no better than pirates, who ought to be kept far away from Japan.

Ieyasu responded diplomatically, saying he was pleased the Spaniard had asked nothing for himself, only "for his God and his king." But after the ex-governor had sailed on from Japan, in a ship Adams built, little changed. Persecution only progressively sharpened against Catholics, and trade with Manila was now in Japanese ships, not Spanish.

As for the Dutch, they became the shogun's favorite Europeans, the one Western window in his draconian wall of exclusion. By 1641, after being increasingly restricted, the other troublesome Europeans had been completely expelled. Only the

Dutch, and the Chinese, were allowed to maintain trading stations. Both were on Deshima, an artificial island in Nagasaki harbor, where one Dutch ship arrived each year bearing European goods – including, influentially, books on the latest science and technology, though the Hollanders were too circumspect to include religious works in their stock. From 1641 until 1853, Deshima was Japan's one link with the non-Asian universe.

The Tokugawa peace

After well over a century of almost constant conflict between power-hungry warlords, Japan was ready for peace, and the Tokugawa were ready to impose it. For their two-and-a-half centuries, if not quite the well-regulated, clockwork society its masters envisioned, Japan was without external war and suffered only internal disturbances. With peace came, as it usually does, relative prosperity despite famine years, and considerable cultural creativity. However, poverty and unrest in the countryside only grew worse as the years advanced, even as the commercial sector became more and more prosperous.

It was not a time of peace for Japan's remaining Christians either. The Tokugawa regime, alarmed by news of European expansion, desirous of a society without significant internal dissent, and determined that Japan must cut itself off from the rest of the world, enacted increasingly harsh decrees against Christianity, until by 1623 the religion was subjected to unspeakably cruel persecution. Christians were tortured until they recanted or died, and were forced to spit or stamp on crucifixes. (In 1637 a rebellion broke out in Shimabara in Kyushu, a Christian stronghold, but it was finally suppressed.) Some Christian families remained faithful, however, throughout the long Tokugawa era; when missionaries finally returned in the mid-nineteenth century, they found *Kakure Kirishitan*, "Secret Christians," who, without priests, had kept alive sometimes garbled versions of the Lord's Prayer, the Hail Mary, and the Creed, and who worshiped by such ingenious devices as placing a crucifix behind a Buddhist image.

Buddhism itself was organized and controlled by the Tokugawa government. Each family was required to have membership in a Buddhist temple. Every temple, in turn, was made a branch of a well-regulated major temple, like Mount Koya in Shingon, Mount Hiei in Tendai, the two Honganji in Jodo-Shinshu, or their major auxiliaries, which trained and supplied priests for the local level. Japanese Buddhism had no geographical divisions of responsibilities, like the diocese or district in many Christian churches; each priest and local temple looked to its main temple for guidance and, if need be, the resolution of difficulties.

By this process the new Kamakura schools, like the Pure Land and Nichiren sects, were "tamed" and placed under central authority. At the same time, the Tokugawa ordinances meant that Buddhism now was at least a nominal part of the life of every village and family. Even Zen broke out of its mold to become more widely popular in the wake of renowned preachers like Hakuin or poets like Basho. However, the real "religion" of the Tokugawa regime, though the House formally embraced Pure Land, was Confucianism. It is clear that, during the Tokugawa centuries, Buddhism held steady while Shinto and Confucianism grew in influence.

A Neo-Confucian society

In medieval China, a new school of Confucian philosophy arose. It continued the ancient sage's humanistic emphasis on a harmonious social order and the realization of one's true inner nature as the supreme good. But, influenced by Taoist and Buddhist thought, the tradition now took on a more metaphysical cast. What ultimate view of nature, and of humanity, best led to true humanism and the good society? According to Zhu Xi (1130–1200), the leading Neo-Confucianist, the key is the discovery and contemplation of *li* (Japanese, *ri*) or fundamental principles. Everything has its own *li*, and it is from the supreme *li* of heaven (*tenri* in Japanese), earth, and humankind that all else derives. The second most important Neo-Confucianist, the idealist Wang Yangming (1472–1529), considered the *li* to be ultimately in the mind.

Either way, Neo-Confucianism had definite political and social implications, for it envisioned a coherent cosmos in which the nature of ultimate reality, the universal *li*, is expressed reflexively in society and the human individual. These two are not at odds, but ultimately harmonize; an individual's *li* is that of his or her place in the social order. The human family functions well when everyone moves harmoniously in accordance with his or her true inner nature, as though in a great dance. One's true inner nature, and that of the universe, can become known through self-discipline and clear-eyed introspection, and the wise person will undertake self-examination.

The fundamental Neo-Confucian social idea, then, was that the order of human society is natural, no more and no less than a part of the natural order of the cosmos. One can no more change society than one could change the laws of nature. Acceptance of one's role – parents over children, husband over wife, older brother over younger brother; one's social rank and one's duties as a subject of the state, with mutual obligations all around – is simply like accepting gravity. To reject them is to go against nature, which can only bring dire consequences.[5] This perspective was highly congenial to the Tokugawa Bakufu in its desire for peace and stability after a time of troubles. Confucianism as interpreted by Neo-Confucianism was its official ideology. But enough variations in interpretation and schools of thought (some at odds with the official ideology) appeared to make for a yeasty intellectual life.

Hayashi Razan (1583–1657) was the Tokugawa court teacher favored by the shogunate as an official advisor. His family became hereditary heads of the Confucian academy in Edo. A close follower of Zhu Xi, Hayashi taught that the universal *li* – which became for him almost monistic, like a universal essence behind all appearances

– is inherent in nature, yet must be cultivated in humans, in the sense we must realize the universal consciously in our true nature. When this is correctly done, society creates itself after the right order. Yet each person will act with the sense of freedom that comes from doing what is truly natural to that person. (One could no doubt also see, in such a realization of one's true social nature and role, the product of a system of education and social organization built to create powerful but voluntary inner constraints.) At the same time, Hayashi vehemently criticized other views, such as those of Buddhism, Taoism, and rival schools of Confucianism like that of Wang Yangming.

The last had his own school in Japan. Its chief figure was Nakae Toju (1608–1648), who said that one should act by the mind or will and its intuitions; the *li* are not external, but are ways by which the mind understands and categorizes the world.

Other Confucian thinkers were in the Kogaku ("Ancient Learning") tradition, which challenged Neo-Confucianism by endeavoring to go back to earlier Chinese sources, to Confucius himself or even before. As might be expected, these scholars were less mystical and more this-worldly, even materialistic. Yamaga Soko (1622–1685), for example, taught that the universe is without beginning or end, changing eternally through the flux of yin and yang. Human nature is neither good nor bad; actions must be guided by both self-interest and the common good. Nonetheless, Yamaga is most famous for his military concerns and his codification of the ethics of Bushido, the "Way of the Warrior," based on *giri*, or irrevocable obligation and loyalty. (Falling out of favor with the shogun, he was exiled to the castle of Lord Asano, where he instilled the latter's samurai with that sense of loyalty which was to lead nearly fifty of them to avenge their lord in the famous episode of the forty-seven *ronin*.)

Ito Jinsai (1627–1705) proposed that the universe is basically energy, and all is in a continual process of change. Everything then is naturally good, for action is good. Death is the only bad change, but death does not really exist, for the universe is a living being, and what we call death is only a change in status of a tiny part of that universal and immortal organism. The great virtue is humaneness, expressed by love.

Ogyu Sorai (1666–1728) was more pessimistic. Like the ancient Chinese school called Legalism, he was more concerned with how to regulate society than how to let it freely follow *li*. The Tao, or universal flow, is not in nature but was created by the philosophers; in other words, it is a social construct, and the way to truth is not through reason or the contemplation of *li* but through the study of history. We discern what is socially good through experience and learning the lessons of the past, not through speculation.

The Tokugawa regime, believing it was following nature and reinforcing earlier precedents, divided society rigorously into four classes: samurai, peasants, craftsmen, merchants. This was theoretically in order of their comparative importance and productiveness; after the ruling class came the farmers, since they were the obviously highly productive sources of sustenance for all; merchants, traditionally looked down on by Confucianists, were lowest since they only dealt in goods produced by

The forty-seven *ronin*

In 1701 the Asano *daimyo* was provoked by an insult from one of the shogun's corrupt counselors, who had not received an expected bribe, into drawing his sword within the Edo palace. The visitor, quickly condemned, was compelled to take his own life; his estate was confiscated. Forty-seven of his retainers, now *ronin* or masterless samurai, vowed to avenge their lord. This led to a long intrigue, which included the leader of the *ronin* immersing himself for a time in the pleasure quarters of Kyoto in order to throw off suspicion. In the end vengeance was satisfactorily taken. The colorful story clearly lent itself well to drama, and was immortalized in the *kabuki* and *bunraku* play *Chushingura*, and in many other media down to the present.

others. In fact, in Tokugawa times the peasants were by far the most impoverished and exploited class of all, while many merchants did extremely well, supporting religion and religious arts among other indulgences. The government tried to enforce sumptuary laws to keep them from flaunting their wealth at the expense of the proud but less-fortunate samurai, but this only led them to patronize the brilliant worlds of art and theater that made Edo famous.

The samurai class in the Tokugawa period had an anomalous role. What does a warrior do when there is no war, but he must remain true to his class? Government jobs were insufficient to go around, and the fighting-man generally did not deign to enter trade. Many samurai fell into genteel poverty and, worse, idleness. This condition led, on the one hand, to a self-idealization of their samurai role, incarnated in innumerable Kabuki plays and books like Yamaga's summarizing the values of Bushido.[6] On the other hand, soldiers who feel under-employed and under-appreciated can be a difficult element in any society. Certain samurai, tiring of their subordinate and empty lives under the Tokugawa, came to be among the most active critics of the shogunate, instrumental in its replacement by imperial restoration.

Peasant philosophers

In the Tokugawa era, philosophy also reached the popular level. The burgeoning merchant class, and even the peasants, welcomed teachings that reinforced the virtues of loyalty, hard work, family, and community basic to their lives. Tired of religious corruption and conflict, like their contemporaries in "Age of Reason" Europe and America they were ready for enlightenment grounded in those values together with tolerance, respect for the natural order, a somewhat secular perspective, and a nascent sense of the possibility of progress; Voltaire, Benjamin Franklin and these Japanese moralists were roughly contemporary.

Rangaku

A significant subsect of Tokugawa thought was called Rangaku, or "Dutch Learning." It was based on the scientific instruments, and especially the books, brought by Dutch ships to Deshima. Teaching themselves the Dutch language, even in their isolation a few open-minded scholars acquired remarkable knowledge of Western geography, astronomy, medicine, history, and scientific technology. This "learning" was by intent entirely secular, though as we shall see that in itself can raise religious questions, and furthermore something of the role of Christianity in Europe managed to slip in.

The position of the Rangaku scholars in Japan was usually uncertain. Some thoughtful officials appreciated the new information and technology they procured. Others found "Dutch learning," so much at odds with traditional Chinese and Japanese views of the cosmos, unsettling and likely to lead people to ask unwelcome questions. Some Rangakusha suffered exile or worse. It might be said that, in the Japanese context, Rangaku was an opening wedge for religious and philosophical skepticism in the modern hard-headed scientific sense. As one shogun sympathetic to Rangaku, Tokugawa Yoshimune, put it in 1720:

> People of the red-hair country customarily do things by mental reckoning and by reason; they only use implements they can see; if a fact is not certain, they do not say so, and they do not make use of it.[7]

In Japan as in Europe and America, some pragmatic modernizers were content to keep matters on this level. Others were profoundly disturbed at the implied receding tide of faith.

Shingaku ("Heart Learning" or "Mind Learning") founded by Ishida Baigan (1685–1744), pulled together several stands. He was heavily influenced by the *Warongo* (*Japanese Analects*), a Shinto text published in 1669 as an offshoot of the *Shinto Gobusho* and Ise Shinto. The *Warongo* saw the *kami* through Neo-Confucian eyes, as pure mirror-like beings without beginning or end, to be worshipped with sincerity no less pure. The native gods were themselves the source of buddha-nature, so prior to Buddhism.

Ishida's school thus encouraged worship at Shinto shrines, but based its ethics on Neo-Confucian concepts of cultivating the original purity of mind. Ishida also inculcated proper regard for the social order and its laws, seeing them as a part of the natural order of which human nature is an expression. However, he perceived all classes and occupations as equal, declaring that the merchant living off his merchandise is no different from the samurai living off rents from his rice fields; Shingaku was sometimes call the "Way of the Merchant."[8]

Ninomiya Sontoku (1787–1856) was known as the "peasant sage." Like Franklin, he had a practical side. He vigorously strove to improve the quality of rural life through teaching countrymen how to budget, plan, and cooperate. Philosophically, his fundamental idea was *hotoku* ("returning virtue"), a concept emphasizing the individual's dependence on the larger units of nature and human society, and our obligation to honor that interdependence.

Life, he said, means cooperation. It calls for returning good in gratitude for good received, from the human family, and from the universe itself. At the same time, Ninomiya stressed the value of hard work and the dignity of labor; he wanted to give farmers a sense of pride in their occupation, and to let their diligence be an example for all. While not a radical reformer, he helped spark a desire for a more equitable social order in which those who labor are given a fair portion of respect and reward.[9] (Ninomiya's ideas and impetus are clearly in the background of the nineteenth century "new religions," which emerged out of the same rural milieu as his earlier audiences.)

The renewal of Shinto

Another side of the religious ferment just beneath the surface in Tokugawa Japan was a revival of Shinto, on both intellectual and popular levels. For one thing, this was the result of a perception that Buddhism, now quiescent after the earlier upsurge, was corrupt and out of touch. For another, it was because supporting Shinto, which could hardly be attacked directly because of its association with the sacred imperial institution, was one relatively safe, if indirect, way to protest the authoritarian Tokugawa regime. For yet another, it was a way of affirming nationalism amid increasing awareness of an outside world.

Intellectually, the major Shinto revival school was now Kokugaku ("national [i.e., Japanese] learning"). It carried on the heritage of Yoshida and Watarai Shinto, and laid the foundations of later nationalistic thought. Kokugaku's leading lights were Kada Azumamaro (1669–1736), Kamo Mabuchi (1697–1769), Motoori Norinaga (1730–1801), and Hirata Atsutane (1776–1843). Advocating a rejection of everything foreign, including Buddhism and Confucianism (which set them at odds with the Bakufu), the Kokugakusha called for a return to the ancient ways of the *Kojiki* and archaic Shinto rites, including direct imperial rule.

Perhaps influenced by Taoism, like Laozi they felt that with a recovery of primordial simplicity, virtue would come of its own, without need of Confucian ethics. At the same time, through their study of ancient texts, these schoolmen made immense contributions to Japanese linguistics, historical study, and religious thought. Motoori's painstaking scholarly work on the *Kojiki*, the *Tale of Genji* (on the basis of which he called *mono no aware*, "sensitivity to things," the fundamental Japanese quality), and other texts, was seminal to all subsequent understanding of ancient Japan. Kada Azumamaro wrote detailed accounts of the Daijosai, which were initially suppressed by the Bakufu on the grounds they revealed sacred secrets. Kamo Mabuchi made an especial study of the *Manyoshu*, the earliest major poetry collection, in which he saw the true ancient Japanese spirit revealed.

Hirata on the other hand wrote Shinto theology which showed the influence of Dutch learning, and thus of Christian and Western scientific books. But Hirata turned Western science on its head to serve Japanese nationalism and the revival of Shinto. He argued that Copernican astronomy proved the superiority of Shinto myth, for did not the fact that the earth actually revolves around the sun show the Japanese had been right all along in honoring Amaterasu, the sun goddess and ancestress of the Japanese people, above all other *kami*?

Such thoughts were congenial to another party of Tokugawa-era nationalists, the Mito School of scholars, named after the town northeast of Edo where their academy was located. Producers of a monumental history, the *Dai-Nihon-Shi* (*History of Great Japan*), which glorified the role of the emperor, they emphasized Japanese uniqueness. They said in effect, "Let's take what we can learn from the lessons of European history, but not let it change Japan's special character."

Aizawa Seishisai, one of its prominent figures, wrote in 1825 that while Christianity was evil and the Western barbarians should be exterminated if they ever reached Japanese shores, nonetheless we should understand why Christianity had made the West so powerful in relation to Japan. That was because belief in one God helped a nation unify under one ruler, to whom people were obedient as unto God. Church and state should be one in Japan as well. Therefore, he urged, Shinto should be made into a national faith under an emperor who conjoined the roles of sovereign and high priest, and in which the sun goddess was worshiped like the Christian God.

As misinformed as its views may have been about Western realities, the Mito school, both through the bias of its *Dai-Nihon-Shi* and views like those of Aizawa, provided the ideological foundations of the Meiji Restoration's imperial monarchism. As Ian Buruma has indicated, apparent conservatives like those of Mito were also, in a real sense, Westernizers and modernizers: they simply wanted to borrow a totalitarian side of modern Europe that, as the twentieth century was to prove all too well, was certainly there along with everything else.[10] Their ideal was to make Japan strong enough to take its place in the modern world while remaining true to its own culture.[11]

Then came the *Bakumatsu* ("End of the Bakufu") period, the crisis leading up to the Meiji Restoration, when Shinto shrines were centers of pro-imperial, anti-shogunal activism, on occasion even proclaiming miraculous signs on behalf of the cause.

Pilgrimage to Ise

Turning to popular Tokugawa-period Shinto, very interesting is the mass *Ise mairi*, or pilgrimages to the Grand Shrine of Ise. These occurred, apparently spontaneously, about every sixty years starting 1650. Pilgrimage to Ise was always popular in those days; usually the great majority of travelers on the Tokaido road running south from Edo would be Ise-bound. By all accounts these wayfarers were light-hearted, with every intention of enjoying the journey and the merry inns along the way as well as praying at the Grand Shrine, for Shinto was by no means a religion demanding only serious intensity.[12]

Yet once in a while something special would break out: an *okage-mairi*, "Pilgrimage under divine grace." Rumors would sweep the country that Ise amulets, or a sacred sword, or even silver coins, were falling from heaven. Then, in a kind of mania, whole households and businesses would depart overnight for Ise. Children might leave without notifying their parents and without provisions. The lively apprentices of Edo would just disappear, on a *nuke-mairi*, "secret pilgrimage," perhaps leaving a note saying, "Gone to give thanks." Inns were jammed; the procession reminded one observer of an endless line of ants. In April and May of 1705, 3,620,000 worshipers were said to have come to Ise.[13]

While probably not conscious on the part of most ordinary pilgrims, it is possible there was a political meaning to these mass surges to the shrine of the imperial ancestors parallel to the Kokugaku and Mito resuscitation of imperial thought, as well as an understandable urge to take a vacation from the humdrum of daily life in a hardworking society. These great journeys of faith were, significantly, to Ise, to the shrine of the ancient imperial goddess. No such pilgrimages ever besieged the Toshogu, the garish shrine in Nikko to the spirit of Tokugawa Ieyasu, built at extravagant public expense by his successors – though this shrine and temple complex is now a favorite of tourists, who are especially intrigued by its famous three monkey bas-relief, hands over eyes, ears, and mouth: "See no evil, hear no evil, speak no evil."

Religion and popular culture

How was religion represented in Tokugawa cultural life? Sometimes visibly, sometimes not, for like eighteenth-century Europe, Japan under the last shoguns seemed on the surface to be mainly devoted to secular delights, in reaction against the stormy religious scenes of earlier times. Take the Genroku period, 1688–1704, considered the absolute apex of Edo culture, epitomized by Kabuki; *ukiyo-e*, "floating world pictures" of the passing scene, including studies of actors and famous beauties; and *bunraku* puppet theater.[14] We can here mention only three Genroku-era writers whose work in different ways evokes the spirit of the times: Basho, the Zen haiku poet, discussed in the chapter on Zen; the novelist Ihara Saikaku; and the writer of *bunraku* dramas, sometimes called the Shakespeare of Japan, Chikamatsu Monzaemon.

The enormously popular Ihara Saikaku (1642–1693) was not a religious writer, but rather a how-we-live-now story-teller who said he was tired of nature and cherry blossoms, and wanted to display instead the life of the worldly, pleasure-seeking, now-prosperous great cities, of the merchant princes who made them go and the demi-monde of actors, geishas, footloose artists, and hangers-on they supported. The titles of his erotic picaresques like *Koshoku ichidai otoko* (*The Life of an Amorous Man*, 1682), and *Koshoku gonin onna* (*Five Women Who Loved Love*, 1686) say it all.[15] But in his later work, especially *Nihon Eitaigura* (*The Eternal Storehouse of Japan*, 1688), we see the darker side of a society devoted to money and the pleasure it buys; with both humor and bitterness, Saikaku depicts the battles of townsmen to make fortunes, the despair of those who fail and cannot pay their bills, and the struggle of others just to keep afloat.[16] In all this there is doubtless a spiritual message the Buddha would have understood.

Chikamatsu Monzaemon (1653–1725) wrote Buddhism more explicitly into his dramas, though usually in a highly conventional and sentimental way; that in itself bespeaks his times. Take for example *Shinju ten no Amijima* (*The Love Suicides at Amijima*, 1720) about the love between a whining, weak paper-seller named Jihei (who has a wife and children) and a prostitute, Koharu. Though there is little to admire in them, through the magic of his art Chikamatsu manages to make us believe in the reality of their love. At the end, when they are caught, they determine to commit suicide together. The narrator, to the twanging strings of the *samisen* (a banjo-like instrument), tells us that the sincerity of their love may have won the pair rebirth together, from a single lotus-blossom, in the Pure Land.[17]

Town and country

Now let us glance at rural popular religion. Life in the countryside during the Tokugawa period was hard. As always, crops and weather were uncertain, and domain lords collected heavy taxes. Sometimes hunger forced peasants into such extreme expedients as infanticide or selling daughters into prostitution. Or, driven to desperation, peasants rose up in resistance, even though reprisals were often harsh, entailing torture, execution, exile.[18] Folk plays based on these events often portray resistance leaders as heroes who knew what the cost would be, but believed the benefit to the community would in the end be worthwhile. In Japan, there is a long tradition of figures from samurai to peasants who face certain defeat, and usually death, for the sake of honor and justice. Something in the Japanese character is capable of responding to them even more than to successful heroes; the historian of Japanese literature Ivan Morris has summarized this theme in a book entitled *The Nobility of Failure*.[19]

Times of year came when village people enjoyed themselves as well. Then as now, New Year was the biggest of all annual celebrations. Small pine trees were brought down from the mountains and set up at household gates. *Omochi*, round rice cakes, were made, eaten, and offered to *kami* of hearth and granary, and to the ancestral spirits inscribed in the family Buddhist altar. In the snowy north, as we have seen, strange masked intruders might appear at the door, like tricks-or-treaters, frightening children until given refreshments.[20]

At village shrines throughout the year, festivals for seed-time, mid-summer, and harvest as well as New Year provided occasion for the local *kami* to welcome his or her *ujiko*, parishioners, to a day of festivity. Processions, dancing, contests, and a carnival atmosphere would enliven the mood. Fertility dances, explicit and obscene by Western standards (and for that reason now seen only in the most remote parts of the country) might be enacted in spring festivals by young men from the best families. All would watch the ribald performances with amusement and in the hope their energy would help the crops to flourish.

The major popular, village-level Buddhist event was, and still is, the previously mentioned *obon* dances held in July. This festival, imported from China, marked a time when it was believed the souls of the dead returned to earth. The dances were performed to welcome and entertain them: graceful processional and circle steps, done by men and women alike, to the accompaniment of flute, drums, and samisen. Buddhist priests would also chant sutras and present food offerings. (Notice how Shinto and Buddhism harmonized, each dealing with its own sphere: the *kami* were concerned with fertility and the turn of the seasons, the buddhas with the state of the dead and their return.)

Urban Buddhism had its popular centers too. One example is the Asakusa temple to Kannon in Edo (Tokyo), then as now in the heart of a popular entertainment district always overflowing with people looking for traditional amusements. As often as not fun-lovers may slip into the temple for a change of pace, perhaps muttering a prayer to the goddess and then returning to the street, for she is very much at the heart of easy-going Asakusa. In the view of a scholar like Nam-lin Hur, the parallel realms of entertainment, drama, and religion were not far apart in traditional Japan.[21]

The most sacred image of this temple, allegedly dredged up already miraculously carved by fishermen back in the reign of the Empress Suiko (592–628), is what is known as a *hibutsu* or "secret buddha," a figure so numinous that it is not revealed at all, or perhaps (as at Asakusa) only once a year, when the temple would inevitably be thronged with awe-struck worshipers. In Edo alone, we have records of several great exhibitions a year of special images of Kannon besides Asakusa.[22]

Significantly, perhaps, the Asakusa Kannon temple was adjacent to a temple to Benten (or Benzaiten), the only female deity among the often-portrayed Shichifukujin or "Seven Lucky Gods," to be described later. Benten was not as great as the mighty Kannon, but as a patron of literature, art, and happiness, usually depicted playing a *biwa* or Japanese lute, she was popular, above all among entertainers and their devotees. These gods of fortune, favorites with the affluent mercantile classes, grew in popularity in the Tokugawa era.

Popular Buddhism was lively. Many of the special devotions, displays of *hibutsu* and other powerful images, and pilgrimages around circuits of temples which kept believers and contributions coming into famous sanctuaries, were doubtless organized by priests with one eye on the ledger, but nevertheless they testify to widespread if often shallow spiritual yearning. Images of Amida and Shaka (the historical Buddha) or of some such relic as the Buddha's tooth, or the staff of Kobo daishi, would also be put on display from time to time. These would be heralded by banners, posters, and much promotion by the clergy, and toward the sacred showing would come, in the words of a contemporary, "a continuous stream of people in succession like ants seeking sweets."[23]

Many colorful religious figures might be seen along the Tokaido leading south from Edo toward Ise and Kyoto, and not only Ise pilgrims. Engelbert Kaempfer, a doctor attached to the Dutch facility at Deshima, in his highly informative *History of Japan*, based on observations made in 1691, tells of a number of them.[24] He rather liked the *bikuni*, begging nuns, who for a few coins would sing songs and otherwise entertain passers-by; though they shaved their heads, they were not always as devout as might be expected. One could also see on city street corners (though Kaempfer does not mention these) *komuso*, mendicant monks playing flutes, with the head of each covered by a basket, completely concealing his identity. It was said this was to enhance egolessness; some also alleged it was because they were samurai out of favor with the regime, who did not want to be recognized, or conversely that they were spies.

Most intriguing of all to Kaempfer were the *yamabushi*, mountain priests of the Shugendo order. Long-haired, roughly but colorfully dressed, these strong and vigorous men went along pounding the ground with huge staffs, iron rings attached to them rattling, sometimes blowing trumpets made of large shells that produced an explosive sound.

So was Tokugawa Japan, for all its surface appearance of order and peaceful stability, alive with diverse intellectual and spiritual movements just below the surface. Official Confucianism was there, so also were half-subversive kinds of Shinto, poetic Zen, sentimental Pure Land, and even mountain priests seeming to have stepped out of the archaic past.

Key points you need to know

- Japan was torn by internal warfare during the fifteenth and sixteenth centuries
- Christianity first arrived in 1549 and was initially successful, but began to be persecuted at the end of the century, to be finally extirpated for the most part
- During the Tokugawa period the official philosophy was Neo-Confucianism, but registration at a Buddhist temple was required, and a revival of nationalist Shinto (Kokugaku) laid a foundation for later nationalism
- Popular Tokugawa religion included mass pilgrimages to Ise, visits to temples of Kannon, and in the countryside *obon* dances and New Year celebrations.

Questions for study

1. During the Sengoku ("Country at War") period, why was there a revival of Shinto and what were its characteristics?
2. What was Oda Nobunaga's attitude toward religion?
3. Why did many Japanese initially accept Christianity in the sixteenth century?
4. Why did Japan's leaders later turn against Christianity?
5. What kind of influence did the Dutch have on Japan?
6. What was Buddhism like during the Tokugawa period, both institutionally and on the popular level?
7. Discuss the main themes of Tokugawa Confucianism, distinguishing between different schools and authorities.
8. What was the message of popular Confucian teachers?
9. What were the major objectives of Kokugaku Shinto thinkers?
10. What was the role of Ise in Tokugawa Japan?
11. Describe village-level popular religion in this era.

Further reading

Bellah, Robert N., *Tokugawa Religion*. Glencoe, IL: Free Press, 1957.

Boxer, C. R., *The Christian Century in Japan, 1549–1650*. Berkeley, CA: University of California Press, 1967.

Burns, Susan L., *Before the Nation: Kokugaku and the Imaging of Community in Early Modern Japan*. Durham, NC: Duke University Press, 2003.

Cooper, Michael, *They Came to Japan: An Anthology of European Reports on Japan, 1543–1640*. Berkeley, CA: University of California Press, 1965.

Earl, David Magarey, *Emperor and Nation in Japan: Political Thinkers of the Tokugawa Period*. Seattle, WA: University of Washington Press, 1964.

Harootunian, Harry D., *Things Seen and Unseen: Discourse and Ideology in Tokugawa Nativism*. Chicago, IL: University of Chicago Press, 1988.

Hibbett, Howard, *The Floating World in Japanese Fiction*. New York: Oxford University Press, 1959. [an anthology of Tokugawa fiction]

Matsumoto, Shigeru, *Motoori Norinaga, 1730–1801*. Cambridge, MA: Harvard University Press, 1970.

Nosco, Peter, *Remembering Paradise: Nativism and Nostalgia in Eighteenth-Century Japan*. Cambridge, MA: Harvard University Press, 1990.

Ooms, Herman, *Tokugawa Ideology*. Princeton, NJ: Princeton University Press, 1985.

Smith, Robert J., *Ancestor Worship in Contemporary Japan*. Stanford, CA: Stanford University Press, 1974.

Smith, Warren H., *Confucianism in Modern Japan*. Tokyo: Hokuseido Press, 1973.
Vaporis, Constantine Nomikos, *Voices of Early Modern Japan: Contemporary Account of Daily Life During the Age of the Shoguns*. Boulder, CO: Westview Press, 2013.

Electronic Resources

Wikipedia, "Ikkō ikki." https://en.wikipedia.org/wiki/ikkō-ikki

"Ise Shinto," *Encyclopedia of Shinto*. http://eos.kokugakuin.ac.jp/modules/xwords/entry.php?entryID=594

"Christianity," *Japan Guide*. www.japan-guide.com/e/e2298.html

John E. Van Sant, "Rangaku Medicine and 'Foreign' Knowledge in Late Tokugawa Japan," *Southeast Review of Asian Studies*, Vol. 34 (2012), pp. 207–14. http://www.uky.edu/Centers/Asia/SECAAS/Seras/2012/17_Rangaku_Medicine.pdf

"Confucianism in the Edo (Tokugawa) Period." www.willamette.edu/~rloftus/neoconfucianism.html

Kallie Szczepanski, "The 47 Ronin." http://asianhistory.about.com/od/japan/p/47ronin.htm

Michael Hoffman, "Japan's 'Hidden Christians,'" *The Japan Times*, Dec. 23, 2007. www.japantimes.co.jp/life/2007/12/23general/japans-hidden-christians/#.vw411su37tR

Robert N. Bellah, address at "Symposium on the 270th Anniversary of the Founding of Shingaku: Shingaku and Twenty-first Century Japan" (Oct. 15, 2000). www.robertbellah.com/articles_4.htm

"The Kokugaku (Native Studies) School," *Stanford Encyclopedia of Philosophy*. http://plato.stanford.edu/entries/kokugaku-school/

Wikipedia, "Mito Domain." https://en.wikipedia.org/wiki/Mito_Domain

"Asakusa," *Japan Guide*. www.japan-guide.com/e/e3004.html

Shousei Suzuki, "The Ise Pilgrimage." http://web.japan.org/tokyo/know/pilgrimage/ise.html

"Chikamatsu Monzaemon (1653–1725)." www.washburn.edu/reference/bridge24/Chickamatsu.html

9 *The rising sun and the dark valley*

From the Meiji Restoration until 1945

In this chapter

This chapter will look at the background and course of development of the Meiji Restoration of 1868, especially in terms of its religious impact. We will then see how the extreme nationalism and militarism of 1930–1945 emerged, and consider the ideologies that underlay it.

Main topics covered

- Religious aspects of the Meiji Restoration and its background
- Shinto and imperial ideology in the Meiji period
- Meiji Buddhism and Christianity
- The "Dark Valley" ideology and its spiritual dimensions, especially modern "emperor worship" and Bushido
- The role of Shinto, Buddhism, and Christianity in wartime Japan.

Behind the Meiji Restoration

Was the Meiji Restoration a religious event? That depends on how one regards the role of religion in human life. It is possible to consider changes in religious consciousness as fundamental, deep-level motors in history. One can also argue for rivalry over economic or political power as the real force, and say religious partisanship is no more than a mask, or after-the-fact rationalization, for such very human drives. Or it may be, as is more likely, that history is fueled by a complex mixture of faith and fortune-hunting, and moreover that the engine driving each individual "player" may run on a different ratio of these energies.

In the first half-century after 1800, the Tokugawa shogunate seemed to be getting more and more hidebound and unresponsive, as one might expect from a regime that had been in power more than two centuries. Economic problems and discontent in the countryside mounted, but the government had no new ideas on how to cope. Most serious of all, steadily increasing Western presence in East Asia beset a regime made for another time. Britain defeated ancient China in the notorious Opium War of 1839–1842, changing the balance of power in the East. The major powers all rushed in to demand commercial and missionary rights in both reclusive empires, China and Japan. Foreign intrusion on this scale, abetted by nineteenth century technology, was something for which Japan was unprepared, and the Bakufu was at a loss as to how to react.

Matters reached a new level in 1853, when the "Black Ships" of Commodore Matthew Perry of the United States arrived in Uraga harbor demanding a treaty. Refusing to obey Japanese orders to leave, Perry declared he would deliver documents sent by President Fillmore to the shogun by force if necessary. Eventually, on March 31, 1854, recognizing they had no alternative, the Japanese signed a treaty granting minimal concessions and opening the door for further agreements in the future. They were quickly compelled to make similar treaties with other Western powers. "Round-eyes," in the form of consular officials and commercial agents, made their appearance on Japanese streets.

Japan was polarized by these dramatic and unwelcome developments. The imperial court of the Emperor Komei adamantly opposed giving the foreigner any toehold in the sacred land, and in this he was, at the time, supported by such powerful *daimyo* as the Lord of Mito (patron of the academy of such staunch nationalists as Aizawa) and by a number of fiery young samurai – their cry was *"Sonno joi!"* ("Revere the Emperor; expel the barbarian!") The southern fiefs of Choshu and Satsuma were especially hosts to such pro-imperial and – in view of Bakufu accommodationism – anti-shogunate sentiments. By 1864 the situation had deteriorated into sporadic civil war between the two sides.

Between two worlds

The Bakumatsu ("End of the Bakufu") era, roughly 1853–1868, was difficult. The uncertainty that hung in the air, together with hard economic times and civil warfare, produced what by some accounts was a strange yet almost playful end-of-the-world mood in popular culture, when nothing seemed to matter anymore. The shogunal government lost authority; the old religious institutions, Shinto and Buddhist, seemed no better able to respond to the crisis. Popular Japan was caught up in what Robert J. Lifton described as a "revolutionary immortality" mood, which often goes with radical changes in society. Then ordinary time seems to stop in a reversal of all structures, as though the world were being turned upside down.[1]

In 1867, at the very end of the old regime, Ise *taima* or talismans were reported falling in many places. In the last of the great *okage-mairi* mass pilgrimages to Ise, many thousands thronged the roads to the Grand Shrine amid disorder suggestive of a minor apocalypse. Women dressed in male garb and men in female attire. The pilgrim parades often turned into the *ee ja naika* (roughly, "anything goes") dances frequent in the period, when hungry and dispossessed people would dance chanting into the homes of the rich to take what they required. But we are also told that at Ise coins were thrown about as though money had no more meaning, and frenzied or comic music and dance went on day and night, people forgetting time and value in scenes beyond description.[2] One is not surprised to realize it was in this era, or just before it, that several of the major "new religions" of Japan, such as Kurozumikyo, Tenrikyo, and Konkokyo, first emerged, for times of social stress and rapid change often produce new revelations and new faiths.

Then, in 1866 and 1867, following unexpected deaths in Edo and Kyoto, the embattled nation suddenly had both a new shogun and a new sovereign, the fifteen-year-old Meiji taking the imperial throne. (Indeed, the almost simultaneous deaths of the ineffective Tokugawa Iemochi, only twenty, and the implacable emperor were so unexpected questions have been raised as to whether that of Komei, at least, was natural.) Imperial radicals seized the palace early in 1868 and declared restoration of direct imperial rule, the Meiji *ishin*. More fighting followed, but the forces of restoration soon prevailed; by now the country was ready for a new start of some sort.

In the meantime, the largely young and restless imperial party had changed. The more they saw of the Westerners – and some had even secretly traveled to Europe or America – the more they realized Japan could no longer simply retreat into insular fantasy. The cry was now not just *Sonno joi*; it was also *Bunmei kaika*, "Civilization and enlightenment," meaning Japan must match the rest of the world in these respects. And, the Meiji restorationists would add, equal it in industrial and military strength. Only then would Japan's unique culture be safe.

Yet the ideology of nationalistic imperialism was still alive as well. The Japanese emperor, now freed from the trammels of the shogunate, sun-descended and divine sovereign for ages on ages undying, would legitimate by his sacred mystique that which must be done to modernize the nation and make it a mighty world power. Thus, on the one hand, the new government would move to enhance Shinto, as the religion which ultimately validated imperial rule, through its imperialist mythology and its court and national rites; on the other hand, fresh leadership would update Japan by importing the latest Western learning and technology. It was an unstable mix, and one that in the end would lead to disaster. But in the Meiji era it seemed to work.

Constructive traditionalism was fairly common in the nineteenth century, especially in monarchical settings. Many cultures were torn between rapid social and technological change on the one hand, and a need to idealize the past on the other, as a sort of nostalgic compensation, and to suggest that present rulers still represented legitimacy and an ancient heritage even as they presided over change. Consider the vogue for King Arthur and chivalry in Victorian England, or for the Wagnerian Teutonic past in Wilhelmine Germany, both not disconnected with cults of empire and of the gentleman, or the hero.[3] At the same time many "medieval" or "ancient" rituals were likewise revived in both church and popular Western culture including, in England and North America, the virtual reinvention of Christmas, Valentine's Day, and Halloween as holidays. So was Shinto imperialism in Meiji Japan also.

The old and the new

On April 6, 1868, an imperial edict announced the restoration of various imperial Shinto rites, often from the *ritsuryo*,[4] that had long been in abeyance under the shoguns. The official position was that these rites helped restore the ancient concept of *matsurigoto*, or *saisei itchi*: government and (Shinto) religion as one inseparable unity. To some extent that amounted to what has been called the "invention of tradition," the creation or revival in a disproportionate way of myths, customs, rites, and attitudes from the distant past so as to legitimate present institutions.[5]

The next day, April 7, came the much more famous "Charter Oath" or declaration of five guiding principles by the young emperor, proclaimed to the accompaniment of exclusively Shinto rituals. They deserve to be cited:

1. Deliberative assemblies shall be widely established and all matters decided by public discussion.
2. All classes, high and low, shall unite in vigorously carrying out the administration of affairs of state.
3. The common people, no less than the civil and military officials, shall each be allowed to pursue their own calling so that there may be no discontent.
4. Evil customs of the past shall be broken off and everything based on the just laws of nature.
5. Knowledge shall be sought throughout the world so as to strengthen the foundations of imperial rule.

The democratic mentality suggested by the first three was, needless to say, not always honored, and the fourth principle clearly left much to be defined and debated. The fifth, however, quickly became a guiding theme in Meiji life. Just as, much earlier in the Nara period, young Japanese had gone to China to gain both the technical and spiritual knowledge that enabled Japan to catch up with the great continental civilization, so now – with China itself stagnated and deeply humiliated – they fanned out to Europe and America. They returned with what it would take to run railroads, build factories, form an army and navy able to face down any other power, administer a modern state and discuss the latest philosophies, whether pragmatism or idealism, with fellow scholars in either of the Cambridges (England and Massachusetts), or Paris or Berlin. As for the Westerners' religion, Christianity, that was a more complex issue which will be discussed a little later. For as we have seen, although Christianity might seem – and was seen by some – to be basic to Western civilization, at the same time the whole Westernizing enterprise rested on the restoration of ancient Japanese imperial Shinto for its theoretical justification.

In fact, the new Meiji government went through a rapid and rather confusing (both to us and people at the time) series of false starts and changes of course in religious policy. At first a revitalized government Shinto department, under a shifting series of names, was established, and it appeared that Shinto was being aggressively promoted as the state religion. Government-sponsored teachers were sent out to indoctrinate the people in Shinto, with special emphasis on the divine origin of the imperial line.[6] At the same time, Buddhism was forcefully separated from Shinto (*shinbutsu bunri*):

Figure 9.1 The Meiji Emperor Mutsuhito (Harper's Monthly, September 1876. © Stocksnapper / Shutterstock.com)

Buddhist priests were no longer allowed to serve in shrines, and the symbols and images of one religion were not permitted in the houses of worship of the other, to extirpate any hint of *honji suijaku* (*kami* as Japanese manifestations of buddhas). In a reversal of Tokugawa policy, families were required to be registered not as members of a Buddhist temple but with a Shinto shrine. In some places, inflamed by the slogan *haibutsu kishaku* ("abolish Buddhism, destroy Shakamuni"), mobs attacked priests and temples.

This phase, however, was at its height only 1869–1871. By the early 1870s, the government recognized that extreme reactionary and anti-Buddhist policies were non-productive for at least three reasons: Buddhist priests and many laypeople were by now aroused in all their potential political strength and prepared to campaign against *haibutsu*; the government's real concern was modernization, not religious quarrels; and the Western nations were pressuring Japan to prove its commitment to "enlightenment and civilization" by meeting Western standards of religious freedom.

Indeed, Jason Ananda Josephson, in *The Invention of Religion in Japan*, has pointed out that this confrontation forced Japan to define religion, and the several strands of Japanese religion, in ways that had never been required before.[7] As we have seen, traditional Japanese did not even have a word or concept meaning anything like the modern western understanding of "religion" or "a religion" as a distinct component of culture or national life separate from custom, government, and all else. The need to do this did not always produce precise results, and led to issues remaining down to the present.

By the end of 1871 a new Daikyoin (Ministry of the Great Teaching) was set up to administer both faiths and to teach a combined Shinto and Buddhism, with strong Confucian overtones, as a unified Japanese religion. The Kyobusho, or Board of Religious Instruction, was established in 1872 to present ethical education that abandoned exclusive emphasis on Shinto and, it was hoped, conjoined all religions in a single higher outlook. Nonetheless shrines and temples were still kept distinct, with their separate priesthoods and without *honji suijaku* doctrines or admixture of symbols. But this apparent combining of religions also produced largely negative reactions, and lectures by the national teachers were poorly attended. In 1875 the Daikyoin was abolished, and the Kyobusho in 1877. Direct interference by the Meiji government in religion ended for the time being.

Shinto remained a key part of state policy on the ideological level, particularly in regard to the imperial institution. The constitution of 1889, in force until 1945, granted the Japanese religious freedom, "within limits not prejudicial to peace and order and not antagonistic to their duties as subjects." This charter established an elective parliament, but made clear that in theory its purpose was merely to assist the "sacred" and "inviolable" emperor who had promulgated it, and in whose mystical being all power resided. In practice democracy was sufficiently hedged to keep real power in conservative, "establishment" hands.

The famous "Imperial Rescript on Education" of 1890 began: "Our Imperial Ancestors have founded Our Empire on a basis broad and everlasting ..." then proceeded to moral exhortations couched largely in Confucian terms: filial piety, respect for the Constitution, guarding "Our Imperial throne coeval with heaven and earth." Copies of the document were hung in all schoolrooms in the realm alongside the emperor's portrait; students and teachers made daily obeisance to both.

At the same time, the government from time to time issued statements and policies which seemed to declare Shinto, especially on the level of the major national rituals and shrines like Ise, to be not a religion, but simply a set of "foundational" rituals and symbols of a patriotic nature. That assumption conveniently allowed the state to require the participation of schoolchildren, soldiers and sailors, government officials, and on occasion all citizens, in indoctrinating Shinto-type practices, such as the schoolroom imperial obeisances, while at the same time telling the world that Japan observed religious freedom.

The non-religious characterization of Shinto meant, however, that it was considered unseemly for Shinto priests, particularly those at the great imperial shrines, to talk too much about their practice as a religion of the *kami*. Understandably, some religiously sincere Shintoists were discontented. The "above religion" view of Shinto and the ideological dominance of Ise Shinto were reasons why openly religious "sectarian" forms of the *kami*-faith emerged, and were grudgingly recognized by the state, in the Meiji era. Izumo Taisha-kyo ("Teaching of the Izumo Grand Shrine"), for example, was founded by the outspoken Senge Takatomi, a member of Senge family, hereditary chief priests of that western rival to Ise as a national shrine. Its mission was to honor Okuninushi, chief *kami* of Izumo's very ancient cultus, but not a deity highly placed in the Ise pantheon.

The most painful example of government control of Shinto was undoubtedly the mandatory shrine mergers of 1906–1912. For reasons of administrative convenience, especially in assuring that shrines were mainly seen as outposts of state ideology and the imperial cult, rather than as "religious" bastions of localism and so possible centers of resistance, numerous small rural or neighborhood places of *kami*-worship were forcibly merged into larger regional entities. Many were the stories of villagers weeping and dispirited as they watched beloved *kami* compelled to move, and the god's former home demolished. The number of Shinto shrines declined from about 193,000 in 1906 to 110,000 six years later.[8]

What was happening overall was that Shinto was being changed from a religion of innumerable hometown *kami* concerned mainly with particular places and families, to a faith of Japan's national identity, and above all of the sacred character of its sovereign. Shinto as traditional religion fell victim to Japan's increasing secularization and political needs.[9] *Fukko* or "restoration of antiquity" Shinto was all well and good for Kokugaku scholars nostalgic for a glorious past and concerned with determining what was *really* Japanese.[10] But hardheaded Meiji industrialists, militarists, and adept politicians wanted only as much of this as would help meet their perceived need for a world-class economy, army and navy, and standing in the family of nations – and for a docile, hard-working citizenry laboring to make that happen.

The emperor as religion

What this called for was a definite national spiritual focus, and what could that be but the emperor? Shinto of itself was not effective as a national ideological center, nor was Buddhism, but one element of Shinto could be lifted out. Ito Hirobumi, the basically conservative principal creator of the 1889 constitution and a major figure in Meiji politics, put it this way:

> What is the cornerstone of our country? ... Though Buddhism once flourished and was the bond of union between all classes, high and low, today its influence has declined. Though Shintoism is based on the tradition of our ancestors, as a religion it is not powerful enough to become the center of the country. Thus in our country the one institution which can become the cornerstone of our constitution is the Imperial House.[11]

But though the new imperialism may have taken birth in such quasi-political considerations, it quickly became foundational to education and ideology, as we have seen in the Education Rescript. By 1910 a schoolbook linked imperialism and Confucian filial piety through sentiments like these:

> It is only natural for children to love and respect their parents. ... Our country is based on the family system. The whole country is one great family, and the Imperial House is the Head Family. It is with the feeling of filial love and respect for parents that we Japanese people express our reverence toward the Throne of an unbroken imperial line.[12]

Many similar expressions of reverence for the Imperial House could be cited, and they became more and more intense, and quasi-religious, as the twentieth century advanced. What did it all mean, and where was it leading?

Certainly the Meiji leaders wanted Japan to catch up with the rest of the world. Yet they, and many Japanese, felt a compensating sense that in some way Japan also had to be special, and that its spiritual heritage, including the role of the emperor, was central to that uniqueness. *Nihon seishin*, the Japanese spirit, gave the nation the power to do what it wanted to do, and become what it wanted to become, in an alien world.

However, once let out of the bottle the imperial genie could not be put back in, at least not until utter disaster arrived. The time would come when the imperial ideology would appeal to the disadvantaged and discontented as well as the complacent leaders of society. We will turn to that side of the issue in a moment. First, however, a look at other religions in Meiji Japan.

Meiji Buddhism

If Shinto became more ingrown and aligned to nationalism, Buddhism went the other way, to become more international in awareness and open to reform in the Meiji era, more than making up for centuries of isolation and stagnation.

Change was pushed by the Meiji state itself. In 1872, legislation allowed Buddhist priests to marry (heretofore all had been expected to be celibate, except for Shugendo priests, and for Jodo-Shinshu clerics, who could follow the example of their founder, Shinran), to eat meat, to dress and let their hair grow long as they wished rather than take the robe and tonsure.[13] (The following year the same privileges were legally granted Buddhist nuns, though in practice there was no way they could accept them without leaving the convent.) From the government's point of view, these changes may have been intended to demystify Buddhism, as part of its policy of putting it in its place and exalting Shinto. Initially the right to marry in particular evoked a great range of reactions among priests, from passionate resistance to enthusiastic acceptance, as might have been expected.

The transition was most difficult in those denominations with a strong monastic tradition, Shingon, Tendai, and Zen, rather than Nichiren and Jodo-shu, more oriented to temple pastorates. But within a generation or two most priests were married in Japan (almost alone among Buddhist countries), the incumbency of temples had become largely hereditary, and as we will see priests' wives came to have a special, if anomalous, role. The character of Buddhism subtly but decidedly changed.

Other reform movements appeared within Buddhism itself. Progressives became particularly aware, with the "opening" of Japan, that Buddhism was an international and not just an insular religion, that Japanese Buddhists needed to relate to Theravada as well as Mahayana co-religionists, and that the faith was now a part of an advanced, but largely non-Buddhist, world. Some advocated the restatement of Buddhist doctrine in light of new scholarship on the Buddha and the religion's original sources, and no less in response to its growing encounter with Christianity and modern science.

There were those who thought Buddhism, with its profound metaphysics, could hold its own very well in the contemporary marketplace of ideas, but the right words had to be found – in Sanskrit and Western languages as well as East Asian. In this endeavor Jodo-Shinshu was initially the most active of Japan's denominations. The Nishi Honganji sent Shimaji Mokurai with a group of scholars to observe Western religion 1873; after visiting Europe, some returned by way of America, but Shimaji himself proceeded to the Middle East, including a tour of the Holy Land, before making a pilgrimage of Buddhist sites in India on his way back to Japan. On the other hand, the Higashi Honganji sent Nanjo Bunyu to learn Sanskrit under the famous Max Muller in England, and other Buddhists studied in Europe and America.

Jodo-Shinshu was also concerned early with ministering to the spiritual needs of Japanese immigrants in Hawaii and mainland America. The Higashi Honganji established missions for Japanese in Hawaii 1899, and in Los Angeles 1904. To this day probably at least half the Japanese-Americans who are active Buddhists worship in the Buddhist Church of America. (This denomination is Jodo-Shinshu, though with notable flexibility it has adapted features of Protestant Christianity; the visitor will find Protestant-type hymns with Buddhist words, Sunday Schools, and Sunday morning services which, though Buddhist, have a characteristic Protestant structure.)

Other groups were not far behind. Nichiren Buddhism came to Hawaii in 1902, and to California 1914. Shingon was in Hawaii by 1902, later on the mainland. Zen, with its rather different story in the West because of its appeal to Westerners as well as Japanese immigrants, has already been mentioned. Among the most remarkable and influential of the wandering Buddhist seekers and scholars of Meiji Japan (note his wandering to Theravada Ceylon) was the redoubtable Zen monk Soyen [Soen] Shaku (1859–1919), who wrote of himself in 1888:

This fellow was a son of Nobusuke Goemon Ichenose of Takahama, the province of Wakasa. His nature was stupid and tough. When he was young, none of his relatives liked him. When he was twelve years old, he was ordained as a monk by Ekkei, Abbot of Myo-shin Monastery. Afterwards, he studied literature under Shungai of Kennin Monastery for three years, and gained nothing. Then he went to Mii-dera and studied Tendai philosophy under Tai-ho for a summer, and gained nothing. After this, he went to Bizen and studied Zen under the old teacher Gisan for one year, and attained nothing. He then went to the East, to Kamakura, and studied under the Zen master Ko-sen in the Engaku Monastery for six years, and added nothing to the aforesaid nothingness. He was in charge of a little temple, Butsu-nichi, one of the temples of the Engaku Cathedral, for one year and from there went to Tokyo to attend Kei-o College for one year and a half, making himself the worst student there; and forgot the nothingness that he had gained. Then he created for himself new delusions, and came to Ceylon in the spring of 1887; and now, under the Ceylon monk he is studying the Pali language and Hinayana Buddhism. Such a wandering mendicant! He ought to repay the twenty years of debts to those who fed him in the name of Buddhism.[14]

This worthless fellow (but those who know something of Zen philosophy may catch a double meaning in the nothingness he gained and lost) did something to repay those debts when, in 1893, he came to Chicago to attend the World's Parliament of Religions, a seminal event that did much to popularize Eastern religion in the West. Returning to Japan, he taught Zen in Kamakura, where among his students were D. T. Suzuki, who did so much to spread knowledge of Zen worldwide, and Senzaki Nyogen, who was later to spend many years in America as a Zen teacher. Soyen returned to America in 1905 as a guest of Mr. and Mrs. Alexander Russell of San Francisco; Mrs. Russell was reportedly the first American to study *koans* formally. Another student of Soyen's, through his student Sokatsu, was the already-

Daisetz Teitaro Suzuki

Daisetz Teitaro Suzuki (1870–1966) deserves particular mention. When Soyen Shaku was at the World's Parliament of Religions, a publisher, Paul Carus, asked him for a translator of Asian spiritual literature; the monk recommended Suzuki, who subsequently lived in Carus' home in LaSalle, Illinois, for several years. He married an American woman, Beatrice Lane, who would later author a book on Mahayana Buddhism.

D. T. Suzuki himself is very widely known for his books, and lectures throughout the world, on Zen. These were the initial introduction to that tradition for advocates like Alan Watts, and Suzuki undoubtedly did more than anyone else to make Zen seem very special to innumerable Westerners.

To be sure, Suzuki had his own approach; neither a monk nor a scholar in the strictest academic sense – though very learned in many languages – he presented Zen as he saw it, with a Taoist flavor and in a way that at least spoke to the concerns of Western existentialism and psychoanalysis. In the Rinzai tradition himself, he emphasized *koan* work, and the cultural side of Zen, far more than *zazen*. Curiously, he barely mentioned the Sotoist Dogen, despite the latter's eminence in the eyes of most other interpreters of Japanese Zen. But Suzuki is immensely significant, and in the latter years of his long life was probably the most important exponent not only of Zen but of Japanese culture generally in the world.

mentioned Sasaki Sokei-an, who brought Zen across the Pacific. He came in 1906, and after many vicissitudes opened the First Zen Institute in New York in 1930, the first formal Zen center primarily catering to Westerners.[15]

Returning to Meiji Buddhism, one other name and event ought to be mentioned. They are Henry Steel Olcott (1832–1907) and his two visits to Japan, 1889 and 1891. The American Olcott was a co-founder (1875) and first President of the Theosophical Society, which did much to circulate knowledge of Eastern spirituality in the West. After settling at the society's international headquarters in India, Olcott "took pansil," formally becoming a Buddhist according to his lights, perhaps the first American to do so. He became deeply concerned with the situation of Buddhists, initially in Ceylon (Sri Lanka), as they struggled under colonialism and the onslaughts of Christian missionaries. Taking up their cause with the tireless energy and irrepressible self-confidence of the Victorian enthusiast, Olcott was sometimes called a "missionary in reverse." As he tried to interpret the ancient religion in contemporary terms, he constructed a Buddhist catechism, designed a Buddhist flag, and traveling to various Buddhist countries endeavored to promote understanding and cooperation among its various divisions.

It was for this "ecumenical" purpose that Olcott, accompanied by a leading Theravada Buddhist spokesman, came to Japan at the invitation of Noguchi Zenshiro, a Buddhist reformer who had visited him in India. Olcott's lectures to Buddhist priests and monks in Japan calling for greater worldwide Buddhist unity of spirit and practical cooperation did not result in any dramatic changes. But the interest on the part of such an exceptional westerner made news, and undoubtedly increased awareness on the part of attentive Japanese that their faith was no longer the parochial matter of as recently as the Tokugawa era, when foreigners could not visit nor Japanese leave the island nation, but part of a living world community and a world spiritual force.[16]

Christianity returns to Japan

As soon as Japan had been "opened" by the treaties subsequent to Commodore Perry's visit, Christian missionaries were naturally eager to enter. They first came in 1858, the best known being the Presbyterian J. C. Hepburn, who opened a school and clinic that year in Kanagawa. He also began a translation of the Bible into Japanese. (Hepburn is well known for creating the system of transliteration of Japanese into roman letters still in use with slight modifications, including in this book.) However, Christianity was formally prohibited as a religion until 1873, though the first church was opened in 1872; before then Hepburn and other missionaries were unable openly to conduct worship for Japanese. They quickly discovered, though, that demand for Western education and medicine was overwhelming; by means of schools and clinics they won many friends. Roman Catholicism also returned to Japan about the same time. An order of nuns opened an orphanage in 1872, and churches soon followed.

Indeed, in a real sense social services, then churches, have been the story of Christianity in Japan. As we have noted already, the number of formal converts has been small. Such Meiji converts as there were often came from the samurai class. Some samurai families, feeling bypassed by a changing society, were willing to look into new roles and new challenges, including the up-to-date educational opportunities the missionaries offered. Christianity has retained respect for its educational, medical, and other institutions, and for its moral values; far more Japanese consider themselves Christians, or sympathizers, in some spiritual sense than appear on church roles.

The dark valley

What about the role of religion in the modern period of extreme nationalism, militarism, and war, roughly 1930–1945, a time spoken of by many Japanese as *kurotanima*, the "dark valley"? To understand the dark valley and its spiritual ideology, a little history is necessary. Up until around 1930, matters had looked relatively promising for advocates of progress and democracy. Japan's successful war with Russia, 1904–1905, her annexation of Korea in 1910, and her victorious role on the Allied side in the First World War, had given the empire recognition as a world power, even though many Japanese still sensed racist antipathy, especially in the "oriental exclusion" immigration policies adopted by the United States, Canada, and Australia. The era of the Taisho emperor, who had succeeded Meiji in 1912, was sometimes spoken of as "Taisho democracy."

In 1926 the sickly Taisho was followed by Hirohito (1901–1989), who ironically took the era-name Showa, "Enlightened Peace." The first two decades of his long reign were anything but that, though war may have not been the desire of this still-controversial figure. The fundamental problem was an expanding population, and rising expectations, in a country with very limited natural resources. This made the anti-Japanese immigration policies of other countries especially galling. Then the onset of the Great Depression in 1929 terribly exacerbated matters. As export markets collapsed, numerous rural and working-class families suffered real privation, even near starvation, and voices among them began calling for any solution, however radical or violent.

Those voices came particularly from younger officers in the army. They themselves were largely from hard-pressed country families, and their zeal for suffering Japan was coupled with rage against the *zaibatsu* (industrial monopolists) and their privileged cronies in the traditional ruling class. They demanded radical answers – but answers consistent with the Bushido values they also honored. These army men were quite prepared to accept, and indeed glorified, violent and military means to solving Japan's problems. (That set them against the communists who were also noisy at the time, but were soon silenced.)

What suited the needs of the officers and the small number of intellectuals who supported them was an extreme version of the Meiji imperial ideology, the Kodo or "imperial way" doctrine that the emperor must rule directly, and that unhampered the divinely-guided "imperial will" would lead Japan to its ultimate glorious destiny. They readily assumed the corollary to this teaching, that now the pure imperial intent was being hindered by traitorous counselors to the throne, who must be removed by any means necessary. Once rid of timid placemen in the corridors of power, Japan would boldly seize by force of arms the markets, areas for immigration, and sources of raw materials it required.

This faction never completely controlled the government, nor even the armed forces; the navy, generally officered by more moderate and sophisticated men who were better aware of the realities of Japan's position in the world, was often a reluctant partner. Some civilian statesmen and senior army officers were contemptuous of the militants' ill-informed zeal and correctly predicted disaster at the end of the road they would have Japan take. That the radicals were able to put Japan on that road nonetheless was due to three factors. First, they did not hesitate to use assassination to terrorize

A major ideologue of Kodo outlook was Kita Ikki (1883–1937). Advocating Asian nationalism, he proposed that Japan should lead a united and free Asia. But fulfilling this role depended first on radical change in Japanese society. A military coup would be needed to rid the country of existing incompetent leadership, and substitute an authoritarian regime based on a direct relationship between the emperor and the people. The emperor would next suspend the constitution, declare martial law, and authorize a national reorganization parliament, free from corrupt businessmen and politicians. The new state would then nationalize principal industries, confiscate excess wealth, and enact land reform to benefit the peasants. All this would strengthen the nation and enable Japan to fulfill its destiny to liberate Asia from Western imperialism, and develop a "Showa Restoration" society based on a true *kokutai* or national polity. Kita inspired the 1936 attempted coup, mentioned below, and was executed for his part in 1937.[17]

their opponents. Second, beginning in Manchuria in 1931, when army hotheads seized Mukden in that territory, and soon the whole of it, without authorization from Tokyo, they presented the government with the option of either caving in to the extremists or facing down the army and its "grass roots" supporters. Nervous politicians usually found accepting a *fait accompli* more palatable. Third, because in Japan the cabinet ministers for the army and navy were uniformed officers, and without their support it was difficult to form or sustain a cabinet, they could put substantial leverage on the government when it came to policies, and budget priorities, important to them.

The sacred imperial institution was central from the Meiji Restoration to 1945, but the segments of society that most promoted it and its ideology changed over those years. At the time of the Restoration it was rebellious *daimyos* frustrated by the weakness against foreigners of the shogunate – seen as usurping the emperor's role – who exalted direct imperial rule. Then, once in power, those same *daimyos* and their allies wanted the emperor to legitimate their rule, as they learned from the foreigners and transformed Japan. By the time of the Meiji constitution, a conservative political establishment coopted the throne to conserve its power. But in the 1930s, imperialism became a "reformist" cause in the hands of angry younger officers who believed they represented the disadvantaged; they wanted to use the emperor against the "establishment" rather than for it. Like the European fascism of the same period, with which Japanese nationalism had obvious similarities, that cause combined traditionalist symbols with present-day protest, populism, and militaristic fervor.[18]

The river of violence rose in 1930, when a self-styled patriot shot the prime minister on his return from the London Naval Conference, where he had accepted limitations on Japan's sea forces. After the 1931 "incident" in Manchuria, more industrialists and political figures were killed by extremists, including another prime minister in 1932; the situation has been called "government by assassination." Then on February 26, 1936, some 1,500 soldiers led by junior officers butchered several politicians and senior officers, and seized a section of Tokyo in preparation for a *coup d'état*. They were suppressed and the chief mutineers hanged, but an atmosphere of edgy tension at home increasingly accompanied expansionism abroad. In 1937, in another "incident," Chinese and Japanese troops began fighting near Peking (now Beijing); soon the Japanese had occupied most of northeast and coastal China, and – though long undeclared – war was underway in earnest. Most of the rest of the world looked askance, embargoing shipments of oil and other military necessities to Japan.

Now the island empire claimed to be misunderstood and unfairly treated, and moreover declared itself called to lead all East Asia in a struggle against European colonialism. By 1940 the high-riding militarists were unable to resist the temptation posed by the rich French and Dutch colonies (French Indo-China, now largely Vietnam, and the Netherlands East Indies, now Indonesia), vulnerable because their homelands were under Nazi occupation. The British were busy fighting Hitler elsewhere, and the U.S. was presumed unprepared. In 1940 Japan joined the Axis powers and, on December 7, 1941, expanded the war with its attack on the U.S. naval base at Pearl Harbor, Hawaii. The Pacific War, as it is called in Japan, followed, ending with Hiroshima, Nagasaki, and surrender, all in the almost-apocalyptic month of August, 1945.

Figure 9.2 Zen monks of Eiheiji, Japan, 1938 (Xinstalker; Public Domain: Wikimedia Commons)

National foundations

These moves were not without philosophical and spiritual buttressing. In 1937, as we have seen, the Ministry of Education issued an important document called *Kokutai no hongi*, or *Fundamentals of National Polity*. Its arguments are of some interest.

The text begins by stating that the "various ideological and social evils of present-day Japan" are the result of ignoring fundamental principles and pursuing the trivial, and this deviance essentially stems from the perverse but pervasive influence of European and American culture, especially those rationalist and positivist doctrines derived from the Enlightenment. They put supreme value on the abstract liberty and equality of separate individuals, ignoring the historical, racial, and national context which gives meaning to the individual. In the West, excessive individualism has led to "a season of ideological and social confusion and crisis." It was reaction to the "deadlock" of individualism that then gave rise to European totalitarianism and nationalism.

Japan, however, is established on another basis than Western confusion. Its "nationalism" and "totalitarianism" are said to be different, more benign, indeed more like mysticism or the harmony of a well-ordered family, than the Western equivalent. "Our country is established with the emperor, who is a descendant of Amaterasu Omikami, as her center, and our ancestors as well as we ourselves constantly have beheld in the emperor the fountainhead of her life and activities." Serving the emperor and his "great august will" gives life its rationale and is the source of morality. That means casting aside one's "little" self and becoming a part of the greater "self" of the state under the emperor. This is not a master–servant relationship of mere obedience, as of one individual to another, but a profoundly mystical loss of the self in something greater, "dying to self and returning to [the] One," a natural development of the great Way. It is no less an extension of filial piety, for the Imperial Household is the head family of the nation.

We note, then, the use of Shinto in this document in the myth of Amaterasu, of Confucianism in the concept of filial piety, and of Taoism in reference to the Way (Tao) and return to the One. The text next exalts above all the virtues of Bushido, especially of the warrior's "spirit of self-effacement and of meeting death with a perfect calmness." This ideal has some roots in Zen and its ideal of the adept's total awareness and non-attachment to life or death. But Buddhism as such is not much mentioned in the *Kokutai no hongi*.[19] We have noted before that a basic Bushido text like the *Hagakure* explicitly contrasts the way of the warrior and that of the Buddhist priest, and by implication distances itself from real Buddhist values.

However, despite their allegiance to what some nationalists still regarded as a foreign faith, most Buddhists diligently supported the war effort. Buddhist chaplains were assigned to every regiment of the Imperial Army, and many also served as medics. The Myowa Kai, a pan-Buddhist organization, provided services to imperial troops and the war effort.

Note again the centrality of the imperial office to the spirituality of nationalism. Here is how it was put by one bluff soldier who rose to the highest political office under the emperor, that of prime minister, for most of the Pacific War years. When asked in parliament early in the war whether he was becoming a dictator, Tojo Hideki responded:

> It is only when I am exposed to the light of His Majesty that I shine. Were it not for this light I should be no better than a pebble by the roadside. It is because I enjoy the confidence of His Majesty and occupy my present position that I shine. This puts me in a completely different category from those European rulers who are known as dictators.[20]

On the local level, these sentiments were accompanied by increasing conformity and mobilization (creation of a *gunkoku* or "military state") at home, in education, and by the dreaded Tokko or "thought police," assigned to censor subversive notions in film, radio, the print media, and wherever they might occur. One area to be watched, of course, was religion.

In 1940 a religious organizations law placed all religious bodies under the Home Office, forcing them to combine: all Shinto sects were reduced to thirteen, Buddhist to twenty-eight, and the thirty-three Protestant churches required to unite into one. The faiths were to support the war effort both by patriotic expression, including acknowledgment of the imperial divine lineage, and in practical ways. Those that refused to be so regulated, such as the Salvation Army, Jehovah's Witnesses, and some Nichiren Buddhists, suffered severe persecution.

Most religions, however, supported the war with apparent enthusiasm. Pilgrimages to Ise were up by 25 percent the New Year after Pearl Harbor, and pilgrims were said to be exuberant. As it happened, a great Shinto and imperial event occurred in November of 1940, at the high tide of imperial ideology: the alleged 2600th anniversary of the establishment of the Empire at Kashiwara by Jimmu Tenno, the first sovereign in the undying line. According to *The Japan Times*, the sovereign made a public appearance, and there were processions, dances, the carrying of portable shrines, and Shinto ceremonies throughout Tokyo.

A companion article, "New Shinto Board to Guide Thought," tells us that the occasion was taken to create a new Shinto Ritual Board intended to emphasize that Shinto rites were the foundation of the state and of education, and to mobilize 15,000 Shinto priests in the service of the nationalistic cause.[21]

Priests also took jobs in war plants – in some cases replaced by women serving at Shinto and Buddhist altars for the first time in a thousand years.[22] Brian Victoria, in his illuminating book *Zen at War*, offers photos of Zen novices marching and training with wooden weapons under Imperial Army officers like all schoolboys, and presents quotations from numerous prominent Zen and other Buddhist spokesmen vigorously supporting the war and its objectives. The previously-mentioned all-

Buddhist Myowa Kai, for example, issued a statement on July 28, 1937, containing the following lines in response to criticism of Japanese aggression by Chinese Buddhists:

> In order to establish eternal peace in East Asia, arousing the great benevolence and compassion of Buddhism, we are sometimes accepting and sometimes forceful. We now have no choice but to exercise the benevolent forcefulness of 'killing one in order that many may live.' … In general it can be said that Chinese Buddhists believe that war should absolutely be avoided no matter what the reason. Japanese Buddhists, on the other hand, believe that war conducted for a [good] reason is in accord with the great benevolence and compassion of Buddhism.[23]

As for Japan's Christians, without quite embracing imperial divinity, Roman Catholics set up a "National Committee of Catholics for Foreign Propaganda" for the purpose of "enlightening Catholics of other countries in regard to the nation's true aims and motives," and the Executive Committee of the (Protestant) National Christian Council declared its "utmost loyalty to Imperial aims, and to accomplish the unity and peace of the Far East, in reverential loyalty to the Imperial Will."[24]

In the end, however, all this became rubble and hunger, and Japan was ready for a new start.

Key points you need to know

- The Meiji Restoration of 1868 meant a revival of Shinto, especially imperial, Buddhism turning outward, and the arrival of Christian missionaries
- The new Meiji government experimented with several religious policies, but ended up mainly promoting imperialist Shinto and Confucian morality
- Documents of the extreme nationalistic and militaristic period, like the *Kokutai no hongi*, cited Bushido values
- During the Second World War, Shinto sects, Buddhism, and Christianity were forced to merge into a few denominations, and to support the imperial ideology.

Questions for study and discussion

1. What religious and philosophical ideologies lay behind the Meiji Restoration?
2. Why was support for the imperial office important to the Meiji reformers?
3. What and why was the popular response to the Bakumatsu period?
4. How did the Meiji government attempt to use Shinto?
5. Why was its religious policy so uncertain at first?
6. Why did the spiritual role of the emperor become the main focus of nationalism?

7. What happened to Buddhism in the Meiji period?
8. Discuss the reintroduction and role of Christianity in Meiji Japan.
9. How did the extreme nationalists justify the use of violence at home and abroad?
10. Discuss the basic philosophy of the *Kokutai no hongi*. How and why did it criticize western individualism?
11. Discuss the role of Shinto, Buddhism, and Christianity during the Pacific War.

Further reading

Bellah, Robert, *Imagining Japan*. Berkeley, CA: University of California Press, 2003.

Gluck, Carol, *Japan's Modern Myths: Ideology in the Late Meiji Period*. Princeton, NJ: Princeton University Press, 1985.

Hall, Robert King, and John Owen Gauntlett, *Kokutai no Hongi: Cardinal Principles of the National Entity of Japan*. Cambridge, MA: Harvard University Press, 1949.

Hardacre, Helen, *Shinto and the State 1868–1988*. Princeton, NJ: Princeton University Press, 1989.

Havens, Thomas R. H., *Valley of Darkness: The Japanese People and World War Two*. New York: Norton, 1978.

Holtom, Daniel Clarence, *Modern Japan and Shinto Nationalism*, rev. ed., Chicago, IL: University of Chicago Press, 1947.

Inglehart, Charles W., *A Century of Protestant Christianity in Japan*. Rutland, VT and Tokyo: Tuttle, 1959.

Jansen, Marius, *The Making of Modern Japan*. Cambridge, MA: Harvard University Press, 2000.

Kishimoto, Hideo, *Japanese Religion in the Meiji Era*. Tokyo: Obunsha, 1956.

Kitagawa, Joseph M., *Religion in Japanese History*. New York: Columbia University Press, 1990.

Kosaka, Masaki, *Japanese Thought in the Meiji Era*. Tokyo: Pan-Pacific Press, 1958.

Ruoff, Kenneth J., *Imperial Japan at its Zenith: The Wartime Celebration of the Empire's 2,600th Anniversary*. Ithaca, NY: Cornell University Press, 2014.

Thomas, Julia Adeney, *Reconfiguring Modernity: Concepts of Nature in Japanese Political Ideology*. Berkeley, CA: University of California Press, 2001.

Victoria, Brian (Daizen), *Zen at War*. New York and Tokyo: Weatherhill, 1997.

Electronic Resources

Wikipedia, "Bakumatsu." https://en.wikipedia.org/wiki/Bakumatsu

"Izumo Taisha." www.japanesemythology.jp/izumo-taisha/

"Shinto sect [Izumo Taishakyo] to mark 97th year in Hawaii," *Honolulu Advertiser* Dec. 28, 2002. http://the.honoluluadvertiser.com/article/2002/Dec/28/il/il22a.html

"Shinto History," BBC [see on Meiji Shinto]. http://www.bbc.co.uk/religion/religions/shinto/history/history_1.shtml

Wikipedia, "Haibutsu Kishaku" [smashing Buddhism]. https://en.wikipedia.org/wiki/Haibutsu_Kishaku

Wikipedia, "Shinbutsu Bunri" [separation of Shinto and Buddhism]. https://en.wikipedia.org/wiki/Shinbutsu_bunri

Wikipedia, "Hirohito." https://en.wikipedia.org/wiki/Hirohito (Presents much material unfavorable to the Emperor in relation to World War II.)

"Japan: Hirohito warned attack on Pearl Harbor would be 'Self-destructive,'" *The Guardian*, Sept. 10, 2014. www.theguardian.com/world/2014/sep/10/japan-emperor-hirohito-pearl-harbor-attack-biography (A somewhat more favorable view than the preceding site. Both offer new biographical material released by the Imperial Household in 2014; more is to come.)

"Selections from the *Kokutai no hongi (Fundamentals of our National Polity), 1937*." http://afe.easia.columbia.edu/ps/japan/kokutai.pdf

Wil Deac, "The Rise of Militaristic Nationalism [in Japan]." www.historynet.com/the-rise-of-militaristic-nationalism-november-96-world-war-ii-feature.htm

Note: Researchers will find a number of reviews and discussion online of Brian (Daizen) Victoria's *Zen at War*, cited in the bibliography, a source of much important new information on the Buddhist establishment in Japan and its support of Japan's role in World War II. In general Victoria's forcefully presented material is accepted, although there are criticisms of his interpretation of D.T. Suzuki. The postings are too numerous to list and discuss here, but though like all such are to be used with caution, they are suggested to students with an interest in the topic.

10 Chanting and dancing

Shugendo and the "new religions" of Japan

In this chapter

This chapter will survey Shugendo, a number of the "new religions" of Japan, and look at their common characteristics.

Main topics covered

- Shugendo
- Tenrikyo
- Konkokyo
- Omoto
- Seicho no Ie
- World Messianity
- Perfect Liberty Kyodan
- Nichiren groups: Soka Gakkai, Reiyukai, Rissho Kosei Kai
- Examples of the "new new" religions: Agonshu, Shinnyoen, Mahakari, Gedatsu, Aum Shinrikyo
- Common characteristics of Japanese new religions.

Mountain priests

The bringing together in this chapter of one of the oldest forms of Japanese religion, the *yamabushi* or mountain priests of Shugendo, with one of the newest, the so-called "new religions" founded in the last two centuries, is not as odd as may seem. For the ways in which many of the latter had direct or indirect connections with mountain priests, or at least with the kind of shamanistic spirituality they represented in Japan, is striking. Illustrative of this linkage is our first example of a new religion – though one of the oldest of the "new" – Tenrikyo, whose headquarters in Tenri City have already been described in Chapter 2. Its foundress, Nakayama Miki, was initially possessed by the High God while serving as a medium assisting a *yamabushi* in a healing rite for her son.

We have already met the *yamabushi*, whose roots go back far in Japanese religious history, inspired by the earliest meetings of esoteric Buddhism and shamanistic Shinto. The Tokugawa period might be called their golden age. Then, after the Kamakura faith-based Buddhist movements had settled down, and peace made pilgrimage and the rhythms of rural life easier, they permeated the popular religion of large areas of Japan. Essentially, the priests of the several *yamabushi* orders, associated tenuously with Shingon or, more often, Tendai, spent winters in the mountains doing spiritual and ascetic exercises, and initiating new adherents. They then returned to the villages to practice faith-healing, divination, and other magic, give religious instruction, and lead pilgrimages to their sacred sites. The initiations might include such trials as leaping over fires, standing under waterfalls, being suspended by the heels over sheer cliffs for "a peek into eternity," or meditating in solitude all winter – sometimes for long periods in total darkness, when eyes and mind become accustomed to seeing visions.

I once had the opportunity to observe the "winter peak," an important Shugendo rite, at one of the remaining *yamabushi* sites, Mount Haguro in northern Japan, on New Year's Eve and night. This Tendai-related *yamabushi* order (mostly workaday men for whom Shugendo is an avocation and spiritual path) ascends the mountain three times a year for seasonal rituals, known as "peaks." The summer peak is thronged with pilgrims. The autumn peak is important as the time of initiation and promotion for members of the *yamabushi* order: candidates undergo a series of dramatic and tangible experiences imitating death, descent into hell, and rebirth; it culminates in a ritual fire or *goma*. The winter peak (with which the spring peak is now combined) is a lively New Year's Eve celebration. It ends a period of ascetic confinement for the chief priests, and involves divination for the coming twelvemonth.

Mount Haguro is in Japan's *yukiguni* or "snow country." At that time of year the sacred mountain was white with drifted snow, its white and the deep green of the evergreen forests along the winding upward road contrasting dramatically. The winter peak outdoor ceremonies were held on a large snowy field in front of a commodious Shinto shrine; around the clearing were walls of dark pine. On the other side of the ritual area were two lodges, built back-to-back. The order is divided into two wings, each with its own lodge. This meant that most of the rites would have a duplicate, twofold character. Some would involve a jocular rivalry between the two. This interesting doubling is reminiscent of the twofold repetition of the most sacred Shinto rites of Ise and the Daijosai. At Mount Haguro, ritual contention between the two sides plays the universal role of such sacred combat at New Year: symbolic struggle between the old and new year, and divination of whether the coming seasons would be good or bad.

Within each lodge, a lower hall was filled with milling order members taking a break between events; refreshments were available, in the form of roasted sweet potatoes and warm sake. A higher floor contained an altar and the seat of that section's *matsu-hijiri* – the *yamabushi* elder who that night had completed one hundred days of residence as a hermit and ascetic.

Activities began about 2 p.m. as the *yamabushi* entered the area noisily blowing conch shells. They were dressed in black-and-white checked blouses, white pantaloons, and high black hats resembling the *eboshi* worn by Shinto priests. Around their necks were curious cases and mirrors like breastplates. At 3 p.m. a Shinto service was held.

Then, in front of the shrine interest centered around two large straw "insects," said to ward off harm to the coming year's crops. Standing on top of them, *yamabushi* threw down *shimenawa*, sacred straw ropes, to pilgrims, who would put them over their house doors to keep evil away; the snowy scramble was often rough.

That evening a series of curious events ensured. First the two sides stood on two facing piles of straw and, each jumping up as he spoke, shouted humorous insults at one another. Then, in the main shrine hall, two lines of *yamabushi* alternatively circled about in a dance step said to represent the crow sacred to Mount Haguro. Next, a man disguised as a giant rabbit entered, reportedly an envoy of Mount Gassan, "Moon Mountain" (the rabbit is associated with the Moon in Japanese folklore), a nearby sacred mountain. The "rabbit" sat between two low tables as *yamabushi* came up to him in two lines, each placing a hand on a table. The animal would try to hit the hands with a fan before the other could pull it back. This was divinatory; I was told that each *yamabushi* represented a month of the coming year; if his hand was hit, that month would be bad.

Meanwhile, another contest had developed outside as each side tried to pull its giant straw "insect" into a fire. Judges would determine which did this first and best.

By now it was about midnight. Another competition ensued to see which side could light the new, pure fire for the new year first, using only gunpowder and old-fashioned flint and steel implements. In all these contests, it was said the winning side would be the one whose *matsu-hijiri* had accumulated the most spiritual power during his confinement on the peak.

The last rite, after midnight, was peculiar: the *kuni-wake*, or "division of the country." It commemorated an ancient jurisdictional dispute between these Mount Haguro *yamabushi* and the *yamabushi* of Kumano to the south, the other major Shugendo lineage. A priest representing Haguro stood beside a beam set in the ground at a 45-degree angle. He spoke in low, menacing tones to a group of four *yamabushi* about twenty feet off who were standing in for Kumano. The latter then came up one by one in a kind of dancing step to challenge the Haguro priest. Putting his hand across the beam, he repeated his angry, growling tones; the others retreated. This was alleged to reaffirm Haguro's exclusive right to serve northern and eastern Japan.

Coming down from their "peaks" to minister in the countryside, these priests would have been an important part of Tokugawa-era spiritual life, as we will see in the case of the founding of the Tenrikyo "new religion." Now they are less influential, thanks to modernization and Meiji-era suppression, though later we will get a glimpse of a contemporary Shugendo initiation. NHK, Japanese national television, was present at the rite described above to give millions across the country a taste of this colorful, still-living segment of Japan's spiritual past.[1]

Tenrikyo

One of the earliest and in some ways most paradigmatic of the major new religions, now claiming nearly two million members, Tenrikyo was founded by a farmer's wife named Nakayama Miki (1798–1887).[2] Its defining revelation occurred in December 1838.[3] Shuji, the eighteen-year-old son of Miki, had had a severe pain in his leg for over a year, which greatly inhibited his helping with the farm work. Though the Nakayamas were landowners and prominent in their village, times were hard and the family not so exalted as to be spared arduous labor in the fields. Shuji was a strong young man otherwise, and his ailment, which kept recurring, a serious matter. A *yamabushi* was retained to do *yosekaji* or ritual incantations on the youth's behalf.

The procedure in these rituals was for a female assistant serving as medium to go into trance, holding two sacred staffs with *gohei* or Shinto zigzag paper hangings on it; a diagnosis of the affliction would be received from a *kami* who possessed her and spoke through her lips. At the ritual on December 9, 1838, the usual medium, Soyo, was not available. Miki took her place. In trance, the woman's face reportedly took on an appearance of tremendous majesty, and the voice that spoke through her was not that of one of the many *kami*, but a Being who said "I am the True and Original God. Miki's mind and body will be accepted by me as a Divine Shrine, and I desire to save the world through this body."[4]

In other words, something new and unexpected was present: the voice of a monotheistic supreme God who, using Miki as an earthly vehicle, would deliver the world.[5] This development was, needless to say, highly disconcerting to the assembled family, and especially to the *yamabushi*, but Miki refused to come out of trance until they had accepted her new vocation. The family discussed the matter in the usual Japanese family-conference way, Miki sitting in her hieratic pose all the while. Finally after three days her kin came to consensus that they had no choice but to accept the god's requirement, and the strange destiny this would bring to her, to her distraught husband Zenbei, and their three daughters. When Zenbei then bowed before the deity in the shape of his wife and declared, "I offer Miki to you," she arose.

From then on nothing was the same. At first Miki seemed virtually mad, insisting on giving away all her possessions, on one occasion almost drowning herself in a well. But gradually she stabilized, giving sewing classes, becoming known in the neighborhood as a spiritual healer, all the while going into a light trance from time to time and speaking the words of God in a stentorian voice.

In time the basic teachings of Tenrikyo emerged. The original creator God is now trying to call humankind back to himself, and so to the *yokigurashi*, the joy in which the Parent had meant us to live. But we have allowed our minds to be covered by *hokori*, "dusts," that have brought forgetfulness and various vices. Oyasama ("worthy parent," an honorific title for the foundress) was chosen to be the means by which he recalls us.

In the *Ofudesaki*, the scripture she composed under inspiration, she recites the Tenrikyo story of creation, and describes the dances which would be the religion's basic rite. As we saw in Chapter 2, the greatest dances are performed in the main temple, around the Kanrodai, the pillar which according to Oyasama marks the place where the creation began. (The temple is on the former site of the foundress' home, not far from Nara.) Dances performed in branch churches present sweeping gestures that indicate the wiping away of the dusts. Another practice is *osazuke*, a commonly-performed healing rite consisting of stroking gestures made just above the body of the patient. Otherwise, worship in Tenrikyo churches is definitely of the Shinto type, with altars (including one to the foundress) and offerings made in a way characteristic of that religion.

As befits a religion emphasizing *yokigurashi* and of which the main rite is dancing, Tenrikyo has no strict or stern moral code, but says live a happy life and encourage others to be happy. Let life have a festive, celebrative flavor. The faith affirms *karma* (*innen*) and reincarnation. It has no belief in a future life other than one's next embodiment, the quality of which will depend on the *karma* one creates in this life. But unlike the Buddhism which sees reincarnation as a gloomy doctrine, indicating one is chained to the wheel of *samsara*, for the Tenrikyoist rebirth is something about which to be optimistic and joyous. All in all life is getting better and better. Indeed, soon a wonderful transition will occur, when *kanro* or sweet dew will fall into a basin atop the Kanrodai, the world will become paradisal, everyone will live to be 115, then painlessly die and be quickly reborn to another long and joyous life.

Sociologically, Tenrikyo centers around Oyasato, the town surrounding the Jiba or headquarters community with its temple housing the Kanrodai. Members and prospective members come for training and to do *hinokishin*, volunteer labor. *Itte hitotsu*, roughly "group spirit," is very important to Tenrikyo, as it is to popular Japanese culture. Oyasato is now a vast complex, including not only the headquarters building and dormitories for pilgrims, but institutions including schools from kindergarten through university, and a modern hospital combining spiritual services with the best contemporary medicine.

I have spoken of Tenrikyo as a "pilgrimage faith," since it seems to me this is an effective metaphor for its essence: its lifeblood is the incoming of members from around the world to Oyasato for training and spiritual renewal, and it sees life as a pilgrimage in time, lifetime after lifetime in this world, till one reaches the earthly paradise somewhere in the future.

Initiation as a *yoboku* (said to mean "timber"), a Tenrikyo "missionary" or committed member, lay or clergy, is obtained by means of a simple but definite process, called *honseki*. It must be accomplished at the Jiba, hence linking the faith worldwide to the sacred site. One must affirm the Tenrikyo faith, then listen to the same basic lecture on it nine times (said to represent the nine months in the womb before birth), and after that receive *osazuke*, which the *yoboku* can then bestow on others. Often this visit to the Jiba is combined with *shuyoka*, a three-month training program involving classes, *hinokishin* or volunteer labor, together with a deep experience of the Tenrikyo community and its worship.

Entry into Tenrikyo then has three defining qualities:

- first, it is a definite process, telling one that this faith is not just something one is born into, but means a definite personal commitment and initiatory experience;
- second, the process is, on the other hand, not complex and esoteric but fairly easy, indicating the religion is open to virtually everyone regardless of education or social status;
- third, it tells us that being a Tenrikyoist means maintaining an intimate connection to a particular sacred place and community.

These are features we will find typical of all the new religions.

Tenrikyo clearly has links in its very founding to shamanistic Shugendo, and just as clear ideological roots in Tokugawa Shinto and Neo-Confucianism (in the very term *tenri* "heavenly principle"). These are no doubt as interpreted by Ishida Baigan and especially by the "peasant sage," Ninomiya Sontoku (his idea of *hotoku*, giving return for grace received, is also important to Tenrikyo and most of the new religions), as well as in Buddhism in the concepts of *karma* and reincarnation. But there are also new emphases.

One is monotheism, belief in one God. The idea of one supreme God may have foreshadowings in Japan in the Confucian Heaven, in Buddhist Oneness and particularly the popular figure of Amida (Miki was raised in Pure Land), in some medieval Shinto ideologies, and even by means of underground Christian influences. But there is no doubt that Tenrikyo, like the other new religions, was monotheistic or monistic in a new, decisive way, especially in that it emphasized the one God as Creator of the world at a definite point in time, and made this creative act and its recollection central to teaching and worship. In this it is more like the Western monotheistic religions, Judaism, Christianity, and Islam, though whether any direct influence from them reached Miki is hard to prove one way or the other.

Her mention brings up another feature very important in Tenrikyo, and common in other new religions: a charismatic founder, often a woman and often possessing shamanistic characteristics (a powerful initiation experience by God or the gods; ability to enter into trance and utter divine words – *kamigakari* or divine possession; ability to heal and prophesy; sometimes ecstatic singing and dancing).

Before proceeding to further features of the new religions, however, let us examine more briefly other examples. We cannot cite all of them, but our list does include the largest and best-known.

Konkokyo

Some twenty years after Miki's initial experience of the True and Original God, a farmer named Kawate (or Akazawa) Bunjiro (1814–1883; now known by the posthumous name of Konko Daijin), whom life had brought many misfortunes, received a similar revelation. From it the religion of Konkokyo ("Golden Light Teaching") was born.[6] Kawate, always religious, had worshipped devoutly at Shinto shrines and Buddhist temples, as well as carefully following horoscopes and geomancy. His village had also been deeply influenced by Shugendo *yamabushi*. Kawate was impressed by a *sendatsu* (guide) of a mountain sect who, going into trance, was possessed by a deity, becoming an *ikigami* (living god) able to do miracles and transmit revelations. Later Bunjiro was to see himself in this role.[7]

He believed that a serious illness he underwent in 1855 was punishment from a god called Konjin, an often dangerous folk deity of Taoist background who ruled the northeast. But through praying to Konjin, Kawate was healed, and realized that the directional guardian was not entirely malevolent. The pious farmer developed a more and more profound relationship with this mysterious being, receiving instructions (*shirase*) from him about many matters, practical as well as spiritual. Then, in 1859, the deity revealed to him that he whom Kawate had called Konjin was actually Tenchi Kane no Kami, the one true God of the universe, and the Creator from whom all things derive. Konkokyo dates its origin from this event.

Although long registered as a Shinto sect for legal reasons, Konkokyo was and is in effect an independent monotheistic faith of a half-million members, whose central teaching is the reciprocal relationship between humanity and God, comparable to the *hotoku*, "returning virtue," of Ninomiya Sontoku, the Neo-Confucian "Peasant Sage." Konkokyo stresses that God, as loving parent, shares our suffering and joy. There is also a great deal of emphasis on the presence around us of ancestral spirits, *mitama*, who guide and protect, and with whom one can have a close relationship.

Worship is basically of the Shinto type, though directed to the one God and with more emphasis on the sermon at services than is usual in Shinto. A special feature of Konkokyo is *toritsugi* ("mediation"), a practice by which a minister, sitting at a designated place in the church, hears confessions on the part of believers and conveys them to God. It has been compared to Catholic confession. *Toritsugi* in Konkokyo reminds us that a particular characteristic of the new religions is concern for the personal problems and spiritual needs of ordinary members. These are religions one joins as an individual, and from which one can receive individual help.

The Omoto Group

This group of new religions started in 1892, but climaxed in the twentieth century. The foundress of Omoto (meaning "Great Source") was, like Miki and Kawate, of simple rural background. Deguchi Nao (1836–1918) suffered a life of great hardship.[8] Both at home and after marriage, she lived in desperate poverty. Of her eight children, two girls went mad, two boys ran away, three children died. She was widowed at thirty, and had to make a living selling rags. Deguchi had some contact with Konkokyo. Finally, in 1892, when she felt at the limit of her strength, she received a highly eschatological revelation from the Konkokyo God, Konjin or Tenchi Kane no Kami. This mighty deity told her that the destruction of the world was at hand, but that he would send a saving Messiah. A new paradisal world would then be constructed by God in place of this highly imperfect planet. The world renewal (*yonaoshi*) would also create the kingdom of the coming Buddha, Miroku (Sanskrit: Maitreya).

Poor and uneducated, regarded in her village as insane, Deguchi Nao was herself unable to do much with this dramatic teaching beyond talking about it, and beginning to write her scripture, *Ofudesaki*. She had only a small circle of followers. However, in 1898 a remarkable figure entered her life. Ueda Kisaburo (1871–1948), a striking and original religious practitioner, who had done *yamabushi*-type asceticism in the mountains, and also studied Spiritualism, happened upon the strange woman. He began organizing her movement, in the process marrying her one remaining available daughter, and changing his own name to Deguchi Onisaburo.[9]

Onisaburo made Omoto widely known, as he published extensive materials of a Spiritualist and power-of-mind or "positive thinking" description, also developing dramatic healing rituals and worship scenarios. He furthermore made pronouncements on public affairs, sometimes considering himself an incarnation of Miroku and an equal to the emperor. On one occasion he pointedly rode a white horse, considered an imperial prerogative; on another he went to Mongolia in a failed attempt to establish a Utopian state under himself as a living buddha. His positions ranged from pacifist to far right, but amid the turbulence of the first half of the twentieth century in Japan neither extreme was congenial to the authorities, and he and Omoto were often in trouble. Omoto headquarters were raided by police in 1921; Onisaburo spent 1935–1942 in jail. After the war the movement, much decreased by defections and persecution, reformed itself as a sect devoted to culture and world peace.

Several movements were in some way inspired by Omoto. They are now bigger than the original, in large part because they avoided Onisaburo's incautious political moves. The three that will be considered here might each be considered to have developed one facet of his remarkably fertile religious creativity: Seicho no Ie his positive thinking side, Sekai Kyusei Kyo the healing and eschatological side, PL Kyodan the cultural.

Seicho no Ie

Seicho no Ie was founded by Taniguchi Masaharu (1894–1985), a one-time active member of Omoto who left following the police crackdown of 1921. In 1928, after reading a book by the American "New Thought" writer Fenwicke Holmes,[10] *The Law of Mind in Action*, he reported a brilliant and joyous religious experience, in which he realized that the perceived world is merely the product of our five senses and our negative thoughts, and that the real world, created by God's infinite wisdom, is perfect and eternal. Taniguchi became a prolific writer and lecturer in this "inspirational" vein. It remains to add that Taniguchi often identified himself with rightist causes in Japan. In the 1930s and during the Pacific War he wrote inspirational material in support of the imperial cause, and even afterwards advocated such symbolic acts as displaying the Japanese flag and observing nationalistic holidays. But the essence of his teaching was on another plane.

He declared that we are perfect children of God, and only see and experience ill because of our thoughts. If you want to be happy, change your mind! One's environment will mirror the mind, bright or drab, hopeful or depressing. Sin and sickness have no reality in themselves.

Taniguchi offered a form of meditation called *shinkosan* to help us realize this true nature. However, Seicho no Ie, though rightly regarded as among the new religions, has functioned less as a formal religious denomination than an educational movement, spreading its message through books, lectures, seminars, and retreats. In Japan, where plural religious identity is common, this has mattered little; the message has reached millions; three million followers are claimed. Its relatively few overseas churches, including several in the United States, have generally organized like other churches with Sunday morning services.

Sekai Kyusei Kyo

Often called by its English name, the Church of World Messianity[11] is most famous for its healing practice called *jorei* (roughly, "divine light"). It also affirms that the divine light is coming more and more strongly into the world, and that a far better New Age is about to dawn. "Natural" farming (without fertilizers or insecticides) is advocated. The group maintains several large gardens in the Japanese style, considered among the most beautiful in Japan, as foretastes of what the world will be like in the New Age.

The founder of this movement was Okada Mokichi (1882–1955), now called Meishu-sama. Of impoverished background, he tried several business ventures in Tokyo, but suffered reverses and was completely ruined by the great earthquake of 1923. At the same time, he had become involved in Omoto. After the earthquake, he plunged into that movement wholeheartedly, holding teaching and leadership positions. Yet Okada also believed that he had been granted visions of Kannon on mountaintops, who told him that he had a special work to do for the salvation of humanity. He went his own way more and more, finally breaking with Omoto in 1934. He formed a "Japan Kannon Association," Kannon being very important to him then. Later, as the New Age advanced, Miroku became more significant. In the meantime, Okada acquired some measure of fame – as well as controversy – as a spiritual healer.

The spiritual healing practice of *jorei* consists simply of holding the cupped hand, like a lens to focus light, over the afflicted area of a person's body. World Messianity people say that as the New Age light increases in the world, the time the hand needs to be held has grown less and less. The technique can also be used to heal non-medical situations. I recall hearing some World Messianity followers in Los Angeles say they practiced *jorei* on a particularly dangerous exit in the city's freeway system, and that the accident rate subsequently went down significantly.

Perfect Liberty Kyodan

The English title Perfect Liberty was adopted in 1946, at a time when everything English and American had great prestige in the defeated nation.[12] But the religion has deep roots in prewar Japan. The ultimate founder was Kanada Tokumitsu, a fairly prosperous Osaka merchant seriously interested in esoteric Shingon Buddhism and the *yamabushi*-type mountain faiths associated with it, especially Mitake-kyo, a Shinto sect emphasizing pilgrimage to a sacred peak of that name. He established a group, Shinto Tokumitsu Kyo, to promote certain teachings his experiences had garnered. After his death in 1919, it was taken over by a disciple, a former Zen priest called Miki Tokuharu (1871–1938). Named Hito no Michi ("Way of Man") in 1931, the movement now came less to stress esotericism than right family and social relations. In 1936 the leadership role of *oshieoya* ("teaching parent") passed to his son, Miki Tokumitsu (1900–1983). Both father and son spent time in prison under the nationalistic government; Tokumitsu survived and essentially reconstructed the religion as PL Kyodan after the war, then using only the initials.

Although Perfect Liberty has many beautiful dancelike ceremonies and festivals with fireworks, Tokumitsu's basic principle was not esotericism but "Life is Art." In his life and work he stressed the importance of seeing one's life – including one's marriage, work, and play – as a work of art, designed with an eye to harmony, expression of beauty, and the gradual creation of an earthly paradise. The "life is art" theme may have ultimate roots in the Shingon concept of art as a manifestation of the buddha-nature, but it certainly also is related to the spiritual importance Onisaburo and Omoto gave to art. Perfect Liberty churches try to feature classes in traditional Japanese arts, and provide facilities for sport, also part of a balanced artistic life.

Two further concepts are important to understanding Perfect Liberty: *mishirase* and *mioshie*. These may be translated as "divine warning" and "divine instruction." If, as PL assumes, humanity is an expression – one might say a work of art – of God, then everything that happens to us is a part of that divine work, though some strokes of the Painter's brush – sickness, reverses, unhappiness – are meant to be warnings, messages that something is wrong and should be changed. If we need guidance on how to do so, we can receive divine instruction from the *oshieoya* or his representative. A definite way to do this is offered; a believer can write his or her question on a prepared form, and give it to the minister who will forward it appropriately. When the answer returns the minister takes that document to the petitioner's home and presents it in a solemn and reverent manner.

In Japan Perfect Liberty has sometimes been called the "golf religion," because when possible churches of this denomination like to provide golf courses on their grounds, as witness to the importance of sport and play, along with work, study, family life, hobbies, and everything else in a balanced life that is a living work of art. But there is more to it and its 934,000 members than golf alone.

The Nichiren Group

All three of the older and larger Buddhist groups usually considered to be among the new religions come out of the Nichiren tradition. They are Soka Gakkai (once by far the largest of all the new religions), Rissho Kosei Kai, and Reiyukai.

Soka Gakkai[13]

Earlier, in Chapter 2, we took the opportunity to visit a meeting of Soka Gakkai, in the form of Nichiren Shoshu of America. In Chapter 6 we traced the career of Nichiren himself and the Nichiren movement in medieval Japan. Now let's bring the story up to date, and see how Nichirenism gave birth to a group that, though technically part of the older Nichiren Shoshu denomination until 1991, for all intents and purposes was a "new religion," and in its heyday the most successful of all.

This remarkable modern upsurge of Nichiren Buddhism really began in 1928, when a Japanese schoolteacher and educational philosopher named Makiguchi Tsunesaburo (1871–1944) was converted to Nichiren Shoshu, which as we have seen was the most "extreme" form of Nichiren Buddhism, believing Nichiren to be none other than the buddha for the present, and the Lotus the only authoritative sutra for this "third age" of Buddhism, all other buddhas and scriptures being now obsolete. Makiguchi was joined by a younger disciple, Toda Josei (1900–1958). Two years later, in 1930, they formed a group called, initially, Soka Kyoiku Gakkai, "Value-Creation Education Society," based on a combination of Makiguchi's own educational philosophy and Nichirenism.

The former was a sort of educational pragmatism. In brief, Makiguchi believed that the traditional triad of values in western thought, Goodness, Beauty, and Truth, should be amended to Goodness, Beauty, and Benefit. The Japanese teacher argued that not all that is true benefits humanity, or can even be known, but we can know what is of use to us, and imparting that should be the real end of education. The goal of worthwhile pedagogy should not be just transmitting some abstract ideal of truth, but serving the real good of the individual and of society.

Makiguchi and Toda held that Nichiren Buddhism complemented this vision well, since unlike "pie in the sky" religions, it taught that all realms of buddha-nature are united in the present, as a source of power for a joyful, prosperous life here and now. It gauged religions not in terms of their abstract truth, but in their power to convey present benefit, and by this test Nichiren Shoshu came out way ahead.

Soka Gakkai was not at first a religious movement. During the 1930s it was simply a small discussion group, though most of the participants were Nichiren Shoshu. But in 1942 the government, avid for totalitarian control, tried to force all Nichiren sects to unite, and all to participate in Shinto worship as an expression of patriotism. Makiguchi and Toda refused, and were imprisoned; the older Makiguchi died in prison in 1944.

But Toda, released in 1945, believed that he had attained full enlightenment while in confinement and was full of eagerness to reconstruct Soka Gakkai on a mass basis. The spiritual vacuum after defeat, and the prestige one like him who had resisted what was now a thoroughly discredited regime could claim, gave him the opportunity he needed. A whirlwind of energy, utterly dedicated, he took full advantage of it. His version of Nichiren Buddhism, and that of the movement for the first twenty-five or thirty years after the Second World War, was dogmatic and exclusivistic, presenting itself as the one true Buddhism and one true religion in the world.

The group's name was changed to Nichiren Shoshu Soka Gakkai, and it became a lay teaching and evangelistic organization within the Nichiren Shoshu denomination. But it had its own structure, meetings for worship and cultural life, its own chain of command, its own publications, though nominally it acknowledged the authority of the older group and its priests. So effective was its promotional efforts that soon Soka Gakkai had five times the membership of the rest of Nichiren Shoshu, a strange relationship which was ultimately to lead to problems, but which worked at the time to make long-quiescent Nichiren Shoshu suddenly the largest Buddhist denomination in Japan, claiming some three million households by 1962, and 7,500,000 households[14] in 1970, the peak year of its rapid growth. The movement had also spread around the world.

How did it accomplish this? First, Soka Gakkai organized in a thoroughly modern way into prefectural, city, district, and block groups. The old-fashioned Buddhism of family temples tucked away in remote villages or on side streets was not for it. Instead, this new Buddhism for the third age of the Dharma was participatory. Neighborhood leaders kept track of members and prospective members, caring about their problems. Soka Gakkai neighbors made sure the zeal of their co-religionists did not flag, and that non-members were not allowed to forget they could join this welcoming and supportive group too. Members were rarely at a loss for something to do; one had the opportunity to take part in lively meetings and activities virtually every night of the week.

Nor was there anything musty about these activities. While of course dynamic chanting of the Daimoku and Gongyo (passages from the sutra) rang through Soka Gakkai halls and homes, this was a modern, streamlined form of Buddhism for today. No ethereal meditation amid incense and gongs, no ascetic diet or celibacy. Local centers sponsored art classes, sports teams, and music (especially marching bands and *min-on*, popular music) ensembles. Soka Gakkai activities were good places for outgoing young people to meet others of their kind.

And there was the practice of *shakubuku*, "break and subdue," winning new converts to "true Buddhism." Needless to say, this was controversial. In the 1950s, in its eagerness to gain a large base under Toda Josei's uncompromising leadership, it was said that the upstart sect used intolerant, unfair arguments against other religions, and high-pressure tactics. Shakubuku practitioners were accused of calling prospective converts at all hours of day and night, even of threatening to boycott the businesses of those who would not come around. One convinced family member was supposed to give the others no rest until they joined too.

On the other hand, Soka Gakkai made no secret of its promise of immediate, tangible benefits from the practice: healing, prosperity, wishes granted. Shakubuku enthusiasts made house calls, circulated literature everywhere, filled the streets with parades, and the largest stadia with conventions. These were vast rallies, intended to generate enthusiasm more than anything else with the help of chants, cheers, marching groups, and banners.

Critics murmured darkly that something about the movement seemed fascistic, with its firm discipline, true-believer mentality, and after 1964 even its own political party, the Komeito. Yet many, in those hardscrabble days and after, yearned for a cause as vigorous and positive as Soka Gakkai. The Nichiren sect was the only religion to make much impact on Japan's restless, rootless, searching young people and working-class families in the postwar years, the only faith to offer an effective alternative to the Marxist youth and labor organizations also burgeoning then. Soka Gakkai fought and sometimes won titanic organizing battles with communist-oriented unions and student bodies.

After Toda's death, the presidency of Soka Gakkai fell to Ikeda Daisaku (1928–). He had joined the movement in 1947, partly out of a fervent aversion to war and the

An appreciation of Japan's wartime suffering and postwar crisis of values gives one a perspective on the appeal of Soka Gakkai. I once had the opportunity to visit the home of an impoverished woman in Tokyo. She had lost all her own family to the atomic bomb in Hiroshima, and had since been abandoned by her husband, who left her with a small child. She supported herself and the child by selling newspapers on a street corner. When I entered her tiny home, I found the living room was dominated by a huge *gohonzon* (the Nichiren Shoshu object of worship, you will recall), and she pressed Soka Gakkai literature into my hand. When she was left alone amid the devastation of postwar Tokyo, it was Soka Gakkai friends who cared for her and her child as individuals. Now she had a perpetual optimism and cheerfulness despite everything; I am sure she was much borne up by Nichiren Shoshu faith, and by the support of other members in her neighborhood.

then-recent militarism in Japan; his older brother had been killed on the Burmese front. Then, as times changed in the 1960s and 1970s, Ikeda gradually led Soka Gakkai away from its narrow, quasi-fanatical mentality, and from the characteristic Nichiren nationalism – seeing Japan as the earth's spiritual center – toward more emphasis on its cultural, world peace mission. He spoke often of "Buddhist Humanism," and the Daimoku faith as the foundation of a "Third Civilization" – a new world for the third age of the Dharma, in which the planet would finally find peace, prosperity, culture, and happiness for all. Ikeda's proudest accomplishments were his dialogues with world leaders and religious figures, including the Pope and the Dalai Lama, and the great world peace conventions sponsored by Soka Gakkai, which included distinguished delegates from many faiths and nations.

At the same time, there were problems. Not only was Soka Gakkai plagued by criticism and by declining levels of membership and participation as Japan became more prosperous and secularized, but the movement suffered tension between the technically lay leadership of Soka Gakkai and the priests of Nichiren Shoshu, the parent but much smaller (apart from Soka Gakkai) religious sect. The latter demanded authority which the lay group saw as unwarranted interference in their vast, modern, smoothly-running organization, including the administration of a great new temple, the Taisekiji, being built at the foot of Mount Fuji. On the other hand, Soka Gakkais contended that Nichiren Shoshu priests, now mostly married and passing on their high positions by heredity, sometimes to persons with no true calling and unworthy of priestly office, were in effect little better than privileged laymen and had no real right to rule over the spiritual lives of Soka Gakkai members.[15]

Eventually, Ikeda resigned as president of Soka Gakkai in 1979 as a consequence of these struggles.[16] In 1991 Soka Gakkai and Nichiren Shoshu separated, to make Soka Gakkai International, as it is now called, an independent spiritual organization claiming some ten million individual followers in Japan, and another million and a half in other countries. But the number of active followers was thought to be much less.

Reiyukai[17]

This group, whose name means "Friends of the Spirits Association," was founded between 1919 and 1925 by Kubo Kakutaro (1890–1944) and his sister-in-law Kotani Kimi (1901–1971). It now has over a million and a half members. Kubo was a Nichiren Buddhist who accepted the Lotus Sutra as the ultimate source of religious authority and practice. However, he was alarmed both by the decline in traditional values he saw around him, and by signs of forthcoming disasters. At the same time, he was concerned by what he perceived to be the inability of traditionl Buddhist clergy, Nichiren and otherwise, to provide moral leadership in this situation. He therefore concluded that a new lay organization was the only solution.

To Kubo's mind, a fundamental cause of the crisis was inadequate veneration of the spirits of ancestors, which causes them distress and makes them unable to advance spiritually toward buddhahood on the other side. Augmented ancestrism would both promote the family ethic important to him, and by making ancestral spirits happier, enlist their aid in the improvement of our lives and the well-being of the world. This Reiyukai does by rites centering on the recitation of portions of the Lotus Sutra. The benefits extend not only to one's own family ancestors, but to all ancestral spirits.

The energetic promotion of Reiyukai fell mainly to Kotani Kimi, who worked particularly in poorer sections of Tokyo, not only teaching the faith but also engaging in practical work of nursing and spiritual healing; she is regarded as a manifestation of the future buddha, Miroku, even as Kubo was a buddha for our time. Perhaps Reiyukai especially appealed to the poor because, in a family-oriented society like Japan's, having recognized ancestors and high family values provides a sense of worth. Reiyukai has also supported political causes usually regarded as conservative.

Rissho Kosei Kai

The founder of this Nichiren movement, whose name means "Society Establishing Righteousness and Harmony," was Niwano Nikkyo (1906–1999), at one time a minor leader in Reiyukai. By 1938, the year he founded Rissho Kosei Kai, he had come to have misgivings about the older organization. Though it is also a lay organization, with no clergy-laity distinction, it does have teachers and officials. R.K.K. emphasizes reincarnation, declaring that adversities are caused by karmic effects from previous lives or from the bad deeds of ancestors; these can be reversed through ancestral veneration, spiritual growth, and good deeds, including what is now called bodhisattva practice. Originally Niwano had used divination practices to determine particular past evils to be overcome.

Figure 10.1 The Rissho Kosei Kai Great Sacred Hall (Lombroso; Public Domain: Wikimedia Commons)

One distinctive R.K.K. practice is the *hoza*, Dharma circle or, as it is sometimes called, "circle of harmony." This is in effect group counseling. Members sit in a circle, present their personal problems, and receive advice from others. *Hoza* is surely another example of the way in which the new religions, in contrast to older faiths that tend to give many people a sense of being remote and impersonal, express concern for individual lives, even those of the humblest. The movement has some 3.1 million members.[18]

The "new" new religions

Since the 1970s several more new religions, sometimes called *shin-shinshukyo* or "new new religions," have arisen or, if founded earlier, have grown dramatically.[19] The new spiritual upsurge has two characteristics.

First, one side of it is closely aligned to the world-wide "New Age" movement. (In Japan, the term "Spiritual World" [*Seishin Sekai*] is preferred to "New Age.") "New Age," in Japan as elsewhere, is largely a matter of books and centers devoted to positive thinking, UFOs, psychic phenomena, reincarnation (of course, not as unconventional in Buddhist Japan as in lands of Christian spiritual background), and translations of such writers popular in the West, ranging from Edgar Cayce to George Gurdjieff.

The other side of the new-new religious world is the appearance of new groups of Buddhist background largely based in esoteric or Vajrayana Buddhism, that is,

Shingon together with Tibetan antecedents, rather than Nichiren like the earlier "new" Buddhisms. Several of these will be considered briefly: Agonshu, Shinnyoen, Mahikari, Gedatsu, and the notorious Aum Shinrikyo, now renamed Aleph.

On the "New Age" side, let us look at the prolific writings of Okawa Ryuho, who calls his teaching *Kofuku no kagaku*, "The science of happiness," and heads an Institute for Research in Human Happiness.[20] He has written as many as two or three books a year, most of them "channeled" from angelic beings. At the peak of his popularity (now said to be in decline), his works crowded Japanese bookstores, and his lectures drew large crowds. Okawa claims to have received revelations from angels, and to know the Eternal Buddha, whom he calls the Lord El Cantare, who guides humanity forever. In the past this buddha's consciousness has manifested in Shakyamuni Buddha and Hermes in Greece; it now speaks through Okawa Ryuho.

That sage has made various predictions about the future. War will come in the Middle East – perhaps already fulfilled – Japan will become a religious center; by 2200–2300 robots will run most industries; in 2300–2400 the United States will sink into the ocean, and Atlantis will arise again to take its place. In addition to teaching of this sort, Okawa emphasizes the importance of love defined as giving love to others, the Buddhist compassion; of learning wisdom not only as knowledge but as practice; and of self-reflection in order to get rid of mental impurities. It is evident that Okawa's teaching has much in common with western "New Age" thought, but tinctured by Japanese spirituality, especially Mahayana Buddhism.

Another important figure of this sort is Hosoki Kazuko, a prominent figure in Japanese media, including magazines, bestselling books, and television, in which she offers advice based on her divination practice to celebrities and members of the audience. Her method of divination is based on what she calls "six-star astrology," and includes an emphasis on ancestor worship, which she declares is an essential practice if one is to change one's destiny as it is initially presented in her oracles. She insists that her teachings are not "religion," but simply "natural" to the Japanese people.[21] We will return to this theme of "naturalness" as over against "religion" in Japan today.

Agonshu

This esoteric Buddhist sect was founded in 1978 by Kiriyama Seiyu (1921–), a charismatic individual who is believed to act as an intermediary between followers and the spiritual world. In 1955 he took a kind of lay ordination in Shingon; in 1970 Kannon, through a dream, told him to focus on *goma* (fire ritual) rites and become a leader. The group's name comes from *Agon* (Pali: *Agama*), ancient Buddhist texts, which Kiriyama interprets in an esoteric way. He stresses that bad happenings stem from bad *karma*, either individual or ancestral. These can be reversed, ancestral spirits released from their bondages, and wishes granted through *goma* rituals. Agonshu performs massive, spectacular *gomas* outdoors, with two huge fires, one for each of the two esoteric mandalas, especially on February 11 (Kenkoku or "Founding of the Nation" day, Japan's national holiday). These theatrical rites draw millions of participants, who add wooden sticks with their petition inscribed to the fire, though of course many are not among the some 300,000 actual adherents the group reports.[22]

Shinnyoen

This is also a subsect of Vajrayana or esoteric Buddhism, and regards itself as a lay order. It was founded by Shinjo Ito (1906–1989), who had been both a Shingon priest and an aviation engineer, and his wife Tomoji (1912–1967) in 1936. The stated purpose was to make esoteric practice available to ordinary laypeople, and complementary to a life of service in ordinary society. Central to the group's activity are conferences called *sesshin*, in which followers receive guidance through a spirit medium, *reinosha*, recognized by the organization. Their messages emanate from a spiritual world wherein dwell the spirits of the departed.

An interesting feature of Shinnyoen is that two of the founding couple's sons, Chibun and Yuichi, who died at ages three and fifteen respectively, are believed to have sacrificed themselves to take on the sufferings of others, and now act as guides and guardians in the spirit world. The mediums' contact with that realm is not direct, but only through the assistance of the *ryo-doji*, the "two children." The name Shinnyoen means "Garden of the True Tathata," that is, of the original buddha-nature, the essential nature of all things.[23]

Mahikari

Mahikari, "True Light," is an offshoot of Sekai Kyuseiko or World Messianity.[24] It was founded by Okada Kotama (1901–1974), in 1959. Okada had been a member of World Messianity, but believed he received a revelation in 1959 from Su, a hitherto unknown deity who is the true Creator of the universe. Although he created it benign, the world has become polluted; it can be purified by channeling divine light through the palm of the hand, a practice comparable to *jorei* but called *mahikari no waza* in this group; it can also be transmitted through amulets called *omitama*. This movement has effectively spread overseas, having centers in America, Europe, and elsewhere, but has split into two groups since Okada's death.

Gedatsu

This somewhat older religion stems directly from the Shugendo tradition, as its founder, Okano Shoken, had been a prominent *yamabushi* priest. He started the Gedatsu movement in 1929. Drawing freely from Shinto as well as esoteric Buddhist symbolism, he created a temple designed to enshrine the souls of the highest universal being, Tenjinshigi, together with Fudo and ancestral spirits. Striking ceremonies of the esoteric Buddhist sort, and simple walking exercises, calm negative energies, purify emotions, and generate peace.[25]

Aum Shinrikyo/Aleph

This notorious group was founded by Matsumoto Chizuo (1955– ; later Asahara Shoko) in 1987. He had been a member of Agonshu, and was deeply involved in yoga and esoteric spirituality, especially that of Tibetan Buddhism, based on spiritual experiences he reportedly received in the Himalayas. These interests separated him somewhat from the mainstream of Japanese Buddhism. Even more so did a fascination with prophecy, especially in the New Testament book of Revelation and the writings of Nostradamus. These works led him to make bold predictions, including World War III and the destruction of Japan in the late 1990s.

So far as spiritual life was concerned, Asahara offered his followers a series of three initiations: earthly, astral, and nirvanic. All centered around devotion to the guru, Asahara, symbolized by such acts as drinking his bath water or imbibing a little of his blood. Some of those who had entered the highest initiation undertook the monastic life. The group also maintained a rural center, a hospital, and several businesses.

Aum Shinrikyo is best known for its release of nerve gas in five Tokyo subway cars on March 20, 1995, killing twelve people and injuring more than 5,500. The reason for this attack is not entirely clear, but certainly it had to do with Asahara's apocalyptic prophecies. Some said it was to spark World War III, leading to a new age; some to create a political crisis in Japan in which Asahara would be made emperor; some to divert attention from other crimes, including alleged murders and other gas incidents directed at supposed enemies of the group. Perhaps all three. Asahara and a number of members were arrested, but generally refused to talk; the leader himself was sentenced to death.[26]

This sensational crime had two effects. Although Aum Shinrikyo managed to regroup, changing its name to Aleph in 2000, its membership fell by more than four-fifths, to around 1500 in 2007. Second, the episode created a great amount of public concern in Japan about religious groups, especially new and unusual ones, and particularly Aum. Cases of discrimination against Aum members, even those who had not been been found guilty of any crime, such as refusing to admit their children to schools, were widely reported. Police surveillance became common, aided by legislation specifically allowing this in the case of Aum. Many civil libertarians were concerned, fearful of a return to the situation before 1945. In the end a more moderate outlook prevailed, although Japanese are now more than ever aware of the possible dark side of religion, and observers have remarked on a "post-Aum" era in Japan in which "religion" as such, particularly Buddhism and the New Religions, is under suspicion and in significant decline; some "spiritual" teachers like Hosoki

Kazuko emphasize they are "not religious." But perhaps the post-Fukushima image of religion, especially in its rescue operations, will mitigate that decline somewhat.

Common characteristics of the new religions

In addition to two already mentioned, a tendency toward monotheism and founding by a charismatic, shaman-like figure, often a woman, here are several more:

- A simple but definite process of entry, such as we noted in the case of Tenrikyo, which makes evident that this religion is an individual choice requiring an individual action, not solely something one is born into.
- Each centers on a single, simple, sure practice which anyone can perform or receive, and which a sufficient number of followers experience as producing discernible results, such as *osazuke* in Tenrikyo, chanting the Daimoku in Soka Gakkai, *toritsugi* in Konkokyo, or *jorei* in World Messianity. Any new religious movement requires a practice, and a corresponding sense of experience and results, adequate to compensate for the felt loss one may have in breaking religiously with one's family and community. Nonetheless, these simple techniques often will be based on familiar popular religion concepts and practices, like ancestrism, chanting, and *hotoku* (returning virtue; showing gratitude for blessings received).
- A this-worldly outlook, focused on benefits, and in some cases even an afterlife, here on earth, rather than in an otherworldly heaven or hell. The new religions tend to be optimistic, saying something like Tenrikyo's *yokigurashi* (the joyous life) is possible now, and foretelling a new age of earthly joy, like that of Omoto's apocalyptic, the Third Civilization of Soka Gakkai, or in Tenrikyo's reincarnation, or hinted at in Sekai Kyusei Kyo's paradisal gardens. Perhaps, emerging in a age of unprecedented modernization and progress, they are saying their religion accepts the modern world and can do it even better.
- Most have a sacred center, like Tenri City or Gedatsu's great temple complex, which is a place of pilgrimage and provides scattered members with a sense of the religion's numbers and vision.
- Unlike the older religion's sometimes antiquated organization, they tend to have a tight and thorough organization based on modern corporate or governmental models, supported by a up-to-date use of mass media – magazines, newspapers, radio, TV, and now the internet – to advertise the religion and communicate with members.
- Most put an emphasis on healing. Spiritual healing, including the solution of family and emotional problems, was usually a very important part of the religion's early mission; sometimes it has since been downplayed in favor of other messages, but remains a part of the program.
- Most seem to have a subjectivist outlook, stressing that the individual makes his or her own world by thoughts, positive or negative, though proclaiming also the

religion's worldview, rites, and perhaps meditation practices can greatly help one to improve and purify one's thoughts.

- In propagating the religion, they tend to use rhetoric of enthusiasm and testimony more than reasoned theological arguments. One hears people say, "This religion did this and that for me, I'm extremely grateful and want to share its benefits," rather than, "Let's look at it logically, and then you can see it's got to be true." This is of course generally true of popular religion (rather than academic philosophy or theology), since there feeling and testimony communicate most effectively.

Nearly all of these characteristics point toward something we have already observed, that in contrast to a tendency of the older faiths to be impersonal, clerical, academic, and tradition-ridden, these new religions have a way of making ordinary people believe they are concerned about them and their problems individually, and have a technique, and a fellowship, that can help. It's as though the older faiths say, "Let's talk about your grandparent's shrine or temple"; the newer ones, "Let's talk about *you* and your life now."[27]

The relation of new religious movements to modernity, both in Japan and elsewhere, is complex. On one hand, in pointing toward a better – even Utopian – eschatological future here in this world, they seem to take up the promise of progressivism, saying in effect, whatever science and technology can do, we can do even better. In offering a simple but definite process of entry on the basis of individual choice, in providing individuals with spiritual practices they can do themselves, and in showing concern for the problems of ordinary individuals in today's vast impersonal cities, they reflect the increasing individualism of modern times.

On the other hand, some critics would see the "irrational," magical practices of new religions as anti-modern, carryovers from a benighted past. Other sociologists, however, have pointed out that magic simply represents a technique, and that ours is an age of technique – scientific, technological, bureaucratic – in which knowing the right way to do something is more important than faith or philosophical belief. In this light, the "magic" that seems to be resurging in many movements is just an alternative technique, one that can be wielded by anyone who knows how.

Why alternative? Another aspect of modernity is that for many ordinary people, the brave new world of science, technology, and bureaucracy presents more than anything else a vast, gray, routinized, impersonal environment in which one cries out for some corner of one's life in which there is color, magic, fantasy, an alternative reality. Some find in religion the means to access such a reality, and the more contrasting it is to the everyday world, the better. In considerations like this, I think some insight can be gained into the remarkable power and persistence of magical, miracle-purveying, seemingly incredible, "fundamentalist" religion in a world in which some thought, far too prematurely, that science and secularization would send the gods scurrying. Despite the "post-Aum" mood, the Japanese new religions, and new-new religions, are one venue in which magic is still afoot.

Key points you need to know

- Shugendo is the religion of the *yamabushi* or mountain priests, adepts who practice austerities and initiations in the mountains, and come down to function as healers and diviners in the villages. Shugendo had a role in the founding of some of the new religions
- Tenrikyo and Konkokyo are among the oldest new religions, centering on a new revelation from the one God
- The Omoto group, including Seicho no Ie, World Messianity, and Perfect Liberty Kyodan, emphasize respectively power of mind, a coming new age, and "life is art"
- The Nichiren group, especially Soka Gakkai, has grown powerfully, but suffered difficulties
- Many "new new" religions, including Agonshu, Shinnyoen, Mahikari, Gedatsu, and Aum Shinrikyo, are based on esoteric Buddhism rather than Nichiren
- The Tokyo subway gas attack by Aum Shinrikyo members led to serious questioning of religion in Japan
- Common features of new religions include a single deity or power, a charismatic founder, emphasis on healing, a sacred center, a subjectivist outlook, and use of the rhetoric of enthusiasm and experience.

Questions for study and discussion

1. What does Shugendo tell us about the deep structures of Japanese religion, and about Japanese popular religion?
2. How would you interpret the origin of Tenrikyo in terms of its time and place?
3. Why do you think many of the founders of new religions were women?
4. Why did Deguchi Nao and Omoto have such a strongly apocalyptic outlook?
5. Why did Omoto lead to several other new religions?
6. Why were the "older" new religions of Buddhist background based on Nichiren Buddhism?
7. Why do you think the "new new" religions of Buddhist background tend to be based instead on esoteric Buddhism?
8. How would you summarize general characteristics of the new religions in your own words?
9. How would you epitomize their appeal in a few words?
10. What are some deep-level reasons why you think religion persists in the modern world?

Further reading

Note that the bibliography below gives only general books on the new religions as a group, not books on individual religions. Books on the individual religions are suggested in notes to that group. Generally the notes cite only recent independent scholarly works. Most of the new religions now provide English-language websites and numerous publications, to which the student is referred for further information from the religion's perspective.

Baffelli, Erica, *Media and New Religions: Japanese Religion and Culture*. New York, NY and London: Routledge, 2015.

Clarke, Peter B., *Japanese New Religions in Global Perspective*. Richmond, UK: Curzon, 2000.

Clarke, Peter B., ed., *Bibliography of Japanese New Religions*. Richmond, UK: Japan Library, 1999.

Earhart, H. Byron, *A Religious Study of the Mount Haguro Sect of Shugendo*. Tokyo: Sophia University, 1970.

Ellwood, Robert S., *The Eagle and the Rising Sun: Americans and the New Religions of Japan*. Philadelphia, PA: Westminster Press, 1974.

Hardacre, Helen, *Kurozumikyo and the New Religions of Japan*. Princeton, NJ: Princeton University Press, 1986.

Kisala, Robert, *Prophets of Peace: Pacifism and Cultural Identity in Japan's New Religions*. Honolulu, HI: University of Hawaii Press, 1999.

McFarland, H. Neil, *The Rush Hour of the Gods*. New York, NY: Harper & Row, 1970.

Miyake, Hiroshi, *Shugendo: Essays on the Structure of Japanese Folk Religion*. Ann Arbor, MI: Center for Japanese Studies, University of Michigan, 2001.

Offner, Clark B., and Henrikus van Straelen, *Modern Japanese Religions*. Leiden: E. J. Brill, 1963.

Stalker, Nancy K., *Prophet Motive: Deguchi Onisaburo, Oomoto, and the Rise of New Religions in Imperial Japan*. Honolulu, HI: University of Hawaii Press, 2008.

Thomsen, Harry, *The New Religions of Japan*. Tokyo and Rutland, VT: Tuttle, 1963.

Electronic Resources

Inoue Nobutake, "Recent Trends in the Study of Japanese New Religions." http://www2.kokugakuin.ac.jp/ijcc/wp/cpjr/newreligions/inoue.html

Ian Reader, "Japanese New Religions: An Overview." http://www.wrs.vcu.edu/SPECIAL%20PROJECTS/JAPANESE%20NEW%20RELIGIONS/Japenese%20New%20Religions.WRSP.pdf

"Tenrikyo," http://en.tenrikyo-resource.com/wiki/Tenrikyo (Official site.)

"Konkokyo: Our Faith," www.konkokyo.or.jp/eng/bri/our_faith/religious_beliefs.html (Official site.)

"Frequently Asked Questions About Oomoto." http://www.oomoto.or.jp/English/enFaq/indexfaq.html (Official site.)

Meishu-sama, "Sekai Kyusei and Myself." http://jinsai.org/english/meishu_sama/history/histjins11.php (The Founder's own account of the religion, from 1950.)

"Perfect Liberty Kyodan," *A Collection of Wisdom*. http://www.rodneyohebsion.com/perfect-liberty-kyodan.htm

"Reiyukai America." http://www.reiyukai-usa.org (Official site.)

"Happy Science North America" (Okawa Ryuho). http://happyscience-na.org/about/ryuho-okawa (Official site.)

Peter B. Clarke, "Agonshu," in J. Gordon Melton and Martin Baumann, eds., *Religions of the World: A Comprehensive Encyclopedia of Beliefs and Practices*. Santa Barbara, CA: ABC-CLIO, 2010, Vol. 1, pp. 51–3. https://books.google.co.uk/books?isbn=1598842048 (Go to page number.)

Wikipedia, "Shinnyo-en." https://en.wikipedia.org/wiki/Shinnyo-en

Wikipedia, "Mahikari." https://en.wikipedia.org/wiki/Mahikari

"Sukyo Mahikari: Frequently Asked Questions." www.sukyomahikari.org/faq.html (Official site of one of the major Mahikari denominations.)

Holly Fletcher, "Backgrounder: Aum Shinrikyo," Council on Foreign Relations. www.cfr.org/japan/aum-shinrikyo/p9238

http://english.aleph.to/ (Official site for Aleph, successor to Aum Shinrikyo. A bit difficult to use, but interesting.)

11 *Pilgrimages*

Religion in Japan 1945 to the present

In this chapter

This chapter will summarize the situation of religion in Japan during the postwar Occupation, and in the new world of modern, prosperous, and democratic Japan. We will find that while some changes have obtained, tradition has remained strong in religion, despite secularization, and is reflected even in the most recent products of Japanese popular culture.

Main topics covered

- Religion under the postwar Occupation
- Critical Buddhism
- New roles for nuns and wives of Buddhist priests
- The continuation of tradition in such areas as idealization of village life, spiritual achievement as a goal, and the role of symbol and form in worship.
- *Mizuko kuyo* or ceremonies for unborn fetuses
- Religion and recent popular culture, including *anime*.

Religion under the postwar Occupation

August 1945 was, for Japan, a catastrophic month: the atom-bombing of Hiroshima and Nagasaki and then, on the 15th, Japan's surrender. The island nation was defeated, demoralized, and half-demolished. Its citizens had barely enough of the basic necessities to sustain life. The major cities were little but ruins – with the exception of Kyoto, which was spared aerial attack, including possible selection as an atomic bomb target, by intervention of U.S. Secretary of War Henry Stimson. (He had visited the ancient capital sixteen years earlier, while Governor of the Philippines, and had been deeply impressed by the beauty and cultural significance of its countless shrines and temples.)

The Japanese people, however, by now thought of little but survival, wearily going through the motions of life and war like automatons. If ever a country seemed like a blank slate on which a new history, even a new religion, could be written, it was Japan in 1945. But while a fresh start obtained in some areas of national life, in others, including religion, in the end tradition proved as strong as any impulse to change.

Traditionalism was evidenced in the very circumstances of Japan's surrender. Though generally the emperor was not expected to intervene in government decisions, it appears he did play a decisive role in the war cabinet's acceptance of the Allies' terms.[1] His dramatic radio address the next day, about "bearing the unbearable," did much to assure the peaceful reconciliation of his people and remaining troops to the inevitable. In response to the Allies' demand for unconditional surrender, the only condition for which Japan's leaders held out was that the ruler would retain his office as figurehead sovereign of the nation. Whatever ordinary people (or the emperor himself) thought, this consideration seemed non-negotiable to those who had led the disastrous adventure in the sovereign's name, and who no doubt believed he was in some sense the sacred center of Japan's very identity; the throne was therefore essential to the land of the sun's continuation as a nation and people.

Needless to say, vehement opposition to accepting this condition was expressed by many on the Allied side who thought the emperor represented everything they were fighting against in the vicious Pacific War. But other counsels, articulated especially by General Douglas MacArthur, prevailed. They believed that Emperor Hirohito would only be an asset as Japan transited from one era to another. Preserving nominal imperial rule undoubtedly prevented much bitterness, and quite possibly bloodshed.

Otherwise it was initially a new scene, for religion as well as for almost everything else, under the occupation guided by the authoritarian General MacArthur.[2] Although nominally Supreme Commander of the Allied Powers (SCAP), the U.S. commander was for all intents and purposes ruler of the country, and the Occupation a solely U.S. affair during its span from 1945 to 1952. MacArthur was sometimes called the "American Shogun," and his "shogunate" was an intriguing mirror of the American mind in those years of victory and increasing Cold War anxiety, as well as of Japan's complex attitudes toward tradition and change. At first the supremely confident victors wanted nothing so much as to remake Japan on the model of America. The Japanese, as they had many times in the past, in the end took what they wanted from the foreigners and reworked it till it became a part of their own evolving culture.

At its beginning the Occupation imposed much idealistic renovation on the defeated nation. Japan was demilitarized, and the postwar constitution forbade the government to maintain armed forces or engage in war, the first (and thus far only) major state so to do. Land reform broke up large estates, including some belonging to Shinto and Buddhist institutions, in favor of the peasant farmers who actually worked the land. Titles of nobility (except those of the imperial family) were abolished, women were given the right to vote, and the political process became, at least officially, thoroughly democratic. Only those "purged" because of their reputed close association with the wartime regime and its ideology were excluded from electoral roles.

As one would expect from Americans, the reforms put special emphasis on separation of religion and the state. Links between Shinto and the government were abolished under SCAP. Ownership of shrine property, and the appointment of priests, reverted to the local community as represented by elected shrine trustees, rather as though Shinto shrines were congregational churches. Many shrines, and also Buddhist temples and monasteries, lost considerable revenue in the land reforms, but they soon learned to make it up through American-style pledges, fund drives, and money-making enterprises.

On a higher level, the emperor was induced to issue a declaration, on New Year's Day, 1946, renouncing his alleged divinity (in which, as a scientific-minded man – his avocation was marine biology – he perhaps never believed anyway): his celebrated "Declaration of Humanity." The erstwhile high priest of Shinto continued to perform the rituals of his office at the palace shrines, but these were now technically considered personal rather than state acts of worship.

While religious bodies faced financial problems in the impoverished and secularized land, they also for the first time had real freedom to control their own institutional lives. Before 1945, faiths could function legally only if chartered by the state; obtaining that recognition entailed doctrinal conformity to the official mythology and ideology, and much detailed regulation of the religion's internal affairs. Several of the new religions and their leaders suffered severe restriction or persecution in those days. The tiny Christian minority was also hampered on both practical and intellectual levels; during the war, as we have seen, all Protestant denominations were forced to unite into one church for the convenience of the government, and had to recognize in some way the spiritual authority of the emperor. Now churches could do whatever they wished.

Symbolic changes also took place. Shinto holy days were no longer national holidays, being replaced by such innocuous celebrations as Adult's Day, Children's Day, Vernal Equinox, Autumnal Equinox, Culture Day, and the like. The small Shinto altars that had been omnipresent in schools and government offices were removed. Of course ambiguities occurred. At the end of 1945, as Japanese government workers were busy removing their tiny *kamidana*, shoebox-sized shrines on office walls, loudspeakers outside the entrance of SCAP headquarters in the heart of Tokyo were blaring out Christmas carols.

That picture suggests a larger ambiguity: the relation of the Occupation to Christianity. While sincerely promoting religious freedom, Douglas MacArthur and certain other high SCAP officials strongly believed also that Japan needed Christian faith to become truly democratic. The defeat, and therefore the discrediting of the traditional religions that had generally supported the imperial cause, should, they thought, open the way for the empire's evangelization. Urgent calls went out for armies of missionaries to come over to help. On February 24, 1950, MacArthur sent a cable to a stateside convention of Youth for Christ stating:

> My often repeated conviction remains unchanged that acceptance of the fundamental principles of Christianity would provide the surest foundation for the firm establishment of democracy in Japan. Therefore, distribution of scriptures and interdenominational evangelistic rallies carried on in cooperation with established religious missions capable of providing continuing follow-up are highly welcome.[3]

Nonetheless, the expansion of Christianity in Japan on which some pinned great hopes was not to occur. However, the status of Christianity may be reflected in the fact that since 1945 no less than seven Japanese Prime Ministers have been Christian. But whatever they gave in other areas, when it came to religion the Japanese held back. It was the new religions, deeply rooted in traditional Nichiren and shamanistic themes, that grew exponentially in the unhampered postwar spiritual marketplace. At the same time, Shinto did not wither away, as some outsiders expected it would, mistaking its use, or rather abuse, by the extreme nationalists for its essence. Under local control and a voluntary national organization, the Jinja Honcho, *kami* worship reverted to its roots in family affiliations and local communities. Buddhism too recovered and held its own despite growing secularism; Zen, in fact, rose in esteem in Japan in response to the "discovery" of it by some occupation GIs, who on returning home started the midcentury Zen vogue in the West.

The imperial house remained Shinto, and the heady immediate postwar years ended with the Cold War, and especially the onset of the Korean War in 1950. By

An interesting aspect of the early Occupation years was the way in which, despite denials from the palace, persistent rumors made the rounds that the emperor, the empress, the crown prince, or the whole imperial family, were about to be converted to Christianity. Some missionaries imagined that, if this happened, the ruling house would bring the whole nation into the faith with it, in the manner of kings of old. Others, including MacArthur, found their feelings more mixed. While in principle they accepted that, as Christians, they ought to welcome any converts, they realized that a change on the part of a sovereign to a faith other than that of the majority of his subjects could be very divisive, if not disastrous, from the political point of view. It would even be divisive for Christians. What kind of Christian would he become, Catholic, Protestant, or perhaps Quaker like the respected American tutor to the crown prince, Elizabeth Gray Vining?[4] Emissaries of all faiths were reportedly seen entering the palace.

then idealistic reform was less important to the Americans than keeping Japan on the right side against the Soviet bloc, and when fighting commenced in nearby Korea, Japan became a major source of Allied supplies. Indeed, that tragic opportunity did much to start the Japanese postwar economy rolling toward its ultimate place as a world economic powerhouse. Then, when the peace treaty signed in 1951 took effect the next year, Japan again took control of its own destiny.

New thinking about Buddhism

One subsequent response to the militaristic period, the war, and defeat was the emergence of a school of thought called Critical Buddhism, alluded to above in a note on Dogen, which alleged that a fundamental misconception of Buddhism had enabled the participation of Buddhists, including clerics, in war and the warrior mentality, from the days of the samurai up through the Tokugawa and World War II regimes. The culprit was the notion of Original Enlightenment (*hongaku*), basic to Mahayana in the Japanese understanding of it, but in the critics' eyes virtually permission to do whatever you want to do so long as you perceive it as coming out of your enlightened true nature and *mushin*, "no mind."

It is true that the five basic Buddhist precepts for laity – not to kill, steal, engage in sexual misconduct, lie, or use intoxicants – had been interpreted in an easy-going way, with emphasis on the "sincerity" (i.e. the expression of Original Enlightenment) of the act. Thus one could, it is said, be a samurai warrior whose sword repeatedly tasted blood and whose real code was Bushido, an extreme nationalist whose true loyalty was to the emperor, or a *kamikaze* pilot committing suicide as his plane hit an American ship, and still (in one's own mind) remain true to enlightened Buddha-nature.

Instead, Critical Buddhists insisted, we must go back to strict Buddhist ethics – taking the five precepts seriously in their plain meaning – and to compassion. This means, in effect, going back to the Dharma long before it found expression in the metaphysics of Mahayana, or came to Japan. Original Enlightenment, they tell us, one way or another is basic to the experience of virtually all Japanese Buddhism (though they see Dogen as a misunderstood exception) from Kegon to Nichiren. Go back, then, to Therevada Buddha-nature as something attained, not given.

Critics of the critics, while taking the point, have argued that we should not condemn the whole Mahayana tradition for its occasional misuse. Original Enlightenment can be expressed in ways that make for genuine universal compassion. Similar debates, of course, have raged within other religions, which historically have blessed wars even while their core teachings point to love. It has also been argued that Buddhism, by its very nature, has no "essence" or absolute truth, but is itself always a form of critical inquiry.[5]

New roles for Buddhist women

In August 1945, despite the tremendous turmoil of the atomic bombings and surrender, a previously planned five-day conference of Soto Zen nuns was held as scheduled in Tokyo.[6] Nuns of this order had been meeting and agitating for greater equality with monks, and greater responsibilities, for more than twenty years. They had met considerable resistance from monks, imbued with the traditional Buddhist ideas that women are more impure and bear more negative *karma* than men; their place, whether as wives or nuns, is to be subordinate.

However, during the war, nuns had been virtually forced to take on new responsibilities. They had organized care for children evacuated from the cities, worked in war plants, and in general undertook new areas of responsibility and service outside the convent. Now, in 1945, with the war ending, the leadership did not want to lose what had been gained, and that was what this conference was about.

As it happened, in the democratic postwar atmosphere the Soto sect did grant nuns new privileges in respect to education, teaching, administering temples, and control of their own order, though only grudgingly and little by little. Eventually most goals for formal equality were realized by Soto and other Buddhist nuns, though issues of popular attitude and of ultimate control of the tradition remain problematic.[7]

A parallel question was the wives of priests. As we have seen, priests were allowed to marry in 1872, and within a generation the majority were wed. However, the status of their wives was generally low. Celibacy was still seen by most Buddhists as the spiritual ideal; the religious law of most sects mandated it; many priestly marriages were therefore unregistered, amounting to little more than legal concubinage, leaving wives and children few rights. By the Taisho era there was much discussion of this anomalous situation, and some reforms took place. But, again, it took the war to effect substantial change.

During the war, with many priests pressed into military service or war work, wives were permitted to take their husbands' places in the temple, teaching and conducting services. Special seminars trained and ordained them to do this, though only at restricted levels. Like the nuns, wives of priests organized after the war, and saw to it that these advantages gradually became permanent, including the requirement that clerical marriages be official, with protection for the family in event of the priest's death.

Inevitably, the improved status of priests' wives brought them into some conflict with nuns in their own enhanced roles. Some nuns felt that, as real professionals and with higher religious education, they were better qualified than most wives to teach and do pastoral work. Issues like these are being sorted out. In any case, it is clear that in postwar Japan women have greater visibility and prestige in Buddhism than before.

The wives of priests are a definite presence in Japanese Buddhism today. The visitor to an average temple will often encounter a bright, cheerful woman who will greet him or her, show the guest around, and ask if there is any service the temple can perform. Only in time will it eventuate that this is, more likely than not, the wife of the priest. Today, more than 90 percent of Buddhist priests in Japan are married.

On the other hand, the ranks of nuns are aging and thinning; fewer and fewer younger women in today's Japan opt for that life.[8]

Tradition continues

The discussion in this chapter, and in the book generally to this point, should indicate that substantial changes have occurred in Japanese religion since the Second World War: the rise of New Religions, the effects of democratization and land reform, new thinking in Buddhism (and other faiths) in light of the complicity of religion in nationalism and militarism, new roles for religious women, disturbing issues concerning Soka Gakkai and Aum Shinrikyo, together with controversies over religion and the state involving, for example, the Ise and Yasukuni shrines, and the Daijosai. At the same time, note that these points affect chiefly the intellectual, institutional, and public lives of religion, less its practice by the ordinary layperson. We shall therefore now turn to another side of the postwar situation: the continuity of much of popular Japanese religion with its past.

Despite alleged secularization – the supposed lack of interest in, knowledge about, or practice of religion by a very large part of the population, and the quixotic insistence of many Japanese that Japanese religion is dead, or even that Japan has no religion – to all appearance the country remains the "land of the gods and buddhas." Shrines and temples large and small are visible everywhere, and well attended, especially at major festivals and New Year, displaying rites and customs that did not change dramatically in 1945 or since.

So it is that in one important respect Japanese religion is different from, say, the Christian religious world. Traditional Shinto offerings and Buddhist rites are quite unreformed, and though the New Religions may offer new mixes of old ingredients, and at least in the case of Nichiren groups new emphases, the fundamental Japanese shamanistic/chanting/offering platform remains intact.

One may compare this picture with the Christian third of the world, where Roman Catholic worship is quite different in structure and "feel" from the old Latin mass since the Vatican II Council of the 1960s, while Anglican and Protestant services often seem hardly less changed, being much more informal and, in much of the "third world," pentecostal. (I once attended a Roman Catholic mass in Ise not long after Vatican II; the priest was now behind the altar, the liturgy was in Japanese, and laypeople had significant roles in reading scripture and leading prayers. But certainly nothing had changed at the Grand Shrine.)

Despite Japan's well-deserved reputation for innovation in technology, creativity in the arts, and leadership in the ever-changing world of "pop" culture, religious practice remains firmly grounded in the past. Four factors obtain that, in the Japanese context, tend to support religious traditionalism. They will be explored in some detail:

1. The *kokoro no furusato* ("homeland [literally, old village] of the heart" theme and its mystique.
2. Admiration of individual achievement attained through ordeal and self-discipline, like that of the "marathon monks" and the *yamabushi*, for which the spiritual tradition provides structures.
3. The importance of giving concrete, established symbols and forms to religious interactions.
4. The idea of finding the ultimate in the ordinary.

Homelands of the heart

The *kokoro no furusato* theme, as used by such writers as Kino Kazuyoshi[9] and as it resonates in common parlance, suggests the idealized peace and harmony of a traditional village, with thatched-roofed houses and bright green ricefields nestled around ancient shrine and temple. This is a place of family intimacy, traditional virtues, and the regular annual cycle of seed-time and harvest, marked by established festivals and folklore. As a "homeland of the heart" this scene evokes much nostalgia on the part of Japan's urbanites in the bustling, impersonal cities, even though perhaps few of them would actually want to live in a traditional village, and people continue moving from the countryside into the more varied and more exciting life of the industrialized regions.

Traditional religion is an important part of the *kokoro no furusato* mystique. For this reason *matsuri* and visits to family shrines in the old home town continue to draw. It is one reason, too, why "mainstream" Japanese religion remains so unchanged. It is as though amidst so much change – Japan's rapid modernization and urbanization, plus the traumatic war, defeat, occupation, and rebuilding – it is important that one area of life remains stable, providing a link with the past and with eternal Japanese values.

No doubt, as in Europe and America, rural life – though now actually lived by only a small minority – remains closer to the past than do the cities, and this is important. Karin Muller, in her travelogue of contemporary Japan, speaks of a village Buddhist temple in Shikoku, and of the country women who continually frequented them, whether to worship, work, or just visit.

These small, rural temples are more than just a place of worship, they are the heart and soul of the community, like Southern churches in the United States. They [country women] deliver rice balls and bowls of miso soup to neighbors who aren't feeling well, organize everything from festivals to funerals, and build a protective social scaffolding around the elderly.[10]

In fact at the time of her visit Muller found a regular group of two dozen women, average age 76, all but five widows, but "spry and active as teenagers," "laughing often," who foregathered in this temple to pass the time. Even more than many other peoples, the Japanese love to be in groups and do things as groups; certainly a large part of nostalgia for the *furusato* is directed toward the way, in such traditional communities, communities of neighborliness and interaction emerge naturally. In a real sense the whole village is a tightly-knit community, though made up of all ages and stations, or so it is remembered and idealized. Of course, in the city one connects with artificially-constructed groups: school classes, work groups, office groups. They are very likely to have parties and take tours together, above all in Japan, but this is not the same as the lifelong, organic unity of a "homeland of the heart." For this reason there are those who do not want the temples and shrines that are the "heart of the heart" to change.

Paradoxically, though, it may be for this very reason many also do not think of those places of worship as "religious." Was the temple, like a home to those elderly women in a village in Shikoku, "religious" or just like a community center? Ian Reader suggests that in Japan doing "religious" things simply as part of a crowd visiting a shrine or temple is not always thought to count as "religion." If one goes to a shrine on New Year's Eve, and buys a *taima* or *omamori* like everyone else, is this inner devotion or the crowd speaking? In the same way, one may take part in a *matsuri*, even proudly take one's place as a member of the team that, wearing identical *hachimaki* or headscarves, carries the *mikoshi*. In some prestigious shrines, this is a great privilege which confers social status, like being part of a distinguished "krewe" mounting a float in New Orleans' Mardi Gras. Nonetheless, *mikoshi*-bearers do "religion" in a cheerful, socializing kind of way, rather than reverently and devoutly – they may even find themselves scuffling for space if rival teams meet in a multi-*mikoshi matsuri*![11]

But then, it may be this mood is what the people-loving Shinto *kami* understand and like, and is not anti-religious. In any case, it all represents something Japan thinks of as uniquely Japanese, and therefore not really covered by any imported categories, whether "religion" or "not religion." The important thing is that village temple and colorful festival are signs of the homeland of the heart, to be kept alive in their own unchanging reality.

As we have seen in Chapter 1, Ama Toshimaro has argued that the reason the Japanese, though they may take part in many apparently religious activities and may even profess a spiritual sensibility, do not like to call themselves or these practices religious is because, in their view, that would commit them to a particular teaching – while for them all these are just something "natural," part of being Japanese, even just part of being human or of nature itself. Practices from the first shrine visit to a Buddhist funeral are to them "natural religion," not religion in the revealed sense they think occurs in certain sects, or in certain other countries. "Natural religion" seems most comfortable, and what is more natural than a "homeland of the heart" and its sacred cycles?[12]

We may note that contentment with "natural religion," together with a deep sense of family and community identity, helps explain why Christianity and other missionary religions have not been particularly successful in modern Japan. In general, Christianity is respected, but it is extremely difficult psychologically for Japanese to break with family and community, with traditional shrine and temple symbols of identity, to become something else. Polls have indicated that while formal, committed members of established Christian churches are no more than one percent of the population in the early twenty-first century, a percentage several times higher considers themselves Christian in some informal, personal sense.

Indeed, one significant and characteristic modern Japanese movement has been Mukyokai or "No Church" Christianity, founded by Uchimura Kanzo (1861–1930).[13] It has no formal doctrines, services, liturgies, sacraments, or clergy, though it embraces pacifism, and was a center of resistance to Japanese militarism during the 1930s and 1940s. Adherents meet for bible study and quiet prayer. Its some 35,000 followers include a good number of intellectuals and academics. The movement spread to Taiwan and Korea; Ban Ki-moon, the Korean diplomat elected Secretary-General of the United Nations in 2006, is a "No Church" Christian.

Spiritual achievement

Being part of a group is also essential, at least in Japan, to the achievement of something profoundly individual as well – initiation through ordeal. Whether it is "religious" or not, the ascent of a mountain like Fuji traditionally regarded as sacred, and paying nominal respects to shrines along the way up, remains extremely popular. As many as 400,000 people climb Mount Fuji each year, most during the two-month climbing season, July and August.

According to Ian Reader, traditional pilgrimages to more explicitly religious sites, such as the circuit of the eighty-eight temples on Shikoku associated with the founder of Shingon, Kobo daishi, are only becoming more popular.[14] Now the sacred journey can be taken by car or air-conditioned tour bus, so hardly counts as an "ordeal" – though one can still see pilgrims who prefer walking in the traditional way, wearing white garb and a woven sedge hat, carrying a pilgrim staff, begging bowl, and bell. Walking, the circuit takes sixty to eighty days; at each temple devotees climb 108 steps, symbolically wash, strike the temple bell, leave offerings, perhaps burn incense, and pray or chant. At a priests' office in each temple, a pilgrimage book is stamped to indicate the wayfarer had visited that sacred place.

Another important pilgrimage route is to thirty-three temples of Kannon in Saikoku (western Honshu), and of course Ise still draws its thousands, especially

Pilgrimages to the shrines of the *shichi fukujin*, or seven gods of good fortune, have become increasingly popular since the 1970s. Of diverse Taoist, Buddhist, and Shinto derivation, these deities are often portrayed together, frequently in a boat. Here is big, fat, bald, smiling Hotei, god of contentment and magnanimity; Jurojin, of happiness and wisdom, looking like an old Chinese sage though with a weakness for drink; spear-wielding Bishamonten, guardian of the dharma; long-headed Fukurokuji, of longevity; Daikokuten with his bales of rice, of farming and abundance; Ebisu, in elegant court dress, of honesty and prosperity; and *biwa* [a traditional stringed instrument] playing Benten, of music and art (she is the only female, and her shrine at Enoshima in Kamakura is especially popular). Organized tours proceed from the shrine of one to another.[15]

at New Year and the major Ise harvest festival (*kanname-sai*) of October 15–17, though far from as many as in the glory days of the Tokugawa-era *okage-mairi*. But in honor of those times, and no doubt also with an eye to tourism, the local government has recently reconstructed a section of Ise city to reproduce its appearance in the Edo period, when it was alive with colorful inns and shops and waystations to the Grand Shrine – pilgrimage and "homeland of the heart" in one.[16] Pilgrimages to Izumo *taisha*, another very ancient shrine, are also popular, especially with those wishing to find a good marriage partner, said to be a specialty of its *kami*, Okuninushi.

Other group ventures are much more strenuous, and far more mark ordeal and initiation in the classic sense. Karin Muller describes joining a party of contemporary *yamabushi*, practitioners of Shugendo, for a *hiwatari*, or fire-walking rite, in the countryside. For hours the drums beat in a steady, hypnotic rhythm, as the mountain-priests, wearing off-white garments with bright tassels and animal skins hanging down their backs, circle round and round a sandy arena, chanting sutras, refreshing themselves with sake. Finally, at the right moment as the evening darkens, they light a great pile of maple wood, then let it burn down till it becomes glowing embers on the sand. Then, still chanting, the *yamabushi*, and some of the gathered spectators, walk across the red-hot field slowly and deliberately to the other side.

Muller, well aware that most *yamabushi* are part-time practitioners, remarks, "Tomorrow they'll put on their suits and look for all the world like ordinary businessmen, but underneath … I like people with secret lives."[17]

How does one become such a *yamabushi* in today's Japan? Muller also observed a class of trainees at Mount Haguro, where I had visited Shugendo New Year's rites.

During their eight-day training period, the novices were not permitted to bathe, brush their teeth, shave, or change clothes; they were clad identically in white, the color of purity and death. Much of the time silence was kept. For the first forty-eight hours, they fasted, allowed only green tea and a little orange juice. They climbed vigorously up mountains steps and trails, chanted, practiced making *mudras*, and twice each night of the training period experienced *namban-ibushi* – fumigation by red pepper. Red pepper mixed with rice hulls was burned in several large braziers in a sealed room. Soon bluish smoke burning the eyes and nose filled the chamber, creating an insufferable choking sensation. When the doors finally opened, the initiates stumble out, tears streaming, coughing up clouds of the acrid smoke. The experience is said to simulate death by asphyxiation, and so to be in the lineage of the live burials, semi-drowning, and cliff-hanging of Shugendo of old.

Out of some five hundred applicants, only one hundred and fifty were selected for this class. Most were near sixty, the usual Japanese retirement age. They clearly saw the Shugendo training ordeal as a way to begin a new stage of life. Adepts can, of course, go on year after year to higher and higher levels of Shugendo initiation, marked by the color of the pom-pom-like ornaments on their dress. The advanced courses involve still-greater ordeals, like long isolation and fasting, and retreats in which one goes through all the ten stages of existence, from hell to buddhahood.

Why do contemporary Japanese want to undergo this? Muller's group included a university professor, a sailor, businessmen, several musicians, a few Shinto and Buddhist priests, and many others. But significantly, Muller was unable to get the sort of thought-out spiritual rationales one might have expected. Postulants were reluctant to claim a desire for salvation, psychic powers, victory over self, or the like. Answers were rather reminiscent of "natural religion." Shugendo aspirants would say things like wanting to rediscover nature, to experience strict discipline, to give thanks for a daughter who was healed, to get out of the house, to lose weight, to break an addiction. Only one in five mentioned religious beliefs in relation to why he was there, though the head priest, in charge of the training, said, "These mountains are where one's buddha-nature can be found."

Undoubtedly something more is involved, something which in the characteristic Japanese way goes unstated, precisely because it is what is really important. It must have to do with being part of a group, looking the same, doing the same things, profoundly bonded, perhaps for life, by a shared experience; and at the same time testing oneself through discipline and arduous achievement: both touch on very deep structures of Japanese character and religion. Muller got a sense of group bonding plus pride of achievement on the final day of the class, as the successful initiates performed a lively *yamabushi* dance around a great purifying fire, in celebration of their joint "graduation."

To be sure, Shugendo ostensibly is no longer a major part of Japanese life and religion, to the extent it was before its Meiji suppression. Many urbanized, secularized Japanese seem hardly aware that it still exists, despite occasional print and TV specials on the highly photogenic sect. Yet, like the comparable Tendai "marathon monks," the way of the mountain ascetic reflects the significant "ordeal" strand of Japanese spirituality, also found somewhat more moderately in temple-pilgrimage, sacred mountaineering, *zazen* retreats, and much else still in the picture today.

Symbols and forms

The demand for concrete, established forms and symbols in religious interaction supports religious traditionalism. In Japan, religion is something done, not just thought, seen, or believed. Its "doing" is by means of specific objects or gestures that bear religious meaning, and nothing else. You may have noticed that the Shugendo initiation was strong on actual actions, from fire-walking to *namban-ibushi*, laying much less stress on ideas or even meditation. While it would be misleading to say Japanese religion has no ideas or beliefs, it is also true that getting away from thought alone is what it's all about. Religious activity is completed and, as it were, authenticated through a definite object: getting a *taima* or *omamori*, a charm or amulet, from a shrine or temple; writing one's prayer on an *ofuda*, or slip of paper, and posting it at the shrine or temple. Often, at a Shinto shrine, this means putting the petition on the big, ancient evergreen tree that dominates most shrine grounds. (Posted prayers will typically be for simple, everyday concerns: health for a loved one or oneself, success in school or at work, a prosperous business, money to repay debts.)

In the same way, as we have seen, entering a shrine or temple generally means doing certain actions: for Shinto, ritual washing, clapping hands twice, bowing the head in prayer, tossing a coin in the grill. By doing the job in the right way, one feels the visit has been negotiated and completed successfully, just as a proper social call or business transaction requires appropriate courtesies and signings. Activities in a temple, especially in the more esoteric schools, may be more elaborate, with chanting, mudras, and the honoring of diverse images, but the concept is the same: religion involves seeing and doing. Being in a temple or shrine is rarely passive; just as one would not ordinarily visit a friend, and then just stand there without saying or doing anything, so attendance on a *kami* or buddha is not just being there, but interactive. Even in contemplative traditions, such as Zen, *zazen* is a remarkably formal, structured practice by the standards of the more casual of Western religions.

An instructive example of concreteness in Japanese religion is *mizuko kuyo*, the memorial service for a *mizuko* (literally, "water child"), a miscarried or aborted fetus, mentioned earlier in connection with Jizo, the protector of children who is generally invoked in these rites.[18] Although details differ in different temples and Buddhist schools, generally the *kuyo* involves the usual Buddhist funeral service on behalf of the departed, with prayers and sutras chanted to insure a good transition and rebirth.

But there is more. Often the mother will have an opportunity to address the *mizuko* directly, apologizing for the deed, explaining why it was necessary, and wishing it a better situation in its next birth. There will be a naming ceremony for the deceased

Figure 11.1 Jizo figures for the unborn children at Zojoji Temple, Tokyo (© cowardlion / Shutterstock.com)

unborn child. Typically the purchase of a statue of Jizo, poignantly presented with a red bib, and often toys and other objects reminiscent of childhood, assures his protection. At certain temples emphasizing *mizuko kuyo* services, the woman may be led through more elaborate practices, such as blessing a doll or wooden *ofuda* which represents the miscarried or aborted infant; this she takes home, bathes, dresses, and pretends to feed as though a real child, until she feels emotionally able to release it back to Jizo's care and to the other world in preparation for rebirth – which, it is hoped, when appropriate will be to the same mother.

Mizuko kuyo has been very controversial, both in Japan and among Western observers. This way of handling abortion spiritually is recognized to be neither quite "pro-life" nor "pro-choice" as the issues have been defined in the "culture wars" of Europe and America.[19] It respects the emotional and spiritual burden having an abortion places on a woman, recognizes that the *mizuko* is a real person, yet also suggests ways of viewing abortion religiously short of regarding it as murder, but rather as a process in the ongoing flow of life. Some critics both in Japan and elsewhere have alleged that temples specializing in *mizuko kuyo* cynically exploit women under emotional stress, charging high fees for their services; others say that the experience is profoundly therapeutic.

However, some women and local temples in Japan have themselves organized *mizuko kuyo* services when needed, avoiding the excessive fuss and fees of well-known *mizuko kuyo* temples.

In any case, the employment of a definite ritual, and definite objects such as a Jizo image, red bibs, and perhaps a *mizuko*-substitute, brings home the Japanese gravitation toward the tangible and concrete in spiritual interactions, suggesting how it can help in a very difficult situation.

*   *   *

Somehow we are reminded of still another side of contemporary spirituality: an ongoing sense of the supernatural, in the form of spirits and miracles. Despite Japan's "high tech" civilization, or perhaps through recognition that science and technology do not solve all the mysteries of human life, books on psychic phenomena, spirits good and bad, and miraculous healings are recurrent bestsellers; as we have seen, these notions are very important in many of the New Religions, and the New Age or "Spirit World" mentality, especially. One can hear stories of ghosts and other mysteries surprisingly often in everyday conversation, half believed, half not, yet ever fascinating. Even if religion is allegedly not believed in, the supernatural is always around.[20]

No doubt one reason for persistence of belief in ghosts is ancestrism, which of course is normal and mainstream in Japan. A great number of homes, whether particularly religious or not, have a traditional shrine to the family ancestors; whether Shinto or Buddhist, or sometimes both, it will honor the fundamental Confucian concept that filial piety extends beyond the grave, and also allows the intuition that the ancestors are in some sense still alive, watching over their family with spirit eyes, even intervening in some way to guide its fortunes and correct the wayward. One often hears people expressing awareness that their ancestors, *mitama*, are invisibly with them, sending helpful thoughts, happy about some developments and not about others. From here it is clearly only a short step to belief in ghosts in general, realizing that, as Shakespeare wrote, "There are more things in heaven and earth … than are dreamt of in your philosophy."

A moment's reflection will suggest how all the practices and beliefs discussed above – concrete symbols and actions giving *form* to religious transactions, *mizuko kuyo* (which though relatively new pointedly employs very traditional Buddhist forms), and belief/experience of miracles, ghosts, and spirit-ancestors – fundamentally serve to support traditionalism. If set symbols and forms are helpful, they must be recognizable as such, which means they need to be traditional and not just newly invented. The rationale of *mizuko kuyo* is in large part to assist the woman in dealing with the guilt and emotional distress of abortion by placing these feelings in the context of traditional understandings of life and death. Ghosts and miracles, like ancestrism, are also part of a long Japanese heritage of such stories and beliefs, so put the present-day in the context of the past.

At the same time, new symbols can be imported and placed into the mix, just because it is acknowledged that symbols and rituals can be added and subtracted. Adding a few enriches tradition without diminishing traditionalism. A good example

At Christmas, large department stores may be as virtually taken over by lights and Santas as any in the West; some homes and public places set up Christmas trees (there is a huge one in the Kyoto railway station). Gift-giving and a "traditional" Christmas cake have become popular, doubtless to the delight of merchants and bakers. December 24th is a favorite night for dates, and as early as September one can see ads for Christmas eve dinner, concert, and hotel packages.[21] But the Yule festival is generally a secular holiday, with overtones of being sophisticated because it is new (to Japan) and cosmopolitan.

is the recent Japanese appropriation of some "secular" aspects of Christianity. We have mentioned the vogue for Christian weddings; significantly, it is weddings, not funerals, that are superficially Christianized. In Japan the latter have deep association with traditional Buddhist and ancestral beliefs, and usually have more serious and somber religious overtones.

New Year, *Oshogatsu*, only a week after Christmas since the solar calendar was adopted in 1873, is far more traditionally Japanese. Although there may be some drinking, snacking, and dining, compared to elsewhere the four days of the New Year holiday (December 31–January 3) are relatively quiet, thoughtful, family occasions. If possible families return to their *furusato* or home town, and make visits to shrines and temples during the season.

Houses are cleaned, symbolizing a new start, and entrances are decorated with ornaments of pine (symbol of ongoing life), bamboo, and plum trees. On New Year's Eve, *soba* (buckwheat noodles), also said to symbolize longevity, are traditionally served. Shrines and temples are thronged; several million people may visit the most popular, the Meiji Shrine in Tokyo, during the holidays. Properly, one visits temples on New Year's Eve, to leave behind the old; one goes to shrines on New Year's Day to pray for the future. At temples, the bell is solemnly rung 108 times, representing the 108 Buddhist evil attachments to be cast off, just before the New Year commences at midnight. Although the crowds at these places of worship will be immense, and the sites thick with stalls selling snacks and amulets (it is customary to purchase a shrine or temple *taima* or *omamori* to place in one's home for protection during the coming year), they are usually orderly.

Although the Buddha's birthday is commemorated in the spring, as *hanamatsuri* ("flower festival"; interestingly, like Easter, a seasonal rather than historical term), clearly it is the basically Shinto New Year (like the *yamabushi* New Year described earlier) that focuses attitudes toward time: it is cyclical, recurring, but the beginning of a new yearly cycle is a time when, mystically, time returns to the beginning and can be started over again. One can cast off the past, clean house spiritually as well as materially, pray for the future, and set off fresh and new. It is also well to then be within one's own circles of origin, one's *furusato* and family.

Figure 11.2 Japanese women dressed traditionally at Kiyomizu temple in Kyoto (© Perati Komson / Shutterstock.com)

One's dreams on New Year's night are said to be auspicious; the most fortunate is a dream of Mount Fuji. Ghosts may be especially active this night of all. Bruce Feiler, in his account of his time in Japan as a schoolteacher, tells of a junior high school student who said, as they walked toward a small Shinto shrine on New Year's Eve, "Have you ever seen a Japanese ghost? We might see one tonight. They are *really* scary." The boy's older brother added, "All the ghosts dress in white, and they float in green smoke. But they don't have legs, so you can outrun them."

Feiler comments, "As one of the few occasions in the year when work stops and families spend time together, the New Year festival brings out some of the latent religious traditions that still color Japanese life."[22] From the religious studies point of view, this observation is important. The fact that Oshogatsu is the most important annual holiday in Japan, going on for several days while virtually everything else stops, tells us what is really significant in the Japanese festival calendar. It is sacred time appearing the way it does in what Mircea Eliade called cosmic religion. That is, the religious year is centered around the turn of the seasons, rather than (like Passover or Christmas, at least in theory) historical commemorations (the Exodus or the birth of Jesus). In cosmic religion, New Year is the most important event each year, because ritually New Year's Eve is like a return to the chaos before creation, and then New Year's Day is a "re-creation" or fresh start that begins the world anew. Between old and new, a "crack" opens in time, and the order of the world is broken sufficiently to let in ancestral spirits together with a few mysterious visitors from somewhere else, like ghosts.

The sacred in the ordinary

The Japanese belief, reflected as we have seen in art and poetry, that the ultimate is to be found in the ordinary, also supports religious traditionalism in a subtle way: by putting emphasis in a different place than on religious innovation. In practice this emphasis is associated with traditional arts, especially those Zen-related, such as Chado, the "Way of Tea," Kado, the "Way of Flower Arrangement," and the like. Thus, in drinking tea, one is just drinking tea, savoring the flavor and the beauty of the cup, not thinking of anything else – yet lacking nothing. Like traditional religion, these traditional arts continue to find a place in contemporary Japanese life, and for much the same reasons.

Japan, a new world center of popular culture

In the early years of the twenty-first century, a new awareness was arising, almost as it were by stealth, in planetary consciousness: that much of what people, especially young people, do for story-time in this high tech age comes from Japan. Four words say it all: *manga*, *anime*, Nintendo, Sony. These are, it hardly need be said, Japanese comic books, animated movies, and video games manufacturers and publishers.[23]

In Japan itself the universe of these media dominates youth culture. The most dominated persons, called *otaku*,[24] virtually live in the cyberspace of computers and games; extreme cases have been reported of young people who never left their rooms, and had to have meals brought to them while they sat absorbed in the world of the screen, the dream-woman of, say, "Trainman" being far more real than any flesh-and-blood female. More common are those who engage in what they call "cos-play" (costume playing). These dwellers in two worlds maintain regular school or work obligations, but after-hours and weekends both men and women become samurai or spacemen, playacting their favorite fantasies, mixing only with their own kind. All this has become, some Japanese social commentators say, not just a hobby but a way of life, almost a religion – and a four-billion dollar a year industry.

As *manga*, *anime*, and Japanese computer games take hold on one continent after another, challenging other vehicles of popular culture like British music groups or Hollywood movies, no doubt they are increasingly shaping the inner consciousness of their generation around the world. Therefore it is important to appreciate the worldview that underlies these media of popular culture. In doing so we will find themes and figures stepping out of the pages of Japanese mythology and religion now going global.

At first one may find, say, global Nintendo[25] a depressing thought, since in some eyes the games, like *manga*, seem to involve little more than obsessing with mindless, comic-book-level sex and violence. But that is not quite the case. They tell stories, they create alternative worlds, they provide models for oneself – just as does traditional religion.

Four motifs from traditional Japanese religion suggest themselves in a close examination of the *anime*, *manga*, and Nintendo universe. First: the idea of a separate, magical reality which one can enter by a few definite, as it were evocational, gestures which transport one from the everyday to the alternative reality. As we have seen, such special, sacred times and places are very important: the *matsuri*, the sacred mountains of the *yamabushi*, the mandalas of esoteric Buddhism, the Pure Land, the Zen garden … entered through the magic portal of a certain chant, *mudra*, or method of meditation.

Second, in this set-apart world, spirits and supernatural realities are very much alive. Ghosts, *kami*, and the sort of powers evoked in martial arts are part of the other side, calling forth an atmosphere of wonder and dread, where anything-may-happen, however glorious or horrible. (One may also notice the frequent appearance of robots, which may suggest an over-regulated society in contrast to the world of wonder.)

Third, sex and violence are thoroughly mixed in with the beauty and terror, often in wild and grotesque forms. As Susan Napier has acutely observed in her study of *anime*, this is not unlike the world of Shinto. Shinto myth, and above all the *matsuri* or festival, do not merely present some impossibly transcendent *kami*-realm, but mix the human with the divine till they're virtually all one. The festival (like the myths) may contain phallic, violent, ribald, comic, eating, and excessive drinking themes that sometimes disconcert outsiders. But the Shinto idea is that these are all part of life, whether human or *kami*. By bringing them into the pure space of the shrine and the *matsuri* it is shown that in their inner nature they can be unpolluted, as pure as anything else in its own nature.[26] To be sure, Japanese pop media certainly contains repellantly unwholesome, even sadistic, material. Yet there is a non-Western cultural context into which some of this, insofar as it is merely frank and fun and not degrading, can be put.

Fourth, let's note that the central, saving figure in many of these vehicles, perhaps especially *anime*, is often a *shojo*, young girl. The only comparable Western fairy tale heroine I can think of is Dorothy in L. Frank Baum's modern classic, *The Wizard of Oz*. But in Japan a female figure with special powers, seemingly weak but in the end able to redeem the situation, takes us back to Amaterasu and the ancient shamaness, up through certain samurai tales[27] to *anime* like *Spirited Away* and *Princess Mononoke*.

These productions of the great animator Miyasaki Hayao splendidly exemplify all these features. Take *Spirited Away* (2001), *Sen to Chihiro no kamikakushi* in Japanese (the last word, *kamikakushi*, is translated "spirited away," but could literally be "hidden by the *kami*."). While moving from one town to another, the family of a young girl, Chihiro, gets lost and finds its way into a community of gods and spirits, centered around a bath-house where *kami* go to rest and purify themselves. We are immediately reminded of the importance of the public bath in Japanese society, and of washing and purity in Shinto ritual. Chihiro has to work in the baths, but her real challenge is to rescue her parents, who have been changed into pigs by over-eating in a "free" restaurant in this *kami*-town (*karma?* the Circe myth from the *Odyssey?*), and to find their way out. All this she does in the end.

Another Miyazaki *anime*, *Nausicaa of the Valley of the Wind*, though not set in Japan but in a fantasy-land (nor is she the Nausicaa of the *Odyssey*), is still another film by this great creator centered on a strong, heroic young girl.

Princess Mononoke (1997), put into late samurai days, when guns were beginning to come into Japan, essentially tells the story of supernatural guardians of the forest (Mononoke means woodland spectre or ghost, even monster) who battle against the humans in "Irontown" as they try to exploit nature's resources and destroy it, making firearms. San (Princess Mononoke, the Princess of the Spirits) is a human girl raised by wolves but, like a shamaness or *kami*, close enough to the woods to be on its side. She thinks she is a wolf, rides a wolf, and is a leader of forest spirits. San meets a human boy, Ashitaka,[28] who befriends her and convinces her she is human too. Finally, after terrible battles, they create harmony between humans and the forest. But San returns to the forest; Ashitaka helps rebuild the town, but says he will come to visit her. Here is a separate supernatural world, full of wonder and violence, which one can enter; a young girl at the center; and a modern ecological theme.

Mononoke-hime (*Princess Mononoke*) has (like *Spirited Away* and *Nausicaa*) determined women as focal figures on both sides: Lady Eboshi is the ruler of factory-like Irontown, San of the wild. In a Japanese way, the struggle is not represented as dualistically good versus bad as a western parable of the human destruction of nature might be. Lady Eboshi does indeed want to destroy the forest and kill its *kami*, the Spirit of the Forest (Shishigami), for the sake of industry. But she can also be kindly. She rescues lively girls from brothels, as well as heavily bandaged lepers who make guns for her fighters, and she treats both better than they had been before. Mononoke loves the forest, but has too indiscriminate a hatred for all humans. Creatures change sides and character more than once: the true enemy is always hatred and anger, which can turn anyone on either side into a demon. The real background is the unpredictible wildness of nature as it is, the real victor is life itself, which goes on despite total war and destruction – like Japanese life after 1945.

Some might see an odd Shinto versus Buddhism theme in the movie. A major troublemaker is Jigo, a plausible but scheming monk who is too clever by half, and has his comeuppance at the end, while Shishigami, clearly one of the *kami* from the primeval world, manifests simple nobility. But although the Buddhist cleric who is not all he should be is a familiar figure in Japanese literature old and new, one should not read too much into a film meant to be mainly entertainment. All the same, this film hints at the recent, "post-Aum" trend away from Buddhism, toward other, especially primordial, sources of Japanese spirituality.

In both these movies there are motifs from non-Japanese mythology, as well as elements that seem to be modern inventions. But the setting, and something of the spirit, is Japanese.

Like a circle, Japanese religion seems to end where it began: magical women, or young girls, in a man's world.

Questions for study and discussion

1. Why was the imperial institution kept at Japan's surrender in 1945?
2. How did the occupation change – and not change – Japanese religion?
3. What are religious constituents of the *furusato* theme?
4. Why would modern people undergo rigorous *yamabushi* training?
5. When and why does the group aspect of religion maintain tradition?
6. Discuss the situation of Christianity in contemporary Japan.
7. How does one worship at a Shinto shrine, and what does this worship mean to Japanese today?
8. Why does pilgrimage seem to be gaining in popularity today?
9. How is New Year celebrated in Japan?
10. How does "the ultimate in the ordinary" theme maintain traditionalism?
11. How do you assess the meaning of the new Japanese popular culture and its world influence?
12. How would you see the situation of religion in Japan now?

Key points you should know

- The postwar Occupation of Japan brought land reform, some degree of democratization, and full separation of religion and the state, together with rapid growth of New Religions
- The postwar era also brought critical assessment of the *hongaku* doctrine in Japanese Buddhism, and improved status for Buddhist nuns and wives of priests
- In many ways, though, basic features of Japanese religion maintained tradition: rites, the way one worships at a shrine or temple, rural temples as community centers, *matsuri* and festivals
- A burgeoning and much-discussed practice has been *mizuko kuyo*, or services for unborn fetuses
- New Year remains a very important rite, fairly serious and involving visits to temples and shrines
- The influence of some Japanese religion themes can be seen in *anime* and other vehicles of popular culture.

Further reading

Ambros, Barbara R., *Women in Japanese Religions*. New York, NY: New York University Press, 2015.

Covell, Stephan Grover, *Japanese Temple Buddhism: Worldliness in a Religion of Renunciation*. Honolulu, HI: University of Hawaii Press, 2005.

David, Winston Bradley, *Toward Modernity: A Developmental Typology of Popular Religious Affiliation in Japan*. Ithaca, NY: Cornell University, 1977.

Hardacre, Helen, *Marketing the Menacing Fetus in Japan*. Berkeley, CA: University of California Press, 1999. (About Mizuko Kuyo.)

Kitagawa, Joseph M., *On Understanding Japanese Religion*. Princeton, NJ: Princeton University Press, 1987.

Moore, Ray A., *Soldier of God: MacArthur's Attempt to Christianize Japan*. Portland, ME: MerwinAsia, 2011.

Napier, Susan, *Anime: from Akira to Princess Mononoke*. New York, NY: Palgrave, 2001.

Reader, Ian, *Religion in Contemporary Japan*. Honolulu, HI: University of Hawaii Press, 1991.

Robertson, Jennifer, ed., *A Companion to the Anthropology of Japan*. Malden, MA; Oxford: Blackwell, 2005.

Shimazono, Susumu, *From Salvation to Spirituality: Popular Religious Movements in Modern Japan*. Melbourne: Trans Pacific Press, 2004.

Woodward, William P., *The Allied Occupation of Japan 1945–1952 and Japanese Religion*. Leiden: E.J. Brill, 1972.

Electronic Resources

Jolyon Thomas, "Religions Policies During the Allied Occupation of Japan, 1945–1952," *Religion Compass* 8/9 (2014), pp. 275–86. www.academia.edu/8531258/Religions_Policies_During_the_Allied_Occupation_of_Japan_1945_1952

"Reference Guide: Japanese Pilgrims and Pilgrimages." www.onmarkproductions.com/html/pilgrimages-pilgrims-japan.html

"Shugendo Doctrines Costumes and Tools Symbolisme." www.shugendo.fr/en/doctrines-costumes-and-tools-symbolisme

Doug, "Understanding Omamori." http://jkllr.net/2011/04/14/omamori

"Ofuda." wikimoon.org/index.php?title=Ofuda

Anne Page Brooks, "Mizuko Kuyō and Japanese Buddhism," *Japanese Journal of Religious Studies* 8/3–4 Sept.–Dec. 1981, pp. 119–47. https://nirc.nanzan-u.ac.jp/nfile/2226 (Note: The Internet contains numerous useful articles on this topic from various points of view.)

Billy Hammond, "Christmas in Japan." http://tanutech.com/japan/jxmas.html

Ran Matsugi, "A Guide to New Year Traditions in Japan," *Japan Today*. http://www. japantoday.com/category/arts-culture/view/a-guide-to-new-year-traditions-in-japan

Robert Ito, "Reviving Japan's Dreaded and Beloved Ghosts," *The New York Times*, May 20, 2015. www.nytimes.com/2015/05/24/arts/design/reviving-japans-dreaded-and-beloved-ghosts.html

"Kamisama Kiss & Japanese Mythology." www.animenewsnetwork.com/advertorial/2015-01-27/kamisama-kiss-and-japanese-mythology/.83755 (On anime and manga.)

"Interview: Miyazaki on Mononoke-hime." www.nausicaa.net/miyazaki/interviews/m_on_mh.html

Wikipedia, "Japanese Mythology in Popular Culture." https://en.wikipedia.org/wiki/Category:japanese_mythology_in_popular_culture (A guide to Wikipedia articles on this topic.)

Appendix I

Membership figures for Japanese religions

Here are membership figures for the major Japanese religious bodies presented in the Heisei 25 (2014) *Shukyo Nenkan* (*Religion Annual*), assembled and published by the Japanese government Bunkacho (Agency for Cultural Affairs) from figures provided by the organizations themselves.

These figures must be used with considerable caution, especially in comparison with Western religious statistics, because most of them are based on quite different understandings of the meaning of religious membership. Here are a few points to bear in mind.

1. All added together, these memberships come to over the 2014 Japanese population of 127 million. This means that some Japanese count themselves members of two or more religions, a different situation than common in the West.
2. Traditionally, Japan has counted religious membership by households or families rather than by individuals, and if an individual count is required – as it was for this reckoning – households may be simply multiplied by the supposed average size of a family. Obviously, such procedure is bound to include a number of very inactive "members." Nonetheless, the officially reported figures used here by the Bunkacho are often lower than more generous estimates made by publicists for various faiths, or those garnered by open polls.
3. Many Japanese regard membership in a Buddhist temple chiefly in terms of its role as a place to provide funeral and memorial services when needed. Until that occasion arises, membership may be highly nominal.[1]
4. Despite membership figures, many Japanese will say they have no religion, or even that Japan has virtually no religion. Nonetheless, they are likely to take part in festivals or rites, or to pray in the expected way if they find themselves at a shrine or temple, and whether or not it is the faith in which they reported membership. But by all accounts the number of dedicated, regular worshipers is not high.

5. A comparison of the figures below with the previous, 2008 edition of this book, when 2006 reports were used, will indicate noticeable decline in some Buddhist and New Religions groups.

6. The totals for Pure Land, Nichiren, and Zen are higher than those given for the major denominations of each. This is because of many smaller groups under each heading who add to the total. Many of them are technically independent temples in the tradition of one of the denominations, but which do not differ significantly from it in doctrine or practice.

These caveats in mind, here are the reported figures, rounded off, for the major bodies.

Shinto 94 million
Buddhism 47 million
    Nara Buddhist groups 711,000
    Shingon 9.1 million
    Tendai 3 million
    Pure Land 17.9 million
        Jodo Shu 6 million
        Jodo Shinshu 12 million in several lineages
    Nichiren 17.3 million
        Nichiren Shu 3.9 million
        Nichiren Shoshu 500,000
        Rissho Kosei Kai 3.1 million
        Reiyukai 3 million
        Because of splits and defections, Nichiren Shoshu is much smaller than earlier reports, particularly when the then-large Soka Gakkai movement was included in it. Soka Gakkai, now independent of Nichiren Shoshu, is not represented in the *Shukyo Nenkan* except as an educational organization, without membership figures; the group has not released official membership statistics for a number of years. It has claimed as many as 10 million members in the past, a figure critics consider highly inflated.
    Zen 3.1 million
        Rinzai 1 million
        Soto 1.5 million
New Religions (Selected examples. Complete figures can be found on Wikipedia, "Japanese New Religions" https://en.wikipedia.org/wiki/Japanese_new_religions)
        Tenrikyo 1.2 million
        Perfect Liberty 934,000
        Sekai Kyusei Kyo (World Messianity) 836,000

Seicho no Ie 587,000

Agonshu 356,000

Konkokyo 430,000

Gedatsu 108,000

Christianity 959,285

This is the total of reported Catholic, Orthodox, and Protestant denominational membership, which is what the *Shukyo Nenkan* presents. Independent surveys often give as many as 3 million or more self-reported Christians in Japan, or persons most sympathetic to Christianity.

Roman Catholic 444,451

In addition, surveys reveal as many as 30,000 persons who consider themselves *Kakure Kirishitan*, "Hidden Christians," descendants of Catholic converts of the sixteenth century but not reconciled to the Roman Catholic church of today.

Eastern Orthodox 9,897

Protestant 504,947

This figure includes the mainline United Protestant church (Nihon Kirisuto Kyodan, the remains of the coerced wartime union), 123,000; the Nihon Seikokai (Anglican/Episcopal), 51,000; and the Latter-Day Saints (Mormon), 127,000, plus several Baptist, Lutheran, and other bodies. But it does not include figures for the Jehovah's Witnesses, the Mukyokai (No-church movement), and probably some Pentecostal and other independent groups, all believed to be significant but which do not report memberships. In addition, as indicated many additional Japanese think of themselves as Christian but are not formally members of a church.

Appendix II

Japanese religion timeline

8000–200 BCE	Jomon: preliterate religion – animism, fertility cults, perhaps comparable to Melanesian and Polynesian religion.
200 BCE–200 CE	Yayoi: agricultural rites, shamanism; prototypes of Kojiki and Nihinshoki myths; Himiko?
250–552	Kofun: immense tombs; ritual swords, mirrors, jewels; gradual unification under Yamato house; Korean immigrants.
552–710	Introduction of Buddhism and Confucianism; consolidation of largely Buddhist and Confucian state under Shotoku (573–621); Buddhist art flourishes; Horyuji built. 646 Taika reforms; Shinto influence restored. 702 Taiho Code; Chinese-type bureaucratic government and Shinto court rituals.
712	*Kojiki* issued.
710–794	Nara period; first permanent capital; Buddhist high point: six schools in capital, magnificent Buddhist building including Great Buddha; *bosatsudo* leaders in countryside; Dokyo scandal.
794–1185	Heian period. Shingon and Tendai dominant. Shinto and Buddhism largely combined. Great era of Japanese literature.
1185–1392	Kamakura and brief following periods. Shoguns, samurai values. Rise of new Buddhist schools based on faith and idea of *mappo*: Pure Land (Jodo-shu under Honen; Jodo-Shinshu under Shinran), and Nichiren; importation of Zen by Eisai (Rinzai school) and Dogen (Soto).

1392–1568	Ashikaga or Muromachi period. Zen dominant under Ashikaga patronage, but country torn by civil conflict. *Ikko ikki*; new Shinto movements at Ise; pilgrimage. Christianity under St. Francis Xavier arrives 1549.
1568–1600	Momoyama period. Unification under warlords Nobunaga, Hideyoshi, Ieyasu. Christianity tolerated, then persecuted.
1600–1868	Tokugawa period. Official Confucian ideology. Buddhism mandatory but under state control. Rise of *kokugaku* Shinto nationalism. Japan largely isolated.
1868–1912	Meiji period. Theoretical restoration of direct imperial rule; Japan modernizes and becomes world power. Separation of Shinto and Buddhism; Shinto, especially imperial ideology, fostered by state; Buddhism reformed (e.g. marriage of priests) and becomes more international; Christian missions.
1912–1945	Taisho and early Showa periods. Extremist imperial ideologies and State Shinto. During World War II, religions combined and pressured to support the war.
1945–	Late Showa, Heisei periods. Postwar religious freedom and self government; rise of new religions; continuation of much traditional religious life; secularization; issues involving Yasukuni shrine, Soka Gakkai, Aum Shinrikyo.

Notes

1 Encountering the Japanese religious world

1. The word Shinto itself gives an interesting example of how the Japanese language works. It means "The Kami Way," but in Chinese loan words. Shin is the Chinese word xen or shen, meaning deity; the same character, spoken in original Japanese, is pronounced *kami*, the word for Shinto gods with which we are familiar. "To" is actually the Chinese word tao, as in Taoism, meaning in Chinese way or path, and in native Japanese the tao character is pronounced michi. Some Japanese purists, understandably contending that the name of the native Japanese religion ought to be read the Japanese way, have wanted to call it Kami no Michi, the "Way of the Gods," (no meaning "of," with the word order backward from English), but Shinto has stuck, perhaps because that word was only introduced to distinguish this "way" from the other, Butsudo, the Way of the Buddha.

   Interestingly, while in China tao has come to indicate philosophically the broad path down which the entire universe is moving, in Japan *to* or *do* has more often meant a particular art which, in an overused term but one that fits well here, becomes a "way of life." An adept of the "tea ceremony" follows chado, the "tea-way," a practitioner of the martial arts budo, the "way of the warrior"; a worshiper of the ancient gods Shinto, the "*kami* way."

2. Peter Berger, *The Sacred Canopy*. Garden City, NY: Doubleday, 1969, p. 28.

3. The Okinawan religion of the Noro is considered the world's only traditional, mainstream religion led by women as the acknowledged spiritual leaders. See Susan Starr Sered, *Women of the Sacred Groves: Divine Priestesses of Okinawa*. New York: Oxford University Press, 1999.

4. See Mircea Eliade, *The Sacred and the Profane*. New York and London: Harcourt Brace Jovanovich, 1959. But the book I read then was *Images and Symbols*. London: Harvill, 1961.

5. Joachim Wach, *Sociology of Religion*. Chicago, IL: University of Chicago Press, 1944.

6. John A. McKinstry and Asako Nakajima McKinstry, *Jinsai Annai: Glimpses of Japan through a Popular Advice Column.* Armonk, NY and London: M. E. Sharpe, 1991, p. 157.

7. *The Pew Global Attitude Project.* Washington, DC: Pew Research Center, 2002.

8. W. Cantwell Smith, *The Meaning and End of Religion.* New York: Harper, 1978.

9. Toshimaro Ama, *Why Are the Japanese Non-Religious? Japanese Spirituality: Being Non-Religious in a Religious Culture.* Lanham, MD: University Press of America, 2005. Original published in Japanese.

10. "Religion's Response to the Earthquake and Tsunami in Northeastern Japan," *Dharma World*, Oct.–Dec. 2011. www.rk-world.org/dharmaworld/dw_2011octdecreligionsresponse.aspx.

2   *The past in the present*

1. See D. C. Holtom, *The Japanese Enthronement Ceremonies*, 2nd edn. Tokyo: Sophia University Press, 1972.

2. See Robert Ellwood, *The Feast of Kingship: Accession Ceremonies in Ancient Japan.* Tokyo: Sophia University, 1973, pp. 70–1.

3. Ibid., pp. 60–5.

4. Tokyo District Court decision of March 24, 1999. Senrei (Summary of Japanese Case Law) at senrei.com/const3/html

5. In this book the Sanskrit name of Buddhist figures and texts will often be provided in this manner, as will the Chinese equivalent when it might be of help to students. Romanization of Chinese generally follows the Pinyin system now in widespread use.

6. Because the Toji is literally on the wrong side of the tracks from most of the famous sights of Kyoto, off to itself in a nondescript neighborhood, it is often missed by visitors. Be sure to make a point of seeing it on your next trip to Japan.

7. Aldous Huxley, *The Doors of Perception and Heaven and Hell.* New York: Harper & Row, 1990. Orig. pub. 1956.

8. Jan Chozen Bays, *Jizo Bodhisattva: Guardian of Children, Travelers & Other Voyagers.* Boston, MA: Shambhala, 2003, p. xii. The American woman who authored this book was born on the day the atomic bomb fell on Nagasaki, and is now a Zen Buddhist priest and a pediatrician who works with abused children; her special feeling for Jizo is understandable.

9. Marie Mutsuki Mockett, *Where the Dead Pause and the Japanese Say Goodbye.* New York: W. W. Norton, 2015, pp. 159–160, 166.

10. Ichiro Hori, *Folk Religion in Japan.* Chicago: University of Chicago Press, 1968, pp. 203–06.

11. Mockett, *Where the Dead Pause*, p. 198.

12. Ibid., p. 276.

13. Rev. Taiko Kyuma, "The Deep Listening *Gyocha* Volunteer Activities of the Soto Zen Youth Association," in Jonathan S. Watts, ed., *This Precious Life: Buddhist Tsunami Relief and Anti-Nuclear Activism in Post 3/11 Japan*. Yokohama: The International Buddhist Exchange Center, 2012, p. 68.

14. Mockett, *Where the Dead Pause*, pp. 6–7, 121.

15. Ibid., pp. 5–7.

16. Ibid., pp. 28–29.

17. Ibid., p. 30.

18. Jonathan S. Watts, "Introduction: A Buddhist Roadmap to Engaging with Nuclear Energy," in Jonathan S. Watts, ed., *Lotus in the Nuclear Sea: Fukushima and the Promise of Buddhism in the Nuclear Age*. Yokohama: International Buddhist Exchange Center, 2013, p. 82.

19. Cited in Aso Izuta and Kei Sato, "Explaining the Sin of Nuclear Power," in Watts, ed., *This Precious Life*, p. 159.

20. See Mark Michael Rowe, *Bonds of the Dead: Temples, Burial, and the Transformation of Contemporary Japanese Buddhism*. Chicago: University of Chicago Press, 2011.

3 *The way of the* kami

1. Sir Ernest Satow, "The Shinto Temples of Ise," *Transactions of the Asiatic Society of Japan*, vol. I, no. 2 (July 1874), p. 121.

2. See, for example, Kenzo Tange and Noboru Kawazoe, *Ise: Prototype of Japanese Architecture*. Cambridge, MA: MIT Press, 1965.

3. See Robert Ellwood, "Harvest and Renewal at the Grand Shrine of Ise," *Numen*, XV, 3 (November 1968), pp. 165–90.

4. In visiting places of great natural beauty in Japan, I often saw tiny shrines to the minor *kami* of the place, or perhaps just a *shimenawa* (sacred rope) or *gohei* (white strips of paper), indicators of divinity, around a fine old tree or ancient rock. These never seemed to clash with natural beauty, but to add something to it, suggesting someone has recognized here the added glow of the sacred in the natural. Back in the United States, driving through splendid national parks such as Yellowstone or Sequoia, seeing their "beauty bare," I somehow missed those indicators, knowing that in Japan Shintoists would perceive something numinous enough in the geysers of Yellowstone or the giant sequoia trees to sense a bit of *kami* in them, over and above the geological or biological marvel.

5. Ian Reader, *Religion in Contemporary Japan*. Honolulu: University of Hawaii Press, 1991, p. 75.

6. See Karen Smyers, *The Fox and the Jewel: Shared and Private Meanings in Contemporary Japanese Inari Worship*. Honolulu: University of Hawaii Press, 2000.

7. The Meiji Restoration will be discussed later; briefly, in 1868 militant factions, determined that Japan should open itself to the West and modernize industrially and militarily, brought an end to rule in the name of the emperor by shoguns. In theory the reformers "restored" direct power to the young Meiji emperor. On the one hand this meant rapid modernization; on the other the regimentation that process was thought to require was justified by appeal to ancient Shinto myths and ideologies making the sovereign a descendant of Amaterasu and an *ikigami*, "living god," entitled to unquestioning obedience. In support of this doctrine, the Meiji Restoration also brought about a Shinto revival, especially as a nationalistic religion centered on the imperial institution supporting, and supported by, the state. Buddhism, considered foreign, was briefly persecuted, and radically separated from Shinto.

8. Martin Fackler, "Shinzo Abe, Japanese Premier, Sends Gift to Contentious Yasukuni Shrine," *The New York Times*, April 21, 2015. http://www.nytimes.com/2015/04/22/world/asia/shinzo-abe-japanese-prime-minister-sends-gift-to-yasukuni-shrine.html

9. "Japanese MPs make provocative visit to Tokyo's Yasukuni war shrine," *The Guardian*, April 21, 2015. www.theguardian.com/world/2015/apr/22/japanese-mps-make-provocative-visit-to-tokyos-yasukuni-war-shrine

10. See Klaus Antoni, "Yasukuni-Jinja and Folk Religion," in Mark R. Mullins, Shimazono Susumu, and Paul L. Swanson, eds, *Religion and Society in Modern Japan*. Berkeley, CA: Asian Humanities Press/ Nagoya: Nanzan Institute for Religion and Culture, 1993, pp. 121–32. This article points to an alternative interpretation of Yasukuni (also Ankoku: "Pacification of the Country") some have raised: not the orthodox view that these spirits protect the country, but rather that they themselves, having died violently and perhaps vengeful, are pacified. See also John Breen, ed., *Yasukuni, the War Dead and the Struggle for Japan's Past*. New York: Columbia University Press, 2010.

11. John K. Nelson, *A Year in the Life of a Shinto Shrine*. Seattle: University of Washington Press, 1996.

12. Reader, *Religion in Contemporary Japan*, p. 71.

13. David C. Lewis, "Religious Rites in a Japanese Factory," in Mullins, Shimazono, and Swanson, *op. cit.*, pp. 157–70. The above summary is considerably simplified.

14. Ibid., p. 167.

15. The Ainu are a non-Japanese people (indeed, perhaps partly Caucasian) who dwelt in Japan before the present Japanese, but were pushed out by them and now live only in scattered communities on the northern islands of Hokkaido and now-Russian Sakhalin. They are probably the same as, or closely related to, the prehistoric people known as the Jomon (see next chapter), and the medieval Emishi (referred to at the end of this book in connection with the movie *Princess*

Mononoke) driven back by the Japanese. Like the Native Americans, they have left place-names where they themselves have disappeared.

Interlude

1. See, e.g., Sherab Chodzin, *The Awakened One: A Life of the Buddha*. Boston, MA: Shambhala, 1994; David J. and Indrani Kalupahana, *The Way of Siddhartha: A Life of the Buddha*. Boulder, CO: Shambhala, 1982; Maurice Percheron, *The Marvelous Life of the Buddha*. New York: St. Martin's Press, 1960; John S. Strong, *The Buddha: A Short Biography*. Oxford: Oneworld, 2001. The first three are accessible narratives; the study by John S. Strong reflects more critical scholarship.

2. In Japan he has often been referred to as Shakamuni, meaning the Sage (Sanskrit: *muni*) of Sakya (Sanskrit: Sakyamuni). This terminology is especially used in art history, where a figure in a Japanese temple representing the historical Buddha, as over against one of the cosmic buddhas of Mahayana, may be called a Shakamuni, or sometimes just a Shaka, figure.

3. Walpola Rahula, *What the Buddha Taught*. New York: Grove Press, 1974.

4. Unless otherwise designated, words in parentheses are the Japanese for the term.

5. Guy Richard Welbon, *The Buddhist Nirvana and its Western Interpreters*. Chicago, IL: University of Chicago Press, 1968.

6. For an older but useful introduction, see Beatrice Lane Suzuki, *Mahayana Buddhism*. London: D. Marlowe, 1948. Otherwise, good general textbooks on Buddhism such as those in the "Further Reading" section, are probably most helpful for the beginning student.

7. Edward Conze, *Buddhist Thought in India*. Ann Arbor, MI: University Michigan Press, 1967, contains a vivid and provocative introduction to the issues that gave rise to Mahayana.

8. Edward Conze, *Buddhist Texts through the Ages*. New York: Harper & Row, 1964.

9. Among several studies of Nagarjuna are Joseph Walser, *Nagarjuna in Context: Mahayana Buddhism and Early Indian Culture*. New York: Columbia University Press, 2005; and Frederick Streng, *Emptiness: A Study in Religious Meaning*. Nashville, TN: Abingdon Press, 1967.

10. We will see later that, as *hongaku*, "original enlightenment," this idea that all contain the principle of enlightenment from the beginning, has been attacked by the recent school called "Critical Buddhism," which has associated it with failings it sees in Japanese Buddhism.

11. John Schroeder, *Skillful Means: The Heart of Buddhist Compassion*. Honolulu: University of Hawaii Press, 2001.

12. Thomas E. Wood, *Mind Only: A Philosophical and Doctrinal Analysis of the Vijnanavada*. Honolulu: University of Hawaii Press, 1991.
13. Donald Ritchie, *Japan Journals, 1960* (unpublished). Cited in Arturo Silva, ed., *The Donald Ritchie Reader*. Berkeley, CA: Stone Bridge Press, 2001, p. 50.
14. Donald Ritchie, *Ozu*. Berkeley, CA: University of California Press, 1974.
15. Donald Ritchie, *The Films of Akira Kurosawa*. Berkeley, CA: University of California Press, 1965.

4   Early times

1. Koji Mizoguchi, *An Archaeological History of Japan: 30,000 B.C. to A.D. 700*. Philadelphia, PA: University of Pennsylvania Press, 2002. J. Edward Kidder, *Japan Before Buddhism*. London: Thames & Hudson, 1959.
2. Ryusaku Tsunoda, Wm. Theodore de Bary, and Donald Keene, *Sources of Japanese Tradition*. New York: Columbia University Press, 1958, pp. 7–8.
3. Robert Ellwood, "The Sujin Religious Revolution," *Japanese Journal of Religious Studies*, vol. 17, no. 2–3 (June-Sept 1990), pp. 199–216. https://nirc.nanzan-u.ac.jp/nfile/2427
4. Donald L. Philippi, trans., *Kojiki*. Tokyo: University of Tokyo Press, 1969.
5. Ojin was later identified with the Shinto *kami* Hachiman, the deity of one of the half-dozen or so major families of Shinto shrines, like the Inari or Tenjin families already mentioned.
6. W. G. Aston, *Nihongi*. London: K. Paul, Trench, Trubner, 1896; George Allen & Unwin, 1956, part II, p. 65 ff.
7. Tsunoda, de Bary, and Keene, *Sources of Japanese Tradition*, pp. 50–3.
8. I have written of these events through the lens of a peculiar religious episode of the times, with some speculative comparisons to transitions in modern developing nations: Robert Ellwood, "A Cargo Cult in Seventh-Century Japan," *History of Religions*, vol. 23, No. 3 (February 1984), pp. 222–39.
9. See Tsunoda, de Bary, & Keene, *Sources of Japanese Tradition*, ch. v, "Nara Buddhism," pp. 93–110.

5   Magic mountains and the old court

1. Ivan Morris, *The World of the Shining Prince*. New York: Columbia University Press, 1964, p. 114. This book is an excellent introduction to all of Heian culture.
2. See Yoshito S. Hakeda, trans., *Kukai: Major Works*. New York: Columbia University Press, 1972.
3. Jacqueline I. Stone, *Original Enlightenment and the Transformation of Medieval Japanese Buddhism*. Honolulu: University of Hawaii Press, 1999, p. 19.
4. Hakeda, *Kukai*, pp. 151, 154.

5. See Minoru Kiyota, *Shingon Buddhism: Theory and Practice*. Los Angeles, CA and Tokyo: Buddhist Books International, 1978.

6. Taiko Yamasaki, *Shingon*. Boston, MA: Shambhala, 1988, pp. 157–9. The description of the meditation techniques is here somewhat simplified.

7. "Womb of Infinite Space." Though perhaps parallel to Jizo (Kshitagarbha, "Earth Womb"), this figure has far less popular appeal, and is found mostly in esoteric rites like this one.

8. Yamasaki, *Shingon*, pp. 188–9. Order of citations reversed.

9. Robert Redfield, *The Little Community and Peasant Society and Culture*. Chicago: University of Chicago Press, 1960.

10. See Ichiro Hori, *Folk Religion in Japan*, Chicago: University of Chicago Press, 1968, pp. 92–3.

11. These deities were also brought to Japan through Tendai and other sources as well, though they are represented in the Shingon mandalas.

12. See Thomas Cleary, trans., *Stopping and Seeing: A Comprehensive Course in Buddhist Meditation* [by Zhiyi]. Boston: Shambhala, 1997.

13. John Stevens, *The Marathon Monks of Mount Hiei*. Boston: Shambhala, 1988, p. 22.

14. See Burton Watson, trans. *The Lotus Sutra*. New York: Columbia University Press, 1993.

15. Paul L. Swanson, *Foundations of T'ien-T'ai Philosophy*. Berkeley, CA: Asian Humanities Press, 1989.

16. Translation by the author of poem #658. The *Kokinshu* poems are nearly all *waka*, each 29 syllables in the original Japanese. For a complete translation see Helen Craig McCullough, *Kokin Wakashu: The First Imperial Anthology of Japanese Poetry*. Stanford, CA: Stanford University Press, 1985.

17. Stevens, *Marathon Monks of Mount Hiei*.

18. Burton Watson, trans., *The Essential Lotus: Selections from the Lotus Sutra*. New York, Columbia University Press, 2002, p. 18.

19. See Robert Ellwood, "The Saigu: Princess and Priestess," *History of Religions* vol. 7, no. 1 (August 1967), 35–60.

20. Morris, *The World of the Shining Prince*, chapters IV and V.

21. Hori, *Folk Religion in Japan*, 43–4.

6　*Warrior culture, simple faith*

1. Donald Keene, trans. *Essays in Idleness: The Tsurezuregusa of Kenko*. New York: Columbia University Press, 1967.

2. Archibald Ross Lewis, *Knights and Samurai: Feudalism in Northern France and Japan*. London: Temple Smith, 1974.

3. Many popular and scholarly books on the colorful samurai are available. See Stephen Turnbull, *Samurai: The World of the Warrior*. Oxford: Osprey, 2003, and other titles by this author; Richard Storry, *The Way of the Samurai*. New York: Galley, 1978; and Paul Varley, *Warriors of Japan as Portrayed in the War Tales*. Honolulu: University of Hawaii Press, 1994.

4. Donald Keene, ed., *Anthology of Japanese Literature*. New York: Grove Press, 1955, p. 78.

5. For a dissenting view on this analogy, see James H. Foard, "In Search of a Lost Reformation," *Japanese Journal of Religious Studies* vol. 7 no. 4 (Dec. 1980), pp. 261–91.

6. See Robert E. Morrell, *Early Kamakura Buddhism: A Minority Report*. Berkeley, CA: Asian Humanities Press, 1987.

7. Hisao Inagaki, trans., *The Three Pure Land Sutras*. Berkeley, CA: Numata Center for Buddhist Translations and Research, 2003.

8. Allan A. Andrews, *The Teachings Essential for Rebirth: A Study of Genshin's Ojoyoshu*. Tokyo: Sophia University Press, 1973.

9. See Havelock Coates and Ryugaku Ishizuka, *Honen, The Buddhist Saint*. Kyoto: Chionin, 1925.

10. Senchakushu English Translation Project, *Honen's Senchakushu: Passages on the Selection of the Nembutsu in the Original Vow*. Honolulu: University of Hawaii Press, 1998.

11. Alfred Bloom, *Shinran's Gospel of Pure Grace*. Tucson: University of Arizona Press, 1965.

12. From the *Tannisho*, a collection of sayings attributed to Shinran, collected by a disciple. Ryusaku Tsunoda, Wm. Theodore de Bary, and Donald Keene, *Sources of Japanese Tradition*. New York: Columbia University Press, 1958, p. 217; and Taitetsu Unno, trans., *Tannisho: A Shin Buddhist Classic*. Honolulu: Buddhist Study Center Press, 1996, pp. 5, 6.

13. Ibid.

14. Mark L. Bloom and Shin'ya Yasutomi, *Rennyo and the Roots of Modern Japanese Buddhism*. New York: Oxford University Press, 2006.

15. Minor Rogers and Ann Rogers, *Rennyo: The Second Founder of Shin Buddhism*. Berkeley, CA: Asian Humanities Press, 1992.

16. *Ikko* means "one mind" or one focus of thought, referring to the Shinshu practice of the *nembutsu* alone. *Ikki* means uprising or rebellion.

17. Masaharu Anesaki, *Nichiren, The Buddhist Saint*. Cambridge, MA: Harvard University Press, 1916.

18. Jay Sakashita, ed., *Writings of Nichiren Shonin*. Honolulu: University of Hawaii Press, 2004.

19. Nichiren's followers also took up arms in that violent and sectarian age, to their great loss. In 1532, when the Jodo-Shinshu *Ikko ikki* threatened the city of

Kyoto, a Nichiren *Hokke* ("Lotus") *ikki* rose successfully to defend the ancient capital, and ruled it for four years. But in 1536 Tendai *soho*, "warrior monks," offended by this triumph on the part of heretics, swept down to burn all twenty-one of the city's Nichiren temples, as well as much of the city itself; some 58,000 Nichiren followers died in the futile struggle.

20. Burton Watson, trans., *Letters of Nichiren*. New York: Columbia University Press, 1996.
21. Nichiren's concept of a Japanese national mission has had an interesting relationship with modern Japanese nationalistic extremism. In the twentieth-century period of such excess up to 1945, there were those who cited Nichiren as an example, and some Nichiren priests fervently supported the imperial cause. Yet as we will see others, including the father of the wildly successful postwar Soka Gakkai movement, Makiguchi Tanisaburo, based on uncompromising Nichirenism, stood apart from the fervor of those days. Makiguchi was incarcerated by the government and died in prison during the War. He and his followers had refused to worship Amaterasu or distribute talismans from the Ise shrine because of Nichiren's rejection of Shinto and all other worship except that of the Lotus.
22. For a discussion of the changing influence of the *rokudo* system in medieval Japan, see William LaFleur, *The Karma of Words*. Berkeley, CA: University of California Press, 1983.
23. Sir George Sansom, *A History of Japan to 1334*. Stanford, CA: Stanford University Press, 1958, pp. 432–7. Quotes p. 435.

7 Swords and satori

1. Alan Watts, *The Way of Zen*. New York: Pantheon, 1957, p. 3.
2. Philip Kapleau, *The Three Pillars of Zen*. Tokyo and New York: John Weatherhill, 1965, pp. 244–5.
3. Katsuki Sekida, trans., *Two Zen Classics: The Gateless Gate and Blue Cliff Records*. Boston, MA and London: Shambhala, 2005.
4. Adapted from Alan Watts, *The Spirit of Zen*. London: John Murray, 1936, pp. 47–8.
5. Ryusaku Tsunoda, Wm. Theodore de Bary, and Donald Keene, *Sources of Japanese Tradition*, New York: Columbia University Press, 1958, p. 243.
6. Ibid., 243–6.
7. Heinrich Dumoulin, *A History of Zen Buddhism*. New York: Random House, 1963, p. 151.
8. Bernard Glassman and Rick Fields, *Instructions to the Cook* [based on Dogen's manual of the same title]. New York: Bell Tower, 1996.

9. Dogen, "Meaning of Practice-Enlightenment," in Yuho Yokoi, *Zen Master Dogen: An Introduction with Selected Writings*. New York and Tokyo: Weatherhill, 1976, p. 61.

10. Dogen, "A Universal Recommendation for Zazen," in Yokoi, *Zen Master Dogen*, p. 46.

11. Dumoulin, *A History of Zen Buddhism*; Hee-jin Kim, *Dogen Kigen: Mystic Realist*. Tucson, AZ: University of Arizona Press, 1975.

12. It should be noted that much of the rest of Dogen's extensive body of writings is less metaphysical, being very insightful but conventional, practice-oriented homilies on traditional Buddhist topics, such as *karma* and the places of rebirth. The relative value of various of Dogen's writings, and their relationship to the different periods of his life, is a much-debated issue. So is his approach to the doctrine of Original Enlightenment (*hongaku*), the notion, central to most Japanese Buddhism, that (to put it in simple terms) we are enlightened from the beginning, but just don't realize it. A recent school, called Critical Buddhism, to be discussed later, asserts that Original Enlightenment is not original Buddhism, but a Mahayana and especially Japanese perversion, responsible for many of the evils of Japanese Buddhism. They see the right perspective in Dogen, however, so he emerges as a hero. Others perceive other Dogens. See Steven Heine, *Did Dogen Go to China?* New York: Oxford University Press, 2006, for a very thorough summary of debates about the great Soto master. (The question in the title is not meant to be taken seriously – there is no real doubt that Dogen made his famous trip in 1223 – but is a play on the title of another book.)

13. Hubert Nearman, trans. and Daizui MacPhillamy, ed., *The Shobogenzo*. Mount Shasta, CA: Shasta Abbey, 1996, pp. 173–6.

14. Somewhat as learning, both classical and Christian, was maintained in European Benedictine monasteries during the Dark Ages.

15. Michael Cooper, ed., *Southern Barbarians: The First Europeans in Japan*. Tokyo: Kodansha International, 1971, pp. 119, 122.

16. See Herbert Plutschow, *Rediscovering Rikyu and the Beginnings of the Japanese Tea Ceremony*. Folkestone: Global Oriental, 2003.

17. In this book No is always capitalized when referring to the drama, so as to distinguish it from the common English word. In Japanese 'No' means skill or talent.

18. Eugen Herrigel, *Zen in the Art of Archery*. New York: Pantheon, 1953. Original German edition 1948; it was based in turn on a German article of 1936.

19. See Yamada Shoji, "The Myth of Zen in the Art of Archery," *Japanese Journal of Religious Studies*, 2001, vol. 28 no. 1–2, pp. 1–30.

20. See Winston L. King, *Zen and the Way of the Sword*. New York: Oxford University Press, 1993.

21. Yamamoto Tsunetomo, *The Book of the Samurai: Hagakure*. Tokyo: Kodansha, 1979, p. 164.

22. Ibid., p. 71.

23. D. E. Tarver, ed., *The Hagakure*. New York: Writer's Club Press, 2002. p. 3, 38.

24. Cited in Tsunoda *et al.*, *Sources of Japanese Tradition*, p. 791.

25. *Seppuku* is sometimes known in the West by the less elegant (and reverse order) reading of the characters as *hara-kiri*, literally "belly-cutting."

26. Bushido can be compared to the code of chivalry of knights in medieval Europe in significant ways. Without going into specifics, we may note that, first, both made use of certain values and practices of a dominant religion, Christianity and Zen, though in actuality they also carried over ideals of earlier tribal religion, scarcely exemplifying all the virtues of Christ or the Buddha, and in a real sense almost demonstrated an alternative value-system. Second, both were not really codified (in various not-always-consistent books) as an ideal until after the great age of its dominant class, knights and samurai, had come and gone. *Banzai*, literally "ten thousand years [to the emperor]" is a celebrated cheer or war-cry.

27. Ikkyu, *Wild Ways: Zen Poems*. Trans. by John Stevens. Buffalo, NY: White Pine Press, 2003, p. 39.

28. Ibid., p. 82. From Wild Ways, translated by John Stevens. Translation copyright © 1995, 2003 by John Stevens. Reprinted with the permission of The Permissions Company, Inc., on behalf of White Pine Press, www.whitepine.org.

29. Basho, *The Narrow Road to the Deep North, and Other Travel Sketches*. Trans. by Nobuyuki Yuasa. Baltimore, MD: Penguin, 1966. See also *Basho's Haiku: Selected Poems by Matsuo Basho*. Trans. and annotated by David Landis Barnhill. Albany, NY: SUNY Press, 2004.

30. Philip Yampolsky, *The Zen Master Hakuin*. New York: Columbia University Press, 1971, p. 18.

31. Ibid., p. 121.

32. See Yoel Hoffman, *The Sound of One Hand Clapping*. New York: Basic Books, 1975.

33. See James Heisig, *Philosophers of Nothingness: An Essay on the Kyoto School*. Honolulu, HI: University of Hawaii Press, 2001. Some aspects of the Kyoto School have been controversial, especially its alleged relation to nationalism. See Michiko Yusa, "Nishida and the Question of Nationalism," *Monumenta Nipponica* vol. 46 no. 2 (1991), pp. 203–9.

34. Alan W. Watts, *Beat Zen, Square Zen, and Zen*. San Francisco, CA: City Lights Books, 1959.

35. A student of Soyen Shaku and his pupil Sokatsu, Sokei-an came to America in 1906 to begin Zen work. Early efforts had no lasting success, and Sokei-an, possessing an artistic, literary, and rather "bohemian" temperament as well as a deep inner Zen life, spent some time in those circles on the West Coast and

in New York before the time seemed right for him to commence his work as a Zen master. His center moved to new quarters on November 8, 1941 – and a month later, right after Pearl Harbor, was filled with FBI men, and Sokei-an was interned as an enemy alien. His health failed and he died in 1945. Sokei-an's short, pithy lectures – humorous, observant, full of striking original images – are still, in my opinion, among the best in this genre. See *The Zen Eye: A Collection of Zen Talks by Sokei-an*. Edited by Mary Farkas. Tokyo and New York: Weatherhill, 1993.

36. See, for example, D. T. Suzuki, *Essays in Zen Buddhism*. Kyoto: Eastern Buddhist Society; London: Luzac, 1927; *An Introduction to Zen Buddhism*. Kyoto: Eastern Buddhist Society, 1934, and many other works; Reginald Horace Blyth, *Haiku*. 4 vols., Tokyo: Kokuseido, 1949–52 (Blyth was a British teacher of English who spent the war years interned in Japan); Alan Watts, *The Way of Zen*. New York Pantheon, 1957.

37. Jack Kerouac, *The Dharma Bums*. New York: Viking Press, 1958. See also Carole Tonkinson, ed., *Big Sky Mind: Buddhism and the Beat Generation*. New York: Riverhead Books, 1995.

38. Kerouac, *The Dharma Bums*, p. 157. (Penguin edition 1976)

8 *Christ and Confucius*

1. Richard Storry, *A History of Modern Japan*. London: Cassell, 1960, p. 47.
2. Richard Storry, *The Way of the Samurai*. New York: Galley Press, 1978, p. 15; Michael Cooper, *They Came to Japan*. Berkeley, CA: University of California Press, 1965, pp. 60–1.
3. See Michael Cooper, *They Came to Japan*; Philip G. Roberts, *The First Englishman in Japan: The Story of Will Adams*. London: Harvill Press, 1956.
4. Oliver Statler, *Japanese Inn*. New York: Random House, 1961, p. 65–6.
5. A significant difference between Chinese and Japanese Confucianism was that the former saw one's primary loyalty to be to one's parents, and so by extension to the family; if one was forced to choose between loyalty to one's father and loyalty to the emperor and the state, one must choose the parent. But Japanese authorities put it the other way; loyalty to the emperor and the state came first, a priority which was later emphasized by the extreme nationalists as young men, leaving their parents, were sent off to battle and likely death in accordance with the presumed imperial will.
6. However, that term was not used till Meiji times; Yamaga called his books *Shido* (*Way of the Warrior*) and *Bukyo shogaku* (*An Encouragement of Chivalry*). It is interesting to note that similar systematic idealizations of chivalry appeared in Europe then and up through the nineteenth century as actual knighthood became hopelessly obsolete.

7. Cited in Ian Buruma, *Inventing Japan: 1853–1964*. New York: Modern Library, 2003, p. 16.

8. Herman Ooms, *Tokugawa Ideology*. Princeton, NJ: Princeton University Press, 1985, pp. 146, 186–9.

9. On these teachers, see Robert Bellah, *Tokugawa Religion*. Glencoe, IL: Free Press, 1957.

10. Of course the mystical unity of sovereign and subject, or of the individual and the state, was a longstanding theme of the "divine right of kings" position in Europe, and at the time of Aizawa's writing, the 1810s and 1820s, was experiencing something of a revival as a backlash against the French Revolution in the minds of such thinkers as the reactionary political theorist Joseph de Maistre.

11. Buruma, 24–5.

12. Many of the inns along the Ise road, as well as those in the vicinity of many other religious sites in old Japan, were places where prostitution was available. It must be noted that prostitution has long had associations with religion in Japan, as it did in Babylon and other ancient lands. Prostitutes often represented incarnate deities in the ancient world, and union with them was a kind of worship. Though this role disappeared by the Middle Ages in Japan, wandering female shamans, nuns, and the like still retained a sacred/sexual reputation. It is interesting to note that even in Tokugawa times, high-status prostitutes carried the title of a Shinto priest, *tayu*. Nam-lin Hur, *Prayer and Play in Late Tokugawa Japan*. Cambridge, MA: Harvard University Asia Center, 2000, pp. 88–9.

13. For a well-informed fictionalized account of an *Ise-mairi*, see Statler, *Japanese Inn*, Chapter 9. See also Winston Davis, "Pilgrimage and World Renewal: A Study of Religion and Social Values in Tokugawa Japan," Part I *History of Religions*, Vol. 23, No. 2 (November 1983), pp. 97–116; Part II: Vol. 23, No. 3 (February 1984), pp. 197–221.

14. It should be made clear that Japanese *bunraku* puppet theatre is not to be confused with Western puppetry, often considered a rather trivial children's entertainment. *Bunraku* puppets are nearly life-sized, works of expressive art in themselves, manipulated from behind by black-robed artists of consummate skill. The performances, accompanied by haunting traditional music, are quite capable of conveying the profoundest themes of drama.

15. Ihara Saikaku, *The Life of an Amorous Man*, trans. Kengi Hamada. Rutland, VT: Charles E. Tuttle Co., 1956; *Five Women Who Loved Love*, trans. William Theodore de Bary. Tokyo: Charles E. Tuttle Co, 1956.

16. Ihara Saikaku, *The Japanese Family Storehouse or the Millionaires' Gospel Modernized*, trans. G. W. Sargent. Cambridge; Cambridge University Press, 1959.

17. *The Love Suicides at Amijima* is translated and discussed in Donald Keene, *Four Major Plays of Chikamatsu*. New York: Columbia University Press, 1961.

18. Herbert P. Bix, *Peasant Protest in Japan 1590–1884*. New Haven, CT: Yale University Press, 1986.

19. Ivan Morris, *The Nobility of Failure: Tragic Heroes in the History of Japan*. New York: Holt, Rinehart & Winston, 1975.

20. Charles J. Dunn, *Everyday Life in Traditional Japan*. Rutland, VT and Tokyo: Charles E. Tuttle Co., 1969, pp. 78–9. See also Ichiro Hori, "Mysterious Visitors from the Harvest to the New Year," in Richard Dorson, ed., *Studies in Japanese Folklore*. Bloomington, IN: Indiana University Press, 1963, pp. 76–106.

21. See Nam-lin Hur, *Prayer and Play in Late Tokugawa Japan: Asakusa Sensoji and Edo Society*. Cambridge, MA: Harvard University Asia Center, 2000.

22. Kannon was famous in other venues as well; at the great Hasedera temple in Kamakura, an eleven-headed Kannon image presents her (him?) in both male and female guise, while the overwhelming Sanjusangendo temple in Kyoto (present structure 1266), a must for visitors, displays her in 1001 images, all slightly different.

23. Hitoo Murakawa, "Religious Circumstances in the Late Tokugawa and the Early Meiji Periods," *Tenri Journal of Religion*, Vol. 11 (December 1970), p. 50.

24. Engelbert Kaempfer, *History of Japan*. Glasgow: J. McLehose & Sons, 1906. First pub. in English 1727.

9   The rising sun and the dark valley

1. Robert J. Lifton, *Revolutionary Immortality*. New York: Random House, 1968.

2. From Hitoo Marukawa, "Religious Circumstances in the Late Tokugawa and the Early Meiji Periods," *Tenri Journal of Religion*, Vol. 11 No. 9 (December 1970).

3. See, for example, Mark Girouard, *The Return to Camelot: Chivalry and the English Gentleman*. New Haven, CT: Yale University Press, 1981.

4. It will be recalled this was the body of laws and rituals, including details of Shinto rites performed by the court, set up just before the Nara era. Although seldom observed in full this code had never been abrogated, and was theoretically still in force.

5. Eric Hobsbawn and Terence Ranger, eds., *The Invention of Tradition*. Cambridge: Cambridge University Press, 1983.

6. The three principles of the Daikyo or "Great Teaching" of the propagandists at this time were: Revere the *kami* and love the nation; understand the principles of heaven and the way of man [*Warongo* Neo-Confucian in tone]; and serve the emperor and faithfully maintain the imperial will.

7. Josephson, Jason Ananda, *The Invention of Religion in Japan*. Chicago: University of Chicago Press, 2012.

8. Wilbur M. Fridell, *Japanese Shrine Mergers 1906–12*. Tokyo: Sophia University Press, 1973.

9. Carol Gluck, *Japan's Modern Myths: Ideology in the Late Meiji Period*. Princeton, NJ: Princeton University Press, 1985, pp. 138–9.

10. Marius Jansen, *The Making of Modern Japan*. Cambridge, MA: Harvard University Press, 2000, pp. 457–8.

11. Cited in Joseph Pittau, *Political Thought in Early Meiji Japan*. Cambridge, MA: Harvard University Press, 1967, pp. 177–8.

12. Quoted in Wilbur M. Fridell, "Government Ethics Textbooks in Late Meiji Japan," *Journal of Asian Studies* (August 1970), p. 831. This passage and the preceding one are cited in Kenneth B. Pyle, *The Making of Modern Japan*. Lexington, MA: D. C. Heath and Co., 1978, pp. 99–100.

13. Richard Jaffe, *Neither Monk nor Layman: Clerical Marriage in Modern Japanese Buddhism*. Princeton, NJ: Princeton University Press, 2001.

14. *Wind Bell* Vol. 8, No. 1–2 (Fall 1969), p. 1. Note that Ceylon is now Sri Lanka, and "Hinayana" is Theravada Buddhism.

15. For much of this history of Zen in America, see Robert Ellwood, *Alternative Altars*. Chicago, IL: University of Chicago Press, 1979, Chapter 6, pp. 136–66. On Sokei-an, see Mary Farkas, ed., *The Zen Eye: A Collection of Zen Talks by Sokei-an*. Tokyo and New York: Weatherhill, 1993.

16. Stephen Prothero, *The White Buddhist: The Asian Odyssey of Henry Steel Olcott*. Bloomington, IN: Indiana University Press, 1996, pp. 123–7, 129–30. For Olcott's own enthusiastic account, see Henry S. Olcott, *Old Diary Leaves*, Vol. IV. Adyar, Madras, India: Theosophical Publishing House, 1975 (first pub. 1910), pp. 92–148.

17. See George M. Wilson, *Radical Nationalist in Japan: Kita Ikki, 1883–1937*. Cambridge, MA: Harvard University Press, 1969.

18. To be sure, the "tradition" was partly contrived – the "invention of tradition" – though it was certainly believed in by many fanatics.

19. Robert King Hall and John Owen Gauntlett, *Kokutai no Hongi: Cardinal Principles of the National Entity of Japan*. Cambridge, MA: Harvard University Press, 1949. Passages cited in Ryusaku Tsunoda, Wm. Theodore de Bary, and Donald Keene, *Sources of Japanese Tradition*. New York: Columbia University Press, 1958, pp. 785–95.

20. Cited in Robert Bellah, *Imagining Japan*. Berkeley, CA: University of California Press, 2003, p. 182.

21. *The Japan Times and Advertiser*, November 11, 1940, p. 1. Reproduced in *The Japan Times: Front Page 1897–1997*. Tokyo: Japan Times, 1997. See also Kenneth J. Ruoff, *Imperial Japan at its Zenith: The Wartime Celebration of the Empire's 2,600th Anniversary*. Ithaca, NY: Cornell University Press, 2014. This anniversary, of course, was based on the traditional Kojili/Nihonshoki mythology and chronology, which no reputable scholar would take seriously today.

22. Thomas R. H. Havens, *Valley of Darkness: The Japanese People and World War Two*. New York: Norton, 1978, pp. 68–9.

23. Cited in Brian (Daizen) Victoria, *Zen at War*. New York and Tokyo: Weatherhill, 1997, p. 87.

24. Cited in Joseph M. Kitagawa, *Religion in Japanese History*. New York: Columbia University Press, 1990, p. 247.

10 Chanting and dancing

1. On the same trip to the north, I had an opportunity to see something even more remarkable, if possible: a *miira*, or "self-mummified buddha." In a room not generally accessible by the public, at a small mountain temple with Shugendo links, I was shown the wizened, dry, blackened remains of a human being, dead well over a hundred years, clothed in abbatial robes and enshrined seated on the altar. There he received worship as though a buddha, and perhaps he was. Less than a dozen such "mummies" are known, most interred during the Tokugawa period. They were extreme ascetics who, determined in the Shingon manner to become a buddha "in this very body, in this lifetime," ate less and less until, sealing themselves into a stone chamber, they died chanting prayers and mantras. They were then exhumed by fellow monks and enshrined as spiritual victors. See Ichiro Hori, "Self-Mummified Buddhas in Japan," *History of Religions*, Vol. 1, No. 2 (Winter, 1962), pp. 222–42.

2. On Tenrikyo, in addition to chapters in general books on the new religions, cited in Further Reading, see Robert Ellwood, *Tenrikyo: A Pilgrimage Faith*. Tenri: Tenri University Press, 1982; Henrikus van Straelen, *The Religion of Divine Wisdom*. Tokyo: 1954; and *Tenrikyo: Its History and Teaching* and *The Life of Oyasama, Foundress of Tenrikyo*, both edited by the Tenrikyo Church Headquarters, Tenri, 1966 and 1996 respectively.

3. Kurozumikyo, founded in 1814, is the oldest of those movements usually classified as new religions. It is focused on Amaterasu, worshipped as the rising sun, and has strong Ise connections. See Helen Hardacre, *Kurozumikyo and the New Religions of Japan*. Princeton, NJ: Princeton University Press, 1986.

4. These are the words as generally presented by the Tenrikyo church, but there are interesting variants. For a discussion see Robert Ellwood, *Tenrikyo: A Pilgrimage Faith*. Tenri: Tenri University Press, 1982, p. 39, note 2.

5. The names used for the Tenrikyo God are several. He is sometimes Tenri O no Mikoto (The Divine Tenri; the term Tenri, "Heavenly Principle," is Neo-Confucian for the supreme principle); or Tsukihi ("Moon-Sun," a favorite of Miki's, suggesting union of the celestial male-female archetypes), or – now most often preferred by Tenrikyo people – Oyagami, "God the Parent."

6. Delwin B. Schneider, *Konkokyo: A Japanese Religion*. Tokyo: IISR Press, 1962.

7. Susumu Shimazono, *From Salvation to Spirituality: Popular Religious Movements in Modern Japan*. Melbourne: Trans Pacific Press, 2004, pp. 45–6.

8. Emily Groszos Ooms, *Women and Millenarian Protest in Meiji Japan*. Ithaca, NY: Cornell University Press, 1993.

9. See Nancy K. Stalker, *Prophet Motive: Deguchi Onisaburo, Oomoto, and the Rise of New Religions in Imperial Japan*. Honolulu: University of Hawaii Press, 2008.

10. New Thought is that highly influential school of American religious thought which teaches that our thoughts make our world: by thinking health we become healthier, by thinking prosperity we become more prosperous. Fenwicke Holmes was the brother of Ernest Holmes, founder of the Church of Religious Science, a major New Thought denomination which has long maintained a special relation with Seicho no Ie.

11. A neologism adopted by the church, apparently combining Messiah and the "nity" of Christianity – although actually "Christos" *is* the Greek equivalent of the Hebrew "Messiah" or "Anointed One."

12. Marcus Bach, *The Power of Perfect Liberty*. Englewood Cliffs, NJ: Prentice-Hall, 1971.

13. James Allen Dator, *Soka Gakkai: Builders of the Third Civilization*. Seattle, WA: University of Washington Press, 1969; Phillip E. Hammond and David Machacek, *Soka Gakkai in America*. New York: Oxford University Press, 1999; Daniel Metraux, *The History and Theology of Soka Gakkai*. Lewiston, NY: Edwin Mellen, 1988; David Machacek and Bryan Wilson, eds, *Global Citizens: The Soka Gakkai Buddhist Movement in the World*. New York: Oxford University Press, 2000; Richard Hughes Seager, *Encountering the Dharma: Daisaku Ikeda, Soka Gakkai, and the Globalization of Buddhist Humanism*. Berkeley, CA: University of California Press, 2006; James W. White, *The Sokagakkai and Mass Society*. Stanford, CA: Stanford University Press, 1970. Bryan Wilson and Karel Dobbelaere, *A Time to Chant: The Soka Gakkai Buddhists in Britain*. Oxford: Clarendon Press, 1994.

14. Traditionally, Japanese religions have been counted by households rather than by individual members, and sometimes still are.

15. Richard M. Jaffe, *Neither Monk nor Layman*. Princeton, NJ: Princeton University Press, 2001, p. 233.

16. He retained the title of Honorary President, and is said to continue to exercise considerable influence, but was succeeded as president by Hojo Hiroshi.

17. Helen Hardacre, *Lay Buddhism in Contemporary Japan: Reiyukai Kyodan*. Princeton, NJ: Princeton University Press, 1984.

18. Kenneth J. Dale, *Circle of Harmony*. South Pasadena, CA: William Carey Library, 1975; Stewart Guthrie, *A Japanese New Religion: Rissho Kosei Kai in a Mountain Hamlet*. Ann Arbor, MI: Center for Japanese Studies, University of Michigan, 1988.

19. Mark R. Mullins, "Japan's New Age and Neo-New Religions," in James R. Lewis and J. Gordon Melton, eds., *Perspectives on the New Age*. Albany, NY: SUNY Press, 1992, pp. 232–46.

20. Trevor Astley, "The Transformation of a Recent Japanese New Religion: Okawa Ryuho and Kofuku no Kagaku," *Japanese Journal of Religious Studies*, Vol. 22 No. 3–4 (1995), pp. 343–80.

21. Benjamin Dorman, "Representing Ancestor Worship as 'Non-Religious': Hosoki Kazuko's Divination in the Post-Aum Era." *Nova Religio*, Vol. 10 No.3 (February 2007), pp. 32–53.

22. Ian Reader, "The Rise of a Japanese 'New New Religion' – Themes in the Development of Agonshu," *Japanese Journal of Religious Studies*, Vol. 15 No.4 (1988), pp. 235–61.

23. Michiko Nagai, "Magic and Self-Cultivation in a New Religion: The Case of Shinnyoen," *Japanese Journal of Religious Studies*, Vol. 22 No. 3–4 (1995), pp. 301–21.

24. Winston Davis, *Dojo: Magic and Exorcism in Modern Japan*. Stanford, CA: Stanford University Press, 1980.

25. Byron Earhart, *Gedatsu-Kai and Religion in Contemporary Japan: Returning to the Center*. Bloomington, IN: Indiana University Press, 1989; Minoru Kiyota, *Gedatsu: Its Theory and Practice*. Los Angeles, CA and Tokyo: Buddhist Books International, 1997.

26. David E. Kaplan and Andrew Marshall, *The Cult at the End of the World: The Terrifying Story of the Aum Doomsday Cult*. New York: Random House, 1996; Robert J. Lifton, *Destroying the World to Save It: Aum Shinrikyo, Apocalyptic Violence, and the New Global Terrorism*. New York: Henry Holt, 1999; Haruki Murakami, *Underground: The Tokyo Gas Attack and the Japanese Psyche*. New York: Vintage, 2001. Mark R. Mullins, "Aum Shinrikyo as an Apocalyptic Movement," in Thomas Robbins and Susan B. Palmer, eds, *Millennium, Messiahs, and Mayhem: Contemporary Apocalyptic Movements*. London: Routledge, 1997; Ian Reader, *Religious Violence in Contemporary Japan: The Case of Aum Shinrikyo*. Honolulu: University of Hawaii Press, 1998; Richmond: Curzon Press, 2000.

27. An excellent discussion of such general characteristics of the new religions is found in the first chapter, "The World of the New Religions," of Helen Hardacre, *Kurozumikyo and the New Religions of Japan*. Princeton, NJ: Princeton University Press, 1986.

11 Pilgrimages

1. Robert J. C. Butow, *Japan's Decision to Surrender*. Stanford, CA: Stanford University Press, 1954.

2. The discussion of religion and the occupation is based on that in Robert Ellwood, *1950: Crossroads of American Religious Life*. Louisville, KY: Westminster John Knox Press, 2000, pp. 167–71.

3. Cited in William P. Woodard, *The Allied Occupation of Japan 1945–1952 and Japanese Religion*. Leiden: E.J. Brill, 1972, p. 358. This entire book is highly recommended for the topic. For a 1950 evangelical, missions-oriented look at Japan, see Donald E. Hoke, "Crisis Hour in the Orient," and other related articles in *Christian Life*, December 1950, pp. 33–52. Ray A. Moore, *Soldier of God: MacArthur's Attempt to Christianize Japan*. Portland, ME: MerwinAsia, 2011.

4. Her memoir, Elizabeth Gray Vining, *Windows for the Crown Prince*, Philadelphia, PA: Lippincott, 1952, provides an interesting picture of the imperial family in this era.

5. See Jamie Hubbard and Paul Swanson, eds, *Pruning the Bodhi Tree: The Storm over Critical Buddhism*. Honolulu: University of Hawaii Press, 1997.

6. The situation of women, both nuns and priests' wives, is better documented in Soto Zen than in other denominations. Therefore examples tend to be from that tradition.

7. A telling story is that of Aoyama Shundo. Born into extreme poverty in the prewar years, made a novice nun while still a child, after many tribulations she became an abbess, a leader among Zen nuns, and a highly respected spiritual teacher. Her translated book, *Zen Seeds* (Tokyo: Kosei, 1991), contains both a riveting account of her life and splendid Zen meditations.

8. Uchino Kumiko, "The Status Elevation Process of Soto Sect Nuns in Modern Japan," *Japanese Journal of Religious Studies* Vol. 10 No. 2–3 (1983), pp. 177–94; Stephen Grover Covell, *Japanese Temple Buddhism*. Honolulu, HI: University of Hawaii Press, 2005; Richard M. Jaffe, *Neither Monk nor Layman: Clerical Marriage in Modern Japanese Buddhism*. Princeton, NJ: Princeton University Press, 2001.

9. Kino Kazuyoshi, *Kokoro no furusato: tabi to nihonjin*. Tokyo: Kosei Shuppan, 1985. See also Ian Reader, *Religion in Contemporary Japan*. Honolulu, HI: University of Hawaii Press, 1991, pp. 71–2, 238–9.

10. Karin Muller, *Japanland: A Year in Search of* Wa. New York: Rodale, 2005, p. 115.

11. Reader, pp. 174–5. For carrying the *mikoshi*, see Muller p. 41 ff.

12. Toshimaro Ama, *Why Are the Japanese Non-Religious? Japanese Spirituality: Being Non-Religious in a Religious Culture*. Lanham, MD: University Press of America, 2005. Originally published in Japanese.

13. Hiroshi Miura, *The Life and Thought of Kanzo Uchimura, 1861–1930*. Grand Rapids, MI: Eerdmans, 1996.

14. Reader. *Religion in Contemporary Japan*, pp. 157–61; Reader, *Making Pilgrimages: Meaning and Practice in Shikoku*. Honolulu, HI: University of Hawaii Press,

2005; Reader, "Positively Promoting Pilgrimage: Media Representations of Pilgrimage in Japan." *Nova Religio*, Vol. 10, No. 3 (February 2007), pp. 13–31.

15. Reader, *Religion in Contemporary Japan*, pp. 164–67; Reiko Chiba, *The Seven Lucky Gods of Japan*. Rutland, VT: Charles E. Tuttle, 1966.

16. See the articles on various Japanese pilgrimage sites in Linda K. Davidson and David M. Gitlitz, *Pilgrimage: From the Ganges to Graceland, An Encyclopedia*. 2 vols. Santa Barbara, CA: ABC-Clio, 2002.

17. Muller, *Japanland*, pp. 129–31.

18. Helen Hardacre, *Marketing the Menacing Fetus in Japan*. Berkeley, CA: University of California Press, 1997; William R. LaFleur, *Liquid Life: Abortion and Buddhism in Japan*. Princeton, NJ: Princeton University Press, 1992.

19. Richard W. Anderson and Elaine Martin, "Rethinking the Practice of *Mizuko Kuyo* in Contemporary Japan: Interviews with Practitioners at a Buddhist Temple in Tokyo." *Japanese Journal of Religious Studies*, Vol. 24, No. 1–2 (Spring 1997), pp. 121–143; Elizabeth G. Harrison, "Women's Response to Child Loss in Japan: The Case for *Mizuko Kuyo*," *Journal of Feminist Studies in Religion* Vol. 11, No. 2 (Fall 1995), pp. 67–93; Elizabeth G. Harrison, "*Mizuko Kuyo*: The Re-Production of the Dead in Contemporary Japan," in P. F. Kornicki and I. J. McMullen, eds., *Religion in Japan: Arrows to Heaven and Earth*. Cambridge: Cambridge University Press, 1996, pp. 250–66.

20. Michiko Iwasaka and Barre Toelken, *Ghosts and the Japanese: Cultural Experience in Japanese Death Legends*. Logan, UT: Utah State University Press, 1994; and Michael Dylan Foster, *The Book of Yokai: Mysterious Creatures of Japanese Folklore*. Berkeley: University of California Press, 2015.

21. Kate T. Williamson, *A Year In Japan*. New York: Princeton Architectural Press, 2006, n.p.

22. Bruce Feiler, *Learning to Bow: Inside the Heart of Japan*. New York: HarperCollins Perennial, 2004, pp. 121–2.

23. See Susumu Shimazono, *From Salvation to Spirituality: Popular Religious Movements in Modern Japan*. Melbourne: Trans Pacific Press, 2004, Part 4.

24. *Otaku* was originally an honorific form of address, then used sarcastically to mean something like "nerd" or "geek," and finally accepted by the "nerds" for themselves.

25. The three characters used for this word are *nin*, "duty, responsibility, office"; *ten*, "heaven," and *do*, "temple." The meaning has been variously rendered; perhaps it is something like, "the responsibility [for what happens] belongs to heaven" – in other words, "I do the best I can, but in the end it's up to a higher power."

26. Susan Napier, *Anime from Akira to Princess Mononoke*. New York: Palgrave, 2001, p. 30.

27. For example, Minamoto Yoshinaka's wife, Tomoe Gozen, and Minamoto Yoritomo's spouse, Hojo Masako. The *Heike Monogatari* is full of tales of spirited women who fought alongside male samurai; above all, samurai wives were expected

to avenge the deaths of their husbands, even if by devious means, and to commit suicide if dishonored.

28. He is a prince of the Emishi, an indigenous people in Japan who were pressed further and further north and east during the Middle Ages, finally disappearing. Interestingly, Ashitaka's Emishi village seems to have as its main spiritual figure a "wise woman" who is clearly like the ancient shamanesses.

   Princess Mononoke seems to be influenced by the work of Umehara Takeshi. Though criticized by some specialists, his books were bestsellers in Japan. Umehara proposed an ancient Japanese religion, perpetuated in Emishi and Ainu spirituality, and some aspects of Shinto, centered on a Spirit of the Forest, tree spirits, and a desire to live in harmony with all of nature. All beings, animal or human, are spiritual and therefore equal; all spirits can travel back and forth between this and the other world. On Umehara, see Susumu Shimazono, *From Salvation to Spirituality: Popular Religious Movements in Modern Japan*. Melbourne: Trans Pacific Press, 2004, pp. 282–83.

Appendix I

1. Ian Reader tells the story of a Japanese professor, a highly educated and cultured individual, who when asked what Buddhist sect he belonged to, replied, "I do not know: no one in our household has died yet." Ian Reader, *Religion in Contemporary Japan*. Honolulu: University of Hawaii Press, 1991, p. 3.

Glossary of terms

In this glossary the long marks or macrons sometimes employed in transliteration of Japanese are put over the vowels *o* and *u* when that reflects the original.

Budō   The way of the warrior as a spiritual path.

Chanoyu   The "tea ceremony," expression of Chadō, the Way of Tea.

Daijōsai   The ancient imperial accession ceremony; the harvest festival as celebrated by the emperor on this occasion.

Daimoku   The Nichiren chant honoring the Lotus Sutra: *Nam Myōhō Renge Kyō*.

Eightfold Path (Hashōdō)   The way of life taught by the Buddha, culminating in right concentration or meditation.

Four Noble Truths (Shikai)   The basic Buddhist teaching that life is suffering, suffering is caused by attachment, there can be an end to suffering, the way is the Eightfold Path.

Ghosts (Obake, Yūrei)   Important in both popular folklore and the Nō drama, ghosts may be lonely and hungry (the *gaki* of the rokudō), vengeful (like goryō), or represent deep psychological impulses as in Nō.

Giri   A sense of obligation or gratitude owed to another; basic to Japanese ethics.

Gohei   The zigzag strips of paper that denote the presence of deity at a Shintō shrine.

Gohonzon   The rectangular paper object of devotion in Nichiren Buddhism, containing the names of principal buddhas and bodhisattvas in the Lotus Sutra; the Daimoku is written down the center.

Gongen   "Avatar": shrines honoring a major Buddhist figure in the form of a Shintō *kami*.

Goryō   The vengeful ghost of a person, usually of noble lineage, who was unjustly killed.

Haibutsu Kishaku   "Destroy the Buddha" – cry of the early Meiji anti-Buddhist movement.

Haiku   Seventeen-syllable poem often associated with Zen Buddhism.

Hibutsu   "Hidden Buddha" – a Buddhist image so sacred it is only displayed on rare occasions.

Honden   The inner chamber of a Shintō shrine, where the shintai or divine presence is housed.

Honji Suijaku   "Original essence, incarnate appearance": the theory that Shintō *kami* were Japanese manifestations of universal buddhas and bodhisattvas.

Hōtoku   "Repaying virtue"; repayment of obligations, fundamental teaching of Ninomiya Sontoku.

Itako   A shamaness or medium.

Kabuki   A traditional dramatic form, popular in the Tokugawa period and after, often featuring Samurai heroes and themes.

Kaihōgyō   The practice of the "marathon monks" of Mt. Hiei.

Kami   Shintō deities, life-affirming and generally local.

Karma **(Gō, Innen)**   Buddhist concept of cause and effect, governing all conditioned existence, including reincarnation.

Kōan   The riddle-like meditation queries used in Zen.

Kōdō   "Imperial Way": the nationalistic doctrine of direct imperial rule and loyalty to the emperor.

Makoto   Sincerity, purity of heart: a supreme Confucian and Shintō virtue.

Mandala (mandara)   In esoteric Buddhism, a diagram showing the relationship of various buddhas and bodhisattvas.

Mappō   "End of the Dharma": a popular medieval idea that we had entered the last age of the Buddha's teaching, when times were evil and salvation accessible only by faith.

Matsuri   Shintō festival.

Mikkyō   "Secret teaching": esoteric Buddhism.

Miko   In Shintō, 1) a shamaness, 2) a maiden who assists in shrine ceremonies.

Mikoshi   The palanquin in which the *kami* is carried, often vigorously, in festivals.

Mito school   A nationalistic school of Japanese history in the late Tokugawa period.

Mizuko Kuyō   Controversial Buddhist memorial service for aborted and stillborn fetuses.

Mono no Aware "Sensitivity to things," a basic principle of Japanese aesthetics.

Namahage Masked "mysterious visitors" on New Year's Eve in northern Japan.

Nembutsu "Mindfulness of Amida Buddha," the Pure Land chant, *Namu Amida Butsu.*

Nō drama Classic style of Japanese drama, emphasizing subtle gestures and often involving supernatural themes.

Norito Prayer offered in Shintō rites.

Obon Midsummer Buddhist festival of returning spirits, celebrated with dances and offerings.

Ōharai Shintō rite of purification.

On Kindness, favor, justice owed to another, as by a parent to a child; basic to Japanese ethics.

Ri Basic principle of the universe or of entities within it in Neo-Confucian philosophy.

Samurai Warriors or the social class they represented; ideally ruled by a code of honor and readiness for death.

Satori "Surprise": sudden enlightenment in Zen.

Seppuku Suicide performed in a ritual manner for reasons of honor.

Shimenawa In Shintō, a straw rope indicating sacred places or objects.

Shinbutsu Bunri Separation of Shintō and Buddhism, an early Meiji policy.

Shinbutsu Shūgō Conjoining of Shintō and Buddhist divine figures and worship.

Shintai "Kami substitute": the sacred object representing divine presence in a Shintō shrine.

Shintō Worship Characteristically consists of purification, offerings, prayer, and festival or matsuri.

Shintō Year Major events include New Year, the midsummer Ōharai or purification, and the shrine's own special annual matsuri.

Shintō, Features of These include the theme of purity versus pollution, traditionalism, polytheism, the importance of festival or matsuri, and emphasis on the practical and social expression of religion.

Six Places of Rebirth (Rokudō) In traditional Buddhism, one who has not attained Nirvana may, according to his or her *karma*, be reborn in any of six realms: heavenly, human, asuras (fighters), animal, hungry ghosts (*gaki*), the hells.

Three Refuges or Jewels (Sambō) The Buddha, the Dharma or Buddha's teaching, the Samgha or monastic community: affirming taking refuge in them means becoming a Buddhist, and is a common Buddhist practice.

Torii   The distinctive gateway demarcating the precincts of a Shintō shrine.

Ubasoku   From Sanskrit for "disciple": Nara period countryside Buddhist teachers and practitioners close to the common people.

Uji   1) The ancient Japanese clans, with their *ujigami* or patronal deity; 2) as a reading of *aru toki*, Dōgen's deep philosophical concept of the oneness of being and time.

Watarai Shintō   Late medieval school, also called Ise Shintō, influenced by Taoism and Confucianism, emphasizing the *kami* as manifestations of the universal Way, and the virtues of purity and Makoto.

Yogacara (Hossō), Vijñānavāda (Shiki is Japanese for Vijñāna, "Mind" or "Consciousness"), or "Mind Only" (Yuishiki)   Idealistic school of Mahayana Buddhism, teaching that reality as we experience it is a projection of consciousness.

Yoshida Shintō   Late medieval school teaching that the *kami* represent original spiritual reality, and the buddhas are its conditioned manifestations; also organized shrine rankings and governance.

Yūgen   Sense of mystic wonder evoked by Nō and other great art.

Zen art   Forms such as gardens, tea, flower-arrangement, painting, drama, and poetry shaped by Zen values of simplicity and naturalism.

Index

This index includes the following:

1. Names of persons and texts important to Japanese religion
2. Names of major shrines, temples, and other religious sites
3. Names of major *kami*, buddhas, and bodhisattvas
4. Names of denominations, sects, and other religious groups
5. Terms important to understanding Japanese religion

Note: For very commonly-used names like Buddhism, Shinto, Confucianism, etc., only principal discussions are indexed. Buddhist terms, e.g. Four Noble Truths, Mahayana, Pure Land, are indexed as they are generally written in English discourse, with the Japanese equivalent following in parentheses. These terms also appear in the Glossary.

In this index, as in the glossary, the long marks or macrons sometimes employed in transliteration of Japanese are put over the vowels *o* and *u* when that reflects the original, although they are not used in the main text; it's the same word!